MARSHALLESE REFERENCE GRAMMAR

PALI Language Texts: Micronesia

Social Science Research Institute

University of Hawai‘i

Robert A. Blust

Series Editor

MARSHALLESE REFERENCE GRAMMAR

BYRON W. BENDER

ALFRED CAPELLE

LOUISE PAGOTTO

University of Hawai‘i Press

Honolulu

Printed in the United States of America

21 20 19 18 17 16   6 5 4 3 2 1

Library of Congress Cataloging-in-Publication Data

Names: Bender, Byron W., author. |
Capelle, Alfred, author. |
Pagotto, Louise, author.
Title: Marshallese reference grammar / Byron W. Bender, Alfred Capelle, Louise Pagotto.
Description: Honolulu : University of Hawaiʻi Press, [2016] |
Includes bibliographical references.
Identifiers: LCCN 2015046040 | ISBN 9780824859930 pbk. : alk. paper
Subjects: LCSH: Marshallese language—Grammar. |
Marshallese language—Textbooks for foreign speakers—English. |
LCGFT: Reference works.
Classification: LCC PL6255 .B385 2016 | DDC 499/.52—dc23
LC record available at http://lccn.loc.gov/2015046040

Print-ready copy has been provided by the authors.

University of Hawaiʻi Press books are printed on acid-free paper and meet the guidelines for permanence and durability of the Council on Library Resources.

Contents

1. Table titles are shown in SMALL CAPITAL typeface.

Preface

This publication is the result of a long and sustained effort, inexorably entwined with that of the *Marshallese-English Dictionary* since the mid-1960s, when, in turn, coauthors Takaji Abo, Tony DeBrum, and Alfred Capelle assisted in the search for new words, the writing of example sentences, and the grammatical analysis of the interrelations among the various word forms that had been collected. Each returned to positions in the government of the Marshalls after completion of their programs at the University of Hawai'i, and the dictionary was published in 1976 with the four authors listed alphabetically (see References on pages 13–16).

The dictionary (now referred to as the MED) was stored on computer and included a database of some 6,000 example sentences. In the years that followed, coauthors Abo and Capelle worked to amplify these by another 5,000 sentences exemplifying derivatives of the main entries. Earlier drafts of the first three chapters of this reference grammar and the computerized database of sentences from the MED were made available to Louise Pagotto as she produced her monumental 1987 dissertation. We are indeed happy that she has joined us as third author of the reference grammar. Her syntactic insights have helped solve many a thorny problem in Marshallese grammar. Two examples from the summary of chapter 5 might be noted here:

- classes of IMPERSONAL verbs whose subjects are not to be found in the real world, which help explain number agreement in Marshallese
- a key player in many clauses (in addition to the SUBJECT and the OBJECT) known as the CORRESPONDENT, whose presence helps explain many puzzles of Marshallese grammar.

The first and second authors have spent many hours in consultation when both were on the same island, and have remained in constant email contact; since the year 2000, more than 3,200 messages have been exchanged, an average of 200 per year.

In 2009, a major revision of the dictionary went on-line, free from the space restrictions of hard-copy publication and, thus, with the ability to incorporate as example sentences the full text and translation of a novella written by Capelle, and a concordance (and reverse concordance) of all example sentences, to mention just two of the larger space-takers. One can choose between two different alphabetizations in dealing with characters that have diacritic marks, and one can also view the 1976 version on line verbatim. Links make it possible to navigate instantaneously beween English words in the finder list and entries, and between the concordances and the entries. We refer to it now as the MOD, the *Marshallese On-line Dictionary*. It was made possible by the computer wizardry of Steve Trussel, http://www.trussel.com/.

The MOD has greatly facilitated work on the later chapters of the reference grammar. One of the by-products of the concordance that is especially valuable to grammar writers has been the ability to focus in on any word or phrase in all of its occurrences—sometimes numbering in the dozens, or even hundreds—and discover any significant patterns to its occurrences.

Finally, it is important that the reader understand that this grammar of Marshallese is by no means complete. There are many interesting corners yet to be discovered and investigated, with problems to be studied and questions to be answered. We hope that you will find it both helpful and challenging.

MARSHALLESE REFERENCE GRAMMAR

1 Introduction

THE ISLANDS AND THE PEOPLE

1.1 Marshallese is the first language of the original people of the Marshall Islands. These islands are coral atolls located just north of the equator and west of the International Date Line in the Pacific Ocean. The majority of them lie within a 7° square area between the latitudes 5° and 12° north and the longitudes 165° and 172° east—an expanse of water covering some 175,000 square miles. Two uninhabited atolls that lie further north (Pikaar, 12° 15' N, and Bok-ak 14° 35' N) have been traditionally considered part of the Marshalls, as have two inhabited atolls that lie further west: Ānewetak (Eniwetak), 162° E, and Wūjlañ (Ujelang), 161° E). The atolls lie in two chains that run basically north and south—tilting slightly from northwest to southeast. The eastern chain is called the Ratak, and the western the Rālik. There are 17 atolls in the Rālik chain and 15 in the Ratak. The total land area of all the atolls is only 72 square miles. Several do not have lagoons that can be entered by ocean-going vessels, and several are not inhabited year round, but are visited occasionally for the harvesting of fruit or the hunting of game—especially sea birds, coconut crabs, and turtles.

The Atoll Environment

1.1.1 It has often been said that without the coconut, these atolls could not sustain human life for any span of time. Certainly the coconut (which has a tolerance for salt water not shared by most other plants) has provided most of the necessities of life, including the formation of soil, food and drink, clothing and shelter, tools and utensils, and fuel and transport. The breadfruit has given food and material for building canoe hulls. Other key plants in this meager environment are arrowroot, pandanus, and the banana. But if there is another source of food that rivals the coconut in importance it is the sea, with hundreds of species of fish, whales, porpoises, turtles, spiny lobsters, clams, and other varieties of seafood.

The presence of the sea is ever felt on the narrow strips of land fringing the atolls. For a good half of the year it is too rough to permit travel by canoe between atolls, or the catching of larger fish beyond the reef. Its tides determine when other fish may be caught nearer shore, and high winds coupled with spring tides may bring the seas across parts of the land every year or so. The strong trade winds bring a constant salt spray across all but the widest islets and prevent the introduction of food crops native to other regions. Successful navigation of even the shorter distances between atolls presents a problem, because the atolls (which are never more than 10 or 15 feet above sea level) are not visible from more than 5 or 10 miles at sea, and Marshallese navigators learned to use every clue available, including wave patterns, the stars, and the reflection of vegetation against a cloudy sky.

This environment is reflected in the vocabulary of the language. Hundreds of words have to do with the growth and uses of the coconut, including the dishes prepared by mixing it with the other staple plants and fish. There are almost a hundred named edible varieties of pandanus, a plant whose fruit is not eaten in most other parts of the world. There are many names of fish, and dozens of names of methods for catching them. Names for stars and the signs of navigation, names for various cloud formations, names for the various parts of the distinctive canoes and the maneuvers involved in their sailing—all these remind one who reads a dictionary of the language that it is the language of a people who live in an atoll environment. A bit of the environment can also be seen in the grammar of the language: an elaborate set of directional adverbs (see "Directionals" on page 219) are added to verbs to show movement toward the lagoon shore, interior, or ocean side of the islet, or movement landward or seaward, in addition to the directions commonly shown in other languages.

Marshallese Society

1.1.2 It is estimated that when the first Westerners arrived in the islands, there were some 30,000 people living on them—more than 400 per square mile. For such crowded conditions in a limited environment, special customs were developed that specified who had the rights to what land, how the fruits should be divided, what each person's duties were, and how these rights and duties should be passed on from one generation to the next. A great deal of cooperation, sharing, and tolerance were called for.

But there was not enough land to go around, and war was often waged over who should control it. Those who were successful in battle earned the right to be known as chiefs (*irooj*) over those who were conquered, and in turn led these subjects in protecting their lands against others who tried to take them. The chiefs provided protection, security, and day-by-day leadership for the workers (*ri-jerbal*), who in return supported the chiefs with tribute from the land.

Society was organized around clans (*jowi*), which were subdivided into lineages (*bwij*). Each child inherited the lineage of his or her mother and the land rights of that lineage. Members of royal lineages had chiefly rights in the lands of their subjects. Each islet of any size was divided into tracts with definite boundaries and descriptive names; for each tract there was a commoner lineage with worker rights, and a royal lineage with chiefly rights. More powerful chiefs held rights in many tracts on more than one atoll. There was no private property, only lineage property, and there were elaborate rules for sharing, which extended to other lineages in need. Work was done by groups, often within the lineage, but some tasks—such as a porpoise hunt—were done on a communal basis, involving a whole village or atoll.

People were required to marry outside their lineage, and preferably outside their clan. Marriage was permitted with a first cousin whose mother was from a different clan, but marriage with distant relatives or even those of known relationship was prohibited if they happened to stem from the same clan. Marriages were often arranged by elders in such a way as to consolidate land holdings. These considerations often meant that one might marry someone from another atoll, and in the long run it meant that members of a given clan could be found on a number of different atolls. The system of clans and lineages and the same set of customs ran throughout the islands, and there was a great deal of interisland travel. This system has resulted in the great homogeneity of language and culture to be found today over such a broad expanse of ocean.

Life was treasured but perilous. Men were killed in battle, and voyagers were lost at sea. There were strict customs concerning bodily functions and sanitation, but native medicines could not cope with all diseases, and infant mortality was high. A community-wide feast was held to celebrate the birthday of any child who survived the first year. There were beliefs in both good and evil spirits, and legends concerning the demons who haunted more remote islets.[1]

The concerns of such a society are still reflected in the vocabulary of the language. There are several thousand names for the various islets and tracts of land in the atolls, names for several dozen clans, names for the various levels of royalty and for the types of land rights in the feudal society, names for relatives of all sorts within the complex matrilineal kinship system, names for the numerous spirits and demons, and terms for types of tribute and the sharing of food. In the grammar of the language and its use, one can see the deferring of the individual to the group. Elaborate methods have been developed for avoiding the use of people's names in their presence by the substituting of personal demonstratives (4.2.2), and the first person singular possessive pronoun is often avoided by substituting a plural pronoun (*Ewi bok eo arro?* 'Where is my book?' [literally, 'the book belonging to the two of us']). There is an abundance of euphemisms to soften the harsher facts of life, and playing with words is a favorite pastime. No one is more revered than the skillful composer of lyrics for songs and chants, and singing and chanting accompany daily group work projects.

1. A particularly good source for some of these and other legends, and for notes on Marshallese culture, is Jack A. Tobin's *Stories from the Marshall Islands*.

Modern Changes in Island Life

1.1.3 Much of the foregoing picture of life in the islands remains true today, but there have also been many changes since the arrival of the first Western explorers and missionaries, during the successive German, Japanese, and American administrations of the islands, and now during the compact of free association. The germs of Western diseases, even children's diseases, found little resistance in the bodies of island people, and the population fell rapidly to a low point of about 10,000. Warfare was suppressed by the administering authorities, and chiefs no longer filled the role of leading in battle. Land disputes came to be settled instead before a ruling commissioner or a presiding judge. Christianity came to replace many of the earlier beliefs in good and evil spirits. In addition to Christian beliefs, schools established by the missionaries taught the three R's with respect to both a foreign language and the Marshallese language newly set to writing. Copra was traded for imported tools, utensils, foods, cloth, and other merchandise. Foreigners intermarried with islanders, sometimes establishing new clans, and sometimes bringing with them Western rules of patrilineal inheritance. Some lands were sold to foreigners, and some were appropriated by administering authorities. Western medicine, navigation, and boatbuilding began to replace native arts and skills. Western ideas about property ownership and competition began to complicate the older ideals of sharing and cooperation.

Finally a mechanized war on a scale previously unimaginable was fought on the shores, and the populations of several atolls were evacuated to permit the testing of atomic weapons and intercontinental missiles. In the wake of the war came more regular and rapid communication with the outside world. Items could be ordered from a catalog and obtained within days. More foreigners came to the islands to engage in commerce or to work in the system of schools established by the government. More islanders went away to study and to see the foreign lands for themselves. New patterns of government called for the election of representatives and leaders. The outer world had intruded on the earlier way of life so that it could never be the same again, and foreign influences showed no signs of going away—of ever leaving the islands to themselves again.

Modern civilization brought mixed blessings. There was money to be had at the foreign centers in exchange not only for copra but for services. This and the new experiences that awaited them there caused many islanders to leave their homes behind in order to be closer to medical services, Western education for their children, nightly movies, electric lights, taxi rides, airplane trips, indoor plumbing—the amenities of modern civilization. Antibiotics saved lives and helped more children survive infancy; the population grew rapidly and began to approach the old high level of 30,000, eventually exceeding it by far. But the older controls of the home communities could not operate at these new urban centers, and new social problems arose: population densities of several thousand per square mile, juvenile delinquency, vandalism, violence, crime, alcoholism, malnutrition, and suicide.

All these changes have taken place in little over a century. The Marshallese people have survived these changes as a people, and their language has also survived. Although many of them also know other Micronesian languages, or Japanese, or English, Marshallese is still their native tongue. But the vocabulary of the language has changed greatly as the way of life has changed. Words having to do with the lore of native medicine, navigation, magic, religion, astronomy, and the calendar are rapidly being forgotten. New things brought to the islands have brought a new religious terminology. In general the language has taken the foreign word and reshaped it according to its own perceptions and rules: the archaic *steamer* became *tiṃa* 'ship', German *Tabak* became *tōbak* 'cigar', Japanese *sashimi* became *jaajmi* 'raw fish', and English *business* became *peejnej* 'to cheat'.

In contrast with its vocabulary, the grammar of the language has changed little, if any, as will be seen in the chapters that follow. Most of the changes that are taking place in the language (2.5) are caused by forces within the language, not the outside forces that have changed the vocabulary—the new things, ideas, and languages that have been imported to the islands. This is true of languages in general: the words of a language change to reflect the life of its speakers directly, while the rules of its grammar continue along their own independent way.

The biggest threat to the language today comes from global warming and the concomitant rise in sea level. There are already thousands of Marshallese living in migrant communities in the United States. If a wholesale exodus becomes necessary, the language away from the islands will almost certainly go the way of other immigrant languages within a few generations.

THE ORIGINS OF THE MARSHALLESE LANGUAGE

1.2 A legend that is still known in the islands today tells how a god named Ḷowa created the islands and the people. Although the legend seems to be referring to the Marshall Islands of today, it is possible that it could have been referring originally to some other lands where the ancestors of the Marshallese lived before moving to the Marshalls. At any rate, it seems clear that the Marshallese people have been living in their present islands for many centuries.

There are other bits of evidence that give some insight into earlier history. When one compares the physical appearance and the body types of the Marshallese with those of other Pacific islanders, one finds many similarities. Also, their tools and methods of making things are similar. Many of the legends of other Pacific people are much the same as those of the Marshallese. One explanation for these similarities is that the ancestors of all these peoples lived together as one people at some place many years ago. Later their descendants became scattered to other islands as they sailed away in search of new lands, or became lost at sea and came upon new islands by accident. There may be some significance to the fact that *Ḷowa* means literally "Mr. Canoe."

Great similarities can be seen among the languages of the Pacific. Table 1-1 shows some Marshallese words side-by-side with words that have roughly the same meanings from several other Micronesian languages. Notice how similar words with the same meaning from the different languages are (those shown in a given row). Many of them sound even more similar than they look; some of the differences in appearance result from differences in the spelling systems used for each language. But other differences in appearance reflect the fact that a sound may have changed in one language but not in the others, or it may have changed in a different way in the others. Take the word for 'afraid' as an example. It is thought that it was pronounced something like *mataku[2] by the ancestors of the speakers of all these languages when they were all speaking the same language, before they separated and moved to differnt islands. All the languages except Gilbertese dropped the final *u from the end of the word; Gilbertese kept the *u* but lost the *t from the middle of the word. The *t became *j* in Marshallese, but *s* in Chuukese (Trukese) and Pohnpeian (Ponapean). The *k became *g* in Woleaian, and in addition there were vowel changes in some of the languages. Words like these in different languages that come from the same older word in this way are called "cognates." Gilbertese *maaku* is said to be cognate with Marshallese *mijak,* with Pohnpeian *masak,* and so on.

Usually when sounds changed in this way, they changed not just in one word, but in all the words of the older language that had the same sound in the same place within a word. For example, the older word for 'sleep' has been reconstructed as *matudu. Note that the *t in this word also became *j* in Marshallese and *s* in Pohnpeian, just like the *t in *mataku. (The fact that it developed differently in Gilbertese and Chuukese may perhaps be explained by the different vowels following it in the two older words.) Notice how the first consonants of the words for 'forehead' and 'bone' parallel each other in each language: both words have *sh* in Woleaian, *ch* in Chuukese, *t* in Pohnpeian, *d* in Marshallese, and *r* in Gilbertese. Similarly, notice the first consonants of 'sea water' and 'her ear': both have *t* in Woleaian and Gilbertese, *s* in Chuukese and Pohnpeian, and *j* in Marshallese. This sort of regularity of

2. The asterisk (*) before words of parent languages is a reminder that there are no written records of these older words, and that they have been reconstructed by linguists based on their surviving shapes in the daughter languages of today. An asterisk may also be placed before individual sounds that make up such words, with the same meaning, when the sounds are being discussed.

Table 1-1 Selected cognates in Micronesian languages[1]

MEANING	WOLEAIAN	CHUUKESE	POHNPEIAN	KOSRAEAN	MARSHALLESE	GILBERTESE
shoulder	yefar	afar	apere	—	aerā	—
people	yaremat	aramas	aramas	mwet	armej	aomata
nose	boot	pwéét	—	fwā	bọọt	b'airi
blood	cha	ccha	nta	sra	da	raraa
forehead	—	chaamw	tahmw	sro	daṃ	ram'a
bone	shiu	chúú	tih	sri	di	rii
house	imw	iimw	ihmw	-um	eṃ	um'a
her father	temal	seman	seme	tōmwāl	jeman	tamana
her mother	silal	inan	ine	ninā	jinen	tinana
fart	sing	sing	sing	sōng	jiñ	ting
stand up	siutag	wúútá	uhda	tuyak	jutak	—
sea water	tat	sáát	sehd	-tō	-jet	taari
his/her ear	talingal	seningan	salenge	srāl	-jilñin	taniñana
sharp	kang	kken	kang	—	kōkañ	kakañ
eat (it)	gangi	áni	kang	kang	kan, kañ	kana, kañ
sleep	masiur	méwúr	meir	mutul	mājur	matuu
full	mat	mét	med	mōt	mat	—
afraid	metag	mésék	masak	—	mijak	maaku
life	meoiur	—	mour	moul	mour	maiu
worm	mwat	—	mwahs	we	ṃaj	m'ata
eat, food	mwongo	mwéngé	mwenge	mongo	ṃōñā	—
wave	loa	nóó	—	noa	ṇo	nao
tooth	ngii	ngii	ngih	wihs	ñi	wii
root	wagar	waar	—	okā	okar	wakaa
float	ppes	ppi	pei	pātpāt	pepepe	beibeti
her arm	paiul	péwún	peh	pāol	pein	baina
whale	ras	raaw	rohs	loat	raj	—
dream	ttal	ttan	—	—	tōtōṇak	—

1. Words are spelled in the standard orthography for each language, except Kosraean, where some vowel letters have been changed to make them more comparable to those used for the other languages. The letter *h* is used in Pohnpeian to show that a vowel is prolonged. An apostrophe is used in Gilbertese after a *b* or *m* to show that it is pronounced *bw* or *mw,* respectively. The authors are indebted to Ho-min Sohn, Hiroshi Sugita, Kenneth Rehg, and Kee-dong Lee for the information on the first four languages of the table, respectively, and to Ward Goodenough for information on several of the languages. Many more examples are to be found in Bender et al. (2003).

cognate words in several languages leads linguists to conclude that the languages are related, which is to say that they are all continuations of one earlier language, with peculiarities that developed in each of their separate locations. The earlier "parent" language of the languages in table 1-1 is called Proto-Micronesian, even though all the work of reconstructing this older language has not been done yet. Some of the regularities are not so easy to see at first glance, but as one learns more about the reconstructed parent forms and the changes that took place in each daughter language, the relations become more clear. For example, Chuukese *afar* may not appear so similar to Marshallese *aerā* {hayeray} 'shoulder' unless one knows that the word has been reconstructed as *qapara, and that *p generally became *f* in Chuukese but *y* in Marshallese. Also, Chuukese *áni* is more easily related to Marshallese *kan* 'eat it' if one knows that Chuukese generally lost *k at the beginning of a word before *a.

The same kind of regular similarities can be found when Marshallese words are compared with those of other Pacific languages outside Micronesia. Table 1-2 gives words from Hawaiian, Māori, and Fijian that are cognate with Marshallese words. Both Hawaiian and the Māori language of the original inhabitants of New Zealand are classified as Polynesian languages, because of the great similarities between them and the other languages of Polynesia such as Samoan, Tahitian, Tongan, and so forth, similarities of the sort shown in table 1-1 for the Micronesian languages. The reconstructed parent language of these "daughter" languages is called Proto-Polynesian. Fijian is included in table 1-2 as a representative Oceanic language from Melanesia. It seems clear that most of the languages of Melanesia, Polynesia, and Micronesia are continuations of a single reconstructed "grandparent language" that is called Proto-Oceanic. The words reconstructed for this language for each group of cognates in table 1-2 are shown in the last column, preceded by an asterisk to remind the reader that they are reconstructions. They have been reconstructed by examining not just the words from the four languages in table 1-2, but also cognate words from many other Oceanic languages (including the Polynesian and Micronesian languages).

Cognates of Marshallese words can also be found in the languages of Indonesia, Malaysia, the Philippines, Taiwan, and the island of Malagasy (Madagascar) off the coast of Africa. Several of these from Malay and from Tagalog (spoken in the Philippines) are shown in table 1-3. The language that has been reconstructed as the "great-grandparent" of all these languages and those descended from Proto-Oceanic is called Proto-Austronesian. Notice that Marshallese has lost the final consonant from nouns such as *langiC, *limut, *ñamuk, and ñiuR, but kept the consonant at the end of a transitive verb (3.3.2) such as *inum (see tables 3-15 and 3-16 in chap. 3). Languages like Malay and Tagalog are more similar to the parent language in that they have not lost these sounds from the ends of words.

Table 1-2 Selected cognates in Oceanic languages[1]

MEANING	HAWAIIAN	MĀORI	FIJIAN	MARSHALLESE	PROTO-OCEANIC
light	malama	marama	rama	me-ram	*ramaR
hear	-lono	rongo	rogo	roñ	*rongoR
two	lua	rua	rua	ruo	*rua
fish	iʻa	ika	ika	ek, ike-	*ikan
creature	manu	manu	manu-	mānni-	*manuk
breathe	manawa-ea	manawa	—	menono	*mañawa
warm	mahana	mahana	—	māāņāņ	*mapanas
mosquito	—	namu	namu	ņaṃ	*ñamuk
liver	ake	ate	yate	aj	*qatay
road	ala	ara	sala	iaḷ	*salan
cry	kani	tangi	tagi	jañit	*tangis
three	kolu	toru	tolu	jilu	*tolu
eight	walu	waru	walu	ru-wali-tōk	*walu
canoe	waʻa	waka	waqa	wa	*wangka

1. The left single quote (ʻ) in Hawaiian words shows the glottal stop, a quick closure made in the throat. In Fijian the letter *g* is used for the *ng* sound (the same sound as Marshallese *ñ* and Proto-Oceanic *ng*), and *q* is used for a *g* sound that is preceded by an *ng* sound: *ngg*. The author is indebted to Jay Howard, Andrew Pawley, and Steve Trussel for information on the first three languages. The Proto-Oceanic words are taken from Blust and Trussel (Ongoing).

Table 1-3 Selected cognates in Austronesian languages[1]

MEANING	MALAY	TAGALOG	MARSHALLESE	PROTO-AUSTRONESIAN
spirit	hantu	anítu	anij	*qaNiCu
drink	minum	inóm	ilim, inim	*inum (PMP)
louse	kutu	kúto	kij	*kuCu
fly	langau	lángaw	ḷọñ	*laŋaw
sky	langit	lángit	lañ	*laŋiC
five	lima	limá	lima-, -lem	*lima
moss	lumut	lúmot	liṃliṃ	*limut (PMP)
eye	mata	matá	meja-, māj	*maCa
die	mati	matáy	mej	*ma-aCay
mosquito	ñamok	lamók	ņaṃ	*ñamuk (PMP)
coconut	ñiur	niyóg	ni	*niur (PMP)

1. The first consonant in the last two Proto-Austronesian words (ñ) is similar to the *ny* of English *canyon*. The author is indebted to Terry Ramos for information on Tagalog, and to Blust and Trussel (Ongoing) for information on Malay and the Proto-Austronesian (or Proto–Malayo-Polynesian [PMP]) reconstructions.

Marshallese is, thus, thought to be a member of the large family of languages known as Austronesian, which consists of more than 1,000 languages spoken throughout the Pacific Islands and in parts of Southeast Asia, including Taiwan, the Philippines, and Indonesia. (This family was formerly called the Malayo-Polynesian language family.) Only in New Guinea and in a few islands of western Melanesia such as Bougainville are non-Austronesian languages spoken in this part of the world. This means that at some time quite long ago (perhaps 3000 B.C. or even earlier) the ancestors of those who speak the more than 1,000 daughter languages were speaking one language very similar to the reconstructed Proto-Austronesian. The most widely accepted theory as to where these people might have been living and how their descendants came to people the Pacific in later years places the homeland in Taiwan, where a number of tribes speaking Austronesian languages are still to be found.

Not all the languages of Micronesia are descended from Proto-Oceanic or Proto-Micronesian. Palauan and Chamorro are non-Oceanic members of the Austronesian family. It is thought that their closest relatives may be some of the Austronesian languages in the Indonesian area, or in the case of Chamorro, in the central or northern Philippines. Yapese is an Oceanic language, but its early speakers came to Micronesia separately, possibly from the Admiralty Islands. The languages of Kapingamarangi and Nukuoro are Polynesian languages, possibly most closely related to the language of Tuvalu (formerly the Ellice Islands). Although the island of Nauru is not usually included within the geographic area known as Micronesia, it seems clear that Nauruan is one of the daughters of Proto-Micronesian, and could be listed together with the languages in table 1-1. The languages of Sonsorol and Tobi, Ulithi and the islands between Ulithi and Chuuk, and the Carolinian language spoken on Saipan are all close relatives of Woleaian and Chuukese within the same Micronesian family. Similarly, the languages of Pingelap and Mokil are close relatives of Pohnpeian.

Some terms of human kinship (such as "daughter" and "sister") have been used in this section to show an analogy with human families. To review our present understanding, it can be said that Proto-Austronesian is the great-grandparent and earliest known ancestor of the whole large family or clan. (There are several competing theories that relate Proto-Austronesian back a generation further to ancestors of languages of mainland East or Southeast Asia, but to date none has received general acceptance.) All of the more than 1,000 Austronesian languages are descended from this original ancestor. The languages of Melanesia and Polynesia and most of the languages now found in Micronesia are descended from one daughter of Proto-Austronesian: Proto-Oceanic. The languages of Indonesia, the Philippines, Taiwan, Palauan, Chamorro, and so forth are not. They are descended from another daughter. In a later generation, Proto-Polynesian and Proto-Micronesian are two of the daughters of Proto-Oceanic. Thus, it can be said that Pohnpeian, for example, is a sister of Marshallese, Hawaiian is a first cousin, and Chamorro a more distant cousin. Many of the details of this genealogy are still not fully understood, but more is being learned as each of the 1,000-plus Austronesian languages is becoming better documented and compared with the others.

EARLIER STUDIES OF THE MARSHALLESE LANGUAGE

1.3 Very few comprehensive studies of the language have been made to date. Early expeditions such as that reported by Kotzebue (1821) often included individuals who reported on the people of the islands and their customs, and some of the vocabulary of the language referring to the customs was included in their reports. These were not written accurately enough to make it possible to tell whether pronunciation has changed since that time, and not many details of the grammar were given, but the accounts do give an interesting picture of what life was like when contact with the Western world was just beginning.

Several partial studies on the language were published later that century and shortly after 1900 during the German administration, but the most comprehensive work was that of Erdland (1906). Erdland also published several works on the customs of the Marshallese people early in this century, including their beliefs, the status of women, the system of chiefs, and astronomy and navigation. Matsuoka (1929) published one work on the language during the Japanese administration. These earlier works were done before the concept of the phoneme was well known or understood, and they are, therefore, not very helpful to one interested in the sound system of the language, or the exact shape of the words. Nevertheless, they contain valuable information on sentence patterns and some other grammatical and cultural matters before more recent changes took place.

The most important larger works since the beginning of the American administration include the dictionary by Elbert and Carr (1945), the outline of the syntax by Bailey (1967), and the detailed study of verbs by Pagotto (1987). The various other contributions that have been made to an understanding of the sound system are given in more detail in the first section of chapter 2.

SUGGESTED FURTHER READINGS

1.4 Wiens (1962a) is a thorough but technical detailing of the atoll environment. Spoehr (1949) gives a good picture of what life was like in the village of Laura at the west end of Majuro at the end of World War II, and includes much information on Marshallese society in general. Mason (1947) gives an overview of the economic organization of the islands for the same period. Tobin (1952) gives the details of land ownership patterns. Wiens (1962b) gives a very readable and general introduction to the geography of the area and to some political considerations having to do with recent changes. Howells (1973) considers the evidence available as to where the Pacific Islanders came from and how the islands were first settled, then proposes his own stimulating theory. Tobin (2002) gives folktales from traditional storytellers accurately transcribed in Marshallese, and translated into English with helpful notes. Bender (2013) gives an updated view of the peopling of Micronesia. The bibliography compiled by Taylor (1965) is a good source for references on the other writings of Fr. Erdland, and for the other early works on the language, as well as for the general and anthropological works that had been published by that date.

MARSHALLESE DIALECTS

1.5 The remarkable thing about dialectal differences in the Marshallese language is that they are so few and small, and so systematic and understood by all the speakers of the language—that the language is so nearly homogeneous. One would expect much greater diversity to have developed when one considers the vast area over which the islands and speakers are spread, and the long period of time each of the islands seems to have been occupied by the Marshallese people. Yet one finds fewer differences in all of the Marshalls than are to be found within the same lagoon, or on the opposite sides of one and the same island for some of the high-island languages to the west, such as Pohnpeian, Chuukese, and Yapese.

This would seem to be explained by the unified clan system of the islands, and the great amount of interisland travel and marriage between islands observed in 1.1.2. The only dialect division of any significance is that to be found between the two chains, the Rālik and the Ratak. The major difference between the two chains is in their pronunciation of double consonant words (see "Initial Double Consonants" on page 52), yet all speakers know the rules for these different pronunciations, and can readily mimic the pronunciation of the other dialect. There are also occasional vocabulary differences between these two dialects, but often speakers know and can use the word from the other dialect as well as their own.

Table 1-4 gives a few examples of the differences in vocabulary, and differences in pronunciation not involving initial double consonant words. Within each of the chains there are minor differences: the speech of Eniwetak in the west is distinctive in some respects, as is that of Mejit in the east. For example, Mejit people generally pronounce the greeting word as *eọkwe* instead of *iọkwe*. But the total number of all such differences is not many times more than the sample given in the table, and, all things considered, amazingly small. Throughout this book, words and pronunciations peculiar to the Rālik are labeled as western (W), and those peculiar to the Ratak as eastern (E).

Table 1-4 Examples of vocabulary differences between Rālik and Ratak dialects

RĀLIK (W)	RATAK (E)		RĀLIK (W)	RATAK (E)	
koba	bae	'bamboo'	rōña	rōkeañ	'northward'
aṃōn	aṃwin	'wash hands'	jaab	eaab	'no'
aetok	aitok	'long'	itok	wātok	'come'
kiiō	kiin	'now'	aet	iñña	'yes'
kiki	mājur	'sleep'	koṃ	kōmi	'you (plural)'
lọlọ	lala	'hen'	iia	jemāluut	'rainbow'
jowi	jou	'clan'	wat	luwap	'puffer fish'

REFERENCES

Abo, Takaji, Byron W. Bender, Alfred Capelle, and Tony DeBrum. 1976. *Marshallese–English dictionary.* PALI Language Texts: Micronesia. University of Hawai'i Press. Revised ed., 2009 (http://www.trussel2.com/MOD/ [see abbreviations "MED" and "MOD" in table 2-16 on page 56]; [also at http://evols.library.manoa.hawaii.edu/bitstream/handle/10524/19441/index.htm]).

Bailey, Charles-James N. 1967. Transformational outline of Marshallese syntax. MA thesis, University of Chicago.

Bender, Byron W. 1963a. Marshallese phonemics: Labialization or palatalization. *Word* 19:335–41.

———. 1963b. A linguistic analysis of the place-names of the Marshall Islands. PhD diss., Indiana University. (Available from http://www.proquest.com/products-services/dissertations/)

———. 1968. Marshallese phonology. *Oceanic Linguistics* 7:16–35.

———. 1969. *Spoken Marshallese: An intensive course with grammatical notes and glossary.* Honolulu: University of Hawai'i Press.

———. 1981. A fossilized article in Marshallese. In *Studies in Pacific languages and cultures: In honour of Bruce Biggs,* ed. by Jim Hollyman and Andrew Pawley, 209–28. Linguistic Society of New Zealand, Auckland.

———. 1984. Object marking in Marshallese. In *Studies in Micronesian linguistics,* ed. by Byron W. Bender, 443–65. Series C-80. Canberra: Pacific Linguistics.

———. 1990. Lexical transfer from Marshallese to Mokilese: A study in intra-Micronesian borrowing, with Kenneth L. Rehg. *Oceanic Linguistics* 29:1–26.

———. 1991. On the category distributive. In *Currents in Pacific linguistics: Papers on Austronesian languages and ethnolinguistics in honour of George W. Grace,* ed. by Robert Blust, 11–26. Series C-117. Canberra: Pacific Linguistics.

———. 1994. Language reform in a Micronesian context. In *Language reform: History and future,* ed. by István Fodor and Claude Hagège, 85–99. Hamburg: Helmut Buske.

———. 1995. Notes from the field: Lend me your ears! *Oceanic Linguistics* 34:226–232.

———. 1996. Distinguishing between inflection and derivation. In *Reconstruction, classification, description: Festschrift in honor of Isidore Dyen,* ed. by Bernd Nothofer, 199–207. Hamburg: Abera Verlag Meyer & Co. KG.

———. 1998. Markedness and iconicity: Some questions. In *Case, typology, and grammar: In honour of Barry J. Blake,* ed. by Anna Siewierska and Jae Jung Song. Typological Studies in Language 38. Amsterdam: John Benjamins.

———. 2013. The languages of Micronesia. In *Ling 100: Language in Hawai'i and the Pacific*, ed. by Hiroko Sato and Jacob Terrell. Department of Linguistics, University of Hawai'i.

Bender, Byron W., and Alfred Capelle. 1996. Dealing with the ABCs of Marshallese over twenty years. In *Pacific languages in education,* ed. by France Mugler and John Lynch, 36–75. Suva: University of the South Pacific, Institute of Pacific Studies, Department of Literature and Language; Vanuatu: Pacific Languages Unit.

Bender, Byron W., Ward H. Goodenough, Frederick H. Jackson, Jeffrey C. Marck, Kenneth L. Rehg, Ho-min Sohn, Stephen Trussel, and Judith W. Wang. 2003. Proto-Micronesian reconstructions. *Oceanic Linguistics* 42:1–110, 271–358.

Blust, Robert, and Stephen Trussel. Ongoing. *Austronesian comparative dictionary* (online open access site at: www.trussel2.com/ACD).

Capelle, Alfred. 1978. *Pelọk ilo meto ekauwōtata.* [Drifting on a dangerous sea.] Majuro: Marshall Islands Dept. of Education, Curriculum/Learning/ Training Center. [2nd edition, 2008, posted on-line with the MOD]

Carr, Denzel. 1945. Notes on Marshallese consonant phonemes. *Language* 21:267–70.

[Carr, Denzel, and Samuel H. Elbert.] 1945. *Marshallese–English and English–Marshallese dictionary.* 14th Naval District, District Intelligence Office, Marshall-Gilbert Area: United States Navy Department. xxx, 136, 121 pp. Mimeographed. Notes on pronunciation and grammar in introduction. 4,000 entries.

English–Marshallese dictionary. [c. 1963.] [Kwajalein, Marshall Islands.] xvii, 164 pp. No title page. Contains abbreviated entries from Carr and Elbert English–Marshallese section. Introduction contains one-page table of sounds and selected entries grouped topically: adjectives, verbs, numbers and time, animals and insects, etc. Hawaiian and Pacific Collection, University of Hawai'i Library.

Erdland, August. 1906. *Wörterbuch und Grammatik der Marshall-Sprache nebst ethnographischen Erläuterungen und kurzen Sprachübungen.* Berlin: Reimer. x, 247 pp. German–Marshallese 1–71 (3,500 entries, Marshallese–German 73–180 (5,000 entries), ethnographic notes 181–91, grammar 193–228, language practice 229–47. New York Public Library.

[Feeney, Thomas J., S.J.] [c. 1952.] [Likiep, Marshall Islands: Catholic Mission.] 306 pp. No title page. Mimeographed. Contains entries from Marshallese–English section of Carr and Elbert, with some modifications, and some additional entries, especially of a religious nature.

Grace, George W. 1969. A Proto-Oceanic finder list. University of Hawai'i *Working Papers in Linguistics* 1:39–84.

Harrison, Sheldon P., and Frederick H. Jackson. 1983. Higher numerals in several Micronesian languages. In *Studies in Micronesian linguistics,* ed. by Byron W. Bender, 61–79. Series C-80. Canberra: Pacific Linguistics.

Howells, William. 1973. *The Pacific islanders.* xvi, 299 pp. London: Wiedenfield and Nicolson.

Ko, Young Kuk. 1962. The segmental phonemes of Marshallese, including spectrographic study of the vowels. MS thesis, Georgetown University.

Kotzebue, Otto von. 1821. *Voyage of discovery in the South Sea...1815–18.* 3 vols. London: Longmans.

Kroeber, A. L. 1911. The economic organization of the Marshall Islands. Typescript. Honolulu: U.S. Commercial Company.

Mason, Leonard [and Samuel H. Elbert]. 1952. Anthropology-geography study of Arno Atoll, Marshall Islands. Atoll Research Bulletin 10.20–21. Washington, DC: Pacific Science Board.

Matsuoka, Shizuo. 1929. *Study of the language of the Marshall Islands.* Tokyo: Kyodo Kenkyusha.

Matthews, Peter. 1997. *The concise Oxford dictionary of linguistics.* New York: Oxford University Press.

Nida, Eugene A. 1952. Report on orthographic problems in Marshallese. Unpublished MS. New York: American Bible Society.

Pagotto, Louise. 1987. Verb subcategorization and verb derivation in Marshallese: A lexicase analysis. PhD diss., University of Hawai'i (Available from http://www.proquest.com/products-services/dissertations/).

———. 1992. Constraints on causativization in Marshallese: The case for actor conservation in Oceanic languages. *Oceanic Linguistics* 31:251–66.

Rehg, Kenneth L., with the assistance of Damian G. Sohl. 1981. Ponapean reference grammar. PALI Language Texts: Micronesia. Honolulu: University of Hawai'i Press.

Smith, Alfred G. 1951. Wahween jibehhleh kajin Marshall (Guide to Marshallese spelling). Mimeo. Department of Education, Office of the High Commissioner of the Trust Territory of the Pacific Islands.

Sohn, Ho-min. 1973. Relative clause formation in Micronesian languages. *Oceanic Linguistics* 12:393–406.

Sugita, Hiroshi. 1973. Comparison of verb-object relationships in Micronesian languages. *Oceanic Linguistics* 12:353–92.

Spoehr, Alexander. 1949. *Majuro: A village in the Marshall Islands.* 265 pp. Fieldiana, Anthropology, vol. 39. Chicago Natural History Museum.

Starosta, Stanley. 1982. Mandarin case marking: A localistic lexicase analysis. University of Hawai'i *Working Papers in Linguistics* 14/3:43–96.

———. 1988. *The case for lexicase: An outline of lexicase grammatical theory.* London & New York: Pinter Publishers.

Taylor, C. R. H. 1965. *A Pacific bibliography.* 2nd ed. xxx, 692 pp. London: Oxford University Press.

Tikjinere-Dictionary: Kajin Majōl & Kajin Iñlij: Marshallese & English. 1968. Kwajalein, Marshall Islands: Kwajalein Education Committee. xxxix, 170 pp. Content identical to introductory and Marshallese–English sections of Carr and Elbert, except for addition of preface by chairman of Kwajalein Education Committee, which states that discrepancies and questions of original text copy were resolved by Rev. Jude Samson. Hawaiian and Pacific Collection, University of Hawaii Library.

Tobin, J. A. 1952. *Land tenure in the Marshall Islands.* 36 pp. Atoll Research Bulletin 11. Washington, DC: Pacific Science Board.

———. 2002. *Stories from the Marshall Islands (Bwebwenato jān Aelōñ Kein)*. Honolulu: University of Hawai'i Press.
Tsuchida, Shigeru. 1965. Velarization in Marshallese. Unpublished MS. Honolulu, University of Hawai'i.
Wiens, Herold J. 1962a. *Atoll environment and ecology.* xxii, 532 pp. New Haven, CT. Yale University Press.
———. 1962b. *Pacific island bastions of the United States.* v, 127 pp. Princeton, NJ. Van Nostrand.
Willson, Heather. 2008. Subject positions in Marshallese. PhD diss., University of California, Los Angeles.
———. 2010. Passives and resultatives in Marshallese. *Oceanic Linguistics* 49:233–58.
Zewen, François-Xavier N. 1977. *The Marshallese language: A study of its phonology, morphology and syntax.* Berlin: Reimer.

2 The Sound System of Marshallese

INTRODUCTION

2.1 For a language that uses alphabetic writing, as Marshallese does, it is important to determine what the significant sounds of the language are, because there should be a direct relationship between the two, the sounds and the letters used to spell them. Those who speak Marshallese as their first language have an intuitive feeling for what these basic sounds (phonemes) are, and their ears are specially attuned to them through a lifetime of practice. It is unfortunate that they were not more directly involved when the language was first set to writing in 1863 by people from New England and Hawai'i, whose ears were tuned to their own first languages, English and Hawaiian, respectively. The spelling of Marshallese today would be quite different if those Marshallese who worked with them had been in charge.[1]

The sounds. Marshallese has 19 basic consonants, three semiconsonants, and three basic vowels. Each basic vowel has three pronunciations for which different letters are used, making a total of nine distinct vowel sounds and letters. (As we shall see, two of the basic vowels sometimes combine to create a fourth vowel that also has three distinct sounds, but there are no separate letters for these sounds.) Each of the basic consonants, semiconsonants, and vowels will be discussed in terms of how they are produced by the speech organs. The speech organs include the vocal cords in the throat, the mouth (oral) cavity, the nose (nasal) cavity, the roof of the mouth, the tongue, the teeth, and the lips.

The letters. Marshallese words are written in two different ways in this book: in standard spelling and in phonemic transcription. The phonemic transcription is always enclosed in curly brackets to distinguish it clearly from the standard spelling, and is used only when it is important to show the basic sounds in a way that cannot be done with the standard spelling. For as will be seen, although there is a close relation between the two ways of writing, the standard spelling distinguishes more than the three basic vowels, but does not usually represent other basic sounds, especially two of the semiconsonants.

1. See Bender (1994, 1995) for further details.

The standard spelling. The standard spelling used in this book follows as closely as possible the ways in which Marshallese has been spelled traditionally, while also representing the sounds of the language in a regular way. Where there is a conflict between spelling a word according to one of the ways in which it has usually been spelled, and spelling each sound regularly, the conflict has been settled in favor of the latter—following the principle of always spelling each sound in a predictable way. This causes a change in the spelling of some words; for example, what has usually been spelled *drik* 'small' is now spelled *dik,* and what has usually been spelled *yuk* or *yok* is now spelled *eok.* The number of words changed in this way is not great, however, and the advantages gained are many; one can now be more certain as to how to pronounce a printed word, and the spelling is simpler and easier for children to learn to read and write.

The Roman alphabet was first used to spell the Latin language even before the time of Christ, and has since been used to spell other languages, especially those of Western Europe. It does not have enough of the right kind of letters to show each basic sound of Marshallese, and the people who first tried to use it to write Marshallese began to solve this problem by creating new letters that added marks to some of the Roman letters. New letters created in this way include *ā, ō,* and *ñ.* The standard spelling used in this book has created additional letters by the same means. The extra marks do not greatly change the usual shape of words: *tọ* 'sugar cane' still looks much the same as the way it was usually spelled, *to,* and *m̧arm̧ar* 'necklace' looks much like *marmar.* The marks are available for use whenever necessary to prevent misunderstanding, and should be used in permanently printed works to help everyone learn and remember their significance, but may be omitted in informal writing where no misunderstanding will result.

The major decisions as to the standard spelling were made by a committee appointed by the District Administrator of the Marshall Islands in 1971. The Committee on Spelling Marshallese (COSM) met daily from June 30 through July 9. The members included Ajidrik Bien, Atlan Anien, Carmen Milne, John Heine, Kabua Kabua, Mary Lanwi, Rewa Samuel, Takaji Abo, and Tony DeBrum. The committee left some minor matters to the first author, who served as consultant during the meetings.

The phonemic transcription. Scientists who have been studying human language—linguists—have found that each language has its own set of basic sounds called phonemes, and that the inventory of these basic sounds differs greatly from language to language. Thus, for example, while English has an *r* phoneme and an *l* phoneme, Japanese has only one phoneme somewhere between *r* and *l* in pronunciation, whereas at the other extreme, Marshallese has three *r* phonemes and three *l* phonemes! And while English has a number of fricative phonemes (phonemes in which the air escaping through the speech organs makes a hissing, hushing, or other rushing sound) including *f, v, th, s, z,* and *sh,* Marshallese has no fricative phonemes. The one language can be said to be rich in *r* and *l* sounds but poor in fricatives, while the opposite is true for the other. Such differences create problems for someone trying to learn another language. It takes a great deal of effort for a foreigner to learn to hear and pronounce phonemes that present no difficulty for those who learned the language as children. For example, Americans have no trouble distinguishing *s* and *sh* in English, but they experience great difficulty with the several *l* s in Marshallese.

Such problems help explain why earlier Marshallese spelling did not fit the language perfectly, why words pronounced differently were often spelled the same way. Discovering the phonemes of a language is not a simple process, for while speakers have a feeling for the phonemes of their own language, it is not generally a very conscious one, and needs to be combined with training in phonetics to be brought to fuller awareness. And those who are not native speakers of a language have difficulty avoiding all the problems of foreigners just discussed, even though they may have linguistic training. It is unfortunate that those who first set Marshallese to writing heard it through foreign ears and were unable to distinguish a number of the basic sounds, for as we shall see, the spelling they derived fit the language poorly in a number of places.

The phonemes of a language are the basic sounds that serve to make a word with one meaning different in sound from a word with another meaning. For example, there are two *b* (or *p*) phonemes in Marshallese because they are the sounds that serve to make words like the following different from each other:

jaab	'no'	bwā	'fishpole'
jaap	'red snapper'	pā	'arm, hand'
bokbok	'sandy'	lōb	'grave'
pokpok	'cough'	lep	'egg'

In this book the *b*-sound in the first word of each of these pairs is referred to as "heavy *p*." The sound that occurs in the same place in the second word of each pair is called "light *p*" and is written with the letter *p* to distinguish it from the heavier *b*. Each of the phonemes of the language works in this way to make words sound different from each other so that people can know easily which of several words is being said.

A number of individuals have contributed over the years to the discovery of the phonemes of Marshallese. The work of earlier contributors is summarized in some detail in two of the first author's articles (Bender 1963, 1994) listed in the references at the end of chapter 1. These include the first Bible translators; Fr. Erdland (1906); the anthropologist A. L. Kroeber (1911); Denzel Carr and Samuel Elbert, who did most of the work on the

U.S. Navy dictionary (1945); and Eugene A. Nida, Secretary for Translations of the American Bible Society (1952). More recent contributions have been made by S. Tsuchida (1965), C.-J. N. Bailey (1967), Louise Pagotto (1987), and three of the coauthors of the *Marshallese-English Dictionary* (Abo et al. 1975), who have combined the intuitions of the native speaker with training in linguistics, Takaji Abo, Alfred Capelle, and Tony DeBrum (two of whom also served on the COSM).

Compared to the difficulty of discovering the phonemes of a language that has not been previously analyzed, the task of assigning a different letter to each phoneme for use in a phonemic transcription is a fairly simple matter, because it is possible to use different letters for any one sound. It is most important that each phoneme have a letter of its own—different from all the others. Linguists usually begin with the rich assortment of symbols available in the International Phonetic Alphabet, a collection that is supposed to be adequate for representing all the sounds of all the languages in the world. They then make adaptations as necessary to the typewriter keyboard, the fonts of type a printer has available, the symbols readers may be used to in other languages they know, considerations of word shape, and so forth. All these factors played a part in decisions made concerning the symbols used in the phonemic transcription developed for Marshallese and used in Bender (1969). The decision to use {q} and {g} in the phonemic transcription was made in the late sixties in order to store all the information for the *Marshallese-English Dictionary* on the IBM 365 computer at the University of Hawai‘i at a time when many symbols were not available on the computer, and when it seemed desirable to avoid digraphs (double letters) such as *kw* and *ng* in the computer storage. For ease in reference, the same transcription as was used in Bender (1969) was continued in Abo et al. (1976) and in this work, except that {ẹ} has been substituted for {&} and {ę}, and {k^w} for {q}—with the raised *w* also being used for the rounded consonants {n^w}, {g^w}, {l^w}, and {r^w}.

MARSHALLESE CONSONANTS

2.2 The consonants are presented before the vowels because knowing about them is helpful in gaining an understanding of the vowels. The 19 consonants can be divided into three groups: light, heavy, and rounded. Each of these three groups can be further subdivided in two ways: according to whether or not the sound resonates in the nose cavity, and according to which speech organs are brought into play in shaping the sound.

The light-heavy-rounded distinction. Whether a consonant is light, heavy, or rounded depends on the length of the mouth (oral) cavity from the vocal cords at the back end to the lips at the front. We can consider this cavity as a pipe or tube that runs upward through the throat and then bends to run forward through the mouth. When this tube is kept as short as possible by keeping the tongue low and all organs as near their usual positions of rest as possible, the consonants produced are called "light," or *mera.* When the back of the tongue is raised so as to be closer to the back of the roof of the mouth, thereby making the tube narrower and longer, the consonants produced are "heavy," or *eddo.* (In musical terms we can say that light consonants are sharp *(jaab),* and heavy consonants are flat *(būḷāāt).* And when the shape of the tube that produces heavy consonants is made even longer in front by protruding and pursing the lips, the consonants that are produced are said to be "rounded," or *doulul* (see figure 2-1). The open tube that runs from the lips to the bottom of the throat in the mouth of an adult is about 16 centimeters long when pronouncing the vowel *i* in *pi,* but about 18 centimeters long when pronouncing the *u* of *bu.*) This three-way distinction among light, heavy, and rounded is fundamental in the Marshallese consonant system, and is what makes it possible to have three *l*-sounds and three *r*-sounds, for example (*d* stands for the light *r*-sound).

THE THREE *l*-SOUNDS			
LIGHT:	le	{ley}	'Ms., madam'
HEAVY:	ḷe	{ḷey}	'Mr., sir'
ROUNDED:	ḷwe	{ḷʷẹy}	'pool'
THE THREE *r*-SOUNDS			
LIGHT:	det	{det}	'sunshine'
HEAVY:	rōttā	{rettay}	'they are low'
ROUNDED:	rot	{rʷet}	'kind, sort'

Figure 2-1 The tube that runs from the open lips to the bottom of the throat while making vowel sounds

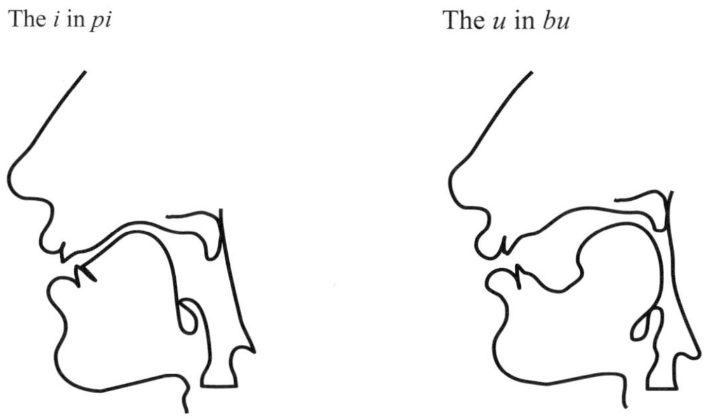

The oral-nasal distinction. An important two-way distinction among consonants concerns whether the sound resonates only in the oral cavity, or in the nasal cavity as well. This is controlled by closing or opening the entrance to the nasal cavity at the back of the mouth. The following pairs of words differ in sound only in this respect:

ORAL:		NASAL:	
baba	'daddy'	m̧am̧a	'mommy'
jaja	'carry on hips'	nana	'bad'
keke	'mature'	ñeñe	'a fathom'

Types of oral closure. The third way in which consonants differ from each other in Marshallese is a five-way distinction having to do with which speech organs are brought into play in shaping the sound by narrowing the mouth down in various ways. (Generally in languages the oral tube is open for vowels but obstructed in various ways for consonants.) For three of the types of closure in Marshallese, the tube is completely closed at some point; for the other two, it is closed either partially or intermittently (with a rapid, fluttering opening and closing). The five heavy oral consonants are used to illustrate the five methods of closure (because there are some consonants missing among the nasals and among the light and rounded consonants in the chart of table 2-1). Figure 2-2 shows the speech organs referred to in this discussion.

Labial stop {b}. Notice that, as the following words are pronounced, the lips are completely closed or "stopped" at both the beginning and at the end of the word.

būb	{bib}	'trigger fish'
bōb	{beb}	'pandanus'
bab	{bab}	'tight'
babbūb	{babbib}	'butterfly'

The {b} sound is termed a heavy oral labial stop—labial referring to the lips that do the closing.

Dental stop {t}. Notice that in the following words the mouth is completely closed at the beginning or the end (or both) by putting the tongue tight against the back of the upper teeth:

tutu	{tiwtiw}	'bathe'
tōt	{tet}	'settled'
tata	{tahtah}	'very'
tūttūt	{tittit}	'breast'

The {t} sound is termed a heavy oral dental stop—dental referring to the teeth against which the tongue brings about the stoppage.

Velar stop {k}. In the words below, it is the back of the tongue that raises to touch the back of the roof of the mouth to close off the oral cavity:

kūk	{kik}	'unripe'
kōk	{kek}	'cracked'
katak	{kahtak}	'learn'
kōkkōk	{kekkek}	'a bird: curlew'

Figure 2-2 The speech organs

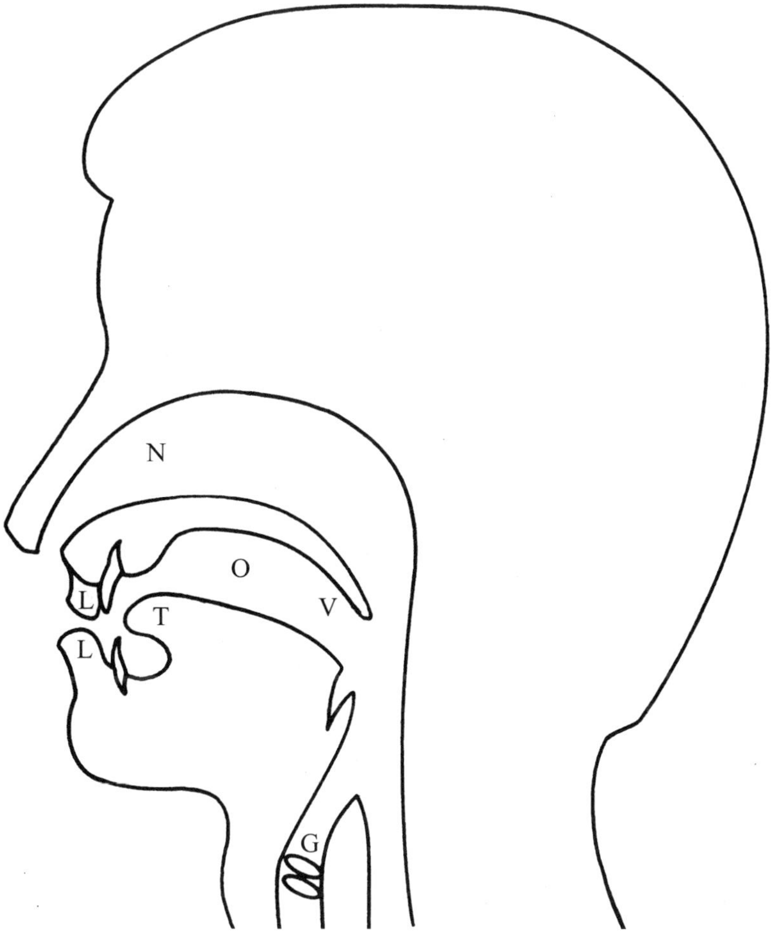

L	lips	V	velum
N	nasal cavity	T	tongue
O	oral cavity	G	glottis (vocal cords)

The {k} sound is termed a heavy oral velar stop—velar referring to the velum at the back of the roof of the mouth, just in front of the opening to the nasal cavity.

Thus, the oral cavity is completely stopped at three places by speakers of Marshallese:

- In front, with the lips, producing the labial stop {b}
- With the tongue tip against the upper teeth, producing the dental stop {t}
- With the back of the tongue against the velum, producing the velar stop {k}

Lateral liquid {ḷ}. For lateral sounds, the oral cavity is not completely closed. Instead, the tip of the tongue is placed against the back of the upper teeth or against the gum ridge just behind them, much as it is for the {t} sound, but the cavity remains open at both sides of the tongue. The following words have this sort of central closure and side opening:

ḷōḷ	{ḷeḷ}	'moldy'
ḷōḷḷap	{ḷeḷḷap}	'old man'
ḷōḷaḷḷaḷ	{ḷeḷaḷḷal}	'knocking; bone-dry (E)'

The {ḷ} sound is termed a heavy lateral liquid—lateral referring to the sides of the tongue where the oral passage is kept open.

Retroflex liquid {r}. For retroflex sounds, the oral cavity is rapidly closed and opened by curling back the tongue and trilling it against the gum ridge behind the upper teeth, as in the following words:

rar	{rar}	'dry leaves over fire'
rōreo	{rereyew}	'clean (E)'
reaar	{rẹyyahar}	'east'

The {r} sound is termed a heavy retroflex liquid—retroflex referring to the curling back of the tongue while performing the trill against the gum ridge.

Most of the terms used to describe the sounds refer to the speech organs involved in their production: *labial,* to the lips; *dental,* to the teeth; *nasal,* to the nose, and so on. A few terms, however, seek to express something of the feeling the sound gives those who hear it. The term *liquid* used to describe the last two sounds is this sort of impressionistic label. It attempts to convey something of what *l* and *r*-sounds have in common, perhaps that like water running, the vowel-like resonance of the oral cavity is never really stopped by these sounds, but continues around the sides of the tongue or between the brief closures of the trill. It is probably not coincidental that the word *liquid* itself begins with a liquid sound.

The terms *light* and *heavy* are also of this latter impressionistic sort. Interestingly, they are translations of the terms invented by some early Marshallese grammarian and now generally used to distinguish, for example, **p** ("*p-emera*" 'light p') from **b** ("*p-eddo*" 'heavy p').

THE CONSONANT SYSTEM

2.2.1 The consonants of Marshallese may be charted as in table 2-1 to show their interrelations. Each consonant is represented by its regular spelling in the chart; its phonemic transcription is also given where there is a difference between the two.

Note the position in the heavy column of the five sounds already introduced: *b, t, k, ḷ,* and *r;* and that although each of the first three—the stops—has a nasal counterpart just beneath it, the labels oral and nasal are not used in the lower part of the chart, among the liquids and semiconsonants. Note also the gaps in the chart indicated by dashes. That there are no rounded labials may be due to the impossibility of further rounding the lips when they are already closed to produce a labial sound. Also, the absence of light velars is probably due to the impossibility of keeping the tongue away from the velum—which is necessary for producing light consonants—while it is against the velum for velar stops. The absence of *tw,* a rounded dental oral stop, is more difficult to explain, because its nasal counterpart *ṇw* does occur, and the most we can say is that it is probably an accidental gap. Finally, the dashes in the semiconsonant row indicate that the light and heavy semiconsonants are not generally represented in spelling by their own distinctive letters. The labels of the chart can be used to describe each sound briefly but distinctively in the conventional ways shown in table 2-2.

Each section that follows presents the consonants that have the same type of closure and gives examples of all light, heavy, and rounded varieties that occur. Examples are chosen and arranged to highlight the sound differences being focused upon and to show each sound at the beginning, in the middle, and at the end of various words. A phonemic transcription is provided for each word as a guide to some of the sound features not shown in the spelling, and each section includes a discussion of how the sounds are spelled.

Table 2-1 Consonant chart

			LIGHT	HEAVY	ROUNDED
STOPS					
	LABIAL				
		ORAL	p	b	—
		NASAL	m	ṃ	—
	DENTAL				
		ORAL	j	t	—
		NASAL	n	ṇ	ṇw {ṇ^{w}}
	VELAR				
		ORAL	—	k	kw {k^{w}}
		NASAL	—	ñ {g}	ñw {g^{w}}
LIQUIDS					
	LATERAL		l	ḷ	lw {ḷ^{w}}
	RETROFLEX		d	r	rw {r^{w}}
SEMICONSONANTS			— {y}	— {h}	w

Table 2-2 Consonant descriptions

p	light labial stop	j	light dental stop	—	
b	heavy labial stop	t	heavy dental stop	k	(heavy) velar stop
—		—		kʷ	rounded velar stop
m	light labial nasal	n	light dental nasal	—	
ṃ	heavy labial nasal	ṇ	heavy dental nasal	ñ	(heavy) velar nasal
—		ṇʷ	rounded dental nasal	ñʷ	rounded velar nasal
l	light lateral	d	light retroflex	y	light semiconsonant
ḷ	heavy lateral	r	heavy retroflex	h	heavy semiconsonant
ḷʷ	rounded lateral	rʷ	rounded retroflex	w	rounded semiconsonant

LABIAL CONSONANTS

2.2.2 As this portion of the consonant chart shows, there are four labial consonants: two oral and two nasal, and two light and two heavy.

LABIAL		LIGHT	HEAVY	ROUNDED
	ORAL	p	b	—
	NASAL	m	ṃ	—

The examples in tables 2-3 and 2-4 show the four labial consonants in various contexts.

Table 2-3 Oral labial consonants: LIGHT VS. HEAVY

{p} VS. {b} INITIALLY					
pi	{piy}	'bee'	bwi	{biy}	'drying rack'
pepe	{peypey}	'decide'	bwebwe	{beybey}	'tuna'
pā	{pay}	'arm'	bwā	{bay}	'fishing pole'
pata	{pahtah}	'war'	bata	{bahtah}	'priest'
puwaḷ	{piwaḷ}	'coward'	bu	{biw}	'gun'
pok	{pẹkʷ}	'tangled'	bok	{bẹkʷ}	'blister; bladder'
pokpok	{pekʷpekʷ}	'cough'	bokbok	{bekʷbekʷ}	'sandy'
pọpo	{pawpẹw}	'coiled'	bọbo	{bawbẹw}	'fishing method'
{p} VS. {b} MEDIALLY					
kapen	{kapen}	'captain'	jabōn	{jaben}	'end of'
kōpa	{kepah}	'incest'	kōba	{kebah}	'copper'
jepe	{jepey}	'basket'	jebwe	{jebey}	'paddle'
{p} VS. {b} FINALLY					
ip	{yip}	'crooked'	ibeb	{yibyẹb}	'gush'
tap	{tap}	'thatch frame'	tab	{tab}	'haze'
jaap	{jahap}	'red snapper'	jaab	{jahab}	'no'
wōp	{wẹp}	'*Barringtonia* sp.'	ob	{wẹb}	'chest'
kap	{kap}	'bolt of cloth'	kab	{kab}	'cup; and'
kōpkōp	{kepkep}	'struggle'	kōb	{kẹb}	'dig'
lep	{lẹp}	'egg'	leb	{lẹb}	'grave'

Table 2-4 Nasal labial consonants: LIGHT VS. HEAVY

{m} VS. {m̜} INITIALLY					
miin	{miyin}	'stingy'	m̧wiin	{m̧iyin}	'this house'
me	{mẹy}	'barricade'	m̧we	{m̧ẹy}	'this house'
mā	{may}	'breadfruit'	m̧wām̧wā	{m̧aym̧ay}	'food (baby)'
māj	{maj}	'eye'	m̧aj	{m̧aj}	'eel, worm'
maaj	{mahaj}	'open field'	m̧aaj	{m̧ahaj}	'march'
mar	{mar}	'bush'	m̧arm̧ar	{m̧arm̧ar}	'necklace'
mō	{meh}	'elastic'	m̧ō	{m̧eh}	'emaciated'
men	{men}	'thing'	m̧ōn	{m̧en}	'house of'
merā	{meray}	'parrotfish'	m̧ōrā	{m̧eray}	'dry'
{m} VS. {m̧} MEDIALLY					
tōmak	{temak}	'believe'	tōm̧a	{tem̧ah}	'light bulb'
imen	{yimen}	'ray fish'	im̧ōn	{yim̧en}	'house of'
limabukwi	{limabik^{w}iy}	'500'	lim̧a	{lim̧ah}	'you women'
{m} VS. {m̧} FINALLY					
nām	{nam}	'taste'	nam̧	{nam̧}	'secondary lagoon'
am	{ham}	'our (EXCL)'	am̧	{ham̧}	'your (SG)'
waam	{waham}	'our vehicle'	waam̧	{waham̧}	'your vehicle'
kijem	{kijem}	'our food'	kijem̧	{kijem̧}	'your food'
ippām	{yippam}	'with us'	ippam̧	{ippam̧}	'with you'

Light and heavy *b* and *m* were not generally distinguished in earlier Marshallese spelling practices, except indirectly through differences in preceding or following vowels, or by the insertion of a following *w.* Most writers used the letter *b* for both oral stops, but some used *p* for the light variety, especially at the end of words. The COSM decided to extend this latter practice consistently throughout words, and to mark the heavier *m.* The committee also decided to continue inserting *w* after heavy *b* and *m̧* before the vowels *i, e,* and *ā* to maintain the usual shape of words such as *bwebwe* and *m̧we.* It should be understood, however, that the letter *w* in such words does not stand for the rounded semiconsonant phoneme {w} as in *wa* or *awa;* it simply emphasizes that the preceding labials are of the heavy variety.

DENTAL CONSONANTS

2.2.3 As this portion of the consonant chart shows, there are five dental consonants: light and heavy oral, and all three nasal varieties.

DENTAL		LIGHT	HEAVY	ROUNDED
	ORAL	j	t	—
	NASAL	n	ņ	ņw {ņ^{w}}

In tables 2-5 and 2-6, the light and heavy oral consonants are contrasted first, then the light and heavy nasals, and finally the heavy and rounded nasals. The light and heavy consonant pair *j* and *t* have been consistently represented in Marshallese spelling practices. The only known exceptions are those of foreign map makers in names such as Jaluit {jalẹwẹj} and Mejit {majẹyẹj}, but such mistakes are understandable because {j} at the end of a word is often unreleased—the tongue remains against the teeth indefinitely—and is, therefore, more difficult for the nonnative to hear as distinct from {t}. (More accurate spellings for these two words would be *Jālwōj* and *Mājeej,* respectively.)

The three *n*-sounds have all been written with a single letter *(n)* traditionally, and in the above spelling the heavy and rounded ones are given a mark to distinguish them from the light ones. The rounded ones are further distinguished from the heavy ones by having a preceding rounded vowel (*u, o,* or *ọ*) as in *boṇ,* or where this is not possible, a following rounded vowel (*u* or *o*) as in *ṇotaan,* or where neither of the preceding is possible, by a following *w* as in *ṇwab.* The rounded {ṇʷ} is a rare sound in Marshallese, and the examples in table 2-6 represent most of the recorded occurrences.

Table 2-5 Oral dental consonants: LIGHT vs. HEAVY

{j} vs. {t} INITIALLY					
jaja	{jahjah}	'carry on hips'	tata	{tahtah}	'very'
jab	{jab}	'not'	tab	{tab}	'haze, fog'
jok	{jekʷ}	'alight'	tok	{tekʷ}	'hither'
jọ	{jaw}	'ignite'	tọ	{taw}	'sugar cane'
jen	{jẹn}	'shrink'	tōn	{tẹn}	'ton'
jep	{jẹp}	'biased'	tōp	{tẹp}	'wood shavings'
jo	{jẹw}	'float loose'	to	{tẹw}	'get off'
jāje	{jayjẹy}	'machete'	tāte	{taytẹy}	'bind'
{j} vs. {t} MEDIALLY					
aji	{hajiy}	'chopsticks'	ati	{hatiy}	'drying rack'
kajin	{kajin}	'language'	katin	{katin}	'carton'
kọọjoj	{kawajwẹj}	'use a blanket'	kọọtot	{kawatwẹt}	'stealing'
{j} vs. {t} FINALLY					
aj	{haj}	'liver'	at	{hat}	'hat'
ij	{yij}	'I am'	it	{yit}	'make fire'
wūj	{wij}	'uproot'	ut	{wit}	'flower'
waj	{waj}	'watch'	wat	{wat}	'puffer fish'
wōj	{wẹj}	'toward you'	wōt	{wẹt}	'rain'
āj	{yaj}	'weave'	āt	{yat}	'name; eyebrow'
bọḷōj	{baḷʷej}	'ballast'	paḷōt	{paḷet}	'ballot'

Table 2-6 Nasal dental consonants: LIGHT vs. HEAVY vs. ROUNDED

{n} vs. {ṇ} INITIALLY					
ne	{ney}	'leg, foot'	ṇe	{ṇey}	'that by you'
naṃ	{naṃ	'secondary lagoon'	ṇaṃ	{ṇaṃ}	'mosquito'
nono	{newnew}	'pound'	ṇo	{ṇew}	'wave'
naajdik	{nahajdik}	'to feed'	ṇajikin}	{ṇahjikin}	'make room for'
nana	{nahnah}	'bad'	ṇa	{ṇah}	'shoal'
{n} vs. {ṇ} MEDIALLY AND FINALLY					
kane	{kaney}	'tasty with'	kaṇe	{kaṇey}	'those by you'
jino	{jinew}	'begin'	jiṇo	{jiṇẹw}	'a sore; snow'
kōnpat	{kẹnpat}	'*Sonneratia* sp.'	kōṇṇat	{kẹṇṇat}	'*Scaveola* sp.'

Table 2-6 Nasal dental consonants: LIGHT vs. HEAVY vs. ROUNDED (continued)

kōnono	{kenewnew}	'speak'	kōṇo	{keṇew}	'*Cordia* sp.'
ennek	{yennek}	'harvest (W)'	eṇṇok	{yeṇṇek}	'sharp pain (W)'
en	{yen}	's/he is to'	eṇ	{yeṇ}	'that'
kankan	{kankan}	'tug'	kaṇ	{kaṇ}	'those'
kwōn	{kʷen}	'you are to'	koṇ	{kʷeṇ}	'compact'
{ṇ} VS. {ṇʷ} INITIALLY					
ṇaṃ	{ṇaṃ}	'mosquito'	ṇwab	{ṇʷab}	'popping sound'
ṇōjje	{ṇejjey}	'snap'	ṇwōj	{ṇʷej}	'snapping sound'
{ṇʷ} INITIALLY, ADDITIONAL EXAMPLES					
		ṇotaan	{ṇʷetahan}		'his/her fault'
		ṇwōmṇwōm	{ṇʷemṇʷem}		'siphon'
		ṇwōmpe	{ṇʷẹmpẹy}		'alcoholism'
		ṇooniep	{ṇeweniyep}		'fairy'
		ṇoṇṇoṇmeej	{ṇʷeṇʷṇʷeṇʷmeyej}		'marrow'
{ṇ} VS. {ṇʷ} MEDIALLY AND FINALLY					
ṃan	{ṃan}	'kill'	mọṇ	{maṇʷ}	'feces'
ṃane	{ṃaney}	'kill him, her'	mọṇe	{ṃaṇʷẹy}	'surgeon fish'
ṃōṇe	{ṃeṇey}	'that house'	ṃoṇe	{ṃeṇʷey}	'deceive him, her'
eṇ	{yeṇ}	'that'	eoṇ	{yeṇʷ}	'go aground'
tōṇ	{tẹṇ}	'ton'	toṇ	{teṇʷ}	'tune; eel'
			boṇ	{beṇʷ}	'clogged'
			kajṇoṇ	{kajṇʷeṇʷ}	'nasal speech'
			mọṇmọṇ	{maṇʷmaṇʷ}	'haunted'

VELAR CONSONANTS

2.2.4 As this portion of the consonant chart shows, there are four velar consonants: two oral and two nasal, and two heavy and two rounded.

VELAR		LIGHT	HEAVY	ROUNDED
	ORAL	—	k	kw {kʷ}
	NASAL	—	ñ {g}	ñw {gʷ}

The examples in tables 2-8 and 2-9 show each sound in various contexts. The {k} and {kʷ} sounds are spelled in these examples according to the most common of traditional practices, wherein both are represented by *k.* However, when the letter *k* stands for the {kʷ} sound, only rounded vowel letters (*u, o,* or *ọ*) may precede it (as in *lukwarkwar, bok,* and *ḷọk*); of the various vowel letters, only *u* or *o* may follow it directly (as in *kur* and *koṇ*). All other following vowel letters (*i, e, a, ā,* or *ō*) must be separated from it by the letter *w,* as in *jukkwe, jokwe, jokwa, jokwā,* and *bọkwōj.* (The letter *w* in such words does not stand for the rounded semiconsonant phoneme {w} as in *iuwe* or *ewi;* it simply marks the preceding *k* as rounded.) Thus, to summarize, the letter *k* stands for {kʷ} rather than {k} if it is preceded by *u, o,* or *ọ* and/or followed by *u, o,* or *w.* Otherwise, it stands for {k}.

Table 2-7 Oral velar consonants: HEAVY vs. ROUNDED

{k} vs. {kʷ} INITIALLY					
ki	{kiy}	'key'	kwi	{kʷiy}	'hot-tempered'
ke	{key}	'yes?'	kwe	{kʷey}	'you (SG)'
keke	{kẹykẹy}	'sew'	kwekwe	{kʷẹykʷẹy}	'scrape'
kōb	{kẹb}	'dig'	kob	{kʷẹb}	'bent'
Kōle	{kẹlẹy}	'Kili Island'	kole	{kʷẹlẹy}	'hungry'
kaḷ	{kaḷ}	'loincloth'	kwaḷ	{kʷaḷ}	'wash'
karkar	{karkar}	'cut copra'	kwarkwar	{kʷarkʷar}	'sardine'
kōṃa	{keṃah}	'cauldron'	koṃa	{kʷeṃah}	'comma'
kōṇ	{keṇ}	'caulk'	koṇ	{kʷeṇ}	'compact'
kūr	{kir}	'call'	kur	{kʷir}	'squirrel fish'
kūtak	{kitak}	's.w. wind'	kutak	{kʷitak}	'rake'
kiin	{kiyin}	'now'	kwiin	{kʷiyin}	'queen'
kūḷatḷat	{kiḷatḷat}	'spoon'	kuḷatḷat	{kʷiḷatḷat}	'c.nut scrubber'
{k} vs. {kʷ} MEDIALLY					
jekaka	{jekahkah}	'a chip'	jokwa	{jekʷah}	'clumsy'
jekākā	{jekaykay}	'hereabouts'	jokwā	{jekʷay}	'driftwood'
likarkar	{likarkar}	'a shell'	lukwarkwar	{likʷarkʷar}	'to chase'
bakōj	{bakej}	'bucket'	bọkwōj	{bakʷej}	'embrace'
{k} vs. {kʷ} FINALLY					
bwilak	{bilak}	'unicorn fish'	bwilọk	{bilakʷ}	'broken'
ek	{yẹk}	'fish'	eok	{yẹkʷ}	'you (OBJ)'
bōk	{bek}	'bring, take'	bok	{bekʷ}	'sand'
ḷak	{ḷak}	'then; lock'	ḷọk	{ḷakʷ}	'away'
laklak	{laklak}	'helmet shell'	lọklọk	{lakʷlakʷ}	'wave tail—fish'

Table 2-8 Nasal velar consonants: HEAVY vs. ROUNDED

{g} vs. {gʷ} INITIALLY					
ñar	{gar}	'coconut'	ñortak	{gʷertak}	'snore'
ñōñatñat	{gegatgat}	'repugnance (E)'	ñoñortaktak	{gʷegʷertaktak}	'snoring (E)'
ñūñ	{gig}	'packed'	Ñoñ	{gʷegʷ}	'Jaluit islet'
{g} vs. {gʷ} MEDIALLY					
tōñal	{tegal}	'sweet'	toñōl	{tegʷel}	'comeuppance'
bōḷñak	{beḷgak}	'split open'	lōḷñọñ	{leḷgʷagʷ}	'terror'
tūññūḷọk	{tiggiḷakʷ}	'ringing'	tuññūlaḷḷọk	{tigʷgʷilaḷḷakʷ	'sink'
			aeñwāñwā	{hayegʷaygʷay}	'clamor'
{g} vs. {gʷ} FINALLY					
būñal	{bigal}	'dusty'	buñ	{bigʷ}	'fall down'
ḷañ	{ḷag}	'storm'	ḷọñ	{ḷagʷ}	'canoe roller'
ṃōñka	{ṃegkah}	'cartoon'	ṃoñ	{ṃegʷ}	'gateway'
mañ	{mag}	'brown coconut'	mọñ	{magʷ}	'pate of the head'
peñpeñ	{pegpeg}	'muscular'	poñpoñ	{pegʷpegʷ}	'cover pandanus'
eañ	{yag}	'north'	eọñ	{yagʷ}	'sprout'

The spelling of rounded *ñ* {g^w} generally parallels that of rounded *k* {k^w} except that a following *w* is inserted only when no rounded vowel letter precedes, so that while 'its tail' {lek^{w}an} is spelled *lokwan* rather than *lokan,* the word for 'canoe roller of' {ḷeg^{w}an} is spelled *ḷoñan* rather than *ḷoñwan.* Similarly, 'to dwell' {jẹk^{w}ẹy} is spelled *jokwe* rather than *joke,* but 'fall down on' {big^{w}it} is spelled *buñūt* rather than *buñwūt.* Like rounded *ṇ* {ṇ^w} (but unlike rounded *k* {k^w}), rounded *ñ* {g^w} is rare, and the words listed in table 2-8 constitute most, if not all, of the instances we have found.

LIQUID CONSONANTS

2.2.5 As this portion of the consonant chart shows, all three varieties of both lateral and retroflex liquids occur.

LIQUIDS		LIGHT	HEAVY	ROUNDED
	LATERAL	l	ḷ	lw {l^w}
	RETROFLEX	d	r	rw {r^w}

Examples of light and heavy laterals are contrasted first in table 2-9, then heavy and rounded in table 2-10. Parallel order is followed for retroflex examples in tables 2-11 and 2-12.

Traditional Marshallese spelling did not distinguish the three *l*'s. The spelling used here marks the heavy and rounded ones to distinguish them from the light ones. The rounded ones are then further distinguished from the heavy ones by having rounded vowels either precede or follow the rounded *l*'s, or where this is not possible, as in *ḷwe,* by inserting a following *w.*

Table 2-9 Lateral liquid consonants: LIGHT VS. HEAVY

{l} VS. {ḷ} INITIALLY					
lōn	{lẹg}	'above'	ḷōñ	{ḷẹg}	'lust'
lañ	{lag}	'sky'	ḷañ	{ḷag}	'storm'
laklak	{laklak}	'helmet shell'	ḷakḷak	{ḷakḷak}	'swagger'
lām	{lam}	'clam organ'	ḷam	{ḷam}	'bay'
lā	{lay}	'to list'	ḷā	{ḷay}	'gravel; file'
lōlō	{lehleh}	'pierce'	ḷōḷō	{ḷehḷeh}	'to wreathe'
lōt	{let}	'clean'	ḷōt	{ḷet}	'which man?'
lokwan	{lek^{w}an}	'its tail'	ḷokwan	{ḷek^{w}an}	'its rear end'
{l} VS. {ḷ} MEDIALLY					
bwilak	{bilak}	'a fish'	būḷak	{biḷak}	'raise; block'
kōlla	{kellah}	'a dump'	kōḷḷā	{keḷḷay}	'pay'
kilaba	{kilahbah}	'suicide'	kūḷaabreej	{kiḷahabreyej}	'gadget'
{l} VS. {ḷ} FINALLY					
al	{hal}	'song'	aḷ	{haḷ}	'sun'
el	{yẹl}	'nest'	eḷ	{yẹḷ}	'take seriously'
āl	{yal}	'shave'	āḷ	{yaḷ}	'coconut milk'
bal	{bal}	'covered'	baḷ	{baḷ}	'boom end'
bwil	{bil}	'hot'	būḷ	{biḷ}	'box fish'
jool	{jewel}	'neglected'	jooḷ	{jeweḷ}	'musical syllable'
pāl	{pal}	'arrowroot season'	paḷ	{paḷ}	'furious'

Table 2-10 Lateral liquid consonants: HEAVY VS. ROUNDED

{ḷ} VS. {ḷ^{w}} INITIALLY					
ḷōt	{ḷet}	'which man?'	ḷot	{ḷ^{w}et}	'die out'
ḷōñ	{ḷẹg}	'lust'	ḷoñ	{ḷ^{w}ẹg^{w}}	'ant'
ḷein	{ḷẹyin}	'this man'	ḷwe	{ḷ^{w}ẹy}	'pool'
ḷọñ	{ḷag^{w}}	'canoe roller'	ḷọñ	{ḷ^{w}ag^{w}}	'house fly'
ḷōb	{ḷeb}	'tail feather'	ḷobḷoba	{ḷ^{w}ebḷ^{w}ebah}	'lavalava'
ḷōjo	{ḷejew}	'nosebleed'	ḷojat	{ḷ^{w}ejat}	'soggy'
{ḷ} VS. {ḷ^{w}} MEDIALLY AND FINALLY					
lōḷñọñ	{leḷg^{w}ag^{w}}	'terror'	loḷātāt	{leḷ^{w}yatyat}	'intellect'
ṃwilin	{ṃilin}	'his/her behavior'	ṃuḷe	{ṃiḷ^{w}ey}	'dove'
peḷaj	{peḷaj}	'flush (poker)'	paḷot	{paḷ^{w}et}	'ballot'
jeḷā	{jeḷay}	'know'	Joḷ	{jeḷ^{w}}	'clan name'
peḷak	{peḷak}	'hut'	poḷ	{peḷ^{w}}	'anus'
taḷōn	{taḷen}	'talent'	tọḷ	{taḷ^{w}}	'singeing strips'
tōḷao	{teḷahwew}	'sitting mat'	toḷ	{teḷ^{w}}	'mountain'
jiḷait	{jiḷahyit}	'slice'	juḷ	{jiḷ^{w}}	'sprout'
jeḷate	{jeḷatey}	'unsnarl it'	ijoḷ	{yijeḷ^{w}}	'to relish'
bōḷoñar	{bẹḷẹwgar}	'coconut kernel'	boḷ	{bẹḷ^{w}}	'core'
bōḷaḷ	{beḷaḷ}	'lightweight'	boḷot	{beḷ^{w}et}	'damp'
būḷab	{biḷab}	'bluff'	buḷaboḷ	{biḷ^{w}aboḷ^{w}}	'*Sonneratia*'
			buḷuḷḷuḷ	{biḷ^{w}iḷ^{w}ḷ^{w}iḷ^{w}}	'bubble'

The light *r* {d} has traditionally been written *dr* with some exceptions. Unfortunately the "person prefix" *ri/rū/ru-* as in *ri-jerbal* 'worker', *ri-Iaab* 'Yapese', *ri-eọñod* 'fisherman', *ri-kaki* 'teacher, preacher', *ri-taktō* 'patient', *ri-Kōle* 'person from Kili', *ruwa* 'sailor', and so on, came to be written generally as a separate word spelled *dri* using the *dr* combination, even though the *r* involved is of the heavy variety. This usage in this one very common prefix has caused some confusion as to which *r* the *dr* combination of letters is really meant to stand for. The *r* has often been omitted from the combination, especially at the end of words as in *ad* 'our', *wōd* 'coral', and so forth, and this practice is extended to all occurrences of light *r* in the spelling used in this volume. Heavy *r* {r} and rounded *r* {r^{w}} are both spelled as *r,* with the rounded one distinguished by a preceding or following rounded vowel, or a following *w,* using the same method already described for rounded *ñ* {g^{w}}.

Table 2-11 Retroflex liquid consonants: LIGHT VS. HEAVY

{d} VS. {r} INITIALLY					
do	{dẹw}	'soaking net'	ro	{rẹw}	'enraged'
de	{dẹy}	'just'	re	{rẹy}	'musical syllable'
da	{dah}	'blood'	ra	{rah}	'branch'
dak	{dak}	'duck'	rak	{rak}	'south'
dāp	{dap}	'moray eel'	rap	{rap}	'rasping sound'
dọọl	{dawal}	'dye'	rọọl	{rawal}	'return'
dāde	{daydẹy}	'tangled'	rā	{ray}	'board, plank'
dej	{dej}	'flee'	rej	{rej}	'they are'

Table 2-11 Retroflex liquid consonants: LIGHT VS. HEAVY (continued)

{d} VS. {r} MEDIALLY					
ṃade	{ṃadẹy}	'spear'	ṃare	{ṃarey}	'marry'
jedān	{jedan}	'coconut sap'	jeran	{jeran}	'his/her friend'
jidaak	{jidahak}	'land a canoe'	jiraak	{jirahak}	'move'
kadek	{kadek}	'intoxicating'	karōk	{karek}	'arrange'
{d} VS. {r} FINALLY					
ad	{had}	'our (INCL)'	ar	{har}	'lagoon beach'
ṃadṃōd	{ṃadṃẹd}	'harvest'	ṃarṃar	{ṃarṃar}	'necklace'
ṃōd	{ṃẹd}	'provisions (E)'	ṃōrṃōr	{ṃerṃer}	'foam'
ñad	{gad}	'gums'	ñar	{gar}	'coconut meat'
jād	{jad}	'rack'	jar	{jar}	'pray'
kadkad	{kadkad}	'throw'	karkar	{karkar}	'cut copra'
pedped	{pedped}	'foundation'	perper	{perper}	'underestimate'
pid	{pid}	'posterior'	pir	{pir}	'slip down'
wōd	{wed}	'coral'	or	{wer}	'fish gills'
wūd	{wid}	'piece'	ur	{wir}	'tumor'
ed	{yẹd}	'baby mat'	er	{yẹr}	'they, them'
eded	{yedyed}	'snooping'	erer	{yeryer}	'canoe part'
id	{yid}	'lei strands'	ir	{yir}	'dislocated'

Table 2-12 Retroflex liquid consonants: HEAVY VS. ROUNDED

{r} VS. {r^w} INITIALLY					
rañ	{rag}	'wild duck'	rọñ	{r^wag^w}	'hole'
rōṃ	{rẹṃ}	'landslide'	rom	{r^wẹm}	'wink'
rōbtak	{rebtak}	'to goose'	roba	{r^webah}	'rubber'
rōbbat	{rebbat}	'they're late'	robba	{r^webbah}	'trumpet'
rōjañ	{rejag}	'encourage'	rojak	{r^wejak}	'boom'
ri-ṃwijbar	{riṃijbar}	'barber'	ruṃwij	{r^wiṃij}	'late'
rijjiit	{rijjiyit}	'receipt'	ruj	{r^wij}	'awaken'
ripija	{ripijah}	'artist'	rup	{r^wip}	'broken'
{r} VS. {r^w} MEDIALLY AND FINALLY					
ṃūrar	{ṃirar}	'reddish'	ṃuri	{ṃir^{w}iy}	'debt, credit'
tūrūn	{tirin}	'bundle of'	turūn	{tir^{w}in}	'near'
erak	{yerak}	'spread mats'	eoreak	{yer^{w}yak}	'level off'
jirab	{jirab}	'hoist'	jurōn	{jir^{w}en}	'handle of'
ṃōrābōt	{ṃeraybet}	'wet clothes'	ṃor	{ṃer^w}	'worn out'
ṃōrṃōr	{ṃẹrṃẹr}	'foam'	ṃur	{ṃir^w}	'hip; chant'
er	{yẹr}	'they, them'	eor	{yẹr^w}	'bleached'
ār	{yar}	'to beach'	eọr	{yar^w}	'oyster'
ir	{yir}	'dislocated'	iur	{yir^w}	'flock; swift'
jiraak	{jirahak}	'move'	ijur	{yijir^w}	'incense'
iññūr	{gigir}	'groan (E)'	iññurñur	{gigir^{w}gir^w}	'crunch (E)'

Semiconsonants

2.2.6 As this portion of the chart indicates, there is a semiconsonant from each of the major groups of consonants—light, heavy, rounded—but only *w* has been written in Marshallese spelling practices to date in some of the words in which the {w} sound occurs.

SEMICONSONANTS	LIGHT	HEAVY	ROUNDED
	— {y}	— {h}	w

Thus, there is a sense in which it can be said that these are the invisible consonants of Marshallese. Nor are they easy to hear, especially for those just learning the language. The {y} is not always as clear as the English y, the {h} is not as breathy as the English *h,* and only the *w*'s at the beginning of a word sound at all like English *w*'s. There are indirect ways in which their existence can be shown. They can be heard to have the same effect on vowels next to them as do the other consonants in each of their groups (2.3), and their presence can be felt through the effects they have on the timing or rhythm of words, especially when they occur in pairs (2.4.3) or next to other consonants (2.4.2). But, because they are not as easy to detect as the other consonants, it is appropriate that they should be called semi-consonants or "half" consonants.

Most languages have similar sounds. As has been noted, in all languages, the oral tube is open for vowels but obstructed in various ways for consonants. The sounds under discussion in this section lie somewhere in between, neither as open as vowels nor as obstructed as other consonants. In some languages, such sounds are called semivowels or glides, but in Marshallese they are called semiconsonants because they behave more like the consonants than like the vowels.

In previous sections, it has been noted that the oral tube is either completely, partially, or intermittently stopped for each of the other consonants. For the semiconsonants, it is simply narrowed a bit or constricted (but not completely closed) at one of three places (or a combination thereof). The constriction may be made by raising the front of the tongue toward the roof of the mouth (the palate) just behind the upper teeth, thereby producing the {y} semiconsonant. Or it may be made by drawing the tongue root back to narrow the throat and by also raising the back of the top of the tongue to approach the velum, thereby narrowing and elongating the back part of the oral tube and producing the {h} semiconsonant. Finally, while maintaining the {h} constriction, one can protrude and round the lips, thereby further elongating and narrowing the total oral cavity and producing the {w} semiconsonant. Note the parallel between {w} and the other members of the rounded consonant group: for example, just as a rounded *ļ* {ḷʷ} consists of a heavy *ļ* with lip-rounding added, {w} can be viewed as an {h} (pharyngeal and velar constriction) with labial constriction added.

The semiconsonants vary in their degree of constriction depending on the closeness of the neighboring vowels. The main difference among the basic Marshallese vowels lies in how close or open they are (see "Dimension 1: high–low" on page 38), and semiconsonants occurring next to close vowels have greater constriction than those occurring next to more open vowels.

Sound Variation among the Consonants

2.2.7 In the preceding sections, it has been noted that place and manner of consonant closure (labial, dental, velar, lateral, retroflex) are significant in distinguishing Marshallese consonants from each other. The consonants are further distinguished by the opening of the nasal cavity (nasalization) and the three-way shaping of the oral cavity into light (palatalized), heavy (velarized), or rounded (velarized and labialized) consonants. There are other distinctions significant in other languages but not in Marshallese that may pose difficulties for Marshallese speakers attempting to learn those languages. One such distinction is the voicing of consonants, which is a most important one in English, for example. English has eight pairs of consonant phonemes that differ primarily in voicing—whether the vocal cords in the throat are vibrating and humming during the closure of the consonant (or at least by the time of its release), or whether they relax and let the air from the lungs pass silently through (even after the consonat has been released, when it is a stop).

Here follow examples of these eight English pairs, together with an indication of what both members of the phoneme pair have in common while differing in voicing. All these terms have already been introduced except for affricate (a combination stop-fricative sound—one that follows full stoppage with a fricative release) and alveolar (the name of the gum-ridge behind the upper teeth).

VOICED:	VOICELESS:	BOTH ARE
bottle	pot	labial stops
dot	tot	dental
got	cot	velar
Jew	chew	palatal affricates
view	few	labial fricatives
then	thin	dental
zoo	sue	alveolar
u<u>s</u>ual	shoe	palatal

Although the three voiced stops (the first sounds of *bottle, dot, got*) do not have the vocal cords vibrating throughout the time of closure (as happens with voiced stops in some languages), the vocal cord vibration for the following vowel begins much more promptly than it does following the voiceless stops of *pot, tot,* and *cot,* where it is postponed until several fractions of a second after the release of the stop, with voiceless breath (aspiration) escaping in the meantime. The Marshallese equivalents ({b}, {t}, {k}) are more similar to the English voiced stops than they are to the voiceless ones, having prompt onset of voicing for the following vowel and no aspiration. And as has been noted, the pairs {b} and {p}, {t} and {j}, and {k} and {k^{w}} differ in ways not involving the matter of voicing, so that they do not furnish the Marshallese speaker learning English a basis upon which to build. Such learners have most difficulty with the voiceless stops, which they do not give as much aspiration as do native speakers of English.

Marshallese stops coming at the end of a word are generally not released, nor are they voiced as much as they might be at the beginning of a word or between vowels, so that the only clues available to distinguish a final {p} from a final {b}, or {j} from {t}, or {k} from {k^{w}} are in the sound of the preceding vowel.

wōp	{wẹp}	'*Barringtonia* sp.'	ob	{wẹb}	'chest'
wōj	{wẹj}	'beautiful'	wōt	{wẹt}	'rain'
bōk	{bek}	'bring, take'	bok	{bek^{w}}	'sand'

Another interesting comparison from the chart of English consonant pairs involves fricatives and affricates, of which Marshallese has none, while English has a total of 10. An examination of English words borrowed into Marshallese gives an indication of the substitutions made by Marshallese learning English. The two English labial fricatives (like the two labial stops) are represented by {p} if the neighboring English sound is a front vowel See "Dimension 2: front–back" on page 38), or by {b} if it is a back vowel or a consonant:

piba	{piybah}	'fever'	pārokōrāāp	{payrewkerayap}	'paragraph'
penkō	{penkeh}	'vinegar'	baḷeboọḷ	{bahḷẹybawaḷ}	'volleyball'
kọpe	{kawpẹy}	'coffee'	taibuun	{tahyibiwin}	'typhoon'
Pāpode	{papewdey}	'February'	bọjet	{bawjet}	'faucet'
pābōḷ	{paybeḷ}	'bevel'	būḷab	{biḷab}	'bluff'

The two dental fricatives are represented by {t}:

Taije	{tahyijey}	'Thursday'	Jabōt	{jabet}	'Sabbath'
tōrej	{teryej}	'thread'	bata	{bahtah}	'Father, priest'

But the remaining four fricatives, the two affricates, and occasionally English *t*—a total of seven English phonemes—are all represented by {j} in Marshallese:

jijāj	{jiyjaj}	'scissors'	jiij	{jiyij}	'cheese'
Jijej	{jiyjẹj}	'Jesus'	jānij	{janij}	'change'
tōjin	{tẹhjin}	'dozen'	jọkleej	{jak^{w}leyej}	'chocolate'
juuj	{jiwij}	'shoes'	bajinjea	{bahjinjeyah}	'passenger'
Eijia	{yẹyijiyah}	'Asia'	juwain	{jiwahyin}	'twine, lace'

Marshallese {j} shows considerable variation in pronunciation from word to word and from speaker to speaker. Although, like the other stops, it is generally not released when at the end of a word, elsewhere it shows a bit of frication in its release, and can, thus, be said to be the closest thing Marshallese has to a fricative or an affricate. The above examples show how it serves to represent six different English fricatives and two affricates in loanwords, and biligual speakers who have mastered these different sounds in their speaking of English often transfer them over to their pronunciation of the {j} phoneme in such loanwords. And having mastered the range of sounds {j} can represent, younger speakers especially tend to pronounce it in a variety of ways in native words as well. Thus, it is not uncommon to hear *jaja,* for example, pronounced as *chacha, sasa, zaza,* or *shasha.* This sort of lisping is called *weejej.*

In contrast to the variability in the pronunciation of {j}, the other consonants are quite stable. The velars, for example, show much less variation in sound than they do in English. English *k* not only varies between aspirated and unaspirated varieties, it also closes at different points, depending on the quality of the neighboring vowel. (As noted in section 2.3, the tongue narrows the oral tube at different points in forming various vowels: the front of the tongue approaches the palate for the front vowel of *keel,* the back approaches the velum for the high back vowel of *cool,* and even when the tongue remains low of the low back vowel of *call,* the resulting narrowest point in the tube is even further back. The initial *k*'s in these words anticipate the narrow points necessary for the following vowels and make their own closure as near as possible; that of *keel* is palatal, that of *cool* is velar, and that of *call* back velar.) Marshallese *k* in contrast is quite stationary and independent of the effects of neighboring vowels, closing against the same part of the velum whether vowels are front or back. If one listens closely to the vowel of *ki* {kiy} 'key', the backness of the closure as compared to English *key* shows up briefly as the back vowel *ū* heard immediately after the *k* release: *k-**ū**-i.* Or in reverse order in the word *iññā* {yiggay} 'yes': *i-**ū**-ññā.* (Some bilingual speakers have mastered the "traveling" *k* of English and substitute it for the stationary *k* of Marshallese, especially in loanwords such as *key.*)

To sum up this section, recall the opening sentence of 2.2 on page 20, "The consonants are presented before the vowels because knowing about them is helpful in gaining an understanding of the vowels." It can be said that whereas English consonants tend to be greatly influenced by English vowels, Marshallese consonants exert great influence on the vowels of the language. This will become evident in the next section.

MARSHALLESE VOWELS

2.3 The vowels of a language often differ from each other along three basic dimensions.

Dimension 1: high–low. For some vowels, the oral tube may be quite open, while for others it may be closed down considerably at some point. (*Open vowels* are also called *low vowels,* referring to the relatively low position of the tongue in the mouth, and *close vowels* are also called *high vowels,* referring to the raising of some part of the tongue.) For example, in the word *aū* {hahih} 'be dying' the first vowel is open or low, and the second is close or high. Some vowels are neither high nor low, but *mid.* In the word *aō* {haheh} 'to swim', the second vowel is higher than the first but not as high as the second one of *aū*; it is termed a *mid* vowel.

Dimension 2: front–back. If the front of the tongue has been raised to approach the palate during the production of a vowel as in *kiki* {kiykiy} 'to sleep', the vowel is termed a high front vowel, while if the back of the tongue has been raised to approach the velum as in *būbū* {bihbih} 'grandma', the vowel is termed a high back vowel. If the tongue remains low in the mouth but with the narrowest portion of the tube nevertheless beneath the palate during the production of a vowel such as that of *kākā* {kaykay} 'these here', the vowel is called a low front vowel. Similarly, if the tongue remains low but with the narrowest part of the tube beneath the velum, the vowel is termed a low back vowel, as in *tata* {tahtah} 'very'. With these two dimensions, it is possible to chart the vowels as follows (if the *ō* of *aō* is established as mid back, and the *e* of *ke* {key} 'question word' is added as mid front):

	FRONT	BACK
HIGH	i	ū
MID	e	ō
LOW	ā	a

Dimension 3: lips rounded–unrounded. While the tongue is in any of the foregoing positions, the lips may be either *rounded* or left in the position that is more usual when the mouth is open, an unpursed, *unrounded* position. While many European languages, for example, have both front and back rounded vowels, Marshallese has only back rounded vowels in addition to the unrounded ones charted above. For example, the vowels in *bubu* {biwbiw} 'divination' are rounded' those in *būbū* {bih-bih}'grandma' are not. The vowel in *mo* {mew} 'to heal' is rounded, that in *mō* {meh} 'elastic' is not. That in *tọ* {taw} 'sugar cane' is, that in *ta* {tah} 'what?' is not. The three vowel letters just introduced— *u, o, ọ* — can be added to the chart as follows:

	FRONT UNROUNDED	BACK UNROUNDED	BACK ROUNDED
HIGH	i	ū	u
MID	e	ō	o
LOW	ā	a	o̧

(Note that the labels of the rows and columns in the chart can be used to identify each letter distinctively: *a* stands for a low back unrounded vowel sound, *o̧* for a low back rounded one, *e* for a mid front [unrounded] one, and so on.)

At the beginning of the chapter it was noted that Marshallese has nine vowel letters but only three basic vowel phonemes. The nine letters in the preceding chart are the nine letters that were referred to; how they relate to a smaller number of basic phonemes (three) will be made clear in the sections to follow.

In reviewing the three possible dimensions of vowel systems just introduced, it should be noted that there is considerable parallel between the narrowing of the vocal tube beneath the palate for front vowels in (Dimension 2) and the palatal constriction of {y} and the other light consonants discussed in 2.2.6 and at the beginning of 2.2. Similarly, there is a parallel between the narrowing beneath the velum for back vowels and the velar constriction of {h} and the other heavy consonants. As will be seen in the sections to follow, whether a vowel has a front or back sound (Dimension 2), and whether a back vowel is rounded or not (Dimension 3) are determined by the consonants on either side of the vowel. Only the height or open-close dimension (Dimension 1) proves to be fundamental to the three vowel phonemes in distinguishing them from each other.

The High-vowel Phoneme {i}

2.3.1 The three letters from the high row of the last vowel chart (on page 38) are all representatives of one high vowel phoneme {i}, which ranges in sound from the *i* of *di* {diy} 'bone' through the *ū* of *būbū* {bihbih} 'grandma' to the *u* of *kuku* {kiwkiw} 'carry on the back', depending on the consonant phonemes on either side of it. This can be more clearly seen when the invisible semiconsonants in these three words are made visible:

di{y}	bū{h}bū{h}	ku{w}ku{w}

Other instances of the high vowel phoneme with invisible neighboring semiconsonants include:

{y}ij	'I am'	{h}ūrōj	'bother'	{w}uñ	'complete'
{y}i{y}	'in, at'	{h}a{h}ū{h}	'to die'	{w}u{w}	'fish trap'

Observe also the following words:

dim	'tight'	kūr	'to call'		kuk	'cook'
nin	'to pound'	tūb	'reward'		kuḷuḷ	'cockroach'
lij	'to mash'	ñūñ	'compact'		rur	'pick flowers'
pil	'a drop'	būḷ	'boxfish'		jiñurñur	'eardrum'

Note that they are arranged in three columns paralleling those above, with those having the *i* letter (and sound) in the first column, those with the *ū* in the second, and those with *u* in the third. Note that unlike the preceding words, these words contain no invisible consonants (semiconsonants); all are visible. Most important, note that all consonants in the first column are light, all consonants in the second column are heavy, and all consonants in the third column (except for the *ji-* of *jiñurñur)* are rounded!

This is the secret of the Marshallese vowel phonemes—how nine seemingly different sounds and letters represent only three phonemes. Each of the three phonemes has three distinct sounds: a front vowel sound when between light consonants, a back unrounded vowel sound when between heavy consonants, and a back rounded vowel sound when between rounded consonants. Thus, the phoneme {i} has an *i* sound in *nin* between light *n's,* an *ū* sound in *ñūñ* between *ñ's* (members of the heavy consonant group), and an *u* sound in *rur* between rounded *r*'s.

This is what was meant by the earlier statement that the fronting, backing, and rounding of Marshallese vowels are all attributed to the effects of neighboring consonants. They determine whether intervening vowels shall have a front or a back sound, and an unrounded or a rounded sound. All that is left for the vowel phonemes to determine is whether their representatives shall be high, mid, or low—matters of tongue height.

To make the point even stronger, it should be noted that it is impossible to have an *ū* or an *u* sound between light consonants; *i* is the only permissible representative of the high vowel phoneme {i} in this environment. Thus, there can be no word *nūn* or *nun* in Marshallese if the *n*'s are of the light variety—only *nin.* Similarly with the other light consonants in various combinations: *jūn, jun, nūj,* and *nuj* are all impossible, and words such as *Juun* 'name of sixth month' and *nuuj* 'news' do not disprove this observation, because as their phonemic transcriptions show, they have invisible w's that cause the rounding of their vowels: {jiwin} and {niwij}, or in mixed transcription, *Ju*{w}*un* and *nu*{w}*uj.*

And similarly with the heavy and rounded consonants: it is impossible to have a short *i* or *u* sound between heavy consonants — only *ū* as in *būb* 'triggerfish' as the representative of the high vowel phoneme {i} in this environment. Nor is it possible to have a short *i* or *ū* sound between rounded consonants—only *u* as in *kuk* 'cook'. This explains why English words like *tin* and *pink* are borrowed into Marshallese with "long" or double vowels, so that there can be an intervening (although invisible) {y} to give the vowels a front sound: *ti{y}in* and *pi{y}iñ,* and similarly why *soup* and *shoes* are borrowed with prolonged *u* sounds as *ju{w}ub and ju{w}uj,* respectively, so there can be an intervening {w} to give the vowels a round sound approximating their sound in English.

Thus far the discussion has been oversimplified in that it has made it seem that the {i} phoneme has only three distinct sounds depending on its consonantal environment. This is because only "pure" environments have been considered, those in which the consonants on both sides of the vowel were in agreement: both consonants were light, both were heavy, or both were rounded. What does the phoneme sound like when it is in mixed environments, when one of its consonant neighbors comes from one group and the other neighbor comes from another?

As might be expected, in such environments the vowel is caught between competing forces, and ends up sounding not exactly like any of the three sounds *i, ū,* or *u,* but as one of a variety of intermediate sounds, depending on the competing consonants. For example, in the word *kij* {kij} 'louse' the vowel is between heavy *k* and light *j.* Heavy *k* calls for it to have the *ū* sound, while light *j* calls for the *i* sound. Which command does it obey? In a sense, both. It is as if the word were really sounded as *kūij,* with the vowel sounding more like *ū* at first just after the *k* but moving to sound like *i* before the *j* is reached. All this happens so rapidly that the actual sound is more like a cross between *i* and *ū.*

The same sort of thing happens in all mixed environments. The preceding example had consonants that differed just one step on the light-heavy-rounded scale, with one light and the other heavy. The situation is even more extreme when the consonants differ by two steps, with one light and the other rounded, as in *iur* {yir^{w}} 'swift; flock', where the vowel sound must travel rapidly the full range from *i* through *ū* to *u: yiūur*^{w}. Or the reverse situation in rounded-light words such as *ruj* {r^{w}ij} 'awaken' and *rup* {r^{w}ip} 'broken': *r*^{w}*uūij* and *r*^{w}*uūip.* Obviously such words should not be written in this way; they would end up being too long and clumsy. One solution would be to always choose one and the same one of the three available letters for all mixed environments, because it is possible to predict the actual sound if one knows the consonants on either side. This is what the phonemic transcription does—the high vowel phoneme is always written as {i} no matter what its precise sound.

But such a solution goes against people's feelings about the letter i, which they have come to associate with the front vowel sound through spelling practices to date, and furthermore there is no traditional way to mark consonants such as *r* as rounded except by writing rounded vowel symbols (such as *u* or *o*) next to them, or by following them with a *w.* A solution more in keeping with tradition is to choose from among all three available letters—*i, ū, u*—depending on the combination of consonants involved, as in the standard spelling.

Table 2-13 shows the choices made for all types of environments, pure and mixed. The consonants preceding the vowel are listed along the left side, and those following the vowel are at the top. Three cover symbols L, H, and R are used for light, heavy, and rounded full consonants; each of the three semiconsonants is shown separately from the other members of its group, because each needs special consideration in spelling because of its general invisibility. The table can be used as follows: if one wants to know how the high vowel is spelled between *p* and *ñ,* that is, following a light and preceding a heavy consonant, one finds the cell in which the L row intersects the H column. Because the cell contains an *i,* this would mean that a word such as {pigpig} would be spelled *piñpiñ,* with *i* as the vowel letter in both syllables. The table summarizes the decisions made with respect to the standard spelling in an attempt to spell the language systematically while departing as little as possible from traditional practices.

Table 2-13 Spellings of the high vowel

THE PHONEME {i}							
	Before:	{y}	L	H	{h}	{w}	R
After:	{y}	i	i	i	ū[1]	i, u[2]	i, u[2]
	L	i	i	i	ū	u	u
	H	i	i	ū	ū	u	u
	{h}	i[3]	ū	ū	ū	u[4]	u[4]
	{w}	i	ū[5]	u	ū	u	u
	R	i	ū[5]	u	ū	u	u

1. {y} preceding this *ū* becomes *i* when it is initial or follows a consonant or *e* or *ā,* thus, creating *iū* sequences.
2. Spelled *i* if the {w} or R is in turn followed by a vowel, as in {yikʷẹlẹy} 'I am hungry', which is spelled *ikwōle; u* if it is final or followed by a consonant, as in {ṃẹyikʷ} 'goods', which is spelled *ṃweiuk.* As the last example shows, {y} preceding such *u*'s becomes *i,* paralleling those preceding the *ū*'s of note 1.
3. {h} preceding this *i* would become *ū* after a consonant or initially, although no examples have been found.
4. Similarly for any {h}'s preceding these *u*'s.
5. When the {w} or R are medial, u (as in *jouj* {jẹwij} 'kindness', *turun* {tirʷin} 'near it').

Following are some additional examples of mixed environments arranged according to types. The types are labeled with the same cover symbols used in Table 2-13, so that L__H refers to the high vowel phoneme in an environment preceded by a light consonant and followed by a heavy one. Note that the words in the right and left columns are mirror images of each other, so that the one pronounced backward should sound like the other.

	L__H			H__L	
liṃ	{liṃ}	'murky water'	ṃwil	{ṃil}	'behavior'
jik	{jik}	'bower'	kij	{kij}	'louse'
it	{yit}	'make fire'	ti	{tiy}	'tea'
ik	{yik}	'joining'	ki	{kiy}	'key'
iñ	{yig}	'fish spines'	ñi	{giy}	'tooth'
jib	{jib}	'swell up'	bwij	{bij}	'lineage'
lik	{lik}	'outside'	kil	{kil}	'skin'
	H__R			R__H	
bu	{biw}	'gun'	ub	{wib}	'tender'
ruk	{rik^w}	'yaws'	kur	{k^{w}ir}	'a fish'
tu	{tiw}	'there'	ut	{wit}	'flower'
	L__R			R__L	
du	{diw}	'to boil'	wūd	{wid}	'piece'
ju	{jiw}	'perpendicular'	wūj	{wij}	'uproot'

These examples illustrate more graphically than Table 2-13 how the high vowel is treated in mixed environments.

A comparison of the standard spelling and the phonemic transcription shows that the vowel is always *i* next to an invisible {y} and *u* next to an invisible {w}, as in *it, ti, bu, ub,* and *du.* An example such as *ūl {hil}* 'dorsal fin' (not included above) shows that in parallel fashion the high vowel is always *ū* next to an invisible {h}. (Only when it is between two different invisible semiconsonants do exceptions to these general statements occur, as in the word *iu* {yiw} 'sprouted coconut'.) As a very rough rule of thumb to help determine which vowel letter should be used in a given mixed environment (reminiscent of the *jaañke* 'jan ken po' game) one can say that invisible semiconsonants outweigh visible ones (and all other consonants), round consonants overrule heavy and light, and—between heavy and light—the consonant preceding the vowel generally overrules the one following it.

THE MID-VOWEL PHONEME {e}

2.3.2 The three letters from the mid row of the chart under Dimension 3 (on page 38) are all representatives of one mid-vowel phoneme {e}, which ranges in sound from the *e*'s of *jememe* {jemeymey} 'antisocial' through the *ō*'s of *ṃōṇōṇō* {ṃeṇehṇeh} 'happy' to the *o*'s of *roro* {rewrew} 'clothesline'. The details of this phoneme parallel in every way those of {i}; only the height of the tongue is different. Mixed transcription (which inserts semiconsonants into the standard spelling) of the above words brings out the role of the semiconsonants in determining the differences in sound represented by the three letters:

jeme{y}me{y} ṃōṇō{h}ṇō{h} ro{w}ro{w}

Other instances of the mid vowel phoneme with invisible neighboring semiconsonants include:

{y}ej	's/he is'	{h}ōr{h}ōr	'slash'	{w}o{w}	'Oh!'
{h}a{y}e{y}	'current'	{h}a{h}ō{h}	'swim'	ru{w}o{w}	'two'

Instances without semiconsonants include:

ded	'size'	tōt	'settled'	tokokkok	'cluck'
jen	'let's'	kōk	'split'	rorror	'dog bark'
men	'thing'	bōb	'pandanus'	ṇok	'wet'
jej	'we are'	ḷōḷ	'moldy'	N̄on̄	'Jaluit islet'

Note how light consonants are again found on both sides of the *e*'s in the first column, heavy consonants the *ō*'s in the second column, and rounded consonants the o's in the third column. Also, paralleling the explanation of the high vowel, words or syllables such as *dōd, dod, tet, tot,* and so on are not possible in Marshallese. The following are a few words borrowed into the language with long or double mid vowels so that an intervening semiconsonant can help give the two vowels the desired sound:

pe{y}en	'pen'	tō{h}ōm	'term'	ko{w}oj	'course'
pe{y}eḷ	'bell'	jō{h}ōt	'shirt'	bo{w}oj	'boat'
re{y}ek	'rake'	jō{h}ōm	'germ'	jo{w}ob	'soap'
re{y}eḷ	'rail'	bō{h}ōr	'pearl'	ko{w}ot	'goat'
te{y}ek	'deck'	nō{h}ōj	'nurse'	ko{w}ontōreak	'contract'

Table 2-14 shows the letters chosen for all environments, pure and mixed.

Table 2-14 Spellings of the mid vowel

THE PHONEME {e}							
	Before:	{y}	L	H	{h}	{w}	R
After:	{y}	e	e	e	ō[1]	e,o[2]	e,o[2]
	L	e	e	e[3]	ō	o	o
	H	e	ō	ō	ō	o	o
	{h}	e[4]	ō	ō	ō	o[5]	o
	{w}	e	ō[6]	o	ō[7]	o	o
	R	e	ō[6]	o	ō	o	o

1. {y} preceding this {ō} becomes *e* when it is initial or follows a consonant, thus, creating *eō* sequences.
2. *e* if the {w} or R is in turn followed by a vowel, as in {yekʷẹḷẹy} 's/he is hungry', which is spelled *ekwōle; o* if it is final or followed by a consonant, as in {jeyerʷ} 'erase', which is spelled *jeor.*
3. Except after light *l,* where *ō* is used, as in *lōn̄* 'above' and *lōn̄* 'many'.
4. {h} preceding this *e* becomes *ō,* as in the place name {yanẹy-jahẹyhẹy} 'Maloelap islet' spelled *Āne-jaōeōe.*
5. Similarly for any *h*'s preceding these *o*'s.
6. When the {w} or R are medial, o (as in *toon* {tewen] 'pass of' or *bukon* [bikʷen} 'district of').

7. No such examples have been found.

Table 2-14 parallels table 2-13 in every way. The mixed environment L__H is one where usage varies greatly. After most of the light consonants, the letter *e* is more common, as in *dekā* 'stone', *deñdeñ* 'hit', *det* 'sunshine', *jebwe* 'oar', *jekjek* 'chop', *jeḷā* 'know', *jerbal* 'work', *jet* 'some', *jete* 'how many', *mekak* 'clot', *meram* 'light', *metak* 'pain', *meto* 'ocean', *nebar* 'praise', *neḷ* 'make weapons', *net* 'squid', *peḷḷok* 'open', *peran* 'brave', *pet* 'pillow'; but after *l* the letter *ō* is more common, as in *lōb* 'grave', *lōñ* 'above', *lōññā* 'riddle', *lōkā* 'surfing', *lōklōk* 'grass', and *lōñ* 'many'. Hence the decision to make light *l* an exception in the L__H environment, as in note 3 to the table.

Following are additional examples of the mid vowel in mixed environments, arranged according to types. As with the high vowel display (in 2.3.1), the left and right columns are mirror images phonemically.

	L__H			H__L	
eb	{yeb}	'dance'	bwe	{bey}	'because'
eṇ	{yeṇ}	'that'	ṇe	{ṇey}	'that by you'
lōt	{let}	'well-sifted'	tōl	{tel}	'to lead'
	H__R			R__H	
toḷ	{teḷʷ}	'mountain'	ḷot	{ḷʷet}	'die out'
to	{tew}	'rope; channel'	wōt	{wet}	'only'
tor	{terʷ}	'kind, type'	rot	{rʷet}	'kind'
ro	{rew}	'the (PL HUM)'	or	{wer}	'fish gills'
ṇok	{ṇekʷ}	'wet'	koṇ	{kʷeṇ}	'orderly'
	L__R			R__L	
mo	{mew}	'to heal'	wōm	{wem}	'pull out'
jok	{jekʷ}	'alight'	kwōj	{kʷej}	'congeal'

THE LOW-VOWEL PHONEME {a}

2.3.3 The three letters from the low row of the last chart in 2.3 (on page 38) are all representatives of the low-vowel phoneme {a}, which ranges in sound from the *ā* of *jāje* {jayjẹy} 'sword' through the *a*'s of *tata* {tahtah} 'very' to the *ọ* of *tọ* 'sugar cane'. The details of this phoneme parallel in every way those of {i} and {e}; only the height of the tongue—in this case, its lowness—is different. Mixed transcription of the above words brings out the role of the semiconsonants in determining the differences in sound represented by the three letters:

jā{y}je{y}　　　ta{h}ta{h}　　　tọ{w}

Other instances of the mid vowel phoneme with invisible neighboring semiconsonants include:

{y}āj	'weave'	{h}añ	'wind'	{w}ọb	'wharf'
{y}a{y}ẹ{y}	'letter ā'	ña{h}	'I'	{w}ọ{w}ọ{w}	'letter o'

Instances without semiconsonants include:

jāj	'snapper; judge'	bab	'tight'	leḷñọñ	'terror'
pād	'stay'	bar	'again; rock'	rọñ	'hole'
lāj	'ferocious'	ḷañ	'storm'	ḷọñ	'house fly'
jāp	'cheek'	tab	'haze'	tọḷ	'singeing strips'
nām	'flavor'	ṇaṃ	'mosquito'	tūṃṃọṇ	'pluck'
jād	'rack'	otar	'order'	otọr	'squall'

Note that light consonants are to be found in the first column—as they were with the high and mid vowels, heavy consonants in the second, and rounded ones in the third. Note also the impossibility of *pad, pọd, bār, rān̄,* and so on.

Table 2-15 Spellings of the low vowel

THE PHONEME {a}							
	Before:	{y}	L	H	{h}	{w}	R
After:	{y}	ā	ā[1]	a[2]	a[3]	ọ[4]	ọ[4]
	L	ā	ā	a	a	ọ	ọ
	H	ā	a	a	a	ọ	ọ
	{h}	a	a	a	a	ọ	ọ
	{w}	ā	a[5]	a	a	ọ	ọ
	R	ā	a	a	a[6]	ọ	ọ

1. Before light consonants and also the heavy consonants *r* and *t,* as in {yar} 'lung' and {yat} 'eyebrow', spelled *ār* and *āt,* respectively.
2. Before heavy consonants except *r* and *t.* {y} preceding this *a* becomes *e* when it is initial or follows a consonant, as in {yag} 'north' and {tekyak} 'arrive', spelled *eañ* and *tōkeak,* respectively.
3. {y} preceding this *a* also becomes *e* when it is initial or follows a consonant, as in {bijyahyah} 'tread water', {kalbewenyah} 'name of Mejit tract', and {bewyah} 'adolescent', spelled *bwijeaea, Kalboonea,* and *boea,* respectively.
4. {y} preceding these *ọ*'s becomes *e* when it is initial or follows a consonant, as in {yar^w} 'oyster', {yenyar^w} 'Ebon islet', and {yag^{w}ed} 'to fish', spelled *eọr, Eneọr,* and *eọñōd,* respectively.
5. When {w} is medial, ọ (as in Jọọn {jawan} 'man's name'.
6. No such examples have been found.

The following are words borrowed into the language with double vowels to permit an intervening consonant to help achieve the nearest possible vowel sound to the English models:

tā{y}āñ	'tank'	ļa{h}aṃ'	lamp'	bọ{w}ọļ	'ball'
pā{y}āñ	'bank'	ba{h}ak	'barque'	bọ{w}ọk	'box'
jā{y}āk	'check'	ka{h}aj	'cards'	jọ{w}ọļ	'salt'
kā{y}āñ	'gang'	ja{h}at	'chart'	kọ{w}ọn	'corn'
pā{y}āñkōļ	'bangle'	ja{h}aj	'charge'	tọ{w}ọk	'drydock'
tā{y}ākji	'taxi'	ṃa{h}ab	'mop'	tọ{w}ọt	'thwart'

Table 2-15 shows the letters chosen to represent the low vowel phoneme in all environments, pure and mixed, and parallels tables 2-13 and 2-14. A comparison of the three tables shows that the low front vowel letter *ā* is used less in its table than its two front counterparts *e* and *i* are in their respective tables. It appears in neither the H__L nor the L__H cells (e.g., *ļap* and *pat* rather than *ļāp* and *pāt*), nor does it appear in the {y}__H (see note 2) or {h}__{y} cells (*aikuj* rather than *āikuj* for {hayik^{w}ij}). All the decisions summarized in these tables were made in the interests of following traditional spelling practices as closely as possible while being systematic. This is no simple matter because the Roman alphabet that was originally used for spelling Marshallese fit it so poorly.

Following are additional examples of the low vowel in mixed environments, arranged according to types. Again, the left and right columns are mirror images phonemically.

	L__H			H__L	
daṃ	{daṃ}	'forehead'	ṃad	{ṃad}	'loiter'
jar	{jar}	'pray'	raj	{raj}	'whale'
jab	{jab}	'not'	baj	{baj}	'just'
lañ	{lag}	'sky'	ñal	{gal}	'knead'
jañ	{jag}	'cry'	ñaj	{gaj}	'fragrant'
pat	{pat}	'swamp'	tap	{tap}	'frame'
paļ	{paļ}	'furious'	ļap	{ļap}	'large'
naṃ	{naṃ}	'lagoon'	ṃan	{ṃan}	'kill'
eaļ	{yaļ}	'coconut milk'	ļā	{ļay}	'gravel'
ār	{yar}	'lung'	rā	{ray}	'board'
	H__R			R__H	
tọ	{taw}	'sugar cane'	wat	{wat}	'a fish'
ļọk	{ļak^w}	'the last'	kwaļ	{k^{w}aļ}	'wash'
rọ	{raw}	'testicle'	war	{war}	'barren'
	L__R			R__L	
jọ	{jaw}	'ignite'	waj	{waj}	'watch'
eọ	{yaw}	'tattoo'	wā	{way}	'injection'

The High-mid Derived Vowel {ẹ}

2.3.4 It was noted at the beginning of the chapter that two of the vowel phonemes sometimes combine to create a fourth vowel that has three distinct sounds in the same way as the other three vowels do, but for which there are no separate letters in the standard spelling. The two vowels that combine to create the fourth vowel are {i} and {e}, and the sounds created in this way are intermediate between them—hence the name "high-mid." The letters used to represent it are the same as those used for the mid vowel: *e, ō,* and *o.* How the high and mid vowels combine to create this vowel is discussed in 2.5.3; the emphasis in this section is on giving examples of the vowel in various environments and on showing that it does contrast in sound with both its high and mid sources.

Following are three minimal triplets (sets of three words that differ in only one sound each) that show these contrasts among each of the front, back, and back rounded sounds:

ki	{kiy}	'key'	aū	{hahih}	'dying breath'	tu	{tiw}	'where'
ke	{kẹy}	'porpoise'	aō	{hahẹh}	'mine'	to	{tẹw}	'get off'
ke	{key}	'when'	aō	{haheh}	'swim'	to	{tew}	'rope'

Following are examples of the high-mid vowel with semiconsonants in mixed transcription:

{y}e{y}	's/he'	{h}ōññōñ	'interjection'	{w}o{w}	'pale'
{y}ed	'baby mat'	ra{h}rō{h}	'clean area'	ño{w}	'stone fish'
de{y}	'just'	{h}ōn	'vitamin'	ro{w}	'angry'

Further examples without semiconsonants follow:

med	'cooled off'	rōṃ	'crumble'	rọkrok	'scratch'
jej	'no more'	kōb	'dig'	kor	'frightened'
lel	'struck'	ḷōñ	'lust'	ḷoñ	'ant'
lem	'bailer'	rōk	'south'	ḷor	'undergrowth'
pej	'pandanus key'	bōt	'naughty'	boñ	'night'
pel	'boxfish'	kōt	'rotten'	koṃ	'you (PL)'
mej	'dead'	ṃōṃ	'desire'	kob	'bent'
jen	'shrink'	ṃōk	'tired'	jukok	'open oven'

Note, as with the other three vowels, the occurrence of light consonants in the first column, heavy consonants in the second, and rounded consonants in the third. Here follows a listing of some of the loanwords with medial semiconsonants in mixed transcription:

ke{y}ej	'case'	kō{h}ōb	'curve'	bo{w}oḷ	'full'
ke{y}ek	'cake'	nō{h}ōb	'nerve'	ko{w}oḷ	'gold'

Because the high-mid vowel is spelled the same as the mid vowel, table 2-14 summarizes its spellings as well. One of the main reasons for merging the spelling of the two is that the high-mid vowel is unstable and there is considerable interchanging of it with the mid vowel as one moves from one dialect to another, or from the speech of one person to another. For example, the following are a few of the words that are treated differently in the two major dialects:

		RĀLIK PRONUNCIATION	RATAK PRONUNCIATION
irooj	'chief'	{yirewej}	{yirẹwẹj}
ṃōk	'tired'	{ṃẹk}	{ṃek}
mo	'healed'	{mẹw}	{mew}
mō	'elastic'	{mẹh}	{meh}

A number of other words show the same sort of variation in pronunciation although it cannot be pinned down so tightly to the two major dialects. In the following sample, the pronunciation with the wider currency is given first:

		ALTERNATIVE PRONUNCIATIONS	
bukelōlō	'kneel'	{bik^{w}eylehleh}	{bik^{w}ẹylehleh}
ajjinono	'whisper'	{hajjinewnew}	{hajjinẹwnẹw}
appeleñleñ	'bothered'	{happelẹglẹg}	{habbilegleg}
jeleñleñ	'intense'	{jẹlẹglẹg}	{jilegleg}
jeṃjerā	'be friends'	{jẹṃjeray}	{jẹṃjẹray}
jo	'float loose'	{jẹw}	{jew}
jeḷo	'grasshopper'	{jẹyḷẹw}	{jeyḷew}
jedpanit	'serpent'	{jedpanit}	{jẹdpanit}
jepukpuk	'keg'	{jepik^{w}pik^{w}}	{jẹpik^{w}pik^{w}}
jepleklek	'scattered'	{jẹplẹklẹk}	{jepleklek}
jeje	'sail into the wind'	{jeyjey}	{jẹyjẹy}
jitōñ	'designate'	{jiteg}	{jitẹg}
koko	'ringworm'	{kewkew}	{kẹwkẹw}
kino	'fern'	{kinew}	{kinẹw}
kūrōn	'accelerate'	{kiren}	{kirẹn}
ḷōke	'cross over'	{ḷẹkẹy}	{ḷekey}
mede	'chisel'	{medey}	{mẹdẹy}
mije	'stay by'	{mijey}	{mijẹy}
nono	'pound'	{newnew}	{nẹwnẹw}
pọljej	'a dish'	{paḷ^{w}jej}	{paḷ^{w}jẹj}
kwōlej	'plover'	{k^{w}ẹlyẹj}	{k^{w}elyej}
tooj	'break off'	{tẹwẹj}	{tewej}
orjib	'to molt'	{werjib}	{wẹrjib}
ineknek	'decorate'	{yineknek}	{yinẹknẹk}

There is also some sporadic (irregular and unpredictable) interchange of the high-mid vowel with the high vowel:

bwijin	'flock'	{bijin}	{bẹjẹn}
jinjin	'curse'	{jinjin}	{jẹnjẹn}
kanijnij	'swear'	{kanijnij}	{kanẹjnẹj}

and with the low vowel:

baj	'just'	{baj}	{bẹj}
nājin	'child of'	{najin}(E)	{nẹjin}(W)
waj	'toward you'	{waj}	{wẹj}
kaab	'curve'	{kahab}	{kẹhẹb}

but these latter interchanges are not nearly so frequent as those with the mid vowel. All the interchanges taken together do help show the instability of the high-mid vowel and give support to the decision not to attempt to spell it with separate letters in the standard spelling. Although all of the preceding examples have been sporadic or unpredictable (there is no general rule that the mid and high-mid vowels can be switched freely in all words containing one of them—only some), sections 2.5.3 and 2.5.4 present systematic and predictable alternations (interchanges) between the high-mid vowel and each of the other three vowels that help clarify why it is said to be a secondary or derived vowel.

In view of its instability, it is fair to ask whether it should be given any status at all. The three minimal triplets presented at the beginning of this section show that it does function as the sole feature in differentiating some words; here follow a few more pairs of words in which it contrasts with the mid vowel as further indication of the load it does bear:

HIGH MID VOWEL			MID VOWEL		
ae	{hayẹy}	'gather'	ae	{hayey}	'current'
me	{mẹy}	'fortress'	me	{mey}	'which'
wōt	{wẹt}	'rain'	wōt	{wet}	'only'
or	{wẹr}	'lobster'	or	{wer}	'fish gill'
jojo	{jẹwjẹw}	'little chicken'	jojo	{jewjew}	'flying fish'
bok	{bẹk^w}	'book'	bok	{bek^w}	'sand'
eo	{yẹw}	'wet'	eo	{yew}	'the'
leñ	{lẹg}	'above'	leñ	{leg}	'many'
tōl	{tẹl}	'nit'	tōl	{tel}	'to lead'
jen	{jẹn}	'shrink'	jen	{jen}	'let's'
wōn	{wẹn}	'turtle'	wōn	{wen}	'who?'
kor	{k^{w}ẹr}	'frightened'	kor	{k^{w}er}	'rattle'
ṇo	{ṇẹw}	'stone fish'	ṇo	{ṇew}	'wave'
bo	{bẹw}	'missile'	bo	{bew}	'twins'
lo	{lẹw}	'embarrassed'	lo	{lew}	'tongue'
po	{pẹw}	'a fish'	po	{pew}	'caught'
ro	{rẹw}	'infuriated'	ro	{rew}	'the'
je	{jẹy}	'belly'	je	{jey}	'avoid'
le	{lẹy}	'albatross'	le	{ley}	'bear fruit'

Interestingly, the high mid vowel is the vowel in a set of interjections that follow a common pattern:

ōrrōr	{hẹrrẹr}	'pleasure; displeasure'
ōḷḷōḷ	{hẹḷḷẹḷ}	'unwillingness'
ōkkōk	{hẹkkẹk}	'apprehension'
ōttet	{hẹttẹt}	'pain; pleasure'
ōjjej	{hẹjjẹj}	'surprise; disappointment'
bōkkōk	{bẹkkẹk}	'surprise'
ōññōñ	{hẹññẹñ}	'unwillingness'

Here follow a few additional examples of the high-mid vowel in mixed environments arranged according to type, with the left and right hand columns forming mirror images phonemically:

	L__H			H__L	
lōb	{lẹb}	'grave'	bōl	{bẹl}	'taro pit'
pet	{pẹt}	'pillow'	tōp	{tẹp}	'shavings'
lōñ	{lẹg}	'above'	ñōl	{gẹl}	'ocean swell'
eṃ	{yẹṃ}	'house'	mwe	{ṃẹy}	'this house'
ek	{yẹk}	'fish'	ke	{kẹy}	'porpoise'
	H__R			R__H	
bok	{bẹk^w}	'book'	kob	{k^{w}ẹb}	'bent'
to	{tẹw}	'get off'	wōt	{wẹt}	'rain'
bo	{bẹw}	'missile'	ob	{wẹb}	'chest'
ro	{rẹw}	'infuriated'	or	{wẹr}	'lobster'
	L__R			R__L	
po	{pẹw}	'a fish'	wōp	{wẹp}	'*Barringtonia* sp.'
jo	{jẹw}	'float loose'	wōj	{wẹj}	'toward you'

THE PATTERNING OF THE PHONEMES

2.4 The various possible arrangements of the phonemes of Marshallese as displayed in the phonemic transcription will be considered in this section. It will be seen that phonemes are not combined in random order in the make-up of a word, but that certain rules are followed in the combinations. For example, considering just the two major classes of phonemes, consonants and vowels, note that Marshallese words never begin or end with a vowel phoneme, but always with a consonant—at the least, an invisible semiconsonant (which is counted as a consonant in this discussion). Thus, the minimum word in the language can be summarized in the formula CVC, where C stands for consonant or semiconsonant, and V for vowel. All four of the words *bōb* {beb} 'pandanus', *bwe* {bey} 'enough', *eb* {yeb} 'dance', and *e* {yẹy} 's/he' fit this formula in their phonemic transcriptions, and all four can be termed one-syllable words, each having as many syllables as it has vowels. This and other possible patterns for phonemes within words is the subject of what follows.

INITIAL DOUBLE CONSONANTS

2.4.1 An additional vowel and consonant can be added to either side—as it were—of the basic CVC unit to build two-syllable and longer words:

	ADDED	RESULT	EXAMPLE		
BEGIN WITH:	—	CVC	{bey}	bwe	'enough'
PREFIX:	CV-	CVCVC	{jibey}	jibwe	'catch it'
SUFFIX:	-VC	CVCVC	{bẹyẹt}	bweet	'what for?'

But another type of two-syllable word can also be built by simply doubling the first consonant of the basic CVC unit: C_1C_1VC. (Identical number subscripts in the formula are used to show that the two consonants are identical.) Here follow examples of basic stem forms with each consonant doubled, together with their pronunciations in the Rālik and Ratak dialects.

		RĀLIK	RATAK
{bbej}	'swollen'	ebbōj	bōbōj
{ddew}	'heavy'	eddo	dedo
{ggir}	'moan'	iññūr	ñūñūr
{g^{w}g^{w}ertaktak}	'always snore'	eññortaktak	ñōñōrtaktak
{hhabinmakẹykẹy}	'always afraid'	eaabinmakeke	aabinmakeke
{jjew}	'rusty'	ejjo	jejo
{kkag}	'sharp'	ekkañ	kōkañ
{k^{w}k^{w}aḷ}	'sennit'	ekkwaḷ	kokwaḷ
{lliw}	'angry'	illu	lilu
{ḷḷahaj}	'loud'	eḷḷaaj	ḷōḷaaj
{ḷ^{w}ḷ^{w}etḷak^{w}ḷak^{w}}	'always fainting'	eoḷḷotḷọkḷọk	ḷoḷotḷọkḷọk
{mmahan}	'be at anchor'	emmaan	memaan
{ṃṃan}	'good'	eṃṃan	ṃōṃan
{nnaw}	'tasty'	ennọ	nenọ
{ṇṇek}	'sharp pain'	eṇṇōk	ṇōṇōk
{ṇ^{w}ṇ^{w}ejṇ^{w}ej}	'snapping'	eṇṇojṇoj	ṇoṇojṇoj
{ppat}	'feel unworthy'	eppat	pepat
{rray}	'take sides'	errā	rōrā
{r^{w}r^{w}ey}	'insert hand'	errwe	rore
{ttẹr}	'run'	ettōr	tōtōr
{wwan}	'industrious'	eowan	owan
{yyag^{w}edg^{w}ed}	'fish often'	eeọñōdñōd	eọñōdñōd

As the foregoing illustrate, all 19 consonants and the three semiconsonants can appear in double-consonant words of this sort. This is one of the ways in which the semiconsonants can be seen to pattern like the full consonants.

When such words are used as verbs, they may be prefixed with one of the subject prefixes (table 3-10), as in the following sentences:

{yi-lliw	kẹn	ha-n	kar	jakẹw}
I-llu	kōn	a-n	kar	jako.
I-angry	with	his/her	PAST	absence

'I was angry that s/he was gone.'

{ye-ṃṃan	ha-n	jeḷay	kaji-n ṃahjeḷ}
E-ṃṃan	a-n	jeḷā	kaji-n Ṃajeḷ.
It-good	his/her	knowledge	language-of the-Marshalls.

'S/he knows Marshallese well.'

In such sentences, the subject prefixes are attached directly to the bare double-consonant stems, and the resulting forms are pronounced identically in both dialects:

RĀLIK AND RATAK

{yi-}	+	{lliw}	→	{yi-lliw}	illu
I-SUBJ		angry		I-angry	'I am angry.'
{ye-}	+	{ṃṃan}	→	{ye-ṃṃan}	eṃṃan
it-SUBJ		good		it-good	'It is good.'

But when such words are used as nouns, as in the following sentences, they are not prefixed but occur in their bare-stem forms:

{ye-ḷap	haḥẹh	lliw	kẹn	han	kar	jakẹw}
E-ḷap	aō	illu	kōn	an	kar	jako.
it-great	my	anger	with	his/her	past	absence

'I was very angry that s/he was gone.'

{ye-ḷap	han	ṃṃan	han	jeḷay	kajin ṃahjeḷ}
E-ḷap	an	eṃṃan	an	jeḷā	kajin Ṃajeḷ.
it-great	its	goodness	his/her	knowing	language-of-Marshalls

'S/he knows Marshallese very well.'

In these sentences the bare stems {lliw} and {ṃṃan} are shown here in the standard spelling as they would be pronounced in the Rālik dialect. In the Ratak dialect they would be written and pronounced as follows:

Eḷap aō lilu kōn an kar jako.
Eḷap an ṃōṃan an jeḷā kajin Ṃajōḷ.

The Ratak bare-stem forms in these two sentences and the Rālik forms in the preceding two are the same as those given in the listing on page 52 for the various consonants in double-consonant words. All such forms are easily predictable from the basic phonemic shape of the word by applying the following two rules:

Rālik rule. Build a prefix for the word composed of a {y} plus a copy of the vowel phoneme immediately following the first double consonant. (If the vowel to be copied is {a}, substitute {e} as the copy.[2])

2. This is the effect of low-vowel dissimilation discussed in section 2.5.5 beginning on page 92.

Add this prefix to the bare stem, and pronounce and spell the resulting combination according to the usual rules.

{y} PLUS VOWEL COPY		BARE STEM FROM WHICH VOWEL IS COPIED		RESULTING COMBINATION	RĀLIK PRONUNCIATION OF BARE STEM	
{yi-}	+	{lliw}	→	{yi-lliw}	illu	'angry'
{yẹ-}	+	{ttẹr}	→	{yẹ-ttẹr}	ettōr	'run'
{ye-}	+	{bbej}	→	{ye-bbej}	ebbōj	'swollen'
{ye-}	+	{ṃṃan}	→	{ye-ṃṃan}	eṃṃan	'good'

The prefixes created by this rule are "empty" in that they have no meaning; they function only to make the bare stem easier to pronounce. Note that they are sometimes omitted from phonemic transcriptions to emphasize the fact that—unlike the subject prefixes—they have no basic status. (Note also that when the vowel to be copied is the high vowel {i}, the resulting prefix is identical to the 1S subject prefix {yi-} (table 3-10), and when the vowel to be copied is the mid or low vowel ({e} or {a}) the resulting prefix is identical to the 3S subject prefix {ye-}. Thus, the Rālik pronunciation of the bare stem for 'anger' {lliw} is identical to the pronunciation in both dialects of the form for 'I am angry' {yilliw}: *illu.* Similarly, the Rālik pronunciation of the bare stem for 'good' {ṃṃan} is identical to that in both dialects of the form for 'it is good' {yeṃṃan}: *eṃṃan.*

Ratak rule. Copy the first vowel of the stem in the same way as the Rālik rule, but insert it between the double consonants.

BARE STEM FROM WHICH VOWEL IS COPIED	COPY VOWEL	STEM WITH COPY VOWEL INSERTED	RATAK PRONUNCIATION OF BARE STEM	
{l( )liw}	{i}	{l(i)liw}	lilu	'angry'
{t( )tẹr}	{ẹ}	{t(ẹ)tẹr}	tōtōr	'run'
{b( )bej}	{e}	{b(e)bej}	bōbōj	'swollen'
{ṃ( )ṃan}	{e}	{ṃ(e)ṃan}	ṃōṃan	'good'

(Note that as in the Rālik rule, if the vowel to be copied is {a}, an {e} is substituted as the copy.) These two rules together with the usual pronunciation and spelling rules account for all double-consonant stems. Note that, in standard spelling, the copy vowel will often differ in spelling from the vowel copied because of the different consonants between which each stands: for example, in the Ratak pronunciation of {r^wr^wey}, which becomes {r^w(e)r^wey} with the copy vowel inserted, the first (copy) vowel is spelled with an *o* because it lies between rounded {r^w}s, while the second is spelled with an *e* because it lies between a rounded {r^w} and an invisible {y} (which must leave its front effect in a neighboring vowel letter): *rore.*

Both the Rālik and Ratak rules should be viewed as alternative means of making the double consonants pronounceable and hearable in order to preserve the contrast between them and the single consonants. A double consonant consists basically of a closure that is held longer than the closure of a single consonant. For example, between vowels as in the word *bōtta* {bettah} 'to bat' one can hear that the double *t*'s are held longer than the single one in the word *bōta* {betah} 'butter'. But at the beginning of a word there is no way to tell when the closure began in order to time it, because the mouth may have been closed for an indefinitely long period of time before the word was begun. If there were no way to distinguish initial double consonants, the word {m̦m̦an} 'good' would sound just like {m̦an} 'kill', {jjew} 'rusty' would sound like {jew} 'calm period', {ppat} 'feel unworthy' like {pat} 'swamp', and so forth.

Different Micronesian languages solve this problem in different ways. Mokilese changes the first of the two consonants to its nasal counterpart, so that the word for 'sharp' (cognate with Marshallese *ekkañ* / *kōkañ*) is *ngkoang,* while Chuuukese simply pronounces the doubled consonants more forcefully than the single ones. The Gilbertese solution is to keep a vowel between the two consonants, so that the word for 'vomit' (cognate with Marshallese *em̦m̦ōj* / *m̦ōm̦ōj*) is *mumuta*. In fact, it is believed that Gilbertese preserves an earlier stage of what actually happened in the history of each of the languages—that *mumuta* was created from an earlier *muta* by repeating (reduplicating) the first consonant and vowel.

Marshallese and other nuclear Micronesian languages are thought to have participated in the same development while they all—including Gilbertese—were together as a single Proto-Micronesian language, but all except Gilbertese lost the reduplicated vowel as an inherent part of the word and ended up with identical consonants side-by-side. (Other changes that later took place in both Marshallese dialects include the change of the second *u* to {ẹ}, *t* to *j,* and the dropping of the final *a.*) In a sense, the Ratak dialect also preserves this vowel between the consonants when such words are pronounced as bare stems, but the vowel is no longer a basic part of the word and disappears when the word is prefixed. Another way to look at it would be to say that the Ratak rule above reenacts part of the historical reduplication process with its copying of the vowel from the stem—after "reduplicating" the first consonant. As noted in chapter 3, the other half of the historical copying, the copying of the consonant without an intervening vowel to create new words with double consonants—without losing the ones with single consonants from the language—is still a live grammatical process, as, for example, in the word *emmaroro* / *memaroro* {mmahrewrew} 'greenish' created from *maroro* {mahrewrew} 'green'.

Initial consonant clusters in the *Marshallese-English Dictionary* (MED) and in its on-line revision, the *Marshallese On-line Dictionary* (MOD). Table 2-16 shows four entries with initial double consonants as they appeared (excerpted) in the *Marshallese-English Dictionary* (often referred to as the MED),[3] one for each of the four vowel phonemes {i, ẹ, e, a} that occurs immediately following the double consonant. Each of these is followed, in turn, by the treatment of the same data in the *Marshallese On-line Dictionary* (MOD). The following differences can be noted:

In the MED:

- The headwords (and their phonemic counterparts) are abstract forms with initial double consonants that serve both the W and E dialects and show only what is common to both, devoid of the details of pronunciation in either dialect.
- When these words occur unprefixed in example sentences, the same single abstract form is given without the details of dialectal pronunciations.

Table 2-16 Comparison of treatment of initial double consonants in MED and MOD

MED	*ttino*	{**ttinẹw**}. Dial. W: *ittino* {**yittinẹw**}, E: *tūtino* {**titinẹw**}. secret; mysterious; camouflaged; obscure; hidden; covert. *Eḷap an ttino ijo ej kūttiliek ie.* The place he is hiding is secret.
MOD	***ittino***	See ***tūtino***.
	tūtino	{ttinẹw}. Dial. W: *ittino* {**yittinẹw**}, E: *tūtino* {**titinẹw**}. secret; mysterious; camouflaged; obscure; hidden; covert. *Eḷap an tūtino (ittino) ijo ej kūttiliek ie.* The place he is hiding is secret.
MED	*tto*	{**ttẹw**}. Dial. W: *etto* {**yẹttẹw**}, E: *tōto* {**tẹtẹw**}. dig taro. *Ḷōṃaro raṇ rej tto iaraj ṃōñein jota.* Those fellows are digging taro for supper.
MOD	***etto***	See ***tōto***.
	tōto	{ttẹw}. Dial. W: *etto* {**yẹttẹw**}, E: *tōto* {**tẹtẹw**}. dig taro. *Ḷōṃaro raṇ rej tōto (etto) iaraj ṃōñein jota.* Those fellows are digging taro for supper.
MED	*ttoñ*	{**tteg^{w}**}. Dial. W: *ettoñ* {**yetteg^{w}**}, E: *tōtoñ* {**teteg^{w}**}. Sleep soundly. *Eḷap aō kar ttoñ.* I really slept soundly.
MOD	***ettoñ***	See ***tōtoñ***.
	tōtoñ	{teteñ}. Dial. W: ettoñ {**yetteg^{w}**}, E: tōtoñ {**teteg^{w}**}. sleep soundly. *Eḷap aō kar tōtoñ (ettoñ).* I really slept soundly.
MED	*ttal*	{**ttal**}. Dial. W: *ettal* {**yettal**}, E: *tōtal* {**tetal**}. Loudmouth; blabber-mouth; telltale. *Kwōn jab kōṇaan ttal.* Don't be a blabbermouth.
MOD	***ettal***	See ***tōtal***.
	tōtal	{tetal}. Dial. W: ettal {**yettal**}, E: tōtal {**tetal**}. Loudmouth; blabber-mouth; telltale. *Kwōn jab kōṇaan tōtal (ettal).* Don't be a blabbermouth.

3. The hard-copy dictionary published by the University of Hawai‘i Press in 1976. See "References" on page 13.

In the MOD:

- Each of the MED entries appears as two entries, one for the W dialect and one for the E, so that both dialectal pronunciations serve as headwords.
- The W entry is cross-referenced to the E, where all the details are given. When the headword appears unprefixed in an example sentence, it is spelled with its E pronunciation first, and with the W pronunciation appearing in parentheses immediately following.
- The last two points, thus, give precedence to the E (Ratak) dialect, as it is more conservative and historically prior in its treatment of initial double consonants, while the W (Rālik) dialect is more innovative.[4]

MEDIAL CONSONANT CLUSTERS

2.4.2 Double consonants occur medially in words as well, as in *keinabbu* {kẹy-inabbiw} 'papaya', *etto* {yettew} 'a long time', *akki* {hakkiy} 'nail, claw', and so forth. As noted on page 163, these double consonants sometimes function grammatically in "Plural verbs of dimension" such as *remmānni* {remmanniy} 'they are thin' (vs. *emāni* {yemaniy} 'it is thin'), *remmijjel* {remmijjẹl} 'they are thick' (vs. *emijel* {yemijẹl} 'it is thick'), and so forth. Also, the words for 'boy' and 'girl' have double consonants *(ḷaddik, leddik)* unless a demonstrative follows, in which case the consonant becomes single *(ḷadik ro, ledik ro).*

Even though double consonants are pronounced without an intervening vowel (except in the Ratak pronunciation of them initially), the amount of time spent holding the closure is equivalent to the time that would be spent pronouncing a vowel. It is as if there were a silent vowel between the two consonants. Because it is thought that a vowel actually did occur there historically, it is as if the speaker observes a moment of silence for the departed vowel, for as long as it would take to utter the vowel and close again for the second consonant, before actually opening for the real vowel of the next syllable. A blank inserted in the words cited in the last paragraph to mark the position of the unuttered vowel represents the situation graphically: *keinab_bu, et_to, ak_ki, ḷad_dik, led_-dik.* Thus, in terms of the amount of time it takes to say these words, it is as if the first were a five-syllable word, and each of the others a three-syllable word. Or, including the mora of time occupied by the final consonant and the excrescent vowel (2.5.2) that may follow it, the first would be a six-mora word, and the others four-mora words. (See 2.6.1 for a dis-

4. Those innovations resulted in unstable 3-mora words becoming stable 4-mora words (see 2.6.2, beginning on page 104)—probably their root cause. But they also created homonyms with existing inflected forms, as mentioned on page 54 (just before the *Ratak rule*).

cussion of the mora, the amount of time it usually takes to pronounce a short vowel.)

From a mora point of view, in the actual pronunciation of the initial double consonant words, using {ṃṃan} as an example, the Ratak pronunciation *ṃōṃan* has two syllables and is three moras long, while the Rālik pronunciation *eṃṃan* also has two syllables but is four moras long.

Thus far, two ways of expanding on the basic CVC word and syllable have been presented:

(1) put CV- in front of, or put -VC after the basic CVC to make a CVCVC word, or
(2) double the first consonant to make a C_1C_1VC word that is pronounced with three-syllable timing in the Rālik, and with two-syllable timing in the Ratak dialect.

A third way to expand on the basic CVC is to add another CVC to make a CVCCVC word: *jerbal* 'work', *tōprak* 'achieve', *wōtlọk* 'fall', and so on. There are two special types of such words: those in which the two medial consonants are identical (CVC_1C_1VC), as in *ḷaddik* and *leddik,* already cited, and those in which there are two pairs of identical—though not contiguous—consonants, and in which the vowels are identical (or systematically related—see 2.5.4), fitting the formula $C_1V_1C_2C_1V_1C_2$:

ṃarṃar	{ṃarṃar}	'necklace'
ṃwijṃwij	{ṃijṃij}	'cut'
ṃakṃōk	{ṃakṃẹk}	'arrowroot'
meme	{mẹymẹy}	'chew'
ṃōṃō	{ṃehṃeh}	'a fish: grouper'
nono	{newnew}	'to pound'

Such words generally result from the grammatical process known as reduplication, in which a different form of a word is built not by prefixation or suffixation, but by the repeating of one or more syllables, in this case the last—or the only—CVC. Sometimes only the reduplicated form survives; there is no single *ṃak* or *ṃōk* in the language having anything to do with *ṃakṃōk* 'arrowroot'. Sometimes both the reduplicated and unreduplicated forms survive: *ṃarōk* 'put on a necklace' contains the *ṃar* of *ṃarṃar* in unreduplicated form; *ṃwijit* 'cut something' contains the *ṃwij* of *ṃwijṃwij, no* 'pound something' is the unreduplicated form of *nono,* and so on.

The type of reduplication that derives *juujuj* 'wear shoes' from *juuj* 'shoes' can be referred to as right-hand reduplication, where the last three phonemes, the rightmost CVC of {jiwij}, are tacked on the right-hand side of the word to form {jiwijwij}. The reverse process, left-hand reduplication, can be seen in the derivation of *etetal* {yetyetal} 'walk on' from *etal* {yetal} 'go'. As noted at the end of 2.4.1, the process of doubling initial consonants can be viewed as a second type of left-hand reduplication, involving only the leftmost consonant.

The combination of initial consonant doubling and right-hand reduplication constitutes the favorite means in the language of deriving distributive verbs (see page 162):

{piyig}	piiñ	'pink'
{ppiyigyig}	ippiiñiñ (W)	
	pipiiñiñ (E)	'pinkish'
{karijin}	karijin	'kerosene'
{kkarjinjin}	ekkarijinjin (W)	
	kōkarijinjin (E)	'reeking of kerosene'
{k^wiḷab}	kuḷab	'clubhouse'
{k^wk^wiḷabḷab}	ikkuḷabḷab (W)	
	kukuḷabḷab (E)	'frequent a clubhouse'
{k^weweḷ}	kooḷ	'hair'
{k^wk^weweḷweḷ}	ekkooḷoḷ (W)	
	kokooḷoḷ (E)	'covered with hair trimmings'
{kijdik}	kijdik	'rat'
{kkijdikdik}	ikkijdikdik (W)	
	kūkijdikdik (E)	'infested with rats'

The timing of the pronunciation of all medial consonant clusters, whether identical or nonidentical, and whether created by one of the reduplicating processes or already existing in a word (as the *jd* at the middle of *kijdik*), is the same as indicated in the second paragraph of this section, as if there were a vowel between the consonants. And as discussed in 2.5.2, depending on which consonants are involved, an "excrescent" vowel may actually be uttered.

The three ways of expanding on the basic CVC syllable discussed in this section can together account for the formation of all words in the language. For example, the loanword {kawanpiyip} 'corned beef' can be viewed as having been built up as follows:

CVC	{yip}
CV-CVC	{piyip}
CVC-CV-CVC	{wanpiyip}
CV-CVC-CV-CVC	{kawanpiyip}

and the distributive verb derived from it *ekkọọnpiip* (W), *kōkọọnpiip* (E) 'replete with corned beef' involves two further expansions:

CV-CVC-CV-CVC	{kawanpiyip}
C_1-C_1V-CVC-CV-CVC	{kkawanpiyip}
C_1-C_1V-CVC-CV-$C_2V_1C_3$-$C_2V_1C_3$	{kkawanpiyipyip}

Because every consonant is timed as if it had a following vowel, whether or not it does, the number of moras of timing occupied by a word is equal to the number of consonants in its phonemic transcription. Thus, the Ratak pronunciation of the last form {kkawanpiyipyip} has nine moras of timing, and the Rālik pronunciation, with the empty {ye-} prefix, has ten.

Words Beginning in {wiwV} and {yiyV}

2.4.3 As stated in 2.4.1, words beginning in {hh}, {ww}, and {yy} pattern like other double-consonant words in the ways they are pronounced in the Rālik and Ratak dialects. A few exceptions to this generalization should be noted.

The Rālik rule would predict that {hhabinmakẹykẹy} 'always afraid of ghosts' would have an empty {ye-} prefix added in the Rālik pronunciation, and the Ratak rule would call for the copy vowel {e} to be inserted between the *h*'s in that pronunciation. Instead, the copy vowel is {a} in both dialects—because of a special relation between the {h} semiconsonant and the low vowel {a}, both involving retraction of the tongue root. Thus, the two pronunciations can be transcribed as {(ya)hhabinmakẹykẹy} *eaabinmakeke* and {h(a)habinmakẹykẹy} *aabinmakeke,* respectively, where the initial *e* in the Rālik spelling represents the initial {y}, not the following copy vowel {a} (paralleling the spelling *eañ* for {yag} 'north'). (The empty prefix and copy vowels are enclosed in parentheses in the phonemic transcription because they are not considered an inherent part of the word.)

For {ww} and {yy}, on the other hand, the copy vowel is as predicted, so that {yyag^{w}edg^{w}ed} 'always go fishing' receives the empty prefix {ye-} in its Rālik pronunciation (which can be transcribed {(ye)yyag^{w}edg^{w}ed}, and it receives the copy vowel {e} in its Ratak pronunciation {y(e)yag^{w}edg^{w}ed} (both spelled *eeọñōdñōd*). The parallel transcriptions for {wwan} 'industrious' would be {(ye)wwan} *eowan* and {(we)wwan} *owan.* Note that the last Ratak transcription departs from the Ratak rule in that the copy vowel is not inserted between the stem *w*'s to give {w(e)wan}, but is instead prefixed to the stem together with a third {w} of its own: {we-} + {wwan} → {(we)wwan}. This form has four-mora timing, just like the Rālik {(ye)wwan}, instead of the three-mora timing expected.

To summarize these two exceptions to the Rālik and Ratak double consonant rules (2.4.1),

(1) When the double consonant is {hh}, the copy vowel for {a} is {a}, not {e} as with other double consonants.
(2) When the double consonant is {ww}, the copy vowel is added to a third {w} and prefixed (as {we-}), paralleling the Rālik {ye-} prefix, and both dialects have the same timing.

In the {ww} and {yy} stems just discussed, as in other double-consonant stems, the copy vowel is determined by the first vowel after the double consonants. If that vowel is {a} or {e}, the copy vowel is {e}; if it is {ẹ}, {ẹ}, and if {i}, {i}. Only about 15 such words with {ww} and five with {yy} have been found: in addition to {wwan}, there are {wwar} 'beg', {wwat} 'ripe', {wwatrẹyrẹy} 'unripe', {wwej} 'tax', {wwey} 'whistle', {wwir} 'nasal mucous', {wwiy} 'smell of cooking fish', and the following distributives: {wwẹrẹyrẹy} 'always retract the foreskin', {wwahḷak^{w}ḷak^w} 'keep getting up', {wwahyiniyniy} 'laden with copra', {wweg^{w}weg^w} 'chronic homesickness', {wweḷak^{w}ḷak^w} 'fall all over the place', {wwiyin-yin} 'always win', and {wwiywiy} 'pervasive odor of cooking fish'; and in addition to {yyag^{w}edg^{w}ed}, these distributives: {yyeṇ^{w}yeṇ^w} 'always go aground', {yyigtẹktẹk} 'be all twisted', {yyiyeṃahṃah} 'covered with stripes', and {yyiyijyij} 'replete with yeast'.

There is a larger set of words that behave just like the words in {ww} and {yy} just cited, except that the position of the copy vowel in both Rālik and Ratak pronunciations is occupied by the high vowel {i} even though the vowel following the consonants is one of the lower vowels. Because such words behave as if they had an inherent high vowel early in the stem, an {i} is built into their transcriptions between the identical consonants. Thus, they can be identified as a group by their having the initial sequence {wiwV} or {yiyV}, where V is a vowel other than {i}—either {ẹ}, {e}, or {a}: {wiwẹy} 'ride', {wiwetah} 'danger', {wiwah} 'bear much fruit', {yiyep} 'basket', {yiyaḷ} 'road'.

The words in {wiwV} follow the double-consonant pronunciation rules in the same way as those in {ww} do, except that the empty prefixes always have the vowel {i}, and the vowel disappears from between the {w}'s—it is as if it switches places with the first {w} to occupy the position usually occupied by the copy vowel in the empty prefix. Thus:

BASIC FORM OF WORD	DIALECTAL PRONUNCIATIONS	DIALECTAL SPELLINGS	ENGLISH TRANSLATION
{wiwẹy}	{(y)iwwẹy}	iuwe (W)	
	{(w)iwwẹy}	uwe (E)	'ride'
{wiwetah}	{(y)iwwetah}	iuwōta (W)	
	{(w)iwwetah}	uwōta (E)	'danger'
{wiwah}	{(y)iwwah}	iuwa (W)	
	{(w)iwwah}	uwa (E)	'bear much fruit'

The words in {yiyV} follow the double-consonant pronunciation rules in the same way as those in {yy} do, except that the Rālik empty prefix always has {i} in the copy-vowel position (switched from between the {y}'s), and the Ratak pronunciation simply leaves it between the {y}'s (to occupy the usual copy-vowel position in the Ratak pronunciation of double full consonants) and has no prefix. Thus:

BASIC FORM OF WORD	DIALECTAL PRONUNCIATIONS	DIALECTAL SPELLINGS	ENGLISH TRANSLATION
{yiyep}	{(y)iyyep}	iiep (W)	
	{yiyep}	iep (E)	'basket'
{yiyaḷ}	{(y)iyyaḷ}	iiaḷ (W)	
	{yiyaḷ}	iaḷ (E)	'road'

The situation is further complicated by the fact that some {yiyV} words are given the Rālik pronunciation in both dialects; these are indicated in the phonemic transcription by a preposed apostrophe:

	ALWAYS PRONOUNCED IN BOTH MAJOR DIALECTS		
{'yiyah}	{(y)iyyah}	iia	'rainbow'
{'yiyẹk}	{(y)iyyek}	iiōk	'mixture'
{'yiyẹt}	{(y)iyyẹt}	iiet	'least'
{'yiyeh}	{(y)iyyeh}	iiō	'year'
{'yiyen}	{(y)iyyen}	iien	'time'

At the same time, other words in {yiyV} are given the Ratak pronunciation in both dialects; these are indicated with an apostrophe further to the right, before the second {y}:

	ALWAYS PRONOUNCED IN BOTH MAJOR DIALECTS		
{yi'yah}	{yiyah}	ia	'where?'
{yi'yẹy}	{yiyẹy}	ie	'there'
{yi'yahat}	{yiyahat}	iaat	'yard'
{yi'yawat}	{yiyawat}	iọọt	'yacht'
{yi'yak^{w}ey}	{yiyak^{w}ey}	iọkwe	'aloha'

These two meanings for the apostrophe in {yiyV} words that do not show the expected variation in pronunciation for the two major dialects can be remembered in two ways:

(1) The apostrophe can be viewed as a stress (page 100) mark preceding the syllable that is to be pronounced strongly and held longer, and as following ones that are to be passed over quickly, or

(2) when it is further to the left (west on a map), it shows that the word always gets western (Rālik) treatment; when to the right (east), eastern (Ratak) treatment.

It is fair to ask why, among all the consonants, the semiconsonants should show such irregularity when doubled, and although no definitive answer can be given, a few possible explanations do suggest themselves:

(1) Their halfway status has already been noted (2.2.6); they lie somewhere between vowels and consonants. The fact that they follow the double-consonant rules to the extent they do indicates that speakers are attempting to treat them as consonants rather than as vowels, but

the deviations or exceptions that occur indicate that complications are being encountered in the attempt to do so.

(2) Many instances of semiconsonants developed from fuller consonants only relatively recently in the history of the language. This could have helped tip the balance in favor of treating them like the fuller consonants they derive from, or—because processes creating them in doubled form (such as the formation of distributives) are quite ancient—like their forebears had been treated. Instances of both {w} and {y} derive from an earlier *p: the word for 'islet' {yanẹy} *āne* comes from *panua, and the {-gẹwil} *-ñoul* of *joñoul* 'ten', and its multiples, from the *pulu of *nga-pulu, for example. The doublets involving {h} and {k} cited in 2.5.6 (on page 97) suggest that *k is the source for some {h}'s, just as those involving {y} and {p} result from some *p's having become {y}'s (while others remained {p}'s). In addition, the sporadic alternations between {k^w} and {w}, also cited in 2.5.6, suggest that *k is the source for some {w}'s.

(3) Borrowing has complicated the picture. The fact that some {yiyV} words are given the pronunciation of one dialect throughout the islands suggests that there has been borrowing of pronunciation from one dialect to the other, or from a common foreign source, perhaps before the attempt to treat {yy} and {yiyV} words like double full-consonant words became as strong as it is even now. The fact that one dialectal {yiyV} pronunciation fit some loanwords well for use in both dialects ({'yiyeh} for 'year'), while the other fit other loans well for use in both ({yi'yakiyiw} for Japanese *iakiu* 'baseball', {yi'yahat} for 'yard', {yi'yawat} for 'yacht') created further obstacles to using only the one typical pronunciation in each dialect.

Clearly, however, there remains much to be learned on this subject.

"Diphthongs" and "Long" Vowels

2.4.4 A diphthong is a sequence of two different vowels in a word. Strictly speaking, there are no sequences of vowels in Marshallese, because each vowel has a consonant on either side of it, as shown in the phonemic transcription. However, when the consonant standing between two vowels is a semiconsonant, its constriction may be very slight, and the two vowels may sound very much like diphthongs in other languages. (The amount of constriction of the semiconsonant depends in great measure on the consonants on the outer sides of the two vowels. Where they agree with the semiconsonant in heaviness and rounding, very little constriction will be heard, as, for example, in *jein* {jẹyin} 'older sibling of', whose *j* and *n* are light like its {y}. Where they disagree with the semiconsonant, considerable constriction will be heard, as in *jouj* {jẹwij} 'kindness', whose outer consonants are both light but whose medial semiconsonant is heavy and rounded, and, therefore, quite audible.) But the main reason for examining words of the shapes CVhVC, CVwVC, and CVyVC (where the middle consonant is one of the three semiconsonants) in this section is that they reveal several interesting facts about the patterning of the language.

Diphthongs are sequences of two vowels that are not identical, but many languages that have diphthongs also have sequences of identical vowels that are parallel to the diphthongs in many ways. Such sequences are sometimes called "long" vowels, because the sound of the two vowels lasts longer than that of a single vowel. It has already been noted in 2.3.1 (see pages 40 and 48) that Marshallese has sequences of identical vowels separated by a semiconsonant, and a number of examples for each vowel with each semiconsonant were given that had been borrowed from English: *pi*{y}*iñ* 'pink', *ju*{w}*uj* 'shoes', *ke*{y}*ek* 'cake', *kō*{h}*ōb* 'curve', *ko*{w}*oḷ* 'gold', *pe*{y}*en* 'pen', *tō*{h}*ōm* 'term', *bo*{w}*oj* 'boat', *jā*{y}*ān* 'cents', *ḷa*{h}*aṃ* 'lamp', *bọ*{w}*ọḷ* 'ball', and so on. It is clear that whether vowels are double or "long" in this way can make for a contrast between two different words. Consider, for example, the difference in sound and meaning between pairs of words such as *jāān* 'cents' and *jān* 'from', *maañ* 'pandanus leaf' and *mañ* 'coconut beginning to turn brown', or *jook* 'ashamed' and *jok* 'alight'.

Both "diphthongs" (sequences of nonidentical vowels separated by a semiconsonant) and "long vowels" (sequences of identical vowels separated by a semiconsonant) are examined in this section. Because a number of examples of the latter that have been borrowed from English are given in 2.3.1, in this section the question will be considered as to whether there are also such words of native origin. The same question will be asked with respect to the nonidentical sequences: of those occurring, do any seem to be new patterns not in the language originally, but created by the borrowing of large numbers of words from some other language?

Identical sequences

Concerning identical sequences, there are an appreciable number involving each vowel that are not known to have been borrowed. A few examples of each type are given here.

High vowels with intervening {y}: *kiin* 'now (E)', *liin* 'this woman', *lwiit* 'to slurp'; **with {h}:** *kūūk* 'interjection'; **with {w}:** *duuj* 'insert', *tuuj* 'steal someone's spouse', *kuur* 'bird call', *luwi* {liwiy} 'fish chase', *kuwi* {kʷiwiy} 'surgeon fish'.

High-mid vowels with intervening {y}: *kweet* 'octopus', *bweo* {bẹyẹw} 'husk pile'; **with {h}:** *tōōḷ* 'hair bristle'; **with {w}:** *tooj* 'break off of', *doon* 'husking stick', *koon* 'squab', *eoon* {yẹwẹn} 'stanza', *joor* 'pillar', *boor* 'throw wildly', *moot* 'expert'.

Mid vowels with intervening {y}: *ḷeeṇ* 'that man', *mweeṇ* 'that house', *teoḷ* {teyeḷʷ} 'come loose', *deor* {deyerʷ} 'escape', *jeor* {jeyerʷ} 'sideburns; erase', *mweed* 'disenheartened', *teeṇ* 'division', *meej* 'dark colored', *peek* 'dominate', *deel* 'fan', *ṃweo* {ṃeyew} 'the house', *ḷeo* {ḷeyew} 'the man'; **with {h}:** *ōō* {heheh} 'surgeon fish', *rōōj* 'bright colored'; **with {w}:** *towe* {tewey} 'caress', *moot* 'gone forth', *pooḷ* 'surrounded', *kooḷ* 'hair', *tooj* 'conspicuous', *jool* 'neglected', *doon* 'each other', *toon* 'web', *toor* 'swinging', *joot* 'bullet'.

Low vowels with intervening {y}: *tāāñ* 'sex appeal', *kāāj* 'fish hook', *kāāl* 'new', *māāl* 'adze', *wāār* 'crawl', *māār* 'to tell a lie', *jāār* 'fish cooking method'; **with {h}:** *baab* 'suppose', *jaab*, *eaab* {yahab} 'no', *jaad* 'a fish; rather', *baaj* 'taken aback', *maaj* 'open field', *jaak* 'achieved', *raak* 'move', *raan* 'day', *paan* 'red snapper', *naan* 'word'; **with {w}:** *dọọl* 'dye', *rọọl* 'return', *mọọn* 'penetrate', *tọọn* 'apart', *eọọn* {yawan} 'flat, level', *jọọr* 'escape', *mọọr* 'bait', *tọọr* 'flow', *kọọt* 'steal'.

Nonidentical sequences

The sequences of nonidentical vowels that follow are organized according to the first vowel: first, representative examples of the various vowels that follow the high vowel {i} are given, organized according to intervening semiconsonants; then examples of the various vowels that follow the high-mid vowel, and so on.

High vowel {i}. All the other vowels can be found following the high vowel in native words, although examples with intervening {h} are rare. Combinations of the high vowel and the high-mid vowel, **with intervening {y} ({CiyẹC})** include: *kieb* 'spider lily', *mieñ* 'smell of urine', *kie* {kiyẹy} 'canoe part', *lie* {liyẹy} 'this woman', *Pio* {piyẹw} 'Wotje islet'; **with intervening {h} ({CihẹC}):** *ūō* {hihẹh} 'ouch!'; **with intervening {w} ({CiwẹC}):** *juoñ* 'swamp smell', *ruoj* 'shout rhythmically'.

Combinations of the high and mid vowels, **with intervening {y} ({CiyeC})** include: *dien* 'her ear ornament', *nien* 'container for', *jien* 'his/her stomach', *lieṇ* 'that woman', *jieñ* 'erase footprints', *tiek* 'rim', *kien* 'law', *mien* 'place for canoes', *bwio* {biyew} 'noble', *kio* {kiyew} 'orange', *lio* {liyew} 'the woman', *tie* {tiyey} 'lip', *wie* {wiyey} 'pierce'; **with intervening {w} ({CiweC}):** *juon* 'one', *ruo* {riwew} 'two', *tuon* 'trick', *luo* 'a shell', *tuwe* {tiwey} 'possessed by evil spirits'.

Combinations of the high and low vowels **with intervening {y} ({CiyaC})** include: *jiab* 'heart of a palm', *riab* 'false', *pia* 'beer; roe', *wia* 'purchase', *diak* 'tack', *liāp* 'joke; bind', *bwiar* 'stab', *kiar* 'pandanus part', *miar* 'sitting mat', *piọ* {piyaw} 'chilly', *iā* {yiyay} 'ouch'; **with intervening {h} ({CihaC}):** *tūar* 'pandanus blossom'; **with intervening {w} ({CiwaC}):** *puwaḷ* 'coward', *juwa* 'proud', *buwaj* 'halfbeak fish', *buwak* 'birthmark', *luwap* 'puffer fish', *buwat* 'slingshot', *kuwat* 'can'.

High-mid vowel {ẹ}. Only the high vowel is found following the high-mid vowel, primarily in words of native origin, in what is a quite common "diphthong" in the language. The full significance of this is discussed in 2.5.3. Combinations of the high-mid and high vowels, **with intervening {y} ({CẹyiC})** include: *jein* 'older sibling of', *weiḷ* 'oil', *jeib* 'sap bottle', *keid* 'compare', *reil* 'gullible', *kein* 'thing for; these things', *rein* 'these people', *mweiuk* {ṃẹyik^w} 'goods', *jei* {jẹyiy} 'sibling duty'; **with intervening {h} ({CẹhiC}):** *tōū* {tẹhih} 'mackerel'; **with intervening {w} {CẹwiC}):** *jowi* {jẹwiy}, *jou* {jẹwiw} 'clan', *mowi* 'squall', *bouk* 'large dragon-fly', *-ñoul* 'decade', *bout* 'vote', *boub* 'dragon fly', *poub* 'busy', *eub* {yẹwib} 'a game', *douj* 'to ship water', *jouj* 'kindness', *kouj* 'giant octopus', *mouj* 'white', *mour* 'life'.

Mid vowel {e}. Only the low vowel is found following the mid vowel, and only in a handful of examples, half of which have been borrowed. The examples are peculiar in that they all end in a semiconsonant, following two patterns: **{Ceyah}:** *jea* 'chair', *pea* 'pair', *wea* 'wire', and **{Ceyaw}:** *beọ* 'coconut husk', *deọ* 'pretty', and *meọ* 'sour, bitter'. One or two other examples can be formed by adding suffixes to words, as, for example, *kea* {keya-h} 'my figure', but the rarity of "diphthongs" beginning with the mid vowel is striking. The fuller significance of this is discussed in 2.5.3.

Low vowel {a}. All three of the other vowels are found following the low vowel in words of both native and foreign origin. Combinations of the low and high vowels, **with intervening {y} ({CayiC})** include: *āin* {yayin} 'similar to', *aij* {hayij} 'ice', *aik* 'to tow', *jāik* 'catch', *kāik* 'jump over', *pāin ni* 'fronds'; **with intervening {h} ({CahiC}):** *aū* 'to be dying'; **with intervening {w} ({CawiC}):** *jọuñ* 'not add up', *dọuk* 'to lower', *bọun* 'pound; weigh', *lọun* 'a bird', *bọur* 'to lift', *jọut* 'to treat'.

Combinations of the low and high-mid vowels, **with intervening {y} ({CayẹC})** include: *aer* {hayẹr} 'stretched', *ae* {hayẹy} 'collect', *āe* {yayẹy} 'carve', Māe 'May'; **with intervening {h} ({CahẹC}):** *aō* {hahẹh} 'mine; my soul'; **with intervening {w} ({CawẹC}):** *ṃọo* {ṃawẹw} 'a dance call', *ọo* {wawẹw} 'circle', *jọwe* {jawẹy} 'sea bass'.

Combinations of the low and mid vowels, **with intervening {y} ({CayeC})** include: *ael* {hayel} 'unicorn fish', *aen* {hayen} 'iron', *tāo* {tayew} 'pimple', *ae* {hayey} 'current'; **with intervening {h} ({CaheC}):** *aō* {haheh} 'swim'; **with intervening {w} ({CaweC}):** *aoḷ* {haweḷ} 'dispute', *aod* {hawed} 'boat wake', *aol* {hawel} 'a fish', *aop* {hawep} 'a lizard'.

There are two additional "diphthongs" with the low vowel as the first element. These have two intervening semiconsonants, an {h} that closes the first syllable, and a {y} or {w} that opens the second. An excrescent {a} occurs between the semiconsonants according to the Semiconsonant Excrescent Vowel Rule (see page 77), and this makes the {a} of the first syllable sound longer than it does in low-vowel diphthongs that have only one intervening semiconsonant, as the following pairs show:

ṃae	{ṃah(a)yey}	'until'
Māe	{mayẹy}	'May'
jawōd	{jah(a)wed}	'to woo'
jọuñ	{jawig}	'not add up'

The first word in each of these two pairs is an example of the "long" low-vowel "diphthong" with following mid vowel (and intervening {hy} or {hw}). Such words follow the pattern {CahyeC} or {CahweC}. The third person plural possessive forms of words such as *wa* 'canoe', *ra* 'branch', and so forth, can be considered a subtype of this pattern that differ only in that their following vowel is high-mid rather than mid ({CahyẹC}):

koṇaer	{k^weṇah(a)yẹr}	'their duty'
koṇāer	{k^weṇayẹr}	'their catch of fish'

This pattern, with mid (or high-mid) vowel in the final syllable, is of native origin, as can be seen from the three examples that have been given (the first members of the preceding three pairs) and those that follow. Further examples with {y} as the second semiconsonant include: *baeḷ* {bahyeḷ} 'file', *ḷae* {ḷahyey} 'calm', *ṇae* {ṇahyey} 'against', and *kae* {kahyey} 'guy rope'. Examples with {w} as the second semiconsonant include: *bao* {bahwew} 'bird', *dao* {dahwew} 'break a fast', *jao* {jahwew} 'birthmark', *mao* {mahwew} 'bruised', and *pao* {pahwew} 'appearance'. Two others with initial double consonants are: *eḷḷao* {ḷḷahwew} 'seasick (W)' and *eṃṃao* {ṃṃahwew} 'talkative (W)'. The words for 'file' and 'guy rope' show that the pattern has been extended to include borrowed words.

The second "long" low-vowel "diphthong" pattern has a high vowel in the final syllable.

Taik	{tah(a)yik}	'Dike (a man's name)'
tāik	{tayik}	'to roll something up'
rawūn	{rah(a)win}	'go around'
dọuk	{dawik}	'to lower something'

Members of this pattern, like the first words of each of these two pairs, follow the formulas {CahyiC} or {CahwiC}. Because almost all the examples have obviously been borrowed into the language fairly recently, there is good reason to believe that this pattern is an extension of the first one developed to make foreign words sound as much like their sources as possible. Further examples with {y} as the second semiconsonant include: *ṃaiḷ* {ṃahyiḷ} 'mile', *ḷaiṃ* 'lime', *ḷain* 'line', *ṇaib* 'knife', *baib* 'pipe', *baij* 'vise', *jaij* 'size', *raij* 'rice', *taij* 'dice', *jain* 'sign', *kain* 'kind', *wain* 'wine', and *bait* 'to punch'. Examples with {w} as the second semiconsonant include: *Wau* {wahwiw} 'Mother Hubbard dress (from *Oahu*)', *kau* 'cow; look after a sick person', *raut* 'urinate', and with double consonant, *eṃṃawi* {ṃṃahwiy} 'adult conversation (W)'. Only the last two or three examples are not obviously borrowed. Additional examples with more syllables than in the formulas include: *Baibōḷ* {bahyibeḷ}, *jokutbai* {jewk^{w}itbahyiy} 'say goodbye', *jekṃai* {jekṃahyiy} 'coconut syrup', *jibai* {jibahyiy} 'spy', *otbai* {wetbahyiy} 'motorcycle', *Hawai* {hawahyiy} 'Hawaii', and from Japanese *jobai* {jewbahyiy} 'trade' and *wūntokai* {wintokahyiy} 'field events'.

The "long" vowels and "diphthongs" that have been surveyed in this section, generally within a two-syllable framework, are summarized in table 2-17. In this table, all consonants and semiconsonants are omitted, and in the last column headed {a(a)} the second *a* within parentheses is the excrescent vowel in words such as *kain* {kah(a)yin} 'kind'. Rare sequences and those filled primarily by borrowed words are enclosed in double braces: {}. Dashes show sequences that do not occur. The interesting pattern formed by the second and third columns, those headed by {ẹ} and {e}, is discussed at the end of 2.5.3 (page 87).

Table 2-17 Vowel sequences with intervening semiconsonants in two-syllable words

	FIRST MEMBER:	{i}	{ẹ}	{e}	{a}	{a(a)}
SECOND MEMBER:	{i}	i-i	ẹ-i	—	a-i	{{a(a)-i}}
	{ẹ}	i-ẹ	ẹ-ẹ	—	a-ẹ	{{a(a)-ẹ}}
	{e}	i-e	—	e-e	a-e	a(a)-e
	{a}	i-a	—	{{e-a}}	a-a	—

SOUND CHANGES

2.5 Some of the changes of sound that occurred in the past as Marshallese developed from the parent Austronesian language during the last several thousand years are referred to in 1.2. The discussion of sound changes here looks at the changes that are made by speakers using the language today, as they put words and parts of words together in different combinations to form phrases and sentences. Most words differ in sound depending on their location in a sentence, what words are on either side of them, or what words have gone into their own make-up. Speakers are not generally conscious of these changes (because the changes have no effect on the meaning of what is being said), but a study of them can be of considerable interest in showing how the language is in the process of change even today "right before our eyes" and how orderly and systematic that process is.

CONSONANT ASSIMILATION

2.5.1 What happens when two consonants are thrown together, back to back, as the result of two words being joined together tightly in the same phrase? (Because all Marshallese words begin and end in consonants, as the phonemic transcription shows, this happens every time two words are joined.) The answer to this question depends on the nature of the two consonants that are joined, on how similar to each other they are. If they are sufficiently similar, the transition between them is quite smooth, as will be seen in this section. If they are not sufficiently similar, an excrescent vowel is inserted between them, as discussed in 2.5.2.

Similar combinations are of two types: identical and nonidentical. Some examples of identical combinations would be: *jab bōt* 'not naughty', *aṃ ṃōk* 'your tiredness', *lep pidodo* 'soft egg', *am maroñ* 'our power', and so forth. When such pairs of words are uttered as part of the same phrase within a sentence in normal speech, the identical consonants at the joining of the two words are pronounced as if they were in the same word, just like the medial consonant clusters discussed in 2.4.2. Thus, the two *b*'s of *jab bōt* are pronounced like the two of *keinabbu* 'papaya', the two *ṃ*'s of *aṃ ṃōk* like those of *kōṃṃan* 'make, do', the two *p*'s of *lep pidodo* like those of *kappok* 'look for', and the two *m*'s of *am maroñ* like those of *kemmọ* 'jealous', and so forth. Because what happens at the joinings between words within phrases in natural speech (external joinings) generally has the same result as when two consonants are side-by-side within a word (internal joinings), the two types will be discussed together in what follows.

The preceding examples have all been of joinings of identical labial consonants. How about the joinings of consonants that are both labial but not identical? For example, what happens in the phrase *jab maroñ* 'not be able'? The consonant at the end of the first word becomes more like the consonant at the beginning of the second—the first assimilates to the second. Notice that *b* and *m* differ from each other in two ways: *b* is oral while *m* is nasal; *b* is heavy while *m* is light. Thus, for *b* to become completely like *m* involves two changes: *b* must become nasal like *m*, and it must also become light like *m*. When this happens, as it usually does in normal rapid speech, complete assimiliation has taken place. Thus, when speakers set out to say *jab maroñ*, they actually end up saying *jammaroñ*, although they are not especially aware that they have made the change.

Table 2-18 shows all possible labial combinations and their results. The first member of the joining is shown along the left side of the table, and the second is at the top. The resulting combinations are given in the cells where the rows and columns meet. The diagonal from upper left to lower right contains the identical combinations. An arrow in a cell indicates that such a cluster does not occur in normal speech, and points to the cell toward which it assimilates—to the new, more closely related combination that it becomes as a result of assimilation. Sometimes the cell pointed toward also contains an arrow that points onward to another cell, as in the last column, where the resulting combination for the whole column is the *m̧m̧* of the last row. This means that *pm̧, bm̧,* and *mm̧* at word joinings all become *m̧m̧* (the first sounds assimilate completely to the second), and it also means that of the four possible clusters represented by the last column, only one of them, *m̧m̧,* is ever found within a word (internally).

Notice that there are nothing but arrows above and to the right of the diagonal. This means that in all such cases a complete assimilation takes place that results in the combination that is on the diagonal for that column. Notice, however, that there are two cells below and to the left of the diagonal that are occupied by letters (*mp* and *m̧b*). These are the result of partial assimilation, in which the first sound becomes only partly like the second, and in which the identical combination on the diagonal is not the result. For example, the *m* of *item babu* 'come lie down' does not assimilate completely to become *itebbabu,* but only partly to become *item̧babu.* It assimilates to the following *b* in heaviness, but it does not assimilate to the extent of losing its nasality. The only four cells in the whole table whose combinations do not point toward and end up on the diagonal (except for those already on the diagonal) are the four that form a square in the lower lefthand corner. These are the four that have nasals followed by orals. To summarize labial assimilation, it can be said that the first member of a combination always assimilates to the second one, except that nasals do not go so far as to lose their nasality before orals.

Table 2-18 Labial consonant assimilation

		SECOND MEMBER			
		p	b	m	m̧
FIRST MEMBER	p	pp	↓	↓	↓
	b	↑	bb	↓	↓
	m	mp	↓	mm	↓
	m̧	↑	m̧b	↑	m̧m̧

Here are examples for each of the sixteen cells in table 2-18, arranged by rows: The *p* row: *lep pidodo* 'soft egg'; *rup bōro* 'worried' (→ *rubbōro*); *lep mouj* 'white egg' (→ *lemmouj*); *lep m̧ōņakņak* 'brown egg' (→ *lem̧m̧ōņakņak*).

The *b* row: *jab pukote* 'don't look for it' (→ *jappukote*); *jab ba* 'not say'; *jab maroñ* 'not be able' (→ *jammaroñ*); *jab m̧ōj* 'not finished' (→ *jam̧m̧ōj*).

The *m* row: *kōtmānlimpok* 'a flowering shrub'; *item babu* 'come lie down' (→ *item̧babu*); *am maroñ* 'our power'; *item m̧ōñā* 'come eat' (→ *item̧m̧ōñā*).

The *ṃ* row: *aṃ pepe* ‘your decision’ (→ *ampepe*); *jaṃbo* ‘stroll’; *eṃ maroro* ‘green house’ (→ *emmaroro*); *aṃ ṃōk* ‘your tiredness’. (The arrow in parentheses should be read as “becomes”; thus, “*rup bōro* (→ *rub bōro*)” means that *rup bōro* becomes *rubbōro* in rapid natural speech.

The same kinds of assimilation take place when dental consonants come together with some of the other dentals, or with some of the liquids. However, a different result is produced by other combinations of two dentals, or of a dental and a liquid. Instead of the first consonant assimilating to the second either partially or completely, a vowel is inserted between the two consonants in order to make the combination more pronounceable. These excrescent vowels are discussed in 2.5.2. Combinations in which they occur are shown by an “X” in table 2-19.

Table 2-19 contains rows and columns for each of the dental and liquid consonants to show all possible combinations of them with each other. (Only rounded {n^w}, {l^w}, and {r^w} are omitted; what happens to them in combination with other dentals and liquids is discussed later in this section.) The arrangement of the table, with the first member of a combination along the left margin and the second member along the top, is exactly like that of table 2-18. The meaning of the arrows is the same as in that table, and identical clusters again fall along the upper left to lower right diagonal. Notice from the examples below that such identical clusters may either be the original consonants of their words, or they may have been created through the complete assimilation of the first consonant to the second—the first becoming identical with the second. Notice also that there are seven cells that show the results of partial assimilation, where the first consonant has become more like the second, but not completely. These resulting combinations are shown in cells not on the diagonal: *nj, nl, nd, ṇt, ṇḷ, ṇr;* and *ḷt.* The first six of these have nasals that do not lose their nasality—as with the labial nasals—or take on liquid qualities to become completely like the following consonant, although they have changed in heaviness or lightness to become partially

Table 2-19 Dental and liquid consonant assimilation

		SECOND MEMBER							
		j	t	n	ṇ	l	ḷ	d	r
FIRST MEMBER	j	jj	↓	X	X	X	X	X	X
	t	-	tt	X	X	X	X	X	X
	n	nj	↓	nn	↓	nl	↓	nd	↓
	ṇ	↑	ṇt	↑	ṇṇ	↑	ṇḷ	↑	ṇr
	l	X	↓	↑	↑	ll	¯	↓	↓
	ḷ	X	ḷt	↑	↑	↑	ḷḷ	↓	↓
	d	X	X	↑	↑	↑	↑	dd	↓
	r	X	X	↑	↑	↑	↑	↑	rr

like it. The seventh is an *l* that has become heavy like the following *t*, but does not lose its liquid quality or become a stop to be completely like it.

Here are examples for each of the 64 cells of table 2-19, arranged by rows: The *j* row: *ejjab* 'it is not'; *waj ta* 'which watch?' (→ *watta*); *kajnet* 'curious' (→ *kaj(e)net*); *waj ṇe* 'that watch' (→ *waj(ō)ṇe*); *lijlij* 'mash' (→ *lij(i)lij*); *wōjlā* 'sail' (→ *wōj(ō)ḷā*); *kijdik* 'rat' (→ *kij(i)dik*); *pājrōk* 'rudder fish' (→ *pāj(ō)rōk*).

The *t* row: *bat jab uweo* 'that hill over there' (→ *bajjabuweo*); *etto* 'a long time'; *jitnen* 'arrangement' (→ *jit(i)nen*); *ātṇak* 'be named after' (→ *āt(ō)ṇak*); *atlōñ* 'upper jaw' (→ *at(ō)lōñ*); *wūtḷaṃ* 'vain person' (→ *wūt(ū)ḷaṃ*); *ātdik* 'nickname' (→ *āt(i)dik*); *Utrōk* 'Utirik Atoll' (→ *Ut(ū)rōk*).

The *n* row: *penjān* 'its stopper'; *men ta* 'what thing?' (→ *meṇta*); *ennọ* 'it tastes good'; *men ṇe* 'that thing' (→ *meṇṇe*); *wanlaḷ* 'descend'; *jenḷap* 'old chicken' (→ *jeṇḷap*); *jendik* 'young chicken'; *jānruk* 'sprain' (→ *jāṇruk*).

The *ṇ* row: *kōṇ jet kaṇe* 'those caulkings' (→ *kōnjet(ō)kane*); *kōṇ ta* 'what caulking'; *kōṇ nana* 'bad caulking' (→ *kōnnana*); *kōṇṇat* 'a plant: Scaveola'; *letok ṃōk men kaṇ le* 'please give me those things, ma'am' (→ *letok(ō)ṃōk men(ō)le kalle*); *kōṇḷọk* 'caulk away'; *mokwaṇdada* 'a food' (→ *mokwandada*); *kōṇ rot* 'what kind of caulking'.

The *l* row: *bwiljin* 'among' (→ *bwil(i)jin*); *tiltil* 'spotty' (→ *tiḷtil*); *ekkal nana* 'bad design' (→ *ekkannana*); *al ṇe* 'that song' (→ *aṇṇe*); *allok* 'lasso'; *ṃal ḷọk* 'bend away' (→ *ṃaḷḷọk*); *al dikdik* 'small kingfish' (↔ *addikdik*); *al rot* 'what kind of song' (→ *arrot*).

The *ḷ* row: *pọḷjej* 'a food' (→ *pọḷ(ō)jej*); *rāpeḷtan* 'method of' (→ *rāpeḷ(ō)tan*); *kwaḷ nuknuk* 'wash clothes' (→ *kwannuknuk*); *kaḷ ṇe* 'that diaper' (→ *kaṇṇe*); *mānnueaḷ lāj* 'ferocious lizard' (→ *mānnuallāj*); *aḷḷañ* 'gape'; *kaḷ dikdik* 'small diaper' (→ *kaddikdik*); *kaḷ rot* 'what sort of diaper' (→ *karrot*).

The *d* row: *jedjed* 'observe' (→ *jed(e)jed*); *wōtōdtōd* 'diarrhea' (→ *wōtōd(ō)tōd*); *bōd nana* 'bad turtle shell' (→ *bōnnana*); *bōd ṇe* 'that turtle shell' (→ *bōṇṇe*); *mejenkwaad lāj* 'ferocious vampire' (→ *mejenkwaallāj*); *lale kwaar ṃad ḷe* 'don't loiter, Mr.' (→ *lale kwaar maḷḷe*); *kaddoḷ* 'a shell'; *jād rot* 'what kind of drying rack' (→ *jārrot*).

The *r* row: *kurjep* 'a reel' (→ *kur(ū)jep*); *ñortak* 'snore' (→ *ñor(ō)tak*); *bar naajdik* 'feed again' (→ *bannaajdik*); *Arṇo* 'atoll name' (→ *Aṇṇo*); *irḷọk* 'dislocate away' (→ iḷḷọk); *marḷap* 'a plant: Canavalia' (→ *maḷḷap*); *etọọr dān* 'water's running' (→ etọọddān); *er raṇ* 'those people'.

Table 2-20, which shows the various combinations of unrounded velar consonants, is quite simple.

Examples by rows are: the *k* row: *ekkañ* 'sharp (W)'; *ruwalitōkñoul* '80' (→ *ruwalitōññoul*); the *ñ* row: *añkō* 'anchor'; *iññā* 'yes'.

Table 2-20 Velar consonant assimilation

		SECOND MEMBER	
		k	ñ
FIRST MEMBER	k	kk	↓
	ñ	ñk	ññ

The rounded consonants {ḷ^{w}}, {ṇ^{w}}, {r^{w}}, {k^{w}}, and {g^{w}} have been omitted from the preceding charts because it can be said that the results of combinations involving them are the same as those involving their heavy but unrounded counterparts, except that rounding remains in either or both members. For example, *waj rot* 'what kind of watch', in which the *r* is rounded, becomes *waj(ō)rot* with an excrescent vowel as shown in table 2-18 for the *jr* combination, and as in the unrounded example *pāj(ō)rōk.* The *r* remains rounded in the resulting *waj(ō)rot.* Another example, *toḷ ṇe* 'that mountain', in which the *ḷ* is rounded, becomes *toṇṇe,* as shown in the table for the *ḷṇ* combination, and, as in the unrounded example, *kōṇṇat.* Notice that the first *ṇ* of the resulting *toṇṇe* is rounded, this rounding being a continuation of the rounding of the *ḷ* that was replaced by *ṇ.*

Furthermore, there is a tendency in very rapid speech for rounding to spread in either direction through a cluster, especially in identical clusters, so that in *ear itok ke* 'did s/he come?' the unrounded *k* of *ke* becomes rounded like the *k* of *tok* so that *ke* comes to sound like *kwe* 'you'. And as an example of rounding spreading in the other direction, in *bōk kweet ṇe* 'take that octopus', the unrounded *k* of *bōk* becomes rounded like the *k* of *kweet,* and *bōk* comes to sound like *bok* 'sand'. Similarly, in the example above, *toṇṇe* comes to sound like *toṇṇwe.*

Concerning the assimilations that take place within a word, it might be wondered why the word is still felt to have an unassimilated sound in it if the assimilation always takes place. Why, for example, is *jenḷap* 'old chicken' felt to have a light *n* if the word is always pronounced *jeṇḷap* with a heavy *ṇ*? It is because the word is analyzable into two meaningful parts, *jen* and *ḷap,* with the *jen* part (with light *n*) occurring in other words such as *jendik* 'little chicken'. The form *jen* with light *n* is felt to be the basic form. The form *jeṇ* with heavy *ṇ* is the modified or assimilated form that occurs only before other forms beginning with heavy sounds such as *ḷap,* although this modification is not usually felt or noticed. Speakers are not usually aware that any change has taken place.

Speakers of the language may not immediately agree with everything that has been said in this section about assimilation, because these changes are automatic and not consciously felt to be made. Speakers aim to say *jab maroñ,* for example, with a heavy *b* at the end of *jab,* and their brains send a command to the articulatory muscles to do so. But a less conscious portion of the nervous system and the muscles receive the command and amend it (following the rules summarized in tables 2-18, 2-19, and 2-20) by substituting other gestures that are easier to make in the vicinity of the sound that is being assimilated to. Because it is easier to make a light *m* immediately before another light *m* than it is to make a heavy *b, m* is substituted for the *b* command. But neither speaker nor hearer normally notices the substitution, because their attention is focused on the message of what is being said, and the substitution has not affected the meaning of the message. It is only when a student of language comes along and pays more attention to how things are being said—to the details of sound—that these substitutions are noticed.

These assimilatory changes are of special interest to the student of language, because a careful study of them shows that they are anything but random and haphazard. They follow an exact pattern. It can be seen that the nervous system and muscles do not make careless and unpredictable deviations; instead, they follow some very systematic rules as they make substitutions for the original commands coming from the brain.

It should be emphasized again that these assimilatory changes take place only in rapid natural speech. When a speaker slows down unnaturally, as when emphasizing something word-by-word to make it more clear to a child or a foreigner, the substitutions shown in the tables do not take place, and the original commands are actually carried out. This makes it difficult for a speaker to observe these changes in his or her own speech, because the normal tendency in doing so is to slow down and speak more distinctly, thereby making it impossible for the changes to take place. The changes can be better observed in the speech of another who is concentrating on what s/he is saying, and speaking naturally.

These comments about the difficulty of observing changes in ones own speech, and the fact that they generally occur outside of our awareness, are true not only for the consonant assimilations already discussed, but also for excrescent vowels and the other changes to be discussed in the sections that follow.

Excrescent Vowels

2.5.2 In the preceding section it was noted that an excrescent vowel is inserted between certain combinations of dental and liquid consonants: *t* or *j* followed by any of the *n*'s, *l*'s, or *r*'s; any of the *r*'s followed by *t* or *j;* or any of the *l*'s followed by *j* (see table 2-19). The idea of "excrescent" is that the vowel is not a real part of the word, but crops up from within the word to make it easier to pronounce. (English develops excrescent consonants in words such as *something* pronounced "sumpthing" [where the *p* is said to be excrescent] or *lengthen* pronounced "lengkthen" [with an excrescent *k*].) When two consonants in Marshallese are not sufficiently similar as to be easily pronounced together or to assimilate to each other (2.5.1), a vowel is inserted between them to separate them and to give the first consonant a syllable of its own. It was noted in 2.4.2 that medial consonant clusters are timed as if they had a silent intervening vowel; an excrescent vowel can, thus, be viewed as one of these silent vowels that has had its sound restored.

When excrescent vowels are analyzed by acoustic instruments (such as the visible speech machine used to produce voice prints in crime detection), they generally show up in the printed record just as clearly and prominently as the real vowels of the word. But because they are not part of the word as it is stored in the memory of the brain, speakers of the language generally ignore them and tend not to notice them when they speak or when they hear the word. They also usually leave them out of the written form of the word. While they are under discussion in this section, they will be shown enclosed in parentheses in the examples, as they were in the preceding section.

The combinations of consonants examined in 2.5.1 were: the various combinations of labials with each other (table 2-18), combinations of dentals and liquids with each other (table 2-19), and combinations of velars with each other (table 2-20). The consonants in each of these groups are fairly similar to each other. Only among the dentals and liquids are some combinations sufficiently dissimilar that excrescent vowels appear. All the remaining combinations (that have not been considered yet) are of this latter sort; they are so dissimilar that excrescent vowels appear among them all. These include combinations of labials with dentals, liquids, and velars; velars with dentals and liquids; and all combinations of semiconsonants with themselves or other consonants: labials, dentals, velars, or liquids.

LABIAL-DENTAL:	ab(ō)ṇōṇō	'uncomfortable'
	Aj(i)bwirōk	'a pandanus cultigen'
LABIAL-LIQUID:	jeb(ō)laak	'sail away'
	il(i)bōk	'startled'
LABIAL-VELAR:	kab(ō)kab	'use a cup'
	bak(ō)bōk	'knife'
VELAR-DENTAL:	ek(ō)tak	'carry'
	kōt(ō)kōt	'ruddy turnstone'
VELAR-LIQUID:	lōk(ō)lōk	'prickly grass'
	kwaḷ(o)koḷ	'wash'

The exact sound of the excrescent vowels between full consonants such as in these examples can be stated as follows:

Full Consonant Excrescent Vowel Rule. When two full consonants in a cluster are sufficiently dissimilar (any of the preceding five types or any of those marked by an X in table 2-19), compare the vowel phonemes on either side of the cluster, and insert a copy of the higher of the two between the consonants of the cluster. (Exception: if the vowel phonemes on both sides of the cluster are low {a}, insert the mid vowel {e}.) The vowel phoneme thus inserted is pronounced according to the general rules (2.3) of the language.

For example, in the word *ilbōk* there is an *lb* cluster, combining a liquid with a labial, two full consonants sufficiently dissimilar to call for the Full Consonant Excrescent Vowel Rule. A comparison of the phonemes on either side shows one to be high {i} and the other mid {e}: {yilbek}. The higher of the two, {i}, is copied between the consonants ({yil(i)bek}) and is pronounced like other high vowels following a light consonant and preceding a heavy one (*il*{i}*bōk*). The excrescent vowel in this particular word is pronounced just like the first vowel of *libwetōr* 'dimples', but it is not written in the standard spelling.

In the word *kōtkōt* there is a *tk* cluster, combining a dental and a velar, again two consonants sufficiently dissimilar to call for the rule. A comparison of the vowel phonemes on either side of the cluster show them to be identical, both {e}: {ketket}. Therefore, either one may be copied to give {ket(e)ket}, and the excrescent vowel is then pronounced like the first vowel of *tōkeak* 'arrive': *kōt(ō)kōt.*

As an example of the exception to the rule, in the word *kabkab* there is a *bk* cluster, involving a labial and a velar, and, thus, calling for the rule. A comparison of the vowel phonemes on either side of the cluster shows them both to be the low vowel {a}: {kabkab}. The mid vowel {e} is, therefore, inserted between the consonants of the cluster ({kab(e)kab}) and pronounced according to the general rules of the language *(kab(ō)kab),* in this case just like the first vowel in the word *bōkā* 'tide', where the same two consonants (*b* and *k*) are on either side of the mid vowel phoneme.

Of course, speakers of the language do not need to go through this rule step-by-step for each excrescent vowel. Their nervous systems and articulatory muscles carry all this out automatically, and the rule represents a summary of what is done generally outside the awareness of the speaker—a summary to bring out the great regularity and the patterning involved.

There is a different rule for the formation of excrescent vowels between a semiconsonant and a full consonant, or between two semiconsonants.

{h}	ta(a)ta	{tah(a)tah}	'very'
	at(a)at	{hat(a)hat}	'wear a hat'
{w}	tu(u)tu	{tiw(i)tiw}	'bathe'
	ut(u)ut	{wit(i)wit}	'wear flowers'
{y}	je(e)je	{jey(e)jey}	'sail into wind'
	ej(e)ej	{yej(e)yej}	'build up'

These examples all have reduplicated syllables with identical vowels, and that same vowel also appears as the excrescent vowel. But what of examples where the vowels on either side of the cluster differ? As the following examples show, it is the vowel next to the semiconsonant that is copied between the semiconsonant and the full consonant.

{h}	ra(a)rō	{rah(a)rẹh}	'clean an area'
	ekkaar(ō)ōr	{kkahar(ẹ)hẹr}	'lots of *kaar* trees (W)'
{w}	pọ(ọ)po	{paw(a)pẹw}	'bind'
	kọọj(o)oj	{kawaj(ẹ)wẹj}	'use a blanket'
{y}	tā(ā)te	{tay(a)tẹy}	'roll up'
	ekkāāl(e)el	{kkayal(ẹ)yẹl}	'select (W)'

It is as if the semiconsonant were more transparent (or open) and the full consonant more opaque (or closed) to letting the sound of the vowel on the other side flow through and be mirrored in the excrescent vowel.

Finally, the following examples show that when both members of a cluster are semiconsonants, it is the vowel preceding the cluster that is copied to form the excrescent vowel:

wa(a)ini	{wah(a)yiniy}	'copra'
ta(a)unin	{tah(a)winyin}	'for what reason?'
ba(a)o	{bah(a)wew}	'fowl'
ba(a)e	{bah(a)yey}	'bamboo'
bo(o)ea	{bew(e)yah}	'delinquent'
eọ(ọ)eo	{yaw(a)yẹw}	'lash'
wā(ā)we	{way(a)wẹy}	'pick ones way'
we(e)wā	{wẹy(ẹ)way}	'weave pandanus thatch'
kiiō	{kiy(i)yeh}	'now (W)'
mweiie	{ṃẹyiy(i)yey}	'wealthy'

Thus, the following rule can be formulated:

> *Semiconsonant Excrescent Vowel Rule.* When a semiconsonant clusters with a full consonant, the vowel phoneme next to the semiconsonant is copied into the cluster as an excrescent vowel, and pronounced according to the general rules (2.3) of the language. When a semiconsonant clusters with another semiconsonant, the vowel phoneme preceding the cluster is copied.

The insertion of excrescent vowels discussed in this section, and the consonant assimilations of 2.5.1 together constitute the Marshallese means for coping with consonant clusters and making them easier to pronounce. Both changes generally happen beyond the awareness of the speaker and hearer, and both disappear when the speaker slows down appreciably, or otherwise speaks abnormally. In fact, a good test for determining whether a vowel is excrescent or an inherent part of the word is to utter a word extremely slowly. If the vowel disappears, it is excrescent. If it remains, it is not.

Finally, it should be noted that excrescent vowels appear not only within words (where the discussion of this section has focused), but also between words within a phrase in normal speech, where consonant assimilations also take place. Thus, for example, the expression

Kwōj etal ñan ia?
{kʷej yetal gan yi'yah}
Where are you going?

is pronounced normally as

Kwōj(e)etal(ō)ñan(i)ia?
{kʷej(e)yetal(e)gan(i)yiyah}.

The foreigner upon first hearing such an expression and not knowing the shapes or meanings of the individual words hears all these vowels, but has as part of his or her task determining which are "for real" and which would disappear upon slowing down. Those who have learned the language from birth have them all sorted out to the point that they no longer hear or notice the excrescent ones.

CHANGES THAT CREATE THE FOURTH VOWEL {ẹ}

2.5.3 In 2.3 it was noted that the high-mid vowel is in some sense secondary and derived from other vowels. Several of the ways in which it is derived are examined in this section.

There are a number of one or two-syllable words that contain the high-mid vowel {ẹ} in their final syllable. They can be compared with closely related words in which this syllable is not final and contains a different vowel. Such words have an additional syllable that ends with a suffix. (The suffixes on these related words may be the construct suffix (3.2.6) as in *ukōn* 'net of', a possessive suffix (page 124) as in *iṃōn* 'his/her house', or the {-y} suffix that sometimes is the means of deriving a distributive verb as in *ike* {yike-y} 'teeming with fish' (see "Denominal distributive verbs" on page 165):

SHORTER WORD WITH {ẹ} IN SINGLE SYLLABLE			RELATED WORD WITH DIFFERENT VOWEL AND ADDITIONAL SYLLABLE		
eṃ	{yẹṃ}	'house'	iṃōn	{yiṃen}	'his/her house'
ek	{yẹk}	'fish'	ike	{yikey}	'teeming with fish'
el	{yẹl}	'nest'	ilen	{yilen}	'its nest'
bo	{bẹw}	'missile'	buon	{biwen}	'his/her missile'
boñ	{bẹgʷ}	'night'	buñōn	{bigʷen}	'his/her night'
je	{jẹy}	'belly'	jien	{jiyen}	'his/her belly'
lōb	{lẹb}	'grave'	libōn	{liben}	'his/her grave'
lep	{lẹp}	'egg'	lipen	{lipen}	'its egg'
ob	{wẹb}	'chest'	ubōn	{wiben}	'his/her chest'
ok	{wẹk}	'net'	ukōn	{wiken}	'net of'
ōn	{hẹn}	'vitamin'	ūnon	{hinen}	'its nourishment'
pet	{pẹt}	'pillow'	pitōn	{piten}	'his/her pillow'
wōt	{wẹt}	'rain'	utōn	{witen}	'his/her bathing water'

A look at the possessive forms (page 124) of the word for 'house', for example, shows that it can be analyzed as having the stem {yiṃe-}, which is shown separated from the various suffixes by a hyphen in the phonemic transcription:

iṃō	{yiṃẹ-h}	'my house'
iṃōṃ	{yiṃe-ṃ}	'your (SG) house'
iṃōn	{yiṃe-n}	'his/her house'
iṃōd	{yiṃe-d}	'our (INCL) house'
iṃōm	{yiṃe-m}	'our (EXCL) house'
iṃōmi	{yiṃe-miy}	'your (PL) house'
iṃweer	{yiṃẹ-yyẹr}	'their house'

A similar examination of the full paradigm for the other words listed above would show that they, too, have stems following the same pattern ({CiCe}), with a high vowel {i} in the first syllable, and a mid vowel {e} in the second: {yike, yile, biwe, big^{w}e, jiye, libe, lipe, wibe, wike, hine, pite, wite}. On the other hand, the shorter related words have dropped the final syllable containing the {e} and have replaced the {i} of the preceding syllable with {ẹ}.

This suggests the following explanation for what has happened in the history of the language. It was noted in 1.1.2 that the final consonants of the Proto-Austronesian stage of the language were lost in the Proto-Oceanic stage, and that the final vowels that were, thus, left unprotected at the end of the word have since been lost unless the word ends in a suffix. Thus, the final vowel has been lost from the word *eṃ,* which ends in a consonant, but that final vowel is retained in other forms of the word that have suffixes: *iṃō-n, iṃō-ṃ,* and so on. (Even the form for 'my house' *iṃō,* which appears to end in a vowel in its spelling, actually ends in the semiconsonant {h}, as can be seen in the phonemic transcription: {yiṃẹ-h}.)

As noted in 2.6, final vowels were weakened and lost because of the alternating stress pattern that gave prominence to the next to last syllable of the older forms of words, while weakening the last syllable. If the final vowels of the unsuffixed forms of these words had simply been lost, the words would have sounded exactly like other words in many cases. Removing the *-n* suffix and the final vowel *e* from *ilen* 'its nest' would have made it *il,* with the same pronunciation as the word for 'taro sprout'. Similarly, removing the suffix and final vowel from *buon* 'his/her missile' would have made it *bu,* sounding the same as the word for 'gun', and doing the same for *ubōn* 'his/her chest' would have made it *ub,* just like the word for 'tender'. And so forth. This would have made a large number of words sound the same, and might have caused some confusion in communication.

Instead of letting this happen, the language preserved the information carried by the final vowels (which were being weakened and doomed to extinction by the alternating stress rule) by incorporating it into a vowel sound earlier in the word. The process went something like this:

Older form of the unsuffixed word for 'house':	{yiṃe}
Final {e} moves forward in the word, changing places with {ṃ}:	{yieṃ}
Adjacent {i} and {e} merge to form new vowel:	{yẹṃ}
Spelled:	eṃ

The suffixed word for 'house' continued to have two syllables, with {i} in the first and {e} in the second. Only the unsuffixed word, which lost its last syllable, changed the vowel of its first (and only) syllable to {ẹ}, preserving the vowel information from the lost syllable by creating a new vowel sound. (It is appropriate that this new vowel created from the merger of a high vowel and a mid vowel should be pronounced with an intermediate tongue height and called a "high-mid" vowel.)

Parallel changes took place in all other unsuffixed words of this type, so that *el* 'nest' did not come to sound the same as *il* 'taro sprout', *bo* 'missile' did not come to sound the same as *bu* 'gun', and *ob* 'chest' remained distinct from *ub* 'tender', and so on. The result is that all such related pairs of words have different vowel sounds in their first syllables, depending on whether or not there is a second, suffixed syllable: the unsuffixed word for 'house' has the high mid vowel {ẹ}: *eṃ,* while the suffixed word for house has the high vowel {i}: *iṃōn* 'his/her house', and so forth. The *i* of *iṃōn* can be viewed as the older, original vowel that was once in both members of the pair, and the *e* of *eṃ* as the newer vowel that was derived to keep the affected shorter words distinct from other similar words.

The preceding examples all have one syllable in their independent forms, and two (or more) in their suffixed forms. There are other words that show the same pattern of vowel alternation, but have two syllables in their independent forms, and an additional syllable in their suffixed forms:

TWO-SYLLABLE WORD WITH {ẹ} IN BOTH SYLLABLES			RELATED WORD WITH DIFFERENT VOWELS AND ADDITIONAL SYLLABLE		
bōro	{bẹrẹw}	'throat'	būruon	{biriwen}	'his/her throat'
bōlōk	{bẹlẹk}	'leaf'	būlūkōn	{biliken}	'its leaves'
jōtōb	{jẹtẹb}	'spirit'	jitibōn	{jitiben}	'his/her spirit'
kōto	{kẹtẹw}	'wind'	kūtuon	{kitiwen}	'its breeze'

The same kind of derivation can be given for the high-mid vowel in the last syllable of these unsuffixed forms, and an additional change derives the vowel of the first syllable:

Older unsuffixed form for 'throat':	{biriwe}
Final {e} moves forward:	{biriew}
Adjacent {i} and {e} merge:	{birẹw}
First vowel agrees with second:	{bẹrẹw}
Spelled:	bōro

The last change, in which the first vowel changes to agree with the second, is related to the "Vowel harmony" on page 83. It is the only change that did not (and could not) take place in the shorter words examined at the beginning of this section. For some reason, it does not always take place in words where it could, as, for example, in:

bukwe {bikʷẹy} 'knee'	bukwien {bikʷiyen} 'his/her knee'

(If it did take place here, people would say *bokwe* {bẹkʷẹy} instead of *bukwe* {bikʷẹy} for the independent form.)

Another pattern. All the words that have been examined thus far in this section, when suffixed, have the mid vowel {e} in the final syllable before the suffix, and {i} in the preceding syllable, following the pattern {CiCe-}. There are some words that formerly had the opposite order of vowels {CeCi-} and that still show this pattern before suffixes sometimes today. These words also have unsuffixed forms in which the high-mid vowel {ẹ} has been created:

bok	{bẹkʷ}	'bladder'	bokūn	{bekʷin}	'his bladder'
lōb	{lẹb}	'grave'	lōbwin	{lebin}	'pit of'
ok	{wẹk}	'net, trap'	okūn	{wekin}	'trap for'

This pattern could be called "the minority pattern," and the one discussed earlier, "the majority pattern" for the suffixation of words that have high-mid vowels in their independent forms. Only a few words follow this pattern, while most follow the other.

Reanalysis and variation. Notice that the words *lōb* and *ok* are in both lists. They show both patterns, usually with some difference in meaning or usage. Thus, the graves of people usually have the majority pattern, as in *libōn ri-mej eo* 'grave of the dead person', but *lōbwin ḷoñ* 'ant hill' and *lōbwin bwiro* 'pit for preserved breadfruit' have the minority pattern. The construct form of 'net' is usually in the majority pattern, as in *ukōn Kujjae* 'Kosraean net', but with the meaning of 'trap for', the minority pattern can still be found, as in expressions such as *okūmiro* 'trap for the two of you'.

There is evidence that the word for 'night' originally followed the minority pattern, because the cognate word in other Oceanic languages has the mid vowel before the high vowel, and the word in the protolanguage has been reconstructed as *ngpongi. (Both of the *ng*'s of this reconstructed form stand for a velar nasal—the same sound represented by *ñ* {g}. The first *ng* is thought to have caused the following *p* to become heavy rather than light —before it disappeared—in Marshallese.)

The minority pattern is thought to have developed as follows:

Older unsuffixed form for 'night':	{beg^{w}i}
Final {i} moves forward:	{beig^{w}}
Adjacent {i} and {e} merge:	{bẹg^{w}}
Spelled:	boñ

However, for some unknown reason, people later started treating {bẹg^{w}} as if it had had the history of the majority pattern instead, and began saying *buñōn* {big^{w}en} rather than *boñūn* {beg^{w}in} for 'his/her night', and so on.

Today there is considerable variation in the suffixed forms used in constructions: *buñūn inne* {big^{w}in yinney} or *buñōn inne* {big^{w}en yinney} or *boñūn inne* {bẹg^{w}in yinney} 'night before last', for example. The same sort of variation can be found in the suffixed forms of a number of the other examples given in this section. This and the shift from the minority to the majority pattern show that this class of words is undergoing a change at present, and that the original history of the fourth vowel is being lost sight of. It is coming to be treated just like the other three vowels.

A third pattern. One or two other examples are illustrative of the change that is taking place:

armej	{harmẹj}	'people'
armije	{harmijey}	'have lots of people'
ṃakṃōk	{ṃakṃẹk}	'arrowroot'
ṃakṃūke	{ṃakṃikey}	'have lots of arrowroot (plants)'
ṃakṃōke	{ṃakṃẹkẹy}	'have lots of (arrowroot) starch'

The first word in each group is unsuffixed and has the high-mid vowel in the last syllable. The second word in each group is a distributive verb (page 162) derived by using a stem formed according to the majority pattern {harmije, ṃakṃike} and suffixing it with {-y}. (Neither of these stems is the original historical one; both words are thought to have had low vowels originally where the high vowel now occurs: *ṃakṃōk* is derived from the reduplication (2.5.4) of an original *ṃaki,* and *armej* has cognates such as Chuukese *aramas* and Gilbertese *aomata.*) The third word in the second group is a more modern distributive for 'arrowroot', referring to its use in starching clothes. It is formed by the newest pattern, which builds vowels into suffixes, and attaches them directly to the word unchanged. In this case the vowel is copied from the last syllable of the unsuffixed word and attached directly to it: {ṃakṃẹk + -ẹy → ṃakṃẹkẹy}. This is another example of the origin of the fourth vowel being lost sight of, and of its coming to be treated on a par with the other three.

An informal survey made of more than thirty elderly speakers from both island chains as to how they pronounced the suffixed words related to words such as *eṃ* {yẹṃ} 'house' and *ok* {wẹk} 'net' showed the following: everyone followed the majority pattern for *piten* 'pillow of' and *iṃōn* 'house of', and almost everyong followed it for *libōn* 'grave of' and *lipen* 'egg of'. And most speakers followed the majority pattern by saying *utōn* 'rain of', *ūnen* 'substance of', *ubōn* 'chest of', and *ukōn* 'net of', although an appreciable number followed the minority pattern by saying instead *otin, ōnin, obwin,* and *okin,* respectively. On the other hand, almost everyone followed the minority pattern for *toṇūn* 'freshwater eel of'. Most Rālik speakers followed the minority pattern for *elin* 'nest of' and *bokūn* 'bladder of', while most Ratak speakers followed the majority pattern by saying *ilen* and *bukwōn* for these same words. Most Rālik and some Ratak speakers also followed the minority pattern for *bōlin* 'taro pit of' and *pejin* 'placenta of', but most Ratak speakers said *bwilen* and *pijen.* Some speakers distinguished between *pejin* 'placenta of' and *pijen* 'discarded pandanus key of', and a number used *pijin* for the latter. Some used *elin* for 'nest of', but *ilen* for apparel of', and some used *ubōn* for 'chest of a person' but *obwin* for 'thorax of a crab'. And some speakers said both *boñūn inne* 'night before last' but *buñūn ilju* 'tomorrow night'. All in all, the survey confirmed that considerable division in usage is to be found for these words with the high-mid vowel.

Vowel harmony. A second type of change that creates some of the high-mid vowels is one in which a mid vowel in a prefix becomes high-mid in order to agree with a high-mid vowel that is the first vowel in the stem of the word to which it is attached. Or the same sort of thing may happen at the end of a word: a mid vowel in a suffix may become high-mid to agree with a high-mid vowel that is the last vowel in the stem of the word to which it is attached. For example, there are four subject pronoun prefixes (table 3-10 on page 151) that normally contain the mid vowel {e} when the first vowel of the verb to which they are attached is any vowel except {ẹ} (that is, {i}, {e}, or {a}):

kwo-	{k^{w}e-}	'second person SG subject'
e-	{ye-}	'third person SG subject'
je-	{je-}	'first person PL inclusive subject'
re-	{re-}	'third person PL subject'

When these prefixes are attached to a verb such as *maroñ* {mareg^w} 'be able', the first vowel of which is {a}, the vowel of the prefix remains the mid vowel {e}:

kwomaroñ	{k^{w}emareg^w}	'you (SG) are able'
emaroñ	{yemareg^w}	'he/she/it is able'
jemaroñ	{jemareg^w}	'we (INCL) are able'
remaroñ	{remareg^w}	'they are able'

But when they are attached to a verb such as *ṃōj* {ṃẹj} 'finished', the first vowel of which is the high-mid {ẹ}, the vowel of the prefix becomes {ẹ} to agree with it.

kwoṃōj	{kʷẹṃẹj}	'you (SG) are finished'
eṃōj	{yẹṃẹj}	'he/she/it is finished'
jeṃōj	{jẹṃẹj}	'we (INCL) are finished'
rōṃōj	{rẹṃẹj}	'they are finished'

as in the following sentences:

Kwoṃōj ke?
'Are you finished?'

Eṃōj ke an ṃōñā?
'Has s/he finished eating?'

Jeṃōj.
'We're finished.'

Rōṃōj jān aer kọṃat.
'Their deaconship is ended.'

Similarly, the anaphoric object marker of transitive verbs (page 153) is {-ey}, containing the mid vowel {e} when attached to verbs in which the last vowel is any vowel except {ẹ} (that is, {i}, {e}, or {a}):

rupe	{rʷip-ey}	'break it'
pukote	{pikʷet-ey}	'look for it'
kōmatte	{kematt-ey}	'cook it'

But when the last vowel of the verb is high-mid {ẹ}, the suffix vowel becomes {ẹ} to agree with it:

bọrōke	{bawrẹk-ẹy}	'put a stopper in it'
jede	{jẹd-ẹy}	'watch it from a distance'
jeme	{jẹm-ẹy}	'sharpen it'
kajḷore	{kajḷẹrʷ-ẹy}	'empty it completely'

as in the following sentences:

Raar bọrōke mejān bato eo.
'They capped the bottle.'

Raar jede ṃweo ṃokta jān aer deḷọñe.
'They kept a lookout on the house before raiding it.'

Kwōn jeme bakbōk ṇe.
'Sharpen that knife.'

Kwōn kajḷore bato ṇe.
'Get all the water out of that bottle.'

This changing of a mid vowel {e} in a prefix or a suffix to agree with a high-mid vowel {ẹ} in the stem to which it is attached is part of a larger tendency in the language—a tendency against mixing the two different vowels ({e} and {ẹ}) in any one word. The tendency is for all the vowels in a word that are neither high {i} nor low {a} to be either all mid {e} or all high-mid {ẹ}, not some of each.

Here are some examples of agreement among high-mid vowels in a word,

aebōj	{hayẹbẹj}	'drinking water'
wōpeñ	{wẹpẹg}	'empty container'
kōbōj	{kẹbẹj}	'pole for poling canoe'
keememej	{kẹyẹmyẹmẹj}	'remember'
peejnej	{pẹyẹjnẹj}	'business; to cheat'

and here are some examples of agreement among mid vowels in a word:

toḷoñ	{teḷeg^w}	'go to the interior'
oboñ	{webeg^w}	'tray'
dejeñjeñ	{dejegjeg}	'strong; expensive'
ṃōrō	{ṃehreh}	'murder'
jepooj	{jepewej}	'cornet fish'

The only examples to be found of words that contain both mid and high-mid vowels are compound words formed by joining together two separate words or parts of words, as, for example, *jitenbōro* {jitenbẹrẹw} 'sweetheart', which can be divided into *jiten* 'tinder of' with the mid vowel {e}, and *bōro* 'throat' with high-mid vowels {ẹ}. The only other exceptions to the tendency not to mix mid and high-mid vowels in the same word are to be found in certain place-names, such as *Wōnejo-eṇ* {wẹnẹjew-yeṇ} 'a Namorik land tract (*wāto*)'. Such names can no longer be clearly analyzed into meaningful parts, but probably were so composed originally, much earlier in their history.

Vowel assimilation. A third type of change that creates high-mid vowels occurs when words or parts of words are joined so that the mid vowel {e} comes before the high vowel {i} with a semiconsonant between. This can happen when transitive verbs are derived from words that end in a semiconsonant preceded by {e}, that is, words that end in {ey}, {eh}, or {ew}. Below are some examples.

taktō	{takteh}	'doctor'
kaaṃtō	{kahaṃteh}	'carpenter'
jerajko	{jerajkew}	'bleach'
eojojo	{yewjewjew}	'fishing method'
jekajeje	{jekajeyjey}	'coconut syrup'
jememe	{jemeymey}	'grimace'

When the transitivizing increment (see "Transitive and intransitive counterparts" on page 154) is added to such words to form transitive verbs, the mid vowel {e} is raised to {ẹ}.

taktōūk	{taktẹhik}	'to treat someone medically'
kaaṃtōūk	{kahaṃtẹhik}	'to construct or repair something'
jerajkouk	{jerajkẹwik}	'to bleach something'
eojojouk	{yewjewjẹwik}	'to catch fish by the *eojojo* method'
jekajejeik	{jekajeyjẹyik}	'to make sap into coconut syrup'
jememeik	{jemeymẹyik}	'to scowl at someone'

Here are some sentences with the transitive verbs thus formed:

Kwōn taktōūki bwe enañinmej.
'Treat his/her sickness.'

Kaaṃtōūk ṃōk men ṇe.
'Fix that up.'

Kwaar jerajkouk ke nuknuk ko arro?
'Did you bleach my clothes?'

Iar eojojouk ḷañe e.
'I caught this *ḷañe* by the *eojojo* method.'

Kwōn jekajejeiki jekaro ṇe.
'Make that coconut sap into syrup.'

Iḷak itok ñan ṃweo lio ejememeik eō.
'When I got to the house she scowled at me.'

Notice that the six nouns first cited above all end in one of the three semiconsonants preceded by the mid vowel {e}, but that, in the transitive verbs formed by adding {-ik}, the mid vowel has become high-mid {ẹ}.

The same sort of change also happens when verbs beginning in a semiconsonant followed by the high vowel {i}, such as

ūlūlet	{hilhilet}	'talk back'
wiin	{wiyin}	'to win'
ibwij	{yibij}	'to flood (of tide)',

have the third person singular subject prefix added to them as in the following sentences:

Yeūlūlet
'S/he's always talking back.'

Ewiini tep eo.
'S/he won the prize.'

Eibwij tok.
'The tide is coming in.'

Notice that the prefix, which usually has the mid vowel {e}, has this vowel raised to {ẹ} when the first vowel in the verb stem is {i} and the consonant between them is one of the three semiconsonants, as in these examples.

This third type of change results from a strong rule of the language that prohibits the sequences {ehi}, {ewi}, or {eyi} anywhere within a word, or even between words when they are tightly joined together in natural speech. Where such sequences would be created by the joining together of words or parts or words (as in the examples of suffixes and prefixes above), {e} becomes {ẹ} to avoid the prohibited sequences, thus, resulting in {ẹhi}, {ẹwi}, or {ẹyi}, respectively. Like some of the other changes discussed in 2.5, especially the consonant assimilations of 2.5.1, this change takes place automatically and without speakers or hearers being especially aware of it. The last vowel of *taktō,* for example, is felt to be the mid vowel, and the fact that it changes to a high-mid vowel when the {-ik} transitivizing suffix is added in *taktōūk* is not generally noticed.

The second and third changes creating high-mid vowels discussed in this section make it possible to explain the pattern of the second and third columns in table 2-17. In an earlier stage in the history of the language (probably some hundreds of years ago), the table would have had no second row and no second column. The column headed by the mid vowel then contained the two sequences shown in table 2-21.

Table 2-21 Vowel sequences (with intervening {y}, {w}, or {h}) in two-syllable words before the development of the high-mid vowel (compare with table 2-17)

	FIRST MEMBER:	{i}		{e}	{a}	{a(a)}
SECOND MEMBER:	{i}	i-i		e-i	a-i	{a(a)-i}
	{e}	i-e		e-e	a-e	a(a)-e
	{a}	i-a		{e-a}	a-a	—

As some of the second members of {e-e} sequences were raised to high-mid to become {e-ẹ} (by either the first or third changes discussed in this section), the first member also changed to high-mid to agree with it (so that the sequence became {ẹ-ẹ}), in obedience to the tendency or rule against mixing mid and high-mid vowels in any one word. This created the new sequence {ẹ-ẹ} and the need for an additional row and column in such a table: the new (second) column for sequences with {ẹ} as first member, and the new (second) row for sequences with {ẹ} as second member.

Then when the strong rule bringing about the third change of this section began to operate, it had the effect of changing all {e-i} sequences into {ẹ-i} and moving them to the new second column where they now belong, because they have high-mid vowels as first members. The {e-e} sequences whose second members did not become high-mid remained in the third row of the third column, and no {ẹ-e} sequences ever developed to fill the third row of the second column, because there were no rules to create them, and furthermore they would have violated the rule against mixing mid and high-mid vowels in the same word. Earlier {e-a} sequences did not develop into {ẹ-a} to fill the fourth row of the second column because, again, there were no rules that could bring this sort of change about. Thus, the net effect of the changes discussed in this section was to create the new {ẹ} row and the new {ẹ} column of table 2-17, but to empty the first two rows of the {e} column to fill those rows of the {ẹ} column, while leaving the last two rows of the {ẹ} column empty.

One question that remains is what caused the rule prohibiting {e-i} sequences (and permitting instead {ẹ-i}) to begin to operate. As was noted near the end of 2.4.3, there is evidence that many semiconsonants derive from earlier full consonants. Semiconsonants are not as strong as full consonants in preventing the vowels that surround them from influencing each other, and one common influence that vowels may have on each other is that of assimilation: one may become more like the other in some respect. If a sequence {e-i} becomes {ẹ-i}, this can be interpreted as a case of assimilation; the first vowel has become more like the second with respect to height. (High-mid vowels are higher than mid vowels, and of course high vowels are highest of all. A high-mid vowel is, thus, more like a high vowel in height than a mid vowel is.) To give one example, it has been noted that *-ñoul* 'ten' is reconstructed as having been *nga-pulu in Proto-Oceanic.

At some intermediate stage between that parent language and the Marshallese language of today, the *a* had become a mid vowel, and the final *u* had been dropped, so that the word for 'ten' was likely *ñōpul* {gepil}, containing an *ō-u* {e-i} sequence with a *p* between. The *p* was sufficiently opaque to prevent the mid vowel *ō* {e} from assimilating to the following high vowel *u* {i} in height. But when for some reason the *p* became the weaker semiconsonant {w}, this sort of assimilation was no longer prevented. (The *ō*-like vowel probably became more *o*-like (more rounded), and the *u* more *ū*-like (less rounded), together with the development of the {w}.)

Because other *p*'s and other full consonants probably became semiconsonants in a number of other words at about the same time, more and more mid vowels assimilated to following high vowels, until this became the general rule when only semiconsonants intervened. Where full consonants remained, this assimilation did not take place, as in words such as *jebwij* {jebij} 'cut with spurs; kick'. However, there is a tendency in the language today for this assimilation to take place even across full consonants, as, for example, in *etūṃ* {yẹtiṃ} 's/he was too late', where the mid vowel of the prefix {ye-} becomes high-mid before the high vowel of *tūṃ*.

VOWEL ASSIMILATION WITHIN REDUPLICATION

2.5.4 The third and final change discussed in the preceding section, which raises to high-mid a mid vowel followed by a semiconsonant and high vowel, can be interpreted as a case of assimilation. As was noted, it is still a strong and active rule of the language, operating outside the general awareness of speakers of the language.

Another case of vowel assimilation, to be discussed in this section, raised certain low vowels to mid at some time in the past, but is no longer active as such today. However, it has left clear traces in the language for all speakers to know and follow. The traces are seen in reduplicated words in which one syllable is repeated in the syllable that follows, with the consonants of both syllables matching, but with the vowel changed:

ṃakṃōk	{ṃakṃẹk}	'arrowroot'
jāje	{jayjẹy}	'sword, machete'
kọọtot	{kawatwẹt}	'stealing'
ṃōkajkōj	{ṃekajkẹj}	'rapid'
eññajñōj	{ggajgẹj}	'pervasively fragrant (W)'

Examples showing this pattern of reduplication could be multiplied many times over. Note that all contain the low vowel {a} in the first of the two syllables involved in the reduplication, and high-mid {ẹ} in the second.

The theory as to how this pattern developed is as follows: a word such as *ṃakṃōk* was formed from an earlier unreduplicated root *ṃaki,* which when reduplicated became *ṃakiṃaki.* Ignoring the consonants for the moment, note that the second *a* is surrounded by *i*'s, while the first *a* has no *i* preceding it, only one following. The *a* surrounded by *i*'s was assimilated partially in height to those *i*'s by being raised to the mid vowel {e}, while the other *a* (with no *i* preceding it) remained low. The *i*'s were later lost when all original final vowels and those in alternate preceding syllables were weakened in stress (2.6) and lost (1.2). And the mid vowel became high-mid as part of the minority pattern for producing that vowel discussed in 2.5.3, in connection with the loss of the final vowel. To summarize:

Original root:	ṃaki	
Reduplication:	ṃakiṃaki	
Assimilation:	ṃakiṃōki	{ṃakiṃeki}
Minority pattern:	ṃakiṃōki	{ṃakiṃẹki}
Vowel loss:	ṃakṃōk	{ṃakṃẹk}

All such reduplicated words that show the low vowel {a} in the first of the two repeated syllables, and the high-mid {ẹ} in the second, are thought to have undergone this same development. (A few words such as *bakbōk* {bakbek} 'knife' did not follow the minority pattern, for some reason, and their second vowels remain mid.) One bit of evidence that supports this theory is that many of the words with this pattern have corresponding transitive verbs that still keep the high vowel that has been lost in the other form (see “Transitive and intransitive counterparts” on page 154):

daṃdeṃ	{daṃdẹṃ}	‘to lick’
daṃwij	{daṃij}	‘to lick something’
dāpdep	{dapdẹp}	‘to hold on’
dāpij	{dapij}	‘to hold on to something’
rọkrok	{rak^{w}rẹk^w}	‘to scoop up’
rọkuj	{rak^{w}ij}	‘to scratch something’
rarō	{rahrẹh}	‘to clean up’
rakij	{rakij}	‘to clean an area’
tāte	{taytẹy}	‘to wind up’
tāik	{tayik}	‘to wind something up’
pọpo	{pawpẹw}	‘to coil up’
pọun	{pawin}	‘to bind something’
eọeo	{yawyẹw}	‘to lash with sennit’
eọut	{yawit}	‘to lash something with sennit’

The {i} that appears as the last vowel in the transitive forms (the second word in each group above) was spared from being lost by the consonant that follows it (and that prevents it from being the last sound in the word). It is thought that this consonant was itself spared by the object suffix that often follows it, as, for example, in *daṃwiji* {daṃij-iy} ‘lick it’.

There are a number of other reduplicated words that have the low vowel in both parts:

ebbanban	{bbanban}	‘to be continually envious (W)’
ekkotaktak	{kkewtaktak}	‘to be continually raising (W)’
ettōmakmak	{ttemakmak}	‘to be gullible (W)’

Such words generally do not have the high vowel in transitive verbs formed from them:

bane	{baney}	‘to envy someone’
kotake	{kewtakey}	‘to raise something’
tōmake	{temakey}	‘to believe someone’

The theory that derives *ṃakṃōk* from an earlier *ṃaki* would say that these words do not reduplicate in the same way because they derive from earlier forms that probably had final mid vowels: *bane, kotake,* and so forth. They contained no high vowel to cause the *a* to be raised in the reduplicated portion.

An interesting group of words that must have had a final low vowel before reduplication include:

jokwajok	{jek^{w}ajek^w}	'gnat'
m̧winam̧ōn	{m̧inam̧ẹn}	'caterpillar'
bukwabok	{bik^{w}abẹk^w}	'cut'
juwajo	{jiwajew}	'a fish: snapper'

These were formed by reduplicating roots such as {jek^{w}a}, {m̧ina}, {bik^{w}a}, {jiwa}, etc. They are especially interesting in that the final vowel of the first portion was not lost as it was in words of the *m̧akm̧ōk* and *ebbanban* types. The explanation for this is not clear, although it may be significant that the vowel retained was *a,* whereas the ones lost in the other two types were *i* and *e,* respectively. A few other words reminiscent of the *jokwajok* pattern, but less regular, include the following:

wo̧ļaļo	{weļaļew}	'weakling; a fish: bass'
būrabōļ	{birabeļ}	'parable'
wūdado	{widadew}	'a toy'
aduwado	{hadiwadew}	'carry in a basket'

The same sort of interchange between the low vowel {a} and the high-mid vowel {ẹ} as in m̧akm̧ōk also shows up in different forms of some words that are not reduplicated:

pā	{pay}	'arm, hand'
pein	{pẹyin}	'his/her arm'
ro̧	{raw}	'scrotum'
roun	{rẹwin}	'his scrotum'
nājin	{najin}	'his/her child (E)'
nejin	{nẹjin}	'his/her child (W)'

Note that the high vowel {i} is present in these forms that have the higher vowel {ẹ}, so that these can also be considered as cases of assimilation, even though they are few in number and unpredictable. They differ from the reduplicated forms discussed above in that the assimilated vowel is not surrounded by high vowels, only followed by one.

Long a-stem nouns (on page 126) also show raising of a low vowel to high-mid in their first person singular possessed forms. Dropping the *-n* suffix from the third person singular of words such as *waan* {wahan} 'his canoe' and *ko̧ņaan* {k^{w}eņahan} 'his/her duty (E)' shows that the stems of such words should be considered as {waha-} and {k^{w}eņaha-}, respectively. Yet the first person forms have the second {a} raised to {ẹ}: {wahẹh} *waō* 'my canoe' and {k^{w}eņahẹh} *ko̧ņaō* 'my duty (E)'. This can be explained as yet another example of the same pattern of vowel assimilation if the first person suffix is considered to be {-hi}, with the {i} being dropped like other historical final vowels (1.2), after the preceding {a} has assimilated to it by becoming {e}, then further raised to {ẹ} by the minority pattern ("Another pattern" on page 81).

Stem plus suffix:	{waha-hi}	
Assimilation:	{wahe-hi}	
Minority pattern:	{wahẹ-hi}	
Vowel loss:	{wahẹh}	waō

Evidence for this explanation can be found from other languages of the family: the Proto-Oceanic suffix for the first person has been reconstructed as *-ngku, with the high vowel *u*. The *ngk has become {h} and the *u has become {i} in the Marshallese of today: Proto-Oceanic *-ngku became {-hi} in Marshallese.

The vowel assimilation discussed in this section is common in other Micronesian languages. Reduplicated forms with a low vowel in the first part and a higher one in the second can be found in the languages of Sonsorol, Ulithi, Woleai, and Kosrae (for example, Kosraean *laflẹf* 'to scoop'), and low vowels are often raised before a high vowel in other languages such as Chuukese (*paaw* 'arm', *péwún* 'his/her arm'). This process had probably begun in the parent Micronesian language before it separated into the daughter languages of today.

Low-vowel Dissimilation

2.5.5 There is a prohibition in Marshallese pronunciation against two low vowels in the same word with only one full consonant (or a double consonant) separating them. This can be seen at work when words are borrowed into Marshallese from other languages.

JAPANESE	MARSHALLESE		
tama	tōm̧a	{tem̧ah}	'lightbulb'
kama	kōm̧a	{kem̧ah}	'kettle'
baka yaroo	bōkāro	{bekayrew}	'stupid'
sara shiko	jerajko	{jerajkew}	'bleach'
namaiki	nōm̧aiki	{nem̧ahyikiy}	'impertinent'
NEO-MELANESIAN			
kanaka	kōņakō	{kenahkeh}	'native'
GILBERTESE			
Marakei (Atoll)	Merake	{merakey}	'a Mili land tract'
	Merake	{merakẹy}	'a Majuro land tract'
	Merraki	{merrakiy}	'a Bikini land tract'

In each such example, the first of the two *a*'s in the other language becomes the mid vowel {e} in Marshallese. It can also be seen to have taken place in the history of the language.

PROTO-OCEANIC			
*masakit	metak	{metak}	'pain'
*masala	metal	{metal}	'smooth'
*nsakaRu	tōkā	{tekay}	'reef'
*tamana	jemān	{jeman}	'his/her father'
*madama	meram	{meram}	'light'
*waka	okar	{wekar}	'root'
*qapaRa	aerā	{hayeray}	'shoulder'

In these examples the first of two *a*'s in the parent language has become {e} in the language of today.

It sometimes happens that one form of a word may have only one {a}, but that when a suffix is added a second one appears. In such cases, the first one changes to {e}:

māj	{maj}	'eye'	mejān	{mejan}	'his/her eye'
āt	{yat}	'name'	etan	{yetan}	'his/her name'
bar	{bar}	'head'	bōran	{beran}	'his/her head'
ḷọñ	{ḷag^{w}}	'canoe roller'	ḷoñan	{ḷeg^{w}an}	'its roller'

The causative prefix (see "Causative transitive verbs" on page 157) usually has the form *ka-* with the low vowel, but when it is added to stems having {a} as the first vowel, the {a} of the prefix changes to {e}:

kadu	{kadiw}	'short'
kōkaduuki	{kekadiwikiy}	'make it short'
mat	{mat}	'cooked'
kōmatte	{kemattey}	'cook it'

Similarly with the negative prefix *ja-:*

ekkar	{kkar}	'suitable (W)'
jekkar	{jekkar}	'unsuitable'
tāāñ	{tayag}	'attractive'
jetāāñ	{jetayag}	'unattractive'
pakij	{pakij}	'able to stay under water long'
jepakij	{jepakij}	'unable to stay under water long'

Notice also that this is the same sort of situation in which the copy vowel inserted in the dialectal pronunciations of double-consonant words (2.4.1) becomes something different from the vowel copied; when the stem vowel to be copied is {a}, the copy vowel inserted in the preceding syllable becomes {e} instead of the {a} that one would expect:

{nnaw}	'taste good'			
		ennọ	{yennaw}	(W)
		nenọ	{nenaw}	(E)
{bbat}	'late'			
		ebbat	{yebbat}	(W)
		bōbat	{bebat}	(E)

(Notice that as with *jekkar* above, the prohibition extends across double consonants in the Rālik pronunciations: {yennaw}, {yebbat}.)

The only examples that can be found of two *a*'s in the same word separated by only one consonant are when this consonant is a semiconsonant instead of a full consonant:

kāāj	{kayaj}	'fishhook'
jaab	{jahab}	'no'
kọọt	{kawat}	'steal'

or when the first *a* is preceded by an {h}:

apād	{hapad}	'ambush'
apañ	{hapag}	'hinder'
apar	{hapar}	'edge'
aba	{habah}	'harbor'
añal	{hagal}	'attracted'
ajādik	{hajadik}	'walk slowly'
akā	{hakay}	'palsy'

Although as just noted, two *a*'s remain when separated by one semiconsonant *(kāāj, jaab, kọọt),* the first one changes to {e} when the semiconsonant is double:

eowwan	{yewwan}	'to be industrious (W)'
jowwan	{jewwan}	'to be lazy'
eeọñōdñōd	{yeyyag^{w}edg^{w}ed}	'to always go fishing'
jeọñōd	{jeyyag^{w}ed}	'to seldom go fishing'

In earlier sections of this chapter, several kinds of assimilation were discussed, in which one consonant became more like a following consonant, (2.5.1), or where one vowel became more like a following vowel (2.5.3) or like neighboring vowels (2.5.4). The change being discussed in this section is the opposite sort of process, one termed dissimilation, in which a certain vowel (a low vowel) becomes less like a following (identical) vowel (unless certain semiconsonants are present): an {a} becomes {e} when another {a} follows. Irregular dissimilation of certain consonants is fairly common in languages; for example, what would have been *familial* in English became *familiar* to avoid two *l*'s, but a word like *filial* keeps both *l*'s in a parallel place. But regular dissimilation of low vowels (of the sort discussed in this section) is not common, and the explanation as to why it should happen is not clear.

Like many of the other changes discussed in this section, speakers are not always completely aware that this change takes place, and may feel they are saying *tama* (perhaps because of their knowledge of Japanese) or *daṃan* (perhaps because of the existence of *daṃ*) when they actually pronounce *tōṃa* and *deṃan.* Like the change discussed at the end of the preceding section (*ṃakimaki* becoming *ṃakṃōk*), this change must have begun in the parent language before it separated into the daughter languages, because traces of it are still found in the languages of Puluwat, Chuuk, Mokil, Kosrae, and Nauru. But unlike the change of vowel in *ṃakṃōk,* which has ceased to be an active process in the language of today, this change is still very much alive and operates automatically on any new word coming into the language, as with the borrowed words given at the beginning of the section. It is also active today in the languages of Woleai and the Mortlocks.

MISCELLANEOUS CHANGES

2.5.6 Assimilation of consonants standing next to each other in a word or across words is discussed in 2.5.1, including the assimilation of consonants to each other with respect to rounding: for example, the sort of changes that cause *toļ ņe* to come to sound not only like *toņņe,* but even *toņņwe,* or *ear itok ke* to sound like *ear itokkwe.*

Rounding assimilation. Rounding sometimes extends from one consonant to another even across the vowel between. For example, there are two pronunciations of the word for 'school'. One has an unrounded {k}, and the vowel i between it and the preceding j is not rounded: *jikuuļ* {jikiwiļ}. In the other pronunciation, the {k} has been rounded by the influence of the following {w} to become {kʷ}, and the *u* between it and the *j* shows the effects of this rounding: *jukuuļ* {jikʷiwiļ}. Another way to state this is to say that the {k} has assimilated to the {w} in rounding (thereby becoming {kʷ}), and all the vowels of the word are rounded, under the influence of these two rounded consonants. Even the final heavy *ļ* is susceptible to rounding, so that every sound except the j may be rounded in some pronunciations of a word like this.

Other examples of rounding assimilation between consonants across vowels involve the causative prefix *ka-* (page 157). A word like *kawōtlọk* {kawẹtlakʷ} 'cause to fall', formed by adding *ka-* to *wōtlọk* 'fall' may also be pronounced *kọotlọk* {kʷawẹtlakʷ}. In this case again (as in *jukuuļ*) a heavy consonant {k} has become its rounded counterpart by assimilating across a vowel to a following rounded consonant ({w}).

Rounding can, thus, travel freely through a word when the consonants are capable of being rounded. Only the light consonants, and the heavy consonants without rounded counterparts (*ṃ, b,* and *t*), can block this process.

Another type of consonant assimilation across vowels occurs when the second person singular possessive suffix *-ṃ* with its heavy *ṃ* follows stems that have a light *m,* such as *jema-* 'father' or *lime-* (or *nime-*) 'beverage'. In such cases the light *m* in the stem of the word sometimes assimilates to the heavy *ṃ* of the suffix to give forms such as *jeṃaṃ* 'your father' or *liṃōṃ* 'your beverage'. Occasionally the same type of change is also caused when the light *m* in a stem assimilates to the heavy semiconsonant {h} in the first person singular possessive suffix ({-hi}): *jeṃa* {jeṃah} 'my father', *liṃō* {liṃẹh} 'my beverage'. The *m* of these stems always remains light when suffixes with light consonants are added: *jemān* 'his/her father', *jemād* 'our father', and so forth. However, when the dual suffix *-ro* (table 4-2 on page 173) is added, the light *d* of the last form becomes heavy through assimilation, and sometimes also causes the *m* to become heavy, too: *jemārro* or *jeṃarro* 'the father of us two'.

Sporadic alternations. Certain consonants in certain words sometimes change unpredictably to other consonants. These sporadic alternations generally involve closely related sounds. For example, in the first alternation shown below, a heavy (velarized) labial nasal alternates with a rounded (labialized) velar nasal: the two consonants alternating are both nasal, velar(ized), and labial(ized).

{g^w} ALTERNATING WITH {ṃ}

ruṃwij	{r^wiṃij}	
ruñūj	{r^wig^wij}	'late'
uṃtaak	{wiṃtahak}	
uñtaak	{wig^wtahak}	'wring'
pedaṃwijṃwij	{pedaṃijṃij}	
pedañutñut	{pedag^witg^wit}	'resounding'

{k^w} ALTERNATING WITH {w} (BOTH ROUNDED AND VELAR[IZED])

lukweej	{lik^weyej}	
luweej	{liweyej}	'a tree'
ailparok	{hayilparek^w}	
ailparo	{hayilparew}	'cumbersome'
arokrā	{harok^wray}	
arorā	{harowray}	'carry in one hand'
kurjep	{k^wirjep}	
urjep	{wirjep}	'reel'
dienbwijrok	{diyenbijrẹk^w}	
dienbwijro	{diyenbijrẹw}	'final meal'

{l} ALTERNATING WITH {n} (BOTH LIGHT)

limen	{limen}	
nimem	{nimen}	'his/her beverage'
ilimi	{yilimiy}	
inimi	{yinimiy}	'drink it'

{d} ALTERNATING WITH {n} (BOTH LIGHT)

kadu	{kadiw}	
kanu	{kaniw}	'short'

dik	{dik}	
niñ	{nig}	'little'
wūddik	{widdik}	
wūnniñ	{winnig}	'tiny'

{k} ALTERNATING WITH {g} (BOTH VELAR)

dik	{dik}	
niñ	{nig}	'little'
naajdik	{nahajdik}	
naajdiñ	{nahajdig}	'to feed'
ikūr	{yikir}	
iñūr	{yigir}	'sprain; change something'

{j} ALTERNATING WITH {t} (BOTH DENTAL)

pedaṃwijṃwij	{pedaṃijṃij}	
pedañutñut	{pedag^{w}utg^{w}ut}	'resounding'
kij	{kij}	'louse'
ākūt	{yakit}	'delouse'

{g} ALTERNATING WITH {n} (BOTH NASALS)

kañe	{kagey}	
kane	{kaney}	'eat it'

{y} ALTERNATING WITH {h} (BOTH SEMICONSONANTS)

ilūlōt	{yilhilet}	
ūlūlōt	{hilhilet}	'talk back, grumble'
tiār	{tiyar}	
tūar	{tihar}	'pandanus blossom'

{p} ALTERNATING WITH {b} (BOTH LABIAL STOPS)

tip	{tip}	
tūb	{tib}	'reward; prize'
ipnene	{yipnẹynẹy}	
ibnene	{yibnẹynẹy}	'stump; rooty soil'

Doublets. In the preceding examples, there is no difference in meaning between the two pronunciations (except possibly the example with *kij* 'louse', where the prefix {ya-} brings a different meaning to the second form). Sometimes, however, what may begin as two different pronunciations of the same word, like the preceding sporadic alternations, may develop into two different words as slight differences in meaning come to be associated with each of the two pronunciations. Such forms closely related in sound and meaning are called doublets.

{p} DOUBLING WITH {y} (BOTH LIGHT)

pọpo	{pawpẹw}	'to bind, to coil'
eọeo	{yawyẹw}	'to lash with sennit'

popo	{pewpew}	‘to sweep, brush off’
eoeo	{yewyew}	‘to stroke, caress’
pir	{pir}	‘slip down’
ir	{yir}	‘deviate’
{k} DOUBLING WITH {h} (BOTH HEAVY)		
kar	{kar}	‘past tense, conditional’
ar	{har}	‘past tense’
kab	{kab}	‘and’
ab	{hab}	‘but’
ak	{hak}	‘but, or’
a	{hah}	‘but’
takḷọk	{takḷaq}	‘eastward (E)’
taḷọk	{tahḷaq}	‘eastward (W)’[5]
{k^w} DOUBLING WITH {w} (BOTH ROUNDED AND VELAR[IZED])		
bukwabok	{bik^{w}abẹk^w}	‘to cut’
buwe	{biwey}	‘to cut something’
{t} DOUBLING WITH {j} (BOTH DENTAL)		
ukōj	{wikej}	‘turn over’
ukōt	{wiket}	‘translate’
okjak	{wek^{w}jak}	‘toppled’
oktak	{wek^{w}tak}	‘changed’
{t} DOUBLING WITH {d} (BOTH INVOLVE TONGUE TIP)		
ñat	{gat}	‘palate’
ñad	{gad}	‘gums’
bōt	{bẹt}	‘disobedient’
bōd	{bẹd}	‘error’
{t} DOUBLING WITH {r} (BOTH HEAVY)		
iñūti	{yigitiy}	‘to wind, twirl’
iñūri	{yigiriy}	‘to sprain, change’
iñtōk	{yigtẹk}	‘twisted, squirming’
iñrōk	{yigrẹk}	‘twisted, sprained’
{t} DOUBLING WITH {n} (BOTH HEAVY DENTALS)		
būto	{bitẹw}	‘smell of husk soaking pit’
būṇo	{biṇẹw}	‘smell of sexual organs’
{k} DOUBLING WITH {g} (BOTH VELAR)		
itūk	{yitik}	‘rub ones eyes; pluck out eyes’
itūñ	{yitig}	‘rub ones eyes’

5. See table 5-2 on page 220.

No doubt the reader can think of a number of other examples of alternation and doublets. Many of these are thought to be quite old in origin, and to have begun before the Micronesian languages split apart from each other. For example, compared to the alternation in Marshallese between *uṃtaak* and *uñtaak* for 'to wring', islands in the western part of the Truk lagoon have *wúmwúti* and those in the eastern have *wúngúti* as cognate words for the same meaning 'to wring'.

PROSODIC FEATURES

2.6 In addition to using different combinations of consonants and vowels, a language may modify words in other ways to distinguish them from each other. Some languages pronounce the same combination of consonants and vowels on a different pitch or tone of voice as in singing to form different words. Such languages are called tone languages. In Chinese, for example, *ma* (the consonant *m* followed by the vowel *a*) pronounced with a high level pitch means 'mother', while the same combination *ma* pronounced with a high rising pitch means 'hemp', *ma* with a low rising pitch means 'horse', and *ma* with a low falling pitch means 'scold'.

Other languages may pronounce one part of a word more loudly than another to show differences in meaning. Such differences are called differences in stress. In English, for example, there are two-syllable nouns and verb pairs, usually both spelled the same way, in which the noun is stressed on the first syllable, and verb on the second (the last) syllable: *address, contrast, permit, present, rebel,* and so forth: "Do you have your pérmit?", but "Will you permít me to go?" (The louder syllable in such words is usually also said with a higher pitch.)

Other languages may hold a vowel sound longer in one word than in another to show differences in meaning. In German, for example, the main difference in sound between the word *kam* {ka:m} 'came' and the word *Kamm* {kam} 'comb' is that the first word has a long *a* (shown by the colon after the *a* in the phonetic transcription), while the second one has a shorter *a*. Such differences are called differences in length. Some languages may hold some consonants longer than others, although this is usually interpreted as a doubling of the consonant, as it is in Marshallese.

These three ways of showing differences of meaning among words without changing the vowels and consonants are called prosodic features: they may be differences of tone, stress, or length. None of these features is used by itself to differentiate words in Marshallese.

Pitch. This is not to say that the pitch of the voice does not rise and fall as a sentence is spoken in Marshallese, or that some syllables of some words are not pronounced more loudly than others. But such changes do not function to distinguish one word from another as they do in the languages just referred to. Instead, they function to give prominence to certain words within a sentence, and sometimes to help indicate that a sentence is a question or a command, rather than a statement. This use of pitch and stress over the span of a sentence is usually called intonation.

Intonation. Athough intonation in Marshallese has not yet been studied in detail, it is clear that there are at least two major patterns. In the one, a falling pattern, the pitch and loudness both become lower toward the end of the sentence.

Kōm kein turọñ wōt in boñ.
'We used to go skin diving only at night.'

Kwaar pād ia inne?
'Where were you yesterday?'

N̄āāt eo ear itok?
'When did s/he come?'

Wōn eo ear kōṃṃane?
'Who did it?'

All four of these sentences are normally spoken with a falling intonation pattern. Note that the first is a statement, and the other three are questions containing question words such as *ia* 'where?', *ñāāt* 'when?', and *wōn* 'who?'. The falling pattern is usually used with such sentences.

A rising pattern is used with questions of a different sort, those containing the question word *ke.*

Ear itok ke?
'Did s/he come?'

Kōjro maroñ ke jino ilju?
'Could we start tomorrow?'

Such questions may be called yes-no questions. The answers to them will usually contain words such as *aet* or *iññā* 'yes', or *jaab* 'no'. Whether the question word *ke* comes at the end, or earlier in the question, the pitch of the voice rises at the end of the sentence. The sentence contains two indications that it is a yes-no question: the word *ke,* and the rising intonation at the end. These falling and rising patterns are just two of the major uses of intonation in Marshallese. There are a number of other interesting uses of intonation that help communicate something of the attitude of the speaker, which remain to be studied.

Stress. Differences in loudness within a word (differences in stress) have played an important part in the history of Marshallese. In an earlier stage of the language, many words had two syllables, with stress on the first syllable, and with the second syllable weaker. Some longer words were built by joining two two-syllable words together, or by reduplicating a word, to form four-syllable words with the first and third syllables stressed and the second and fourth weak. Thus, two common stress patterns were as follows, using the acute accent (′) to show a stressed syllable, and the breve mark (˘) a weak one:

Two-syllable word: ′ ˘

Four-syllable word: ′ ˘ ′ ˘

An example of a two-syllable word would be *ṃákĭ* (′ ˘) (the original root of *ṃakṃōk*), and an example of a four-syllable word would be the reduplicated form *ṃákĭṃákĭ* (′ ˘ ′ ˘). Other words were built by attaching one-syllable prefixes to these two and four-syllable words to form three and five-syllable words:

Three-syllable word: ˘ ′ ˘

Five-syllable word: ˘ ′ ˘ ′ ˘

Notice that the prefix, coming right before a stressed syllable, was weak, so that all patterns show alternating stressed and weak syllables. An example of a three-syllable word would be *yā-kūtū* (˘ ′ ˘) (the earlier form of *ākūt* 'delouse') and of a five-syllable word *kă-ṃákĭṃákĭ* (˘ ′ ˘ ′ ˘) (the earlier form of *kōṃakṃōk* 'hunt arrowroot').

The final syllables of all such words later became so weakly pronounced that they were lost from the word completely, so that each of the above types of words became one syllable shorter:

		NUMBER OF SYLLABLES		
Before:	′ ˘	2	mājā	
After:	′ Ø	1	mājØ	'eye'
Before:	˘ ′ ˘	3	ākūtū	
After:	˘ ′ Ø	2	ākūtØ	'delouse'
Before:	′ ˘ ′ ˘	4	daninini	
After:	′ ˘ ′ Ø	3	danininØ	'water of'
Before:	˘ ′ ˘ ′ ˘	5	bōtōkōtōkō	
After:	˘ ′ ˘ ′ Ø	4	bōtōkōtōkØ	'blood'

As can be seen, what earlier was a pattern of stressing the next to last syllable became a pattern of stressing the final syllable, after the earlier final syllables had been lost. Not only were the earlier final syllables lost, but other weak syllables came into danger of being lost, too, especially those that were the second from the last (and became next to last when the final syllable had been lost). And many of these other weak syllables were actually lost or became excrescent, depending on the consonants surrounding them. Thus, *dāninin* became *dānnin,* with the *i* between two *n*'s being lost completely, while *bōtōkōtōk* became *bōtōk-tōk,* with the *ō* between the *k* and *t* becoming excrescent. (Such losses of final and third from final vowels is the Vowel Loss Rule referred to in the derivation of *ṃakṃōk* in 2.5.4.)

This is still the prevailing tendency in the language today—to pronounce final syllables strongly, and to pronounce preceding syllables alternately weak and strong, counting forward from the last syllable of the word. Weak syllables that have not already been lost still stand in danger of being lost, especially those that are not the first syllable of the word. The major stress patterns are presented below with words grouped according to the number of moras of time each occupies. A mora is defined as the unit of time equivalent to that occupied by the normal short syllable. Moras are used rather than syllables to measure the length of words in order to avoid confusion. Weak syllables lost from a word may no longer be felt to be syllables, but they still occupy the time (the mora) of a syllable; this is referred to as the "moment of silence observed for a departed vowel" in 2.4.2. Even the syllable lost at the end of words turns out to still occupy one mora when such words are pronounced within a sentence, with other words following closely. For example, *men* 'thing' may be felt to be a one-syllable word, but it occupies two moras in the phrase *men ko* {men(e)kew} 'things' when the excrescent vowel between the *n* and *k* is assigned to it. These moras of final lost syllables are counted in the stress patterns presented below, with *māj* 'eye', for example, listed as a two-mora word having the pattern (′ ˘), just like its syllable pattern before the final syllable was lost. The (˘) part of the pattern is now sounded only as an excrescent vowel when another word follows. Before the various stress patterns are presented, more needs to be said concerning moras and several related matters.

Analyzing Words according to Their Moras

2.6.1 As has been seen, the vowels of some syllables have been lost, but the consonants that preceded them and the time formerly spent in pronouncing them remain. To best understand what has happened and is still happening in the language with respect to these matters, it is necessary to learn how to analyze each word in terms of its moras.

There are as many moras in a word as there are consonants (and semiconsonants) in its phonemic transcription. Therefore, in analyzing a word according to its moras, it is necessary to begin with its phonemic transcription, which will contain all the semiconsonants that may not appear in its spelling. For example, here are the transcriptions of two pronunciations of the transitive verb meaning 'to unload something':

{yaktiwey} eaktuwe

{yakitwey} ākūtwe

The next step is to insert a zero (Ø) after any consonant (or semiconsonant) that is not followed by a vowel in the phonemic transcription as a reminder of the vowel that is missing. Then each mora consists of a consonant followed by a vowel or by zero. The moras are separated by vertical lines:

{ ya | kØ | ti | we | yØ } eaktuwe

{ ya | ki | tØ | we | yØ } ākūtwe

Next, the moras are numbered from right to left, and a breve (˘) is put above all odd-numbered moras, and an acute (′) accent above all even numbered ones. (This backward numbering is necessary because the old stress pattern was counted in the same way, from right to left, alternately weak [˘] and strong [′].)

˘	′	˘	′	˘	
ya	kØ	ti	we	yØ	eaktuwe
5	4	3	2	1	
˘	′	˘	′	˘	
ya	ki	tØ	we	yØ	ākūtwe
5	4	3	2	1	

Finally, if any even-numbered mora contains a zero vowel, its stress mark is switched with that of the mora to its left—its acute accent is replaced by a breve, and the breve of the odd-numbered mora to its left is replaced by an acute. This is necessary for the first pronunciation above, which has a zero vowel in the fourth mora:

	′	˘	˘	′	˘	
→	˘	′	˘	′	˘	
	ya	kØ	ti	we	yØ	eaktuwe
	5	4	3	2	1	

Words of this sort with a zero vowel in an even-numbered mora (which would otherwise receive a strong (′) accent, but which, therefore, has its strong accent switched with the weak accent of the mora to its left) are said to be syncopated. As with beats in music, syncopated words are words that have an uneven beat. The regular pattern of alternating strong and weak stresses (′ ˘ ′ ˘ ′ ˘, etc.) is broken so that two weak stresses instead of one come between a pair of strong stresses. Syncopation occurs only in words that are five moras long, or longer.

Unstable Words and Stable Words

2.6.2 When the moras have been numbered in this way, it can be seen that the first mora is the one at the end of each word from which the vowel has been lost (unless another word follows, when an excrescent vowel may again be inserted). As an odd numbered mora, it is marked with a breve to show that it is weak. Moving forward in the word, the third mora is also marked with a breve as weak. When this mora contains a vowel, as in the first pronunciation above *(eaktuwe),* the vowel is in danger of being lost from this weak position. Such a word is considered unstable, and apt to change to a more stable form, such as that of the second pronunciation *(ākūtwe),* which has no full vowel (only an excrescent vowel sound) in its third mora, and full vowels in its second and fourth moras. Thus, these two types of words can be defined as follows:

- An unstable word is any word with a full (nonexcrescent) vowel in the third mora, counting from the end of the word.
- A stable word is a word that has a zero vowel (nothing more than an excrescent vowel) in the third mora, counting from the end of the word.

Either stable or unstable words may be syncopated, although syncopation can be viewed as a special type of instability, containing an unevenness that the language will tend to eliminate, unless it needs to be kept because of its special effect of sound symbolism, as seen below.

TWO-MORA WORDS, STABLE (ˊ ˘)
2 1

lu	'scold'	el	'nest'
lo	'see something'	men	'thing'

All two-mora words are stable. As has been noted, the mora numbered "1" is not pronounced except when another word follows closely. (This is also true for the final mora of all the patterns that follow but will not be referred to again in connection with those patterns.)

THREE-MORA WORDS, UNSTABLE (˘ ˊ ˘)
3 2 1

lilu	'angry (E)'	jeḷā	'know'
lelo	'see (E)'	kinej	'wound'
kadu	'short'	ṃwijit	'cut something'

All three-mora words are unstable. The first two examples on the left are Ratak pronunciations of double consonant words. The initial weak syllables (the third moras) of these words are in some danger of being lost, like all other weak moras, because this is a position that the pronunciation habits of the language do not permit to be pronounced as strongly and clearly as the following stressed mora. But a counter tendency working against such loss is the need to retain this mora, to keep *lilu* from coming to sound just like the closely related two-mora word *lu* above, to keep *lelo* different from *lo* above, and so on. The Rālik solution to this problem is to change such words to four-mora words: *illu* and *ello* below. The first syllables (the fourth moras) of such words are stressed and no longer in danger of being lost. (It is thought that this is what actually happened in the history of the language, that the Ratak pronunciation of such words is older and was once used by all speakers.) The first syllables (the third moras) of the other three examples (*kadu, jeḷā,* and *kinej*) are also in weak position, and might be lost, too, if it were not necessary to keep them to distinguish these words from others: *kadu* from *du* or *kidu,* for example. Notice what happens to *jeḷā* and *kinej* below when additional syllables are added as prefixes or suffixes. A few more examples of (unstable) three-mora words that have developed alternate stable pronunciations with four moras include the following:

UNSTABLE	(STABLE)	
alen	(annen)	'one more time'
ḷōṇe	(ḷeṇe) {ḷeyṇey}	'that guy'
ōrōr	(ōrrōr)	'interjection'
ōṇōṇ	(oṇṇoṇ)	'interjection'

The four-mora pronunciations (shown in parentheses above) make possible the stressing of the first syllable (the fourth mora), a natural thing to do especially in interjections like the last two examples.

FOUR-MORA WORDS (′ ˘ ′ ˘)
4 3 2 1

STABLE:	FROM UNSTABLE:		
ejḷā	{yejḷay}	(< {yejĕḷay})	's/he knows'
kōnjān	{kẹnjan}	(< {kinĕjan})	'wound of'
dānnin	{dannin}	(< {danïnin})	'water of'
ākto	{yaktẹw}	(< {yakĕtẹw})	'unload'
ektak	{yektak}	(< {yakĕtak})	'carry'
ṃakṃōk	{ṃakṃẹk}	(< {ṃakïṃẹk})	'arrowroot'
okjak	{wẹk^{w}jak}	(< {wik^{w}ĕjak})	'upside down'
emjak	{yẹmjak}	(< {yemĕjak})	'at anchor'
lokjak	{lẹk^{w}jak}	(< {lik^{w}ĕjak})	'tied down'
mwijti	{ṃijtiy}	(< {ṃijïtiy})	'cut it'

(The < sign means 'from', and what follows it is an earlier form of the word.) In the stable pronunciations of these words, the vowel of the third mora is dropped; the earlier (unstable) pronunciations that had a vowel in this mora are shown in parentheses.

In the following unstable words of the same pattern, a vowel is retained in the third mora (marked with a breve in the phonemic transcription):

ekajet	{yekăjet}	'judge'
jekaro	{jekărẹw}	'coconut sap'
l̗ōjabwil	{l̗ejăbil}	'bonito'
m̗winam̗ōn	{m̗inăm̗ẹn}	'caterpillar'
ekadu	{yekădiw}	'it is short'
ubabōj	{wibăbej}	'choked'
ujabōj	{wijăbẹj}	'narrow'
ujal̗oñ	{wijăl̗eg^{w}}	'wide'
kōmalij	{kemălij}	'brain'
jeram̗ōl	{jerăm̗el}	'poor'
ikabwe	{yikăbẹy}	'mackerel'
ikade	{yikădẹy}	'a fist'
utam̗we	{wităm̗ey}	'commitment'
kil̗am̗we	{kilăm̗ey}	'eccentric'
mejate	{mejătẹy}	'path'
ol̗añi	{wel̗ăgiy}	'open the mouth'
atōrak	{hatĕrak}	'lean'
kabwijer	{kabĭjer}	'control'

Other unstable words of this pattern that retain a vowel in the third mora are those formed by the old prefix {hawe-, haye-, hayi-}, as in words such as *aolep* {hawelep} 'all', *aorōk* {hawẹrẹk} 'value', *aelōñ* {hayẹlẹg} 'island', *aetok* {hayetek^{w}} 'long', *aebōj* {heyẹbẹj} 'cistern', *aidik* {hay-idik} 'narrow', and so on. But even including such words, the total number of four-mora words that retain a vowel in the third mora is quite small when compared to the stable group above that do not retain it. The stable group could be increased indefinitely by all reduplicated words that have the pattern of *jāje* {jayjẹy} 'sword', *m̗arm̗ar* {m̗arm̗ar} 'necklace', *oror* {werwer} 'fence', and so forth, and by numerous other words such as *jerbal* {jerbal} 'work', *bōjrak* {bẹjrak} 'stop', *jem̗l̗ok* {jem̗l̗ak^{w}} 'end', and so forth. In fact, stable four-mora words make up the largest single group of words in the language, except possibly for stable two-mora words.

What has prevented this unstable four-mora group from also losing the vowel of their third moras and becoming stable is not entirely clear, although for one thing it should be noted that many of them have the low vowel {a} in this mora. This vowel seems resistant to loss in reduplicated words such as *m̗winam̗ōn, jokwajok, udado,* and so forth, as was noted in 2.4.2. Also, words such as *atōrak* and *kabwijer* may retain vowels in their third moras because they exist alongside related forms that have the vowel shifted to a different, stressable mora: a*tartar, bōjrak.* However, even some of these unstable four-mora words with *a* in the third mora are developing stable pronunciations. For example, *ekajet* 'judge' is also pronounced *ākjet.*

FIVE-MORA WORDS, UNSTABLE (˘ ′ ˘ ′ ˘)
5 4 3 2 1

jedaujij	{jedawĭjij}	'trousers'
kajitūkin	{kajitĭkin}	'ask'
ekabwijer	{yekabĭjer}	's/he controls'
eekajet	{yeyekăjet}	's/he judges'

Words of this pattern that keep a vowel in the third mora are rare, and those that lose the vowel are much more common, of which only a few are given here as examples:

FIVE-MORA WORDS, STABLE (˘ ′ ˘ ′ ˘)
5 4 3 2 1

peoeo	{peyewyew}	'tear'
meoeo	{meyewyew}	'smooth'
bōtōktōk	{betektek}	'blood'
kōmatte	{kemattey}	'cook it'
kūḷatḷat	{kiḷatḷat}	'scrub-shell'
kiḷatḷat	{kiḷatḷat}	'coconut spoon'
ṃōṇakṇak	{ṃeṇakṇak}	'brown'
lelolo	{lelewlew}	'unfaithful (E)'

In a few cases, the loss of the vowel in the third mora tends to obscure the reduplicated origin of words. This happens when the reduplicated portion is not at the end of the word, but further forward, with another mora following it, as in:

	STABLE (˘ ′ ˘ ′ ˘) 5 4 3 2 1	FROM UNSTABLE (′ ˘ ˘ ′ ˘) 5 4 3 2 1	
etetal	{yeteytal}	{ < yetyetal}	'walk'
ememej	{yẹmẹymẹj}	{ < yẹmyẹmẹj}	'remember'

This has happened because in the second forms given, the earlier forms that still show the reduplication clearly, the vowels of the reduplicated portions {yet} and {yẹm} stand in weak position, in the third mora.

FIVE-MORA SYNCOPATED WORDS, UNSTABLE (′ ˘ ˘ ′ ˘)
5 4 3 2 1

As these patterns become longer, fewer of the words in the patterns are simple words or derivatives of simple words, and more are formed by joining together words with the pattern that each has as its own when unjoined. This sometimes results in a syncopated pattern that does not have an even ′ ˘ beat, but may have two weak moras side by side, as with the third and fourth moras of this pattern. The first pronunciation of *eaktuwe,* discussed earlier, follows this pattern. It was formed by joining an old causative form *yákă with *tĭwẹyă (an older form of 'to get off'), each of which had its own stress pattern. Here are other examples of this syncopated pattern:

(´ ˘ ˘ ´ ˘)
5 4 3 2 1

kajjitōk	{kajjitẹk}	'question'
ejjeḷọk	{yejjeḷak^{w}}	'nothing'
allikar	{hallikar}	'clear'
bokkoḷọk	{bẹk^{w}k^{w}ẹḷak^{w}}	'boom'
okkoḷọk	{wẹk^{w}k^{w}ẹḷak^{w}}	'slam'
raññaḷọk	{raggaḷak^{w}}	'astounded'
tūññūḷọk	{tiggiḷak^{w}}	'ringing'
tōññōḷọk	{teggeḷak^{w}}	'ding dong'
taññaḷọk	{taggaḷak^{w}}	'clang'
kūmmūḷọk	{kiṃṃiḷak^{w}}	'shock'
tōmmeḷọk	{temmeḷak^{w}}	'smack the lips'
ñillitok	{gillitek^{w}}	'dizzy'
tuññili	{tig^{w}g^{w}iliy}	'poke'
wōttuōt	{wẹttiwẹt}	'rainy'
turruḷọk	{tir^{w}r^{w}iḷak^{w}}	'sink'
jimmiḷọk	{jimmiḷak^{w}}	'eternity'
merrōḷọk	{merreḷak^{w}}	'rip'
urrūḷọk	{wirriḷak^{w}}	'flare'

Words of this pattern are both unstable and syncopated, and one might expect such a pattern to somehow change to a more even pattern. In several of the examples above this does take place; there are alternate pronunciations of *allikar* as *alikkar* (five moras, stable, and unsyncopated), of *ejjeḷọk* as *ejeḷọk* (four moras, unstable) or *ejḷọk* (four moras, stable). Following are a few more examples of five-mora syncopated words that have either four-mora or five-mora unsyncopated alternate pronunciations that in many cases are also stable:

SYNCOPATED	UNSYNCOPATED	
ajjikub, ajjikup ajjikuk	(ajikub, ajikup ajikuk)	'limp'
tōrreo	(tōreo)	'all the more'
jeppakij	(jepakij)	'poor diver'
ñituwa	(ñiitwa)	'barracuda'
ankoṇak	(anokṇak)	'covet'
jemetak	(jiemetak)	'stomach ache'
turruḷọk	(turuḷḷọk)	'sink'

In other cases the grammar may require the retention of a double consonant at a place where there should be a stressed vowel if the word were to have an even beat. But for most of the examples on the preceding page that do not have alternate pronunciations, syncopation seems to be maintained for the special effect of sound symbolism; most of these examples seem to be somehow onomatopoetic, to be attempting to imitate a sound or a strong feeling that may be associated with a sound.

SIX-MORA WORDS, STABLE (ˊ ˘ ˊ ˘ ˊ ˘)
6 5 4 3 2 1

jujukep	{jiwjiwkẹp}	'barracuda'
jokālōt	{jewkaylet}	'candidate'
kappetpet	{kappetpet}	'hop-scotch'
ellolo	{yellewlew}	'unfaithful (W)'
ānbwinnin	{yanbinnin}	'his/her body'
maroro	{mahrewrew}	'green'
kōkāālel	{kekayalyel}	'choose (E)'

No examples of unstable six mora words have been found.

SEVEN-MORA WORDS, STABLE AND UNSYNCOPATED (˘ ˊ ˘ ˊ ˘ ˊ ˘)
7 6 5 4 3 2 1

jiipkako	{jiyipkahkẹw}	'purser'
kemāltato	{kemaltahtẹw}	'chat'

SEVEN-MORA SYNCOPATED WORDS (ˊ ˘ ˘ ˊ ˘ ˊ ˘)
7 6 5 4 3 2 1

arrukwikwi	{har^{w}r^{w}ik^{w}iyk^{w}iy}	'ticklish'
attūkoko	{hattikewkew}	'eat left-overs'
ekkāālel	{yekkayalyel}	'choose (W)'
kaṃṃweiukiuk	{kaṃṃeyik^{w}yik^w}	'pack goods'
kaadeọeo	{kahdeyawyẹw}	'cobwebs'
keppajojo	{keppajewjew}	'fishing method'

These longer words are stable with respect to their third moras, but syncopated in the higher numbered moras (6 and 5) to the left. The syncopation would seem to be maintained by grammatical considerations. The number of words following this pattern is quite small, and many have alternate pronunciations with six or seven unsyncopated moras, such as the following:

SYNCOPATED	UNSYNCOPATED	
ajjowewe	(ajwewe)	'whistle'
alliñūrñūr	(alñūrñūr)	'mumble'
allijāljāl	(aljāljāl)	'hang'
alluwaḷọk	(aluwaḷọk)	'stare after'
arruñijñij	(aruñijñij)	'groggy'
jādbūtūktūk	(jādbūtbūt)	'spray'
añjuwiwi	(añijwiwi)	'whirlwind'

EIGHT-MORA WORDS, STABLE (ˊ ˘ ˊ ˘ ˊ ˘ ˊ ˘)
8 7 6 5 4 3 2 1

apaproro	{haphaprẹwrẹw}	'indecisive'

EIGHT-MORA SYNCOPATED WORDS (˘ ˊ ˘ ˘ ˊ ˘ ˊ ˘)
8 7 6 5 4 3 2 1

kaammeọeo	{kahammeyawyẹw}	'cheat'

This brief overview of some of the major stress patterns of the language, including some of the changes in the forms of words that have taken place from the loss of a vowel in the third mora, or from the loss of the syncopation that resulted when two words were joined, shows how an old and regular rhythmic pattern of the language is still being observed in the timing with which words are spoken. Although many weak syllables have been dropped, the places they used to occupy in the words remain as moras. Some counter tendencies have also been noted, such as the pronunciation habits that call for a vowel in the third mora to be dropped while the needs of the grammar and communication call for its retention; the similar counter tendencies involved in syncopation; and the obscuring of reduplication by the weakening of a reduplicated syllable, as in *etetal.* Stress is, thus, still a powerful force in the language, even though it does not operate to distinguish one word from another. The stress pattern of a word is predictable from its phonemic transcription; and its stressed and weak syllables do not need to be marked in order to distinguish it from another word, or to point out unpredictably stressed or weak syllables.

Many matters involving stress in the language are still not well understood. For example, when the words for 'boy' and 'girl' were formed by adding the male prefix *ḷa-* (see page 120) and the female prefix *le-* to the word for 'small' *dik,* this would have created three-mora words (˘ ′ ˘) with the *ḷa-* and *le-* in weak position. This was presumably avoided by doubling the *d* to give *ḷaddik* and *leddik,* with the first syllables stressed. This puts these first-syllable prefixes into strong, stressed position. However, when these words are used in phrases with a following demonstrative (table 4-5 on page 179), as, for example, *ḷadik ro im ledik ro* 'boys and girls', the *d* is not doubled, perhaps because the prefixes are no longer in the third mora when the following demonstratives are treated as part of the word:

˘ ′ ˘ ′ ˘

ḷa | di | ke | re | wØ
1 2 3 4 5

With the demonstrative, thus, in effect incorporated into the word, there is no need to double the *d* to move the vowel of the prefix *ḷa-* out of the precarious third mora. However, the double *ḷḷ* of *ḷōḷḷap* 'old man' and *leḷḷap* 'old woman' do not behave in parallel fashion. These and other such matters need further study.

Length. The third possible prosodic feature, length, does not function independently of the consonant and vowel phonemes of a word. As is shown in 2.4.4, what sounds like a long vowel is analyzed as two vowels with an intervening semiconsonant (*maat* {mahat} 'all gone' vs. *mat* {mat} 'satiated; cooked'). And what sounds like a long consonant is analyzed as two consonants (a double consonant) (*ettal* {yettal} 'it leaks' vs. *etal* {yetal} 'go').

SPELLING

2.7 The spelling used in this book is based on the following alphabet, shown in the order in which the *Marshallese-English Dictionary* is alphabetized, together with a phonemic transcription of the pronunciation of the letters when reciting the alphabet, and other names that can be used in referring to the letters in Marshallese and in English.

LETTER AND RECITING PRONUNCIATION		MARSHALLESE TERM OF REFERENCE	ENGLISH TERM OF REFERENCE
a	{hah}	"a"	"a"
ā	{yay}	"ā"	"fronted a" or "a-macron"
e	{yayey}	"āe"	"e"
i	{yiy}	"i"	"i"
o	{wawew}	"ọo"	"o"
ọ	{waw}	"ọ"	"low o"
ō	{heh}	"ō"	"unrounded o" or "o-macron"
b	{biy}	"pi-eddo"	"heavy b"
d	{diy}	"di"	"light r"
j	{jiy}	"ji"	"j"
k	{kiy}	"ki"	"k"
l	{liy}	"li-emra"	"light l"
ḷ	{ḷiy}	"li-eddo"	"heavy l"
m	{miy}	"mi-emra"	"light m"
ṃ	{ṃiy}	"mi-eddo"	"heavy m"
n	{niy}	"ni-emra"	"light n"
ņ	{ņiy}	"ni-eddo"	"heavy n"
ñ	{giy}	"ñi"	"velar n" or "n-macron"
p	{piy}	"pi-emra"	"light p"
r	{riy}	"ri"	"heavy r"
t	{tiy}	"ti"	"t"
u	{wiw}	"u"	"u"
ū	{hih}	"ū"	"unrounded u" or "u-macron"
w	{wiy}	"wi"	"w"

The COSM recommended this kind of regularized spelling because of the following advantages:

1. The ease of children learning to spell.
2. The ease of reading because of consistency and the phonetic basis.
3. The increase of cultural and ethnic pride that can come as the language takes on more of the marks of the major world languages: regularity and consistency reflected in published dictionaries, grammars, and a growing body of literary works.

By "regularity" and "the phonetic basis" the committee was referring to the spelling of each word as it is pronounced according to rules that are as simple and general as possible, usually with one letter for each sound or phoneme. With such a regular spelling, students do not need to memorize the spelling of each new word, as is necessary for a "nonphonetic" language such as English. After the student gets a feeling for the rules by seeing how familiar words are spelled, each new word can be spelled according to the same general principles. (This is also true for more "phonetic" languages such as Spanish, Russian, and German, which children learn to spell much more easily and quickly than English-speaking children can learn to spell English.)

The committee tried to keep the rules as simple as possible, but at the same time tried to make them so that they would change existing spelling practices as little as possible. This second requirement made the rules more complicated than they would otherwise have been. The most complicated part of the rules concerns the vowels, because people have generally used as many as three different letters for each vowel phoneme, and because they have not usually written the semiconsonants at all. The vowel rules are shown in tables 2-13, 2-14, and 2-15.

The consonant rules are much simpler, as the alphabet provides one letter (or a letter with a mark) for each consonant phoneme.

The main complication to the consonant rules concerns the use of the letter *w* to show that a consonant is rounded when this cannot be shown by using a rounded vowel letter such as *o* or *u* next to the consonant, as in the words *kwe* 'you', *ḷwe* 'pond', *aeñwāñwā* 'clamor', and *rwe bōjọ* 'put hands in pockets'. A *w* is also inserted after heavy *b* and *ṃ* before *i, e,* or *ā* only to keep such words looking the same as they have usually been written: *bwebwe* 'tuna', *ṃweo* 'the house'. The letter *w* in words such as *kwe* or *bwebwe* does not stand for the phoneme {w}; it simply functions to show that a consonant such as *k* is rounded, or to keep words with heavy *b* or *ṃ* closer to their usual shape before *i, e,* or *ā* .

One fairly major exception that has been made to the rules involves vowels with a {w} between. Tables 2-13, 2-14, and 2-15 show *ū, ō,* and *a,* respectively, for the w__L environment, resulting in examples such as *wūj* 'pull out of ground', *wōj* 'toward you', and *waj* 'watch'. However, when the {w} is not at the beginning of a word or immediately after a consonant, but has a vowel preceding it, as in *kuuj* {kiwij} 'cat', *jouj* {jẹwij} 'kindness', *booj* {bewej} 'boat', *kọọj* {kawaj} 'blanket', and so forth, the macron is left off the *u* and *o*, and *ọ* is substituted for *a*, thus, making these spellings exceptions to the *kuūj, joūj, boōj,* and *kọaj* that would be called for by the rules. This major exception is extended to the reduplicated syllables in words such as *juujuj* 'wear shoes', *doulul* 'round', *aiboojoj* 'beautiful', *kọọjoj* 'use a blanket', and so forth; otherwise they would appear as *juūjwūj, doūlwūl, aiboōjwōj,* and *kọajwōj,* respectively. This exception can be summed up as follows: substitute *u* for *ū, o* for *ō,* and *ọ* for *a* in the w__L environment when the *w* is preceded by a vowel—when the two vowels together form a long vowel or diphthong (2.4.4)—or when the w__L syllable is a reduplication of a preceding syllable that qualifies for the exception. Generally this results in keeping the spelling closer to usual practices, but there are a few cases where this may not be so, as in *juon* 'one' and *būruon* 'his/her throat', and so forth, which are often spelled *juōn* and *būruōn* as well.

A few words have been made exceptions to the rules. Two such words are *rej* 'they are' and *ren* 'they are to', which according to the rules for the H__L environment (table 2-14) should be *rōj* and *rōn.* The exception is made because these are such common words, and they are usually spelled with the *e.* Another exception involves the high-mid vowel before velar consonants, in a few words such as *iōñ* {yiyẹg} 'north', *iiōk* {'yiyẹk} 'mix', and *kanniōk* {kanniyẹk} 'meat'. The rules (table 2-14) would call for *e* in this y__H environment (as in *tiliekek* 'hide'), but these exceptions, like the preceding ones, have been made in order to avoid making common words look startlingly different. Such exceptions should be as few as possible, because each exception to a rule weakens the rule. If there are too many exceptions to a rule, children in learning to spell will become confused about the rule and unsure what it is—whether, for example, the mid vowel is to be spelled *e* or *ō* in L__H environments: *det* and *jeḷā,* but *lōñ* and *nōṃba.* As more and more children learn this spelling, they may decide to do away with even these few exceptions.

The major difference between the spelling used in this volume and past spelling practices has to do with the marks that have been added to letters. Since the language was first written, marks have commonly been used on four letters: *ā, ō, ū,* and *ñ.* The alphabet presented here uses marks also for *ọ* and the heavy consonants *ḷ, ṃ,* and *ṇ.* Such marks do not change the usual appearance of words drastically, but can often help a reader to distinguish one word from another: for example, *tọ* 'sugar cane' from *to* 'rope', *ḷañ* 'storm' from *lañ* 'sky', *ṃarṃar* 'necklace' from *marmar* 'lots of bushes', and *ṇaṃ* 'mosquito' from *naṃ* 'secondary lagoon'.

The COSM did not intend that these marks should never be omitted. Their recommendation in 1971 said, "The diacritic marks should be used consistently in formal and published works, but should be considered optional and may be omitted in very informal writing, as in personal correspondence, for example, when no misunderstanding of the intended word will result." They also said that the exact shape of the marks used is not important, and must depend on what is available. On a typewriter, for example, some other mark might be used above the letters instead of the macron for *ā, ō, ū,* and *ñ* (making them *ä, ö, ü* and *ṅ,* for example). Underscoring could be used for *ọ, ḷ, ṃ,* and *ṇ* (making them o̲, l̲, m̲, and n̲). Or the apostrophe could be used above the letter for *ọ, ṃ,* and *ṇ,* and the heavy *ḷ* could be typed with a hyphen crossing the *l* (making them *ó*, *ḿ*, *ń*, and ł, for example). Because two letters, *n* and *o*, need to have two different marks (*ñ* vs. *ṇ,* and *ō* vs. *ọ*), it is important that they not be confused. On a computer, much depends on the software and the fonts that are available. In general, the committee recommended a broad, horizontal marking above the letters for *ā, ō, ū,* and *ñ,* and either a single, narrow, and more vertical mark above the letter, or a mark of any shape beneath the letter, for *ọ, ḷ, ṃ,* and *ṇ.*

In 1991 the Nitijeḷā (the Parliament of the RMI) appropriated $20,000 to enable the Jarin Loloorjake Kajin Aelōñ Kein (Marshallese Language Commission) to carry out the provisions of Public Law No. 1983-34, which established the commission and expressed in detail its purpose and functions, one of which was to recommend to the Nitijeḷā a standardized spelling for implementation. In April of that same year the commission unanimously endorsed the spelling in the MED, and in August they accepted the *Report on the Preservation, Development, and Use of Marshallese,* as drafted by the third author and Mr. Harry Ueno, which was then tendered to the Minister of Interior and Outer Island Affairs for introduction to the Cabinet and the Nitijeḷā. In its 1994 session, the Nitijeḷā adopted the MED spelling as the official standard.

SUMMARY

2.8 In this chapter we have identified the consonants, semiconsonants, and vowels that compose the unique sound system of Marshallese, and the phonetic detail of how each is produced. The labels for the phonemes sometimes use letters that do not show up in the standard spelling, such as {y}, {ẹ}, {h}, {k^w}, for example. The relation between each phoneme and how it is represented in the standard spelling has been examined in detail and summarized in general rules to the extent possible. The influence each sound has on its neighbors, and how it is influenced by them is the focus of section 2.5 on sound changes. We have looked at the patterning of stress on words of different length, and we have seen how it makes some words less stable than others, helping explain some of the variation in pronunciation, including that of the two major dialects, Rālik (W) and Ratak (E). Finally, we have summarized some of the developments that led to the spelling used in the *Marshallese-English Dictionary* (MED), in its on-line revision (the *Marshallese On-line Dictionary* [MOD]), and in this volume.

We turn now, in the chapters that follow, to a consideration of meaningful elements of the language: words, phrases, clauses, sentences, and larger cohesive texts. In so doing, we will employ primarily the standard spelling of the language. The phonemes (in { } brackets) will be shown only when necessary to make a particular point about the sounds involved.

3 Marshallese Words and Their Forms

INTRODUCTION

3.1 This chapter surveys the various types of words to be found in Marshallese and the more important characteristics of the two major types. Two sections are organized around the two major parts of speech, nouns and verbs. Other parts of speech, such as pronouns, demonstratives, adverbs, numerals, interrogatives, conjunctions, interjections, and so forth, will be introduced in later chapters. Readers may be familiar with such terms from their study of other languages, because it seems that such parts of speech are to be found in all languages, although the details may differ from language to language. In any event, each part of speech is defined when it is introduced through a range of examples and by observations as to what the examples have in common, both in their form and in the contribution they make to the meaning of sentences in which they are used. In chapter 6 we will learn more of their functions in the larger units they are a part of.

In discussing the form of each part of speech, words are analyzed according to the meaningful parts to be found within them. Some words can be divided into a main part or stem, and either a prefix that precedes the stem or a suffix that follows, or both. For some words, there may be more than one prefix, or more than one suffix. For example, the word *eka-bwilōn̄lōn̄* 'it is surprising' can be analyzed as having the prefix *e-* 'third person singular subject' followed by the prefix *ka-* 'causative' followed by the complex stem *bwilōn̄lōn̄* (formed by reduplication from the simpler stem *bwilōn̄* 'surprised'). The word *limeerro* 'beverage of the two of them' can be analyzed as having a stem *lime-* 'beverage' followed by a suffix *-er* {-yyẹr} 'their' followed by a second suffix *-ro* 'two'.

The term "affix" is used to refer to both prefixes and suffixes, to the parts of a word that either precede or follow the stem. Some affixes are found with one part of speech, and other affixes with another. There are noun affixes, verb affixes, pronoun affixes, demonstrative affixes, numeral affixes, and so forth. The affixes to be found with a given part of speech are presented in the section that deals with that part of speech. Brief attention is also given to some of the other words that may be found together with a part of speech in phrases, although a more detailed examination of the various combinations of words with each other is presented in chapters 4, 5, and 6.

In addition to affixation, another way in which words can differ in their form is by reduplication, when all or part of a word is repeated. For example, compare the word *kijdik* 'mouse, rat' with {**k**kijdik**dik**} 'be teeming with mice or rats' (pronounced *ikkijdikdik* [W] and *kūkijdikdik* [E]). The longer word has been formed by two kinds of reduplication (1) the doubling of the initial consonant, and (2) the repetition of the final syllable. (These reduplicated portions are printed with boldface type in the basic form here.)

In discussing the contribution that words of a given part of speech make to the meaning of sentences in which they are used, it is helpful to separate them into smaller groups or classes. For example, verbs are divided into various classes such as adjectival verbs, distributive verbs, causative verbs, transitive verbs, existential verbs, and so forth. In this chapter, classes are identified and examples given when the class has a distinctive form. Classes based on other differences, especially their groupings within larger units such as phrases and clauses, are discussed in later chapters.

One part of speech can be changed into another by a process known as derivation: nouns can be changed into verbs, verbs into nouns, and so forth. The ways in which these two major parts of speech can be derived receive preliminary discussion in this chapter.

NOUNS

3.2 As will be seen in chapter 6, noun phrases are one of the principal ingredients of many sentences, showing, for example, who or what performed the action of the verb, who or what the action was performed upon, when it was performed, where it was performed, and so on. And although not every noun phrase contains a noun, nouns are nevertheless one of the principal ingredients of noun phrases. Marshallese has both proper nouns (3.2.1) and common nouns. Some common nouns are inalienable (3.2.2) and others alienable (3.2.3). Both inalienable and alienable nouns may be derived from other nouns or from other parts of speech, by several means (3.2.4 and 3.2.5). Many nouns are simple words that cannot be divided into meaningful parts, but inalienable nouns never appear without a suffix that indicates the possessor of the noun. For example, the word *daṃ* 'forehead' cannot be broken down into *d* + *aṃ* or *da* + *ṃ* with any such pieces having a meaning of their own. On the other hand, the word *jeman* 'his/her father' can be divided into *jema-* 'father' and *-n* 'his (or her)', the possessor of the father. However, the *jema-* part is not normally said alone; it must have a suffix such as *-n* to be used as a word. This is why it is written with a hyphen, to show that something—a suffix—must follow for it to be complete. Similarly, the *-n* suffix never stands alone as a word, and its hyphen indicates that it is a suffix and needs a stem to precede it in order to form a word.

There are some other nouns that can be divided into a prefix and a stem. For example, *lọje* 'stomach' may be divided into *lọ-* and *je*. The stem *je* (unlike *jema-*) can also stand alone as a word, as in

(3-1) Kwometak je ke?
'Do you have a stomach ache?'

The exact meaning of the prefix *lọ-* is not easy to determine, although it is found together with several other body parts (3.2.8).

The various affixes that can be found with nouns are discussed together with the types of nouns they occur with. One important prefix (*ri-* 'person from, person who') that derives nouns from other nouns or from verbs and phrases is discussed in 3.2.4, and a suffix that can occur with all common nouns, the construct suffix *-n*, is discussed in 3.2.6. Certain locative nouns are discussed in 3.2.7, and those that take the prefix *lọ-* (as does *lọje* above) are discussed in 3.2.8. Compound nouns are discussed in 3.2.9.

PROPER NOUNS

3.2.1 As in other languages, proper nouns in Marshallese are names: names of places, names of persons, names of clans and other groups and organizations, names of varieties of plants, names of the days of the week, the months of the year, and so forth. Proper nouns are not usually treated like other nouns in the grammar of a language. In Marshallese, for example, they are not possessed either inalienably (3.2.2) or alienably (3.2.3), and they are not usually used in phrases with a following demonstrative (4.2.2). Because of their special status they are written with the first letter capitalized.

Place names. The MED and MOD each contain more than 3,000 names of places in the Marshall Islands (Abo et al. 1976). More than two-thirds of these are the names of tracts *(wāto)* and households *(eoonḷā)* into which islets have been divided, and the remainder are the names of islets, shoals, sandspits, coral heads, rocks, channels, and the districts *(bukwōn)* into which atolls are divided, as well as the names of the atolls themselves. A little over half of the names can still be analyzed grammatically to determine their meaning; the remainder are so old that their original meanings have been lost, although there are legends that furnish possible explanations for some of them. Many that are analyzable involve nothing more than the addition of a demonstrative (4.2.2): *Bok-kaņ* 'those sandspits'. Others have special suffixes showing how an earlier tract was subdivided: *Ankeke-ja-i-rōk* 'south crooked' and *Ankeke-ja-i-iōñ* 'north crooked'. Two other favorite constructions are typified by *Ṃōn-kōñe* 'house of the ironwood tree' and *Lọ-kōñe* 'at the ironwood tree'.

The first of these contains a GENERIC (referring to a general type of place) followed by a SPECIFIC characteristic of the place. The generic *ṃōn* is one of the construct forms (3.2.6) of the word *eṃ* 'house'. An older construct form *ṃwe* {ṃey} without the *-n* suffix (but with the semiconsonant {y} instead) can be found in some place names for 'house of', as in *Ṃwe-det* 'house of sunshine'. Similar archaic construct forms can also be found for most other generics. The most common generics of place names are given in table 3-1, together with both their construct forms and examples. Although generics like *pieo* and *wōja* are not commonly used other than in place names, their original meaning can still be inferred. Notice that several of the generics—*bōran*, *likin,* and *lukwōn*—can be viewed as extensions of names of parts of the human body to names for parts of an island. (There is also great similarity between the word for '*cape of*' {bikien} and '*knee of*' {bik^{w}ien}.) The specifics that make up the second part of these generic-specific constructions are varied, as can be seen from the examples in table 3-1, involving topographic features (*ae* 'current', *ṇo* 'wave', *ḷwe* 'pond'), flora (piñpiñ '*Hernandia* tree') and

Table 3-1 Place-name generics

		CONSTRUCT FORMS			
GENERIC	MEANING	CURRENT	ARCHAIC	EXAMPLE	LOCATION
aelōñ	'island, country'	aelōñin	aelōñi	Aelōñin-ae	Rālik atoll
āne	'islet'	āneen	—	Ānen-oṃ	Ailuk islet
ar	'lagoon beach'	arōn	are	Are-tọ-jāirōk	Erikub islet
bat	'hill'	batin	bati	Bati-Lijarroñ	Wotje tract
bok	'sandspit'	bokwan	bokwā	Bokwā-jine	Malolap islet
bar	'head, rock'	bōran	bōrā	Bōrā-Lōbo	Majuro tract
bōke	'cape'	būkien	būkie	Būkie-Ruwa	Arno tract
—	'surface'	eoon	ewe	Ewe-ṇo	Ujae tract
—	'end'	jabōn	jabwe	Jabwe-jād-eṇ	Arno tract
—	'bottom'	kapin	kapi	Kapi-ḷwe	Majuro tract
lik	'back, ocean side'	likin	liki	Liki-jinre	Mili tract
—	'waist, middle'	lukwōn	lukwe	Lukwōn-wōd	Likiep islet
eṃ	'house'	ṃōn	ṃwe	Ṃwe-Ḷakne	Arno tract
ṇa	'shoal'	ṇaan	—	Ṇaan-merā	Ujae islet
—	'surface'	pikōn	pike	Pike-tōkeak	Likiep islet
pieo	'medicine place'	pien, pieon	—	Pien-mej	Jaluit tract
to	'channel'	toon	—	Toon-turọñ	Ujelang channel
wāto	'tract'	wātuon	wātue	Wātuon-piñpiñ	Arno tract
wōd	'coral'	wōden	wōde	Wōden-el-kaṇ	Arno tract
wōja	'abode'	wōjaan	wōjā	Wōjaan-Etao	Majuro tract
wūn	'base'	wūnin	wūni	Wūni-ḷwe-kaṇ	Arno tract

fauna (*oṃ* 'hermit crab', *jine* 'sand crab', *merā* 'parrotfish'), names of legendary people (*Etao* 'legendary trickster', *Lijarroñ* 'Ms. Deaf'), or other historical or cultural matters (*tōkeak* 'arrival', *mej* 'death', *turọñ* 'spear fishing').

The second construction, typified by *Lọ-kōñe* 'at the ironwood tree', involves the formative *lọ-* 'locative; in, at' discussed in 3.2.8. The specifics found in this construction are also many and varied, as can be seen from the listing of names beginning with *lọ-* in the MED (pages 545–50). The preceding two pages give others that begin with the variant *lo-,* coinciding with the contemporary preposition *lo* in form (*ilo*, with two dialectal variants as given in the MED, can be analyzed as a compound preposition, *i* + *lo*). While the structure of place names with *lọ* ~ *lo* would seem to be that of preposition + noun, their combination results in a noun, one type of the proper nouns known as place names.

Another construction often found in place names involves the basic form of one of the above generics followed by an adjectival (table 3-13) or distributive (see page 162) verb modifying it: *Aelōñ-ḷapḷap* 'great island' (cf. *ḷap* 'great'), *āne-bokbok* 'sandy islet' (cf. *bok* 'sand'), *āne-dekāke* 'stony islet' (cf. *dekā* 'stone'), *āne-kōṇoṇo* 'islet with many *kōṇo*-trees' (cf. *kōṇo* '*Cordia subcordata*'), *āne-kūbwebwe* 'islet with many feces' (cf. *kūbwe* 'feces'). Quite often these names or parts of them are distributive verbs (see "Other affixes" on page 139) derived from nouns, implying a surfeit: *Ṇaṃṇōṃ* 'lots of mosquitos' (cf. *ṇaṃ* 'mosquito'), *Kabokbok* 'lots of sand', *Lo-joñe* 'at the many mangroves' (cf. *joñ* 'mangrove').

As tracts have been subdivided, so have their names, by means of several sets of elements postposed. One of these sets contains three recurring formatives (parts of words that seem to have some meaning): *ja, ra, ka,* which are usually followed by the locative *i* and then by a member of one of the following pairs: *iōñ* 'north' or *rōk* 'south'; *ej* 'up (east)' or *laḷ* 'down (west)'. The meaning of *ja, ra*, and *ka* is felt by speakers to be related to the *j* of *juon* 'one', and the recurring *r* and *k* of the plural human and nonhuman demonstratives (4.2.2) (such as *raṇ* and *kaṇ*), respectively (in spite of the lack of any clear correlation with number or humanness in the names). Examples of these subdividing accretions are: two tracts side-by-side on Ailinglapalap named *Ṃaniddik-ra-i-iōñ* and *Ṃaniddik-ra-i-rōk,* and contiguous Majuro sandspits named *Bok-ja-i-ej* and *Bok-ja-i-laḷ.* Similar subdividing accretions are built from *jit* or *jal* 'facing' followed by one of the following directionals (5.3): *tak* 'eastward', *to* 'westward', *niñeañ* 'northward', *rōkeañ* 'southward', or from *ar* 'lagoon beach' and *lik* 'ocean side', optionally preceded by either or both the formative *ra* and the locative *i* (in that order). Some of the above pairs admit of middle terms: *eoḷap* 'middle' between *iōñ* and *rōk*; and *wōj* 'interior' between *ar* and *lik.*

Other recurring formatives that can be found in the place names, but that no longer have a clear meaning, include *ijo* {yijẹw}, *jekad*, *ilel* {yilyẹl}, and *a* {hah}. Almost 100 loans turned up among the names, ranging from nearby Pacific Islands (*Ṃakin* and *Toorwa* [Tarawa] in Kiribati, *Nonmea* [Nanumea] and *Nuwe* [Nui] in Tuvalu [the former Ellice Islands], *Ṃakil* [Mokil] and *Piñlep* [Pingelap] in the Carolines, for example, to places further afield (*Alajka* [Alaska], *Pāālliiñ* [Berlin], *Jiloon* [Ceylon], *Nupidkin* [New Britain]), including those in Bible lands (*Iten* [Eden], *Jotōṃ* [Sodom], *Jedko* [Jericho], *Kalele* [Galilee]). Non-place-name loans include words such as *Eika* (acre), *Jeḷo* (Sail ho!), *Añkō* (anchor), *Peel* (bell), and *Tūrabōl* (trouble). Almost 200 personal names turn up as place names, or parts of names—three-fourths of these are clearly identifiable as such because of the distinctive male (*ḷa-*) and female (*li-*) personal name prefixes (see the next section): for example, the Majuro tract *Ḷakiḷḷij* 'Mr. Lizard', or the Wotje tracts *Bati-Lijarroñ* 'Ms. Deaf's Hill' (cf. *roñ* {reg^{w}} 'hear', {jarreg^{w}reg^{w}} 'deaf') and *Bati-Lijablo* 'Ms. Not-see's Hill' (cf. *jab* 'not', *lo* 'see'). Many such names are connected with local legends; some obviously may be the results of folk etymology, but the existence of a sizeable body of such names and their paralleling of current personal naming customs would tend to minimize this possibility.

Personal names. One of the most distinctive features of Marshallese personal names is the forming of extended names (*ātlep*) by the addition of a prefix: *li-* for females, and *ḷa-* for males. The light *l* in the female prefix, and the heavy *ḷ* in the male prefix parallel the use of the two *l*'s in the personal demonstratives (see table 4-6 on page 179 and see page 181 for their use as vocatives). Because of this usage in all these words that occur so frequently, the light *l* is sometimes called "the woman *l*" and the heavy *ḷ* "the man *l*."

The vowels of the prefixes do not always remain the same. The female prefix becomes *la-* before names that begin in {h} such as *An* and *Almi*: *Laan* {lahan} and *Laalmi* {lahalmiy}. The pronunciation of the male prefix depends mainly on the first vowel phoneme in the name itself. The mid and high-mid vowels are matched; the prefix is {ḷe-} when the first vowel phoneme in the name is {e}, and {ḷẹ-} when it is {ẹ}: *Jebrọ* {jebraw}, *Ḷōjebrọ* {ḷejebraw}; *Toojio* {tẹwẹjiyẹw}, *Ḷōtoojio* {ḷẹtẹwẹjiyẹw}. The prefix remains *ḷa-* when the first vowel of the name is high or low, except that the low-vowel dissimilation rule (2.4.5) usually raises it to {e} when the first vowel of the name is also low: *Ina* {yinah}, *Ḷaina* {ḷayinah} and *Utaṃwe* {witaṃey}, *Ḷautaṃwe* {ḷawitaṃey}, but *Ṃadi* {ṃadiy}, *Ḷōṃadi* {ḷeṃadiy}, and *Ṃakuj* {ṃahk^{w}ij}, *Ḷōṃakuj* {ḷeṃahk^{w}ij}. The low-vowel dissimilation rule does not operate, however, when the name begins with the semiconsonant {h}: *Aḷi* {haḷiy}, *Ḷaaḷi* {ḷahaḷiy}.

Some names may be used for either men or women: for example, *Badeo*, *Ṃadi*, *An*. They are differentiated by the prefixes, however: *Laan* vs. *Ḷaan*. Some names are never used without the prefixes (for example, *Luubajjōk*, *Luwia*, *Liiñwe*, *Lijen*, *Limuk*, *Lọto*, *Ḷeejed*, *Ḷooran*, *Ḷaiñlen*, *Ḷatni*) and some are never used with them (for example, *Leenut*, *Leleṇ*, *Leñña*, *Luren*, *Lejroñ*, *Ḷọto*, *Ḷōbweāl*). It is probably significant that the latter all begin in one *l* or the other. It may be that they actually contain the prefix, but with the vowel changed from what one would regularly expect. If this is true, then they would simply be additional examples of the former type. Another possibility may be that they are not prefixed in order to avoid too many *l*'s too close together, for ease of pronunciation. But *Lileenut* should be no harder to pronounce than *lilu* (the Ratak pronunciation of {lliw} 'angry'), so this would seem to give more weight to the first explanation.

Concerning those names that can clearly be used with or without the prefixes, the question arises as to the significance or meaning attached to the prefixes. It is sometimes said that they are used to show respect, but if a close examination is made of the circumstances in which they are used, a quite different significance can be seen. Young children use them commonly, parents and children use them with each other, as do spouses. They are not used between taboo relatives or between members of the same sex who do not know each other too well, and they are not used on formal occasions. Thus, they seem to be the marks of close, intimate, informal, and friendly relationships.

Descriptive personal nicknames are formed quite often to refer to special characteristics of people. A name like *Ḷakkadudu* 'Shorty' may be formed by joining the appropriate prefix (*ḷa-* or *li-*) to the distributive verb (see page 162) {kkadiwdiw} derived from *kadu* 'be short' and applied to a man who is especially short. A person with a receding chin may be called *Ḷañitulọk* 'Mr. Diving-teeth', a visiting botanist may be called *Ḷabōb* 'Mr. Pandanus', or an agriculturalist may be called *Ḷōbao* 'Mr. Chicken', and so forth.

The female prefix may be related historically to a prefix that can still be seen in the names of some animals and of some monsters *(mejenkwaar)* and other legendary creatures, although these words never occur without the initial *li-*: *libbūṇōj* 'shrimp', *libbukwe* 'cowric shell', *lijeljelṃak* 'mosquito larva', *lijeṃao* 'owl', *likōb* 'a fish: wrasse', *likōppejdat*, *likaabdoulul,* or *likaaddeboulul* 'trochus shell', *likaakrak* 'maggot', *likaebeb* 'cone shell', *likajjid* 'money cowrie', *likarkar* 'a shell', *luwap* 'puffer fish', *liele* 'trigger fish', *lidid* 'snail', *Lejroñ* 'a monster', *luuj* or *luujrōk* 'a demon', *Lejṃaan* 'a legendary woman and a star', *Liṃanṃan* 'north star', and so forth. A cognate prefix *ni-* can be found in the same sort of words in Chuukese.

Another historic prefix can be seen in a number of women's names: *nei-* {nẹyi-}. This prefix is never separated from the remainder of the word, and may be preceded by the *li-* prefix (for example, *Neiṃōta* or *Lineiṃōta).*

With some such names, the remainder of the word has a meaning of its own (for example, *Neirooj*, rooj 'rose'; *Neimeej*, meej 'dark in color'; *Neikappe*, kappe 'shore'); with others, it does not (for example, *Neiṃōdọ*, *Neibōōj*, *Neipānni*, *Neiwad*, *Neibōn*). Gilbertese has a cognate prefix *nei-* that is still detachable from women's names; they may be said with or without it, like the Marshallese *li-*. A number of Chuukese women's names begin with *niye-*, but like Marshallese *nei* it may not be detached, and the remainders of the words often have a meaning of their own.

Vocatives. Vocatives (words used for calling people or getting their attention) are formed from personal names by adding *-e* {yẹy} after the name: *Jọọn-e* {jawan-yẹy} 'John!' Sometimes if a person does not respond to such a call, *-o* {wẹw} and later *-a* {hah} may be added instead: *"Jọọn-e! ... Jọọn-e! ... Jọọn-o! ... Jọọn-a!"* The added syllable has a higher pitch than the name itself, and a rising intonation pattern.

In addition to this method of forming vocatives, vocative pronouns may also be used at various places in a conversation. These are discussed under "The personal demonstratives as vocatives" on page 181.

Like place names, some personal names are analyzable as to meaning and others are not. Some of those that are analyzable are native Marshallese words such as *lañlōñ* 'joy', *wia* 'buy', *kilmeej* 'black', and so forth. Many others are borrowed from other languages: from German, *Ārṃōṇ* (Hermann), *Atoḷ* (Adolph); from Japanese, *Takaji*, *Jikeru*; from English, *Jekab*, *Jonatan*, *Abner*, and so forth. The words borrowed are not always names in the languages they come from: *Kāāntōḷ* (from 'candle'), *Ejpi* (from S.P. [Shore Patrol]), Empi (from M.P. [Military Police]), and so forth. Very few personal names have been included in the MED, partly because time did not permit a systematic collection, and partly because of the sensitive nature of personal names in Marshallese custom.

Although names may be used to form vocatives, they are not generally used in greetings, with the vocative pronouns being much preferred. They are rarely used in the presence of the individual. Parents may use them in calling children, and teachers or church elders may use them in calling roll. Names are often inherited from deceased ancestors, and surnames are now often created by using the (first) name of one's father. One never asks a surname directly, and even first names are inquired about obliquely, by saying, for example:

(3-2) Kar etan āt eo etarro?
(literally) 'What was the name of the name, the name of us two?'
'What is your name?'

Clan names. The MED contains over 50 names of the Marshallese matrilineal clans. Like the place names, some of these are analyzable as to meaning: *Mekijko* 'Mexico', *RiNaṃo* 'person of Namu', *RiPit* 'person from Kiribati', *Ripako* 'shark people', *Irooj* 'chief', and so forth. Others no longer have such a clear meaning: *Riluut, Joḷ, Tilañ*, and so forth.

Names of plant varieties. For the breadfruit and especially for the pandanus that are found in the Marshall Islands, there are a number of named varieties within one species, similar to apple varieties in English such as Delicious, Winesap, Jonathan, and so forth. These varieties are treated as proper nouns and their names are capitalized in the MED. Like place names and personal names, some are analyzable as to meaning (for example, *M̧aidikdik* 'pandanus cultigen; Ebon tract name' is reminiscent of *em̧m̧aidikdik* 'to whisper') and others are not.

The calendar. Most probably there was a Marshallese calendar before it was replaced by the Western calendar. One can still find vestiges of such a calendar in the vocabulary of the language: *jetñil* 'night of full moon', *jetmar* 'night after night of full moon', and so forth. But the Western calendar is generally used now, with the years named by their number before or after Christ, and with months and days of the week having names borrowed from English, as follows:

(3-3) MONTHS OF THE YEAR

Jānode	{janewdey}	Jul̦ae	{jiwl̦ahyey}
Pāpode	{papewdey}	O̧kōj	{wak^{w}ej}
M̧aaj	{m̧ahaj}	Jebtōm̧ba	{jebtem̧bah}
Eperōl̦	{yeperel̦}	Oktoba	{wektewbah}
Māe	{mayȩy}	Nobōm̧ba	{newbem̧bah}
Juun	{jiwin}	Tijem̧ba	{tiyjem̧bah}

(3-4) DAYS OF THE WEEK

M̧ande	{m̧andey}	Bōl̦aide	{bel̦ahyidey}
Juje	{jiwjey}	Jādede	{jadeydey}
Wōnje	{wenjey}	Jabōt	{jabet}
Taije	{tahyijey}		

INALIENABLE NOUNS

3.2.2 The terms "alienable" and "inalienable" refer to the possession of nouns. Something that is alienable may be taken away from the possessor, or alienated; something that is inalienable cannot. This usage is borrowed from the legal field, where property is said to be alienable if its ownership can be transferred or sold to another. In Marshallese, as in many Oceanic languages, there are two different ways of showing grammatical possession, and nouns possessed in the one way seem less alienable than those in the other. These are the ones discussed in this section.

There are four kinds of inalienable nouns, all of which can be seen as relating to their grammatical possessors in one way or another. Two of them occupy locations in space or time in relation to the possessor: (1) spatial or temporal adjuncts (*ium̧wū* 'under me [lit. in my under-space]', *allōñū* 'my months') or (2) actual parts of a person or place (*peiū* 'my wing, arm, hand, fin', *arin* 'lagoon beach of'). Of the two kinds that are not locatable in time or space, one refers to (3) humans who stand in a kin relation (*jema* 'my father') and the other to (4) one's properties, either tangible or more abstract (*iṃwō* 'my abode', *ṃwilū* 'my character'). Members of this last group include most of what have been called possessive classifiers (see table 4-13).

Possessive suffixes. The grammatical means of showing inalienable possession is through suffixation. Any of the following set of inalienable noun suffixes may be used to show who the possessor is:

(3-5)

SINGULAR			
First Person	(1S)	{-h*i*}[1]	'my'
Second Person	(2S)	{-ṃ}	'your (SG)'
Third Person	(3S)	{-n}	'his, her'
PLURAL			
First Inclusive	(1P.INCL)	{-d}	'our (including you)'
First Exclusive	(1P.EXCL)	{-m}	'our (not including you)'
Second Person	(2P)	{-miy}	'your (PL)'
Third Person	(3P)	{-yyẹr}	'their'

(The abbreviations in parentheses are used to label the various forms.) The basic forms of the suffixes are given in brackets. Notice that each begins with a consonant phoneme (the first two heavy, and the rest light). The inalienable noun stems to which they are attached all end in a vowel phoneme. This vowel is called the STEM VOWEL. Inalienable nouns never occur without one of these suffixes (or the construct suffix [3.2.6]); they have no free form. For example, the word for 'father' always has a suffix attached to it: *jema* {jema-h} 'my father', *jemān* {jema-n} 'his/her father', and so forth. The stem of this noun is the portion that occurs before the hyphen in the phonemic transcription ({jema-}), and the stem vowel is the low vowel {a} that occurs just before the hyphen.

Four stem classes. Inalienable noun stems may be classified into four groups according to their stem vowels: *i*-stems, *e*-stems, short *a*-stems, and long *a*-stems. (For stems that have final {a}, a distinction is made between those that have {aha}, called long *a*-stems, and those that do not, called short *a*-stems.) It is necessary to know to which of these four groups a noun belongs in order to determine all its suffixed forms properly. Although for some inalienable nouns there are similar alienable nouns that may occur as words without a possessive suffix, it is necessary to consider such free forms as being different words (not just the same word without a suffix) for several reasons. For one thing, it is not possible to determine to which of the four groups an inalienable noun belongs by looking at its free, alienable counterpart.

---

1. The *i* of the *-hi* suffix has everywhere been lost along with other word-final vowels, but its effect as a high vowel sometimes lingers on (see "Long a-stems" on page 126).

The alienable counterparts do not usually include a stem vowel, but end in the consonant that precedes the stem vowel of the related inalienable noun. For example, *māj* 'eye' occurs in this form freely without any suffixes. Someone who does not know the language cannot look at this form and predict which vowel should be added to form the inalienable stem for combining with the proper suffix to form the word for 'his/her eye'. The stem vowel could be {i}, {e}, or {a}—or even {aha} could be added. (For this word it turns out to be {a} as in {mejan} *mejān* 'his/her eye, his/her face, its opening' (with the first vowel being raised by low-vowel dissimilation [2.5.5]). Thus, for someone attempting to learn Marshallese as a second language, it is not sufficient to learn just the unsuffixed alienable nouns. Not only do they usually not show a stem vowel; for many inalienable nouns, they (unsuffixed forms) do not exist.

Low vowel dissimilation at work. It is probably better to learn one of the suffixed forms of the inalienable nouns, such as the 3S form, from which the other inalienable forms can be predicted. But it is not always possible to predict the form of the alienable noun from the inalienable one. This is especially true for short *a*-stems, where one cannot tell whether or not the suffixed forms have undergone low-vowel dissimilation (2.5.5), and, therefore, whether the free form has a low or a mid vowel, as with the following two pairs of nouns:

COMMON MEANING:	'all'		'forehead'	
ALIENABLE NOUN:	aolep	{hawelep}	daṃ	{daṃ}
INALIENABLE NOUN (3S):	aolepān	{hawelepan}	deṃan	{deṃan}
BASIC FORM:		{hawelepa-}		{daṃa-}

Both inalienable nouns show the mid vowel {e} as the vowel preceding the stem vowel. If people know only these forms, they cannot be sure whether the alienable counterpart has the same vowel (*aolep,* not *aolāp*), or whether low-vowel dissimilation has taken place (yielding *daṃ,* not *deṃ*). When dissimilation takes place, as it does for *deṃan,* the low vowel {a} will show up in the alienable counterpart (*daṃ*), which has no following {a} to cause dissimilation.

The following derivations from historic {maja} help show that low vowel dissimilation was unable to make vowels in free, unsuffixed forms undergo the same changes that those in suffixed forms did—because the second {a} of {maja}, the cause of dissimilation, had already been a victim of the wide-ranging rule of final vowel loss.

MEANING:	'eye/face'	'my eye/face'	'his/her eye, its opening'
BASIC FORM:	{maja}	{maja-hi}	{maja-n}
FINAL VOWEL LOSS:	{maj}	{majah }	—
VOWEL DISSIMILATION:	—	{mejah }	{mejan}
ACTUAL FORM:	māj	meja	mejān

Note that dissimilation does not take place when the stem vowel is lost from the free form, but that it does take place when the stem vowel is retained in the two suffixed forms.

To be sure about such words, it is necessary to learn both the alienable and inalienable forms. But for most nouns, one can learn an abstract basic form that combines necessary information from both, such as the basic forms given above. It is easy to determine all the forms for 'all' from {hawelepa-}. For the inalienable forms, one adds the basic forms of the suffixes, and for the free form one drops the stem vowel. Deriving the forms for 'forehead' and 'eye' is almost as simple, except that one must remember to apply the low vowel dissimilation rule to the suffixed forms, because they retain the low stem vowel. A basic form of this sort is given for each of the inalienable nouns listed in tables 3-6 through 3-9.

Long *a*-stems. Two special rules are necessary to determine the proper 1S form of long *a*-stems. One of these rules is also necessary for the 1S form of *e*-stems. The rule that applies only to long *a*-stems (the *a*-raising discussed in 2.4.4) raises the final {a} to {e}, and the rule that applies to both (discussed in 2.4.3 in connection with the minority pattern) raises a final {e} to {ẹ}, because of the high vowel in the {-hi} suffix:

MEANING:	'my vehicle'	'my food'	'my eyebrow'	'my catch'
BASIC FORM:	{waha-hi}	{kije-hi}	{yati-hi}	{kʷeṇa-hi}
a-RAISING:	{wahe-hi}	—	—	—
e-RAISING:	{wahẹ-hi}	{kijẹ-hi}	—	—
FINAL VOWEL LOSS:	{wahẹ-h }	{kijẹ-h }	{yati-h }	{kʷeṇa-h }
ACTUAL FORM:	waō	kijō	ātū	koṇa

As the last two words show, neither of these special rules applies to *i*-stems or short *a*-stems, but the rule of final vowel loss always applies to the vowel of the {-hi} suffix after it has done its work of raising preceding vowels. (The high vowel is shown in this suffix in order to explain the raising it causes before being lost; the other suffixes once had final vowels, too, but as nonhigh vowels they had no such effect.) The final vowel loss rule is the same rule that caused the original stem vowel to be dropped from the unsuffixed, free forms.

One other special rule is necessary to determine the proper 3P form of long *a*-stems. It reduces sequences of {ahayy} to {ahy}, so that the basic forms of the stem and suffix of a word like {waha-yyẹr} 'their vehicle' are reduced to the simpler combination {wahyẹr}. A similar rule may operate with the 3P form of *e*-stems, reducing the sequence {eyeyyẹ} to {eyyẹ}, and another raises mid vowels in a stem to high-mid before the 3P suffix, so that the 3P form of {neye-} 'leg' is {nẹyyẹr} *neer*, instead of {neyeyyẹr} *neeier* 'their legs'.

A minor rule is also needed for some of the suffixed forms of three short *a*-stem nouns, those whose basic forms end in the sequence {eya}: {keya-} 'trunk, torso', {weṇeya-} 'price', and {rikewreya-} 'uncle (W)'.

Before the suffixes that begin with a light consonant, the {eya} sequence becomes {aya}; before the two suffixes that begin with a heavy consonant, it remains {eya}. Thus, one says *kāān* {kayan} 'its trunk', but *kea* {keyah} 'my figure' and *keaṃ* {keyaṃ} 'your figure', *oṇāān* {weṇayan} 'its price' and *oṇāāer* {weṇayayyẹr} 'their price', but *oṇea* {weṇeyah} 'my price' and *oṇeaṃ* {weṇeyaṃ} 'your price'. Finally, a minor rule is necessary for two words {waywẹye-} 'shape, manner' and {yẹrṃe-} 'relative' to raise the mid stem vowel to high-mid in all forms: *wāween* {waywẹyẹn} 'her manner', *erṃwen* {yẹrṃẹn} 'her relative', and so forth. An alternative would be to say that their basic shapes are {waywẹyẹ-} and {yẹrṃẹ-} with a high-mid stem vowel, but these would then be the only two ẹ-stems that have been found in the language to date. The rule proposed here for raising a mid stem vowel is the same rule as the tendency discussed under "Vowel harmony" on page 83 that prevents mixture of {e} and {ẹ} in the same simple word. This is also the rule that raises the mid vowels in *neer* 'their legs'.

The spelling of inalienable nouns. The preceding discussion focuses on the phonemic forms of the inalienable nouns. The basic forms and the rules given will together determine all the proper forms of these words as they are spoken. But the words are sufficiently irregular to make for some problems in spelling, although speakers who have a feeling for the phonemes can follow the spelling rules of chapter 2 to get the proper results. The main complications arise as the stem vowel of each form is caught between the consonant that precedes it in the stem (which could be called the stem consonant) and the initial consonant of the suffix. The stem consonant remains the same for each word, but two of the suffix consonants are heavy and six are light. Also, one of the heavy consonants is {h} and one of the light consonants is {y}, and as noted in chapter 2, these semiconsonants cause a number of spelling problems.

Because each of the three short stem vowels may be preceded by light, heavy, or rounded stem consonants, there are nine possible combinations of stem consonants and short stem vowels, and the long a-stems make a tenth type. (For them the stem consonant is always {h}, a heavy semiconsonant.) Representative words of each type are given in tables 3-2 through 3-5, arranged in columns according to the stem consonant, and including three examples of long a-stems.

Contrasts between inalienable and alienable noun counterparts. The main information not contained in the basic phonemic forms is whether or not an alienable noun exists, and if one does, how its meaning may differ from that of the basic inalienable noun. Furthermore, some alienable nouns are not derived by simply dropping the stem vowel, as can be seen from tables 3-6 through 3-9. For example, the alienable noun derived from {bawati-} can be either *bọọt* {bawat} or *bọọti* {bawatiy} 'nose'. The alien-

Table 3-2 *i*-stems

STEM CONSONANT:	LIGHT	HEAVY	ROUNDED
MEANING:	‘skin’	‘outside’	‘near’
STEM:	{kili-}	{liki-}	{tirʷi-}
1S	kilū	likū	turū
2S	kiliṃ	likūṃ	turuṃ
3S	kilin	likin	turūn
1P.INCL	kilid	likid	turūd
1P.EXCL	kilim	likim	turūm
2P	kilimi	likimi	turūmi
3P	kilier	likier	turier

Table 3-3 *e*-stems

STEM CONSONANT:	LIGHT	HEAVY	ROUNDED
MEANING:	‘food’	‘shelter’	‘seat of emotions’
STEM:	{kije-}	{yiṃe-}	{biriwe-}
1S	kijō	iṃō	būruō
2S	kijōṃ	iṃōṃ	būruoṃ
3S	kijen	iṃōn	būruon
1P.INCL	kijed	iṃōd	būruod
1P.EXCL	kijem	iṃōm	būruom
2P	kijemi	iṃōmi	būruomi
3P	kijeer	iṃweer	būruweer

Table 3-4 Short *a*-stems

STEM CONSONANT:	LIGHT	HEAVY	ROUNDED
MEANING:	‘eye, opening’	‘catch’	‘trace’
STEM:	{maja-}	{kʷeṇa-}	{jenkʷa-}
1S	meja	koṇa	jenkwa
2S	mejaṃ	koṇaṃ	jenkwaṃ
3S	mejān	koṇan	jenkwan
1P.INCL	mejād	koṇad	jenkwad
1P.EXCL	mejām	koṇam	jenkwam
2P	mejāmi	koṇami	jenkwami
3P	mejāer	koṇāer	jenkwāer

Table 3-5 Long *a*-stems

MEANING:	‘VEHICLE’	‘DUTY’	‘SOUL, PROPERTY’
STEM:	{waha-}	{kʷeṇaha-}	{haha-}
1S	waō	koṇaō	aō
2S	waaṃ	koṇaaṃ	aṃ
3S	waan	koṇaan	an
1P.INCL	waad	koṇaad	ad
1P.EXCL	waam	koṇaam	am
2P	waami	koṇaami	ami
3P	waer	koṇaer	aer

able nouns derived from {danni-} and {yanbinni-} involve the dropping of a consonant as well as the stem vowel (*dān* 'water' and *ānbwin* 'body'), but the one derived from {yitti-} (also with a double consonant preceding the stem vowel) involves no dropping but the adding of a consonant after the stem vowel (*ittūt* 'breast'). There are many such irregularities. Such unpredictability of form and meaning is one reason for treating the unsuffixed counterparts of inalienable nouns as different words, as alienable nouns derived from them. As such, they behave just like the underived alienable nouns; this and some of the ways they differ in meaning are discussed in 3.2.3. The other reason is the differing ways in which the two types of nouns fit into larger constructions (chap. 4).

In some instances, the alienable counterparts are formed by the dropping of stem vowels:

(3-6)	INALIENABLE		ALIENABLE	
	laļi-	'beneath'	laļ	'earth, country'
	jiki-	'place'	jik	'bower'
	iṃwe-	'home, shelter'	eṃ	'house'
	meja-	'opening'	māj	'eye'
	waa-	'vehicle'	wa	'canoe'

In other instances, they are formed by the adding of the semiconsonant {y} or another consonant:

(3-7)	INALIENABLE		ALIENABLE	
	jibwi-	'grandmother/child'	jibwi{y}	'pet'
	nāji-	'treasure'	nāji{y}	'child-care duty'
	erṃwe-	'relative'	erṃwe{y}	'duty to relatives'
	jema-	'father'	jemā{y}	'father-care duty'
	jera-	'friend'	jerā{y}	'friendship'
	itti-	'breast'	ittūt	'breast'

These examples also bring out some of the differences in meaning to be found between these two types of nouns. Quite often the alienable nouns are more specific in meaning: *wa* refers to canoes, but *waa-* may refer to any means of transportation on land or sea as well as to canoes, *nāji* refers to children but *naji-* may refer to other treasured possessions such as coins, toys, and even ones Bible as well. On the other hand, *nāji* has the added meaning of 'duty of caring for', as do also *erṃwe*, *jemā*, *jerā*, and other alienable nouns such as *nukwi* 'duty towards ones relatives' and *jibwi*, which can mean either 'duty of caring for grandparents or grandchildren' or simply 'pet'. Such differences in meaning, unpredictable differences in form, and the unpredictability as to whether an alienable counterpart exists are the chief reasons for saying that the above pairs (and others like them) are two different words, not just two forms of the same word.

The total number of inalienable nouns is quite small if one does not include those that are derived (3.2.5) from verbs. Because their number is limited and their function in the language is an especially important one, a representative listing including most of them is given in tables 3-8 through 3-11. Each of the four basic types is given in a separate table, the first column of which gives the related alienable noun, if such exists. The four stem types are also differentiated in each table.

Several nouns appear more than once in the tables. Some speakers treat the word for 'cheek' as an *a*-stem, and others treat it as an *e*-stem. Similarly the word for 'neck ornament'. Some speakers treat the words for 'under' and 'interior (of islet)' as *i*-stems, and others treat them as *a*-stems.

From an English point of view there is nothing unusual about body parts or the names of relatives being nouns. That the passage of units of time should be inalienable nouns may seem a bit unusual, but this is Marshallese usage:

(3-8) Jete allōñūṃ ṇai āne in?
how.many month-your on island this
'How many months have you been on this island?'

(3-9) Eor tarrūn ḷalem allōñū ṇai āne in.
there.are about five month-my on island this
'I've been on this island about five months.'

Certainly the most startling from an English point of view is the fact that location and direction words such as 'under', 'above', 'with', 'near', and so forth, are nouns in Marshallese, instead of prepositions as in English. Words such as 'north', 'south', 'inside', 'outside' are not quite so surprising in this respect, because they can be nouns as well as prepositions in English. At any rate, Marshallese grammar presents a world view in which people possess the various spaces about them, so that, for example the English prepositional phrase 'under me' is in Marshallese 'my under-space', 'near me' is 'my near-space', and so forth. Such locative expressions are discussed further in 3.2.7.

Table 3-6 Noun counterparts: Spatial or temporal adjuncts

N_{ALIEN}	$N_{INALIEN}$ (3S)	BASIC FORM	
I-STEMS			
alloñ	allōñin	{hallẹgi-}	'month'
ar	arin	{hari-}	'lagoon beach'
eañ / iōñ	iōñin	{yi'yẹgi-}	'north'
ellor	ellorun	{llẹr^{w}i-}	'shade (W)'
eoḷap	eoḷapin	{yewḷapi-}	'center'
iiō	iiōūn	{'yiyẹhi-}	'year'
—	ioji(n)	{yi'yẹwji-}	'interior (of islet)'
—	iumwi(n)	{yi'yiwṃi-}	'under'
jeṃḷọk	jeṃḷọkun	{jeṃḷak^{w}i-}	'end'
—	jinou(n)	{jinẹwi-}	'beginning'
jik	jikin	{jiki-}	'place'
—	kapi(n)	{kapi-}	'bottom'

Table 3-6 Noun counterparts: Spatial or temporal adjuncts (continued)

N_{ALIEN}	$N_{INALIEN}$ (3s)	BASIC FORM	
lik	likin	{liki-}	'outside'
lōñ	lōñin	{lẹgi-}	'above'
lōlor	lōlorun	{llẹrʷi-}	'shade (E)'
—	pelaaki(n)	{pelahaki-}	'surroundings'
raan	raanin	{rahani-}	'day'
rak / rōk	rōkin	{rẹki-}	'south'
—	toḷọkun	{tewḷakʷi-}	'distant from'
—	turun	{tirʷi-}	'near'
wiik	wiikin	{wiyiki-}	'week'
E-STEMS			
boḷ	buḷon	{biḷe-}	'core, inside'
—	eoon	{yewe-}	'on, above'
iiō	iiōūn	{'yiyehe-}	'year'
—	ikijjien	{yikijjiye-}	'opposite, across from'
—	lọbuḷōn	{lawbiḷe-}	'inside'
—	lukwōn	{likʷe-}	'middle'
SHORT A-STEMS			
eoḷap	eoḷōpān	{yewḷapa-}	'center'
—	eọjān	{yawja-}	'interior (of islet)'
—	ippān	{yippa-}	'company; with'
—	kobban	{kʷebba-}	'contents'
—	pepān	{ppa-}	'company; with (E)'
LONG A-STEMS			
awa	awaan	{hawaha-}	'hour'
—	kōtaan	{ketaha-}	'boundary, between'
—	lowaan	{lewaha-}	'inside'
—	ṃaan	{ṃaha-}	'front'

Table 3-7 Noun counterparts: Body parts

N_{ALIEN}	$N_{INALIEN}$ (3s)	BASIC FORM	
I-STEMS			
addi	addiin	{haddiyi-}	'finger, toe'
akki	akkiin	{hakkiyi-}	'fingernail, toenail, claw'
anbwijban	anbwijbanin	{hanbijbani-}	'right side (W)'
anbwij-maroñ	anbwij-maroñun	{hanbij-maregʷi-}	'left side (W)'
anmiiñ	anmiiñin	{hanmiyigi-}	'right side (E)'
anmọọṇ	anmọọṇin	{hanmawaṇi-}	'left side (E)'
at	atin	{hati-}	'gall bladder'
atlaḷ	atlaḷin	{hatlaḷi-}	'lower jaw'
atlōñ	atlōñin	{hatlegi-}	'upper jaw'
ālki(n)	ālkin	{yalki-}	'back'
ānbwin	ānbwinnin	{yanbinni-}	'body'
ār	ārin	{yari-}	'lung'
āt	ātin	{yati-}	'eyebrow'
baj	bajin	{baji-}	'pubic area'
būtti	būttiin	{bittiyi-}	'wart'

(continued)

Table 3-7 Noun counterparts: Body parts (continued)

N_{ALIEN}	$N_{INALIEN}$ (3S)	BASIC FORM	
bọọt, bọọti	bọọtin	{bawati-}	'nose'
bweọ	bweọun	{beyawi-}	'husk'
bwidej	bwidejin	{bidẹji-}	'soil'
bwij	bwijin	{bijji-}	'lineage'
dān	dānnin	{danni-}	'water'
dāpdep	dāpin	{dapi-}	'trunk, root system'
di	diin	{diyi-}	'bone'
ittūt	ittin	{yitti-}	'breast'
—	jimettanin	{jimettani-}	'half'
jiṃwin ñi	jiṃwin ñiin	{jiṃin ñiyi-}	'chin; close adviser'
jiṃwin pā	jiṃwin pein	{jiṃin peyi-}	'elbow'
kat	katin	{kati-}	'side'
kil	kilin	{kili-}	'skin'
lāñwi	lāñwiin	{laygʷiyi-}	'mouth'
lọpedin pā	lọpedin pein	{lawpedin pẹyi-}	'palm'
lọdiñi	lọdiñin	{lawdigi-}	'posterior (E)'
lọjilñi	lọjilñin	{lawjilgi-}	'ear'
lọñi	lọñiin	{lawgiyi-}	'mouth'
menono	menonoun	{menewnewi-}	'heart'
mọñ	mọñun	{magʷi-}	'pate'
ñad	ñadin	{gadi-}	'gums'
ñat	ñatin	{gati-}	'palate'
ñi	ñiin	{giyi-}	'tooth, eating aid'
pā	pein	{pẹyi-}	'arm, hand, wing, fin'
—	pālin	{pali-}	'wreath, crown'
pāp	pāpin	{papi-}	'frond midrib'
per	perin	{pẹri-}	'tumor, wen'
rọ	roun	{rẹwi-}	'scrotum, testicle'
tudek	tudekin	{tiwideki-}	'stomach, craw, crop'
ut	utin	{witi-}	'flower'
E-STEMS			
bwije(n)	bwijen	{bije-}	'navel'
bōlōk	bwilkōn	{bil(i)ke-}	'leaf, vulva'
bōro	būruon	{biriwe-}	'throat, favorite'
bukwe	bukwien	{bikʷiye-}	'knee'
dede	dien	{diye-}	'ear ornament (W)'
diede	dien	{diye-}	'ear ornament (E)'
jepe, jep	jepen	{jepe-}	'cheek'
jiṃwin ne	jiṃwin neen	{jiṃin neye-}	'heel'
kimej	kimejen	{kimeje-}	'frond'
kole	koleen	{kʷeleye-}	'testicle, nut'
kōd	kōden	{kede-}	'vagina'
lo	loon	{lewe-}	'tongue'
lọpedin ne	lọpedin neen	{lawpedin neye-}	'sole'
lọje	lọjien	{lawjiye-}	'belly'
—	ṃarōn	{ṃare-}	'neck or head ornament'

Table 3-7 Noun counterparts: Body parts (continued)

N_{ALIEN}	$N_{INALIEN}$ (3S)	BASIC FORM	
ob	ubōn	{wibe-}	'chest'
tie	tien	{tiye-}	'lip'
wōl	wilen	{wile-}	'penis'
SHORT A-STEMS			
aerā	aeran	{hayera-}	'shoulder'
aolep	aolepān	{hawelepa-}	'all'
bar	bōran	{bara-}	'head'
daṃ	deṃan	{daṃa-}	'forehead'
jāp, jepā	jepān	{jepa-}	'cheek'
kā	kāān	{keya-}	'torso, trunk, figure'
kimej	kōmjān	{kẹmja-}	'frond'
kooḷ	kooḷan	{kʷeweḷa-}	'hair'
—	lokwan	{lakʷa-}	'posterior'
lọñtōñā	lọtōñan	{lawtega-}	'inside of thigh'
—	ḷokwan	{ḷakʷa-}	'behind, tail'
māj	mejān	{maja-}	'eye, opening; seeing aid'
ṃōra	ṃōran	{ṃara-}	'neck or head ornament'
LONG A-STEMS			
da	daan	{daha-}	'blood'
kōnwa	kōnwaan	{kenwaha-}	'neck'
ra	raan	{raha-}	'branch'

Table 3-8 Noun counterparts: Kin

N_{ALIEN}	$N_{INALIEN}$ (3S)	BASIC FORM	
I-STEMS			
—	jemānjin	{jemanji-}	'wife's sister's husband'
jati	jatin	{jati-}	'younger sibling'
—	jininjin	{jininji-}	'husband's brother's wife'
jei	jein	{jẹyi-}	'older sibling'
—	jibwi	{jibi-}	'grandmother/child'
—	ṃaanin	{ṃahani-}	'brother (of a woman)'
—	nājin, nejin	{naji-, nẹji-}	'child, pet, treasure'
—	nukun	{nikʷi-}	'relative'
—	pāleṃorun	{paleṃorʷi-}	'trusted friend'
—	riin	{riyi-}	'spouse, lover'
—	rilikin	{riyliki-}	'cross-cousin'
E-STEMS			
—	erṃwen	{yẹrṃẹ-}	'relative (W)'
—	inen	{yine-}	'sister (of a man)'
—	jinen	{jine-}	'mother'
—	mañden	{magde-}	'sister's child (of a man)'
—	pāleen	{paleye-}	'spouse'
—	teen	{teye-}	'what relation?'

(continued)

Table 3-8 Noun counterparts: Kin (continued)

N_{ALIEN}	$N_{INALIEN}$ (3s)	BASIC FORM	
SHORT A-STEMS			
—	jemān	{jema-}	'father'
—	jeran	{jera-}	'friend'
—	m̧ōttan	{m̧etta-}	'companion'
—	rukoorāān	{rikewreya-}	'mother's brother (W)'
—	wūllepān	{willepa-}	'mother's brother (E)'
LONG A-STEMS			
—	jim̧m̧aan	{jim̧m̧aha-}	'grandfather'

Table 3-9 Noun counterparts: Properties—tangible or abstract

N_{ALIEN}	$N_{INALIEN}$ (3S)	BASIC FORM	
I-STEMS			
añ	añin	{hagi-}	'powers, stir created'
—	āin	{yayi-}	'similarity'
bablo̧ļ	bablo̧ļun	{bablaļi-}	'enthusiasm'
—	bwiin	{biyi-}	'odor'
—	jōkjōkin	{jȩkjȩki-}	'shape'
kadkad	kadkadin	{kadkadi-}	'status, genealogy'
kij	kijin	{kiji-}	'louse'
jo̧kpej	kupijin	{kopeji-, kupiji-}	'trash'
—	mejļo̧kun	{mȩjļakʷi-}	'favorite'
m̧or	m̧orun	{m̧erʷi-}	'old, worn out things'
m̧wil	m̧wilin	{m̧ili-}	'behavior'
—	wāween	{waywȩyi-}	'shape, manner'
E-STEMS			
—	ainikien	{hayinikiye-}	'sound'
āne	āneen	{yaneye-}	'islet, island'
em̧	im̧ōn	{yim̧e-}	'house, shelter'
el	ilen	{yile-}	'nest, attire'
jalele	jaleen	{jaleye-}	'sauce'
—	kapiten	{kapite-}	'ointment, perfume'
kibwe	kibween	{kibeye-}	'feces'
—	kijen	{kije-}	'food'
kōl	kilen	{kile-}	'technique'
—	kinien	{kiniye-}	'sleeping gear'
leb	libōn	{libe-}	'grave'
—	limen	{lime-}	'beverage'
lep	lipen	{lipe-}	'egg'
—	m̧arōn	{m̧are-}	'neck or head ornament'
m̧weiuk	m̧weien	{m̧ȩyiye-}	'goods, property'
pej	pijen	{pije-}	'placenta'

Table 3-9 Noun counterparts: Properties—tangible or abstract (continued)

—	ruon	{riwe-}	'fault'
N_{ALIEN}	$N_{INALIEN}$ (3S)	BASIC FORM	
te	teen	{teye-}	'sanitary napkin'
—	utōn	{wite-}	'bathing water'
SHORT A-STEMS			
—	abjā(n)	{habja-}	'peculiarity'
aetok	aetokan	{hayetekʷa-}	'height, length'
āt	etan	{yata-}	'name'
—	detta(n)	{detta-	'size, age'
—	ekōjka(n)	{yekejka-}	'what status?'
jar	jeran	{jara-}	'group, crowd'
—	jenkwan	{jenkʷa-}	'footprint, trace'
—	joña(n)	{jegʷa-}	'extent, dimension'
—	kōjeān	{kẹjẹyya-	'disposition'
—	koṇan	{kʷeṇa-}	'catch (of fish)'
—	kōtkan	{ketka-}	'plant'
—	ḷōma(n)	{ḷema-}	'likeness'
—	menwan	{menwa-}	'breath'
eṃṃar	ṃōran	{ṃara-}	'fish basket (W)'
ṃōṃar	ṃōran	{ṃara-}	'fish basket (E)'
ṃōra	ṃōran	{ṃara-}	'neck or head ornament'
—	oṇāā(n)	{weṇeya-}	'price'
—	wōjan	{weja-}	'tool, utensil, machine'
—	tokjā(n)	{tekʷja-}	'importance'
LONG A-STEMS			
—	an	{haha-}	'soul, property'
anemkwōj	anemkwōjaan	{hanemkʷejaha-}	'freedom, independence'
—	daan	{daha-}	'pandanus portion'
—	iaan	{yi'yaha-}	'associate'
—	uwaan	{wiwaha-}	'peer'
—	koṇaan	{kʷeṇaha-}	'duty, contribution (W)'
—	kuṇaan	{kʷiṇaha-}	'duty, contribution (E)'
—	ḷọkjānaan	{ḷakʷjanaha-}	'amazement'
—	ṇotaan	{ṇotaha-}	'defect'
pija	pijaan	{pijaha-}	'likeness, image'
wa	waan	{waha-}	'vessel or vehicle'
—	wōjaan	{wejaha-}	'property, abode'

The construct suffix with inalienable nouns. In addition to the possessive pronoun suffixes, the inalienable nouns also combine with the construct suffix (3.2.6) to show the same sort of inalienable possession by the following proper or alienable noun:

3S PRONOUN POSSESSOR:	waan {waha-n}	'his/her vehicle'
PROPER NOUN POSSESSOR:	waan {waha-n} Jọọn	'John's vehicle'
ALIENABLE NOUN POSSESSOR:	waan armej eṇ	'that person's vehicle'

Note that the form of inalienable nouns with the construct suffix is always identical to the 3S possessive form.

The relation with the word that follows the construct suffix is not limited to POSSESSION. Another common relation is that of ORIGIN, when the following word is a place name:

(3-10) WITH PLACE NAMES:

waan Kujjae	'Kosraean vehicle'
waan Ruk	'Chuukese vehicle'
waan Jepaan	'Japanese vehicle'

When the word that follows is an alienable noun derived from a verb, the relation is one of PURPOSE:

(3-11) WITH DEVERBAL NOUNS:

waan joñak	'example; frame for measuring'
waan bwil	'roller; vehicle for launching'
(i)m̧ōn kemat	'cookhouse'
(i)m̧ōn jar	'church; house of prayer'
jikin jerbal	'place of work'

The word that follows may also be an underived alienable noun. The relation is then one of SPECIFICATION: MODIFYING, SPECIFYING, or NARROWING the meaning of the first noun:

(3-12) WITH ALIENABLE NOUNS

(i)m̧ōn bwidej	'toilet; house of soil'
(i)m̧ōn bao	'chicken house'
kilin wōjke	'bark of a tree'
kilin ek	'fish skin'

Some interesting contrasts between inalienable and alienable construct forms are presented in 3.2.6. And we will find in 3.2.9 that many of the preceding examples are, in fact, compound nouns, even though they are written as two words

ALIENABLE NOUNS

3.2.3 Compared with the fairly small list of inalienable nouns in the preceding section, the number of alienable nouns is quite large. As noted in 3.2.5, the number of both types is increased greatly by the nouns that are derived from verbs, but even so the alienable nouns are much more numerous. The inalienable nouns are only those stems that actually have the possessive pronoun suffixes added to them; even their free counterparts must be considered as alienable nouns. Thus, no exhaustive listing will be attempted; only a few representative examples will be given and discussed.

Unlike some of the inalienable nouns, the meanings of alienable nouns generally parallel those of nouns in English and other European languages: *jokwā* 'driftwood', *mājet* 'match', *peba* 'paper', *bao* 'bird', *booj* 'boat', *waj* 'watch', *ki* 'key', *bwā* 'fishpole', *pileej* 'plate', *men* 'thing', *baajkōḷ* 'bicycle', *māāl* 'axe', *mede* 'chisel', *bu* 'gun', *armej* 'person', *kino* 'fern', *kieb* 'spider lily', *alu* 'a shell', *ṃọle* 'rabbit fish', *ṃōṃō* 'grouper', *kie* 'canoe beam, *lem* 'bailer', and so forth.

There are two subgroups of alienable nouns, human and nonhuman, depending on their use with determiners (table 4-10 on page 185), which have different forms in the plural based on this distinction. Thus, one says *ajri ro* 'the children', but *baajkōḷ ko* 'the bicycles'.

Alienable nouns are possessed by being put in a phrase together with certain inalienable nouns, which thereby serve to classify the possessive relation, as discussed in 4.6. For example, *kijō bao* 'my food, a bird' or 'a bird for me to eat', *koṇa bao* 'my catch, a bird' or 'a bird I caught', *nājū bao* 'my child, a chicken' or 'a pet chicken of mine', *jibū bao* 'my grandchild, a bird' or 'a pet bird of mine'; *aō jāān* 'my property, a coin' or 'a coin of mine', *nājū jāān* 'my treasure, a coin' or 'a special coin of mine'; *ñiū pileej* 'my eating aid, a plate' or 'a plate of mine', *waō baajkōḷ* 'my vehicle, a bicycle' or 'a bicycle of mine', and so forth.

The construct suffix with alienable nouns. Alienable nouns, like inalienable nouns, add the construct suffix (3.2.6) to enter into phrasal constructions with other nouns. Those that end in full consonants add the stem vowel {i} for combining with the suffix: *mājetin* {majet-i-n} *Jepaan* 'Japanese matches, matches made in Japan'. Those that end in one of the semiconsonants generally copy the vowel that precedes the semiconsonant as a stem vowel: *medeen* {medey-e-n} *Jepaan* 'Japanese chisel', *bwāān* {bay-a-n} *Amedka* 'American fishpole', *kinoon* {kinew-e-n} *ut* 'lei ferns', *ṃōṃōōn* {ṃehṃeh-e-n} *kejota* 'supper grouper, grouper for supper'. The high vowel {i} may optionally be used as a stem vowel for such words: *kinoun* {kinew-i-n} *ut*. The same is true for nouns that end in {ah} such as *peba* {pẹybah} 'paper'. The vowel preceding the semiconsonant {h} may be copied to give {pẹybah-a-n}, or the high vowel {i} may be used as a stem vowel. In the latter case, a {y} is also inserted with the stem vowel to give {pẹybah-yi-n}. Thus, one can say either *pebaan kainōknōk* or *pebain kainōknōk* for 'decorating paper'. Furthermore, when the consonant preceding the {ah} is a light consonant, as is the {j} in the word *pija* {pijah} 'artistic creation', the {h} is dropped to give *pijāin* {pija-yi-n}. Note that the {h} is not dropped in {pẹybahyin} because the consonant preceding the {ah} is a heavy one: {b}.

Some nouns may have irregular construct forms. These may involve variation between the majority and minority patterns discussed in 2.5.3 (*lemin wa* vs. *limen wa* 'canoe bailer'), or they may simply be exceptions, usually for very common words such as *bao*, for example: *bawūn* {bahwin} *mejatoto* or *bawōn* {bahwen} *mejatoto* 'birds of the air', rather than the *baoon* {bahwewen} or *baoun* {bahwewin} that would be predicted by the preceding rules.

Four main relations were noted earlier (beginning on page 135) between inalienable nouns with the construct suffix and the words that follow them in a phrase: POSSESSION, ORIGIN, PURPOSE, and SPECIFICATION. Alienable nouns with the construct suffix may have the last three of these relations with the words that follow; their possession is shown by a different means, as noted at the beginning of this section and in 4.6. The examples that follow can be seen to fall into these three general types of relation:

(3-13) a. ORIGIN:

mājetin Jepaan	'Japanese matches'
bwāān Amedka	'American fishpole'
jokwāān lik	'driftwood from the ocean side'

b. PURPOSE:

kinoon wūt	'ferns for leis'
pebaan kainōknōk	'paper for decorating'
baajkōḷin kōkatak	'bicycle for practice (E)'
wūnoon metak bar	'headache medicine'

c. SPECIFICATION:

lemin wa	'canoe bailer'
bawūn mejatoto	'birds of the air'
bawūn laḷ	'poultry'
jokwāān aḷaḷ	'driftwood'
jokwāān bato	'drift bottle'

Verbs used as alienable nouns may be joined by the construct suffix with nouns denoting certain times of the day or night, as in:

(3-14) DEVERBAL CONSTRUCTS WITH TIME PERIODS

kikiin raan	'napping, sleeping in the day'
jerbalin boñ	'night work'
ṃōñein jibbōñ	'breakfast'
ṃōñein raelep	'lunch'
ṃōñein jota	'evening meal'

We will see in 3.2.9 that many of these examples, just like their inalienable counterparts on page 136, are compound nouns, even though written as two words.

The -*ta* suffix. In the Ratak dialect, alienable nouns may be suffixed with -*ta* (closely related to the question word *ta* 'what?, which?'): *meṇta* (< *men-ta*) 'what thing?', *bootta* (< *booj-ta*) 'what boat?', *mājetta* 'what match?', *kabta* {kab(e)tah} 'what cup?', *wata* {wah(a)ta} 'what canoe?', *baota* {bahwew(e)tah} 'what bird?', *medeta* {medey(e)tah} 'what chisel?', and so forth. Notice that the usual rules of consonant assimilation (2.5.1) apply in the preceding examples, with the final consonant being assimilated to the *t* of the suffix, or an excrescent vowel being inserted when called for.

In the Rālik dialect, this suffix has a different form that may be considered as simply -V*t* (*t* preceded by a vowel copied from the last vowel of the preceding stem): *menet* {men-et} ‘what thing?’, *boojet* {bewej-et} ‘what boat?’, *mājetōt* {majet-et} ‘what match?’, *waat* {wah-at} ‘what canoe?’, *baoot* {bahwew-et} ‘what bird?’, *medeet* {medey-et}, and so forth. This vowel copying rule is identical to the vowel copying rule used for the pronunciation of double consonant words (2.4.1) and substitutes the mid vowel {e} when the low vowel {a} is copied: *kabōt* {kab-et} ‘what cup?’. As the examples show, this inserted vowel is written out in the spelling even though it is predictable, just as with the double consonant words.

Other affixes. The person prefix {ri-}, which may be added to any place name to give the meaning ‘person from’, may also be added to a few alienable nouns that can be seen as referring to a place, such as *ruwa* {ri-wah} ‘person from a ship, sailor’ and *ri-āniin* {ri-yanẹy-yin} ‘person from this island’. (It may also be added to at least one inalienable noun {tir^{w}i-} to give forms such as *ri-turuṃ* {ri-tir^{w}i-ṃ} ‘person near you, your neighbor, your spouse’.)

Distributive verbs (see page 162) may be derived from many alienable nouns, with a general meaning ‘be teeming with’. They are derived regularly by doubling the initial consonant and reduplicating the final syllable, less regularly by adding a suffix {-y, -ey, -ẹy} or {-iy} or by combinations of doubling or reduplication and suffixation:

(3-15)	ike	{yikey}	‘teeming with fish’
	armeje	{harmẹjẹy}	‘crowded with people’
	kūkijdikdik(i)	{kkijdikdik(iy)}	‘infested with rats (E)’
	kūkidudu(i)	{kkidiwdiw(iy)}	‘overrun with dogs (E)’
	bōbaoo(e)	{bbahwewwew(ey)}	‘thick with birds (E)’
	bōbaruru(i)	{bbariwriw(iy)}	‘teeming with crabs (E)’

Finally, and most definitively, alienable nouns are often found in phrases with a following determiner or demonstrative (4.2.2):

(3-16)	armej rein	‘these people’
	aelōñ kein	‘these islands’
	wa kaṇ	‘those canoes’
	ṃweiuk ko	‘the goods’
	men in	‘this thing’
	bok kākā	‘these books in particular’

Expansions of these basic phrases are discussed in 4.3.

PERSON NOUNS

3.2.4 A large number of nouns may be derived from other nouns or from verbs by adding the prefix {ri-}. Any proper noun (3.2.1) that is a place name may have the prefix added to derive a noun meaning ‘person from (that place)’:

(3-17)	ri-Mājro	‘person from Majuro’
	ri-Jālwōj	‘person from Jaluit’

ri-Amedka (~ ra-Amedka)	'American (person)'
ri-Nibboñ	'Japanese (person)'
ri-Ruk	'Chuukese (person)'
ri-Pit	'person from Kiribati'

The prefix may be added to an adjectival verb (table 3-13) to derive a noun meaning 'person who has that quality':

(3-18)	ri-nana	'outcast'
	ri-awiia	'barbaric person'
	ri-doebeb	'meddlesome person'
	ri-kadu	'short person'
	ri-jorrāān	'rascal'
	rūkkatak	'learner'
	rūṃṃan	'fine person'

It may be added to certain intransitive verbs (see page 154) to derive a noun meaning 'person who does that activity':

(3-19)	ri-jerbal	'worker'
	ri-lotok	'visitor, guest'
	ri-likbad	'test driver'
	ri-ñortak	'snorer'
	ri-jata	'renter'
	ri-kakkilaajaj	'signaler'
	ri-likjab	'debtor'
	ri-jerawiwi	'sinner'
	ri-liaakḷok	'prosecutor'
	ruwia	'merchant'
	ruuror	'assassin, murderer'
	rūttariṇae	'soldier'

Such intransitive verbs may also have nouns accompanying them:

(3-20)	ri-jekjek wa	'canoe maker'
	ri-pija annañ	'architect'
	ri-kōjerbal armej	'employer'
	ri-koṃṃan bwebwenato	'author'
	ri-jedjed iju	'astronomer'
	ri-ṃwijbar	'barber'
	ri-iiōk pilawā	'baker'
	ri-kōṃṃan baib	'plumber'
	ri-keke nuknuk	'tailor; seamstress'

Occasionally the prefix may also be combined with common nouns, either alienable or inalienable:

(3-21)	ruwa	'sailor'
	ri-turun	'his/her spouse (lit. person near him/her)'

Notice that the sound of the prefix changes, depending on the following consonant: *ru-* before rounded consonants, as in *ruwa*, *rū-* before heavy consonants, as in *rūttariṇae,* and *ri-* before light consonants, as in *ri-jerbal.* Historically, this prefix was usually written as a separate word with the vowel *i,* as in *dri jerbal.*[2] In this book we continue to separate the prefix, using a hyphen, and we ignore the differences in the sound of the vowel, unless (1) the consonant following it is doubled, as in *rūttariṇae, rūkkatak,* and *rūkkāke,* or (2) the following sound is a *w* or a *u,* as in *ruwa, ruwia, ruuror,* and *ruukok,* or (3) the following word does not occur alone without the prefix, like the examples in the following paragraph.

There are some nouns that seem to contain this prefix, but the remainder of the word does not occur alone as a word with a meaning of its own, although it may once have done so. For example, *rūkaki* means 'preacher' or 'teacher', but *kaki* is not a word with a clear meaning of its own.[3] Other such examples include: *rūkorean*, 'his uncle', *rimakaio* 'giant', *rimmenanue* 'leprechaun', and *ruwamaejet* 'stranger'. This is also true of many clan names (most of which begin with {ri}); most are still analyzable, but some are not: *Riluut, Rūbojaar, Rilikijjine*. Possibly the parts of such names following the prefix refer to some forgotten place. Finally, note that the vowel of the prefix changes in a different way in the clan name *Raarṇo* (from ri-Arṇo).

Nouns Derived from Verbs

3.2.5 Verbs may also be used as nouns. As nouns they may occur with the various determiners (4.3), and they may be possessed either inalienably or alienably. Some may be possessed in both ways, with interesting contrasts in meaning. When possessed inalienably, a high {i} stem vowel is added after the stem and before the possessive suffixes or the construct suffix.

Following are some examples of verbs used as nouns together with determiners:

(3-22)	jipañ ko	'aids'	kōṃṃan ko an	'his actions'
	ajej ko	'shares'	aolep jerbal ko	'all tasks'
	aikuj ko	'needs'	ḷōmṇak kein	'these ideas'
	maroñ ko	'powers'	jarom ko	'lightning flashes'
	kweḷọk eo	'the meeting'	uno kein	'these medicines'
	al ko	'the songs'	ṃōñā ko jet	'various foods'

---

2. This spelling with *dr* was unfortunate, as it has caused some confusion as to the sounds represented by the light and heavy *r*'s.
3. A possible history of the word *rūkaki* is that it was first used for the early missionaries who were not only preachers and teachers, but also song leaders who gave the "key" for a song before leading out in it (using possibly a pitch fork or pitch pipe), and were thus *rū-ka-ki* 'person who gives the key' (person prefix–causative prefix–*key*). Today the word is often spelled *ri-kaki.*

Following are some interesting contrasts between the two types of possession:

(3-23)	a.	bōnbōn	'to count'
		bōnbōn ko aer	'their arithmetic problems'
		bōnbōnier	'their calculations'
	b.	maroro	'be green, be blue'
		maroro ko aer	'their blue dyes'
		maroroier	'their blueness'
	c.	nana	'be bad'
		nana ko an	'his/her naughtiness'
		nanāin	'his/her evil nature'
	d.	ekkal	'to build'
		ekkal ko aer	'their buildings'
		ekkalier	'the design of the buildings they build'
	e.	jerbal	'to work'
		jerbal eo an	'his/her job'
		jerbalin	'the things he/she produces'

The first word given in each of these five sets of examples is the basic intransitive or adjectival verb. Next it is shown possessed as an alienable noun, and finally as an inalienable noun. Notice that the meanings in alienable possession refer to things that may be in one's possession at the moment, or to temporary but not necessarily permanent characteristics. On the other hand, the meanings in inalienable possession refer to permanent qualities of the possessors, or to things of which they are the creator: their calculations, their design of buildings, or other fruits of their labors.

There is a common superlative construction in the language into which any inalienable noun derived from an adjectival verb (3.4.4) may be inserted. For example,

(3-24) Ejjeḷọk wōt ṃōṃanin. (E)
'There is nothing (that can compare with) its goodness.'
'It's really good!

Here the adjectival verb {ṃṃan} 'be good' is converted into an inalienable noun and possessed by a 3S possessor (with the stem vowel {i} being added before the suffix). (As the "(E)" indicates, the pronunciation given in the example sentence is that of the Ratak dialect.) Distributive verbs (see page 162 and page 165) that are adjectival can also be converted into inalienable nouns and used in the same construction. In (3-25a) we see the distributive adjectival verb *ike* 'be teeming with fish' (derived from the noun *ek* 'fish'), and in (3-25b) we see this same verb converted into an inalienable noun (by the suffixation of *-in*) and entered into this construction.

(3-25) a. E-ike ānin.
3s-teem.with.fish islet-this
'This island is teeming with fish.'

b. Ejjeḷọk wōt ikein aelōñ ṇe.
'That atoll has more fish than any other.'

This construction seems to be a good test for whether or not a verb is an adjectival verb. If the verb can be put into the frame "Ejjeḷọk wōt ___ -in …," it must be such a verb. This seems reasonable, as adjectival verbs refer to the condition of someone or something, and although some conditions may be only temporary, it should be possible under proper circumstances to view any conditioin as permanent and therefore inalienable.

The Construct Suffix

3.2.6 The fact that this suffix may occur with all inalienable nouns and that its shape is always identical to the 3S possessed form is noted in 3.2.2. Its occurrence with alienable nouns and the shapes of the resulting forms are noted in 3.2.3. There are sometimes interesting contrasts between closely related nouns in the construct form. One concerns the inalienable noun *pijaa-* 'image, likeness' and the alienable noun *pija* 'artistic or photographic creation', which is derived from an intransitive verb of the same form (*pija*) meaning 'draw a picture, take a picture'. The following examples bring out the contrast:

(3-26) Pijaa-n wōn e?
likeness-of who this
'Who is this a picture of?'
'Whose likeness is this?'

(3-27) Pijaō.
'It's a picture of me.'
'It's my likeness.'

(3-28) Pijā-in wōn e?
picture-of who this
'Who drew this picture?'
'Whose artistic creation is this?'

(3-29) Pijaū.
'I drew it.'
'It's my artistic creation.'

In the first question, the construct suffix is added to the inalienable noun stem {pijaha-} to give {pijahẹh} in the reply according to the rules given in 3.2.2). In the second question, the full construct word {yin} is added to the derived noun {pijah}, giving {pijah-yin}, then in normal speech the {h} is dropped because of the preceding light consonant, giving {pijayin} *pijāin*. *Pijaū* is formed by adding a high stem vowel and the 1S possessive suffix to the same noun: {pijah-i-hi}, which becomes {pijahih} according to the same rules.

The same noun stem as in the second question and answer, *pija* 'artistic creation', may also be possessed alienably (3.2.3, 4.6) to give a three-way contrast:

(3-30) An wōn pija e?
property-of who picture this
'Who does this picture belong to?'

(3-31) Aō pija e.
property-my picture this
'It's mine.'

Possession by suffix in the first two pairs of questions and answers is inalienable: people's likeness cannot be taken from them, nor can the fact that they are the creator of something. The alienable possession in the third pair is appropriate for property that can be bought and sold, or given away. The contrast between the second and third pairs parallels that given for the derived noun *jerbal* in 3.2.5.

The form of the construct suffix is always *-n* when attached to inalienable noun stems, making their construct forms identical to their 3S possessive forms. Thus a form like *waan* may be either 'his canoe' or 'canoe of'. But when the construct suffix is attached to alienable nouns, it is necessary to first add a stem vowel (usually the high vowel {i}) between the final consonant of the noun and the -n suffix. (The possible exceptions to this general rule when the final consonant of the noun is a semiconsonant are discussed in 3.2.4.)

In very slow and deliberate speech it is also possible to have the construct suffix as a separate word that follows the noun with the form *in* {yin}, so that one can say, for example, {pẹybah yin jepahan} when speaking slowly, but {pẹybahan jepahan} or {pẹybahyin jepahan} 'Japanese paper' when speaking at normal speed. For a word like *pija* {pijah} 'artistic creation', with the light consonant *j* preceding the {ah}, one would expect in slow speech *pija in*, and at normal speed either *pijaan* or *pijāin*. However, the first of the normal speed alternatives (*pijaan*) seems to be ruled out for this word in order to avoid confusion with the closely related inalienable noun *pijaa-* 'likeness' in its construct form *pijaan*, as the examples at the beginning of this section show.

The construct forms of certain alienable nouns of measure are used with the alienable nouns they measure, as in the following constructions:

(3-32) MEASURES

keijin koḷa	'a case of soft drink'
bọunin raij	'a pound of rice'
pāākin jukwa	'a bag of sugar'
iepin ni	'a basket of coconuts'
kilōkin/kōlkan iaraj	'a *kilōk* of taro' (*kilōk* 'large basket')
kāānin kọọnpiip	'a can of corned beef'
batoun joiu	'a bottle of shoyu'
iaatin nuknuk	'a yard of cloth'
kuwatin jatiin	'a tin of sardines'
kaḷanin karjin	'a gallon of kerosene'

These can be seen as further examples of the relation of specification referred to in 3.2.3. Notice the preponderance of loanwords.

The word *kein* 'thing for doing s.' in (3-33) seems to be a construct form, although the word has not been found in any other forms:

(3-33) INSTRUMENTS

kein jerbal	'tool'
kein kōjjọ	'ignition switch'
kein aō	'life preserver'
kein liklik	'sieve'
kein kaṃool	'certificate'
kein kōṃ	'breadfruit picking stick'
kein katu	'barometer'
kein kakememej	'reminder'
kein kobaatat	'ashtray'
kein kōjañjañ	'musical instrument'

This same construction is used with cardinal numbers to form ordinals (see "The numerals" on page 203). The resulting constructions can all be viewed as instruments of one sort or another, and the relation between the two nouns is one of PURPOSE (3.2.3).

PLACE AND TIME NOUNS

3.2.7 Prepositions such as *i* {yiy} 'at', *ñan* {gan} 'to', and *jān* {jan} 'from' may be used with nouns of location to form locative phrases. In table 3-6 on page 130 a number of inalienable nouns that refer to places or times are listed under the heading "spatial or temporal adjuncts." Those nouns that refer to places may occur with the preposition *i* in phrases meaning 'in or at the place', and with *ñan* or *jān* indicating movement to or from the place. The place nouns in (3-34) already have *i* included within them and are not used without it.

(3-34) SPATIAL NOUNS THAT HAVE {yiy} 'at' BUILT IN

iuṃwin	'under'
ikijjien	'opposite'
ippān	'company; with (W)'

Others may be used with or without *i*, but usually have a higher vowel when *i* is included, as in the following:

(3-35)

WITHOUT *i*	WITH *i*	
eọjān	iojin	'interior (or islet)'
eoon	ioon	'on, above'
eọṃwin	iuṃwin	'under'
eañin	iōñin / iūñin	'north of'
rakin /rūkin	irōkin / irūkin	'south of'

The word *tu* {tiw} may also be used with these place nouns to emphasize the precision of specification of the place or direction. It is often preceded by the preposition *i*.

(3-36) WITHOUT *tu* — WITH *tu*

irearin	'east of'	iturearin	'straight east of'
ilōñin	'above'	itulōñin	'right above'

The word *turūn* {tir^{w}in} or {tiwr^{w}in} 'near' may have been formed originally by adding this *tu* to {r^{w}iy} or {r^{w}in}, because these formatives can still be found in certain place names with a locative meaning such as *Lọrun-kōṇo* {law-r^{w}in-keṇew} 'at the *kōno* tree(s)' and *Lọri-to* {law-r^{w}iy-tew} 'at the channel' (see the last part of 3.2.8).

The examples given above are all in the 3S or construct form, ending in the suffix *-n*. The construct form would normally occur together with a following noun in the same phrase:

(3-37)

iuṃwin bọọk eṇ	'under that box'
ikijjien men kein	'concerning these things'
itulōñin jea ṇe	'right above that chair'

Two of the place words that are often translated 'on' have some interesting contrasts in usage in their construct forms: one is *eoon* or *ioon*, and the other is *raan*, which is the construct form of the inalienable noun *raa-* meaning 'branch' listed in table 3-7 under "body parts." When certain nouns follow, only *ioon* is used.

(3-38)

ioon bok	'on the sand'
ioon jaki eṇ	'on that mat'
ioon jimeṇ eṇ	'on that pavement'

With certain other nouns, *raan* is usually used.

(3-39)

raan kiju eṇ	'on the mast'
raan mā eṇ	'on that breadfruit tree'
raan toḷ eṇ	'on that mountain'

With a number of nouns, either *ioon* or *raan* may be used, usually with some difference in meaning:

(3-40)

raan ṃweeṇ	'on that house'
ioon ṃweeṇ	'on or above that house'
raan toḷ eṇ	'on that mountain'
ioon toḷ eṇ	'on or above that mountain'
raan wa eṇ	'on that canoe'
ioon wa eṇ	'on or above that canoe'

Ioon tends to be used with objects that have flat surfaces, and may mean either 'right on top of' or 'somewhere above, but not necessarily against the top of'. *Raan* tends to be used with high objects such as masts, trees, mountains, and indicates the place 'right on top of' if not actually 'in the branches of'.

Like *raan*, other body parts may be used as place nouns without the preposition *i*:

(3-41) Ta ņe peiṃ, libbuke ke?
'What's that in your hand, a cowrie shell?'

(3-42) Aet, libbuke men e peiū.
'Yes, this is a cowrie shell in my hand.'

(3-43) Ta eņ addiin Jọọn, riiñ ke?
'What's that on John's finger, a ring?'

(3-44) Aet, riiñ men eņ addiin Jọọn.
'Yes, that is a ring on John's finger.'

The preposition *i* may also be used with any place name.

(3-45) iMājro 'at Majuro'
iArṇo 'at Arno'

The preposition *ilo* is used with nouns that denote periods of time. *Jān* and *ñan* are also used with such time words.

(3-46) ilo raanin kakkije eo	'on the holiday'
ilo boñūn Taije	'Thursday night'
jān raan ñan raan	'from day to day'

THE NOUN FORMATIVE LỌ {LAW}

3.2.8 The term "formative" is used for a part of a word (which may be a stem or an affix) that is used as part of a number of words, and that may or may not have a clear meaning of its own. Formatives that do not have clear meanings usually once had a meaning earlier in the history of the language, but that meaning has been lost sight of after the formative was no longer used to build new words. The formative discussed in this section is of this sort; if there is any trace of meaning left for *lọ*, it is some sort of vague locative meaning 'in' or 'at', possibly because of its resemblance to words like *ilo* 'in' or *(i)lowaan* 'inside'.

This formative can be found in certain body parts:

(3-47) lọpiden pā	'palm'
lọpiden ne	'sole'
lọjiliñi	'ear'
lọñi	'mouth'
lọje	'belly'
lọtōñā	'inside of thigh'
lọkwa(n)	'tail (of)'

Of these, only *je* may occur without the formative, and there is no clear meaning difference between *lọje* and *je*. As can be seen in table 1-1 on page 7, the word for 'ear' in the parent language must have been something like *talinga, which is parallel to the Marshallese word for 'ear' without the *lọ-* formative: *jiliñ*. The word for mouth has a variant *lā-ñwi,* which reminds one of the Gilbertese word for 'mouth', *wi*.

The word for 'inside' or 'core' *boḷ* can occur with or without the formative *lọ*: *buḷōn* or *lọbuḷōn* 'inside of'. Other "spatial or temporal adjuncts or bounds" (3.2.1) that may contain the formative *lọ* with the vowel changed are *lowaan* 'inside of' and *lukwōn* 'middle of'.

A formative of the same shape shows up in several words having to do with bodies of water:

(3-48)	lọjet	'ocean'
	loṃaḷo	'lagoon'
	lọmeto	'ocean'

(The vowel of the formative in *loṃaḷo* may be mid because of low vowel dissimilation [2.5.5].) *Loṃaḷo* and *lọmeto* may occur without the formative; *meto* also has the meaning 'navigation', and it has the meaning 'seaward' when part of a COMPOUND DIRECTIONAL (table 5-2 on page 220).

The formative *lọ* is also preserved in many place names: for example, *Lọ-kōñe* 'at the ironwood tree' (3.2.1). Such names are still clearly analyzable and seem to have a locative meaning: *Lọ-bōl* 'at the taro pit', and so on. A number of them have the mid vowel in the formative instead: *Lo-bar* 'at the rock', *Lo-dekā* 'at the stone(s)', etc. In a few place names the formative is found together with what appears to be *turu-* 'near' without the *tu*: *Lọrun-kōṇo* {law-r^{w}in-keṇew} 'at the *kōno* tree(s)', *Lọri-to* {law-r^{w}iy-tew} 'at the channel' (This last name has the archaic construct form without *-n* discussed in 3.2.1). The formative can also be found in the name of at least one pandanus cultigen *Lọpiñpiñ,* which is also the name of land tracts on a number of atolls, one of which was possibly the tract where the cultigen was originally developed.

Finally, what is probably the same formative can also be found in two words meaning 'in public, publicity': *lọbwilej*, and *lọiaḷ* (the last literally 'in the street').

COMPOUND NOUNS

3.2.9 Compound nouns may be formed by following one alienable noun with another, or with a stative verb that modifies the first noun in some way, usually with the relation of specification referred to in 3.2.3. Words for western eating aids furnish some of the examples:

(3-49)	kab kilaaj	'drinking glass (glass cup)'
	kab dekā	'cup (stone or pottery cup)'
	jibuun bọọk	'fork (lit. forked spoon)'
	bọọk aij	'refrigerator (ice box)'

Notice that the order of the head noun and its modifier is the reverse of that of English.

(3-50)	bo̧o̧k peba	'cardboard box'
	wa tipñōl	'sailing canoe'
	wa kōrkōr	'paddling canoe'
	dān m̧ōļo	'cool water'
	dān tōñal	'sweet (not salty) water'
	dān jo̧o̧ļ	'salty water'
	ek jo̧o̧ļ	'salted fish'
	wōn jo̧o̧ļ	'salted turtle'
	armej waan	'worthless person'
	marļap	'a plant: *Canavalia* spp.'
	mar peļe	'a plant: *Iponea tuba*'
	mar kūbwebwe	'a plant: *Wedelia biflora*'
	mar kinenjojo	'a plant: *Vigna marina*'

The things referred to by compound nouns can often also be referred to by the first word alone. A fork is considered a special kind of spoon, and a drinking glass a special kind of cup. The four plant names given above are all considered types of *mar* 'bush, vine'. If someone refers to a *jibuun*, they could be asked a question requiring further specification:

(3-51) a. Jibuun rot?
'What kind of spoon?'

b. Jibuun bo̧o̧k.
'A fork.'

Or they could be asked a question that uses *jibuunin,* the construct form of *jibuun*:

(3-52) a. Jibuunin ta?
'Spoon for what?'

b. Jibuunin ākto m̧ōñā.
'Serving spoon.' 'Spoon for offloading food.'

Following is another pair of examples that contrast further specification with purpose:

(3-53) a. Dān rot?
'What kind of water?'

b. Dān tōñal.
'Sweet water.'

(3-54) a. Dānnin ta?
'Water for what?'

b. Dānnin am̧ōn.
'Water for washing hands.'

Sometimes there is no contrast in meaning between the two kinds of construction:

(3-55)	jokwā bato	jokwāān bato	'drift bottle'
	ek jo̧o̧ļ	jo̧o̧ļin ek	'salt(ed) fish'

And sometimes the second rather than the first part of a compound may be used with full specification: a sailing canoe may be called either *wa tipñōl* or simply *tipñōl*. Similarly, a paddling canoe may be either *wa kōrkōr* or *kōrkōr*.

Compound nouns can be seen as fairly loose and open-ended constructions. Although they are not overly numerous in the language, the way is always open to forming new ones, especially by following a noun with a stative verb:

(3-56)	iien eṃṃan	'a good time'
	jerbal nana	'evil deed'
	wa kilmeej	'dark-colored canoe'

And so forth. No further attempt will be made here to generalize concerning these constructions.

VERBS

3.3 Although, as will be seen in chapter 6, not all sentences have verbs, verbs lie at the heart of many sentences and determine what the other key ingredients in each sentence will be. Some scholars attempt to define verbs by the meanings they convey, such as actions, events, states, conditions, or qualities. Verbs may also express tense, modality, manner, or degree. Another means of defining verbs is to say what is distinctive about their form. Finite verbs appear with a subject prefix, as in (3-57a) below, where *i-aikuj-i* has the prefix *i-* designating a 1S subject. (The subject prefixes are given in table 3-10.) But nonfinite verbs do not appear with such prefixes; in (3-57b) the same subject prefix appears on the helping verb *naaj* 'future', and the nonfinite form *aikuji* (without the *i-* prefix) comes later in the verb phrase, after the helping verb *bar.*

Another part of the definition of verbs has to do with the positions they occupy in the word order of a sentence. We will have more to say on this subject in chapters 5 and 6. There we will also see that finite verbs agree with the subject of the sentence in person and number. Some kinds of verbs have other differences in their forms, in addition to the subject prefixes, as we will see. But first it will be necessary to introduce some of the different kinds of verbs.

(3-57) a. I-aikuj-i roñoul ļalem jāān.
1S-need-TR twenty five cent
'I need twenty-five cents.'

b. I-naaj bar aikuji roñoul ļalem jāān.
1S-FUT again need twenty five cents
'I will again need twenty-five cents.'

Table 3-10 Subject prefixes

PREFIX	BASIC FORM	GRAMMATICAL FORM	ENGLISH TRANSLATION	EXAMPLES WITH PRIME HELPING VERBS		
i-	{yi-}	1S	'I'	ij[1]	in[1]	iar
kwo-[2]	{kʷe-}	2S	'you SG'	kwōj	kwōn	kwaar
e-	{ye-}	3S	'he, she, it'	ej	en	ear
je-	{je-}	1P.INCL	'we, including you'	jej	jen	jaar
kōm	{kẹm}	1P.EXCL	'we, not including you'	kōmij	kōmin	kōm ar
koṃ	{kʷẹṃ}	2P	'you PL'	koṃwij	koṃwin	koṃ ar
re-[3]	{re-}	3P	'they'	rej	ren	raar

1. The subject prefixes replace the initial *e-* {ye-} of the primary helping verbs *ej* {yej} and *en* {yen}; see fn. 2 and 3 on page 177. For 1P.EXCL and 2P, there are special forms for the combinations; see 4.2.1 for a discussion of the 1P.EXCL and 2P forms, which behave more like proclitics than prefixes.
2. The 2S prefix begins with the rounded consonant {kʷ}, so that the vowel of the prefix is spelled with an *o* when the following consonant is heavy or round (*kwokōṇaan, kworiab,* etc.), but with *wō* when it is light (*kwōj, kwōmaroñ,* etc.) and with *a* when it is {h} followed by {a} (*kwaar*). It is recommended that this prefix always begin with *kw* (including the *w* as a clear marker of the second person **singular**).
3. The 3P prefix begins with the heavy consonant {r}, so that the vowel of the prefix is spelled with an *e* when the following consonant is light (*rej, remaroñ,* etc.), but with an *ō* when it is heavy (*rōṃṃan, rōttoon*), or with an *o* when it is round (*rokkut, rowaḷok,* etc.) Before the prime helping verb *ar* {har} and other verbs beginning in {ha}, it is spelled with an *a* (*raar, raabwinmake,* etc.).

HELPING VERBS (ALSO CALLED "AUXILIARIES")

3.3.1 There are three prime helping verbs that, when they occur, generally occur with one of the subject prefixes as the finite verb of their clause: *ej* {yej} 'noncompletive', *ar* {har} 'completive', and *en* {yen} 'optative'. (In the Ratak [E] dialect, *kar* 'nonhabitual past' is also often used instead of *ar* as the 'completive' primary helping verb.)

(3-58) a. E-**j** etal ñan Rita.
'She's going to Rita.'

b. E-**ar** etal ñan Rita.
'She went to Rita.'

c. E-**n** etal ñan Rita.
'She is to go / Let her go / She should go to Rita.'

Unlike these three, the other (nonprime) helping verbs may occur either at the beginning of the clause with a subject prefix, or in a position following one of the three that are always first (when they occur), and preceding the nonfinite form of a main verb. The main helping verbs of this type are given in table 3-11, where they are classified using distinctions generally found in the tense-aspect-mood systems of languages and given simple glosses that may not cover all possible shades of meaning and translations. (The distinction *realis–irrealis* has to do with whether something has actually happened—and therefore is a reality—or may possibly happen.) A sentence may contain sequences of several helping verbs, with any prime one first, if it occurs.[4]

(3-59) b. E-**jjañin kanooj** jeḷā.
'He's still not very good at it.'

c. Ra-**ar jab bar** itok.
'They didn't come again.'

Table 3-11 Classification of Nonprime Helping Verbs

TEMPORAL		NONTEMPORAL	
PAST		DEGREE	
SUBSEQUENT	ḷak 'then when'	INTENSITY	
NONSUBSEQUENT		NEGATIVE	podem 'not even'
HABITUAL	kkein 'used to'	NONNEGATIVE	lukkuun 'really'
NONHABITUAL	kar 'past'		ātin, āteo 'really'
NONPAST			make 'alone'
IMMEDIATE	kab 'just'		kanooj 'very'
NONIMMEDIATE			dọlin 'seriously'
DURATIVE	ja 'still, for now'		baj 'excessively'
NONDURATIVE		NONINTENSITY	jaad 'fairly'
REALIS			kiōk 'nearly'
NEGATIVE	jjañin 'not yet'		bajjek 'a little'
NONNEGATIVE	nañin 'almost'	NONDEGREE	
IRREALIS		NEGATIVE	jab 'not'
NEGATIVE	ban 'will not'	NONNEGATIVE	
NONNEGATIVE	naaj 'will'	ITERATIVE	bar 'again'
		NONITERATIVE	jujen 'therefore'
		INTERROGATIVE	jaaṃ 'why persist?'

Transitive Verbs

3.3.2 Transitive verbs are sometimes defined as verbs expressing an action that is carried from the subject to the object, requiring a direct object to complete its meaning.[5] The four sentences in (3-60) might seem to be transitive by such a definition, but in Marshallese grammar, only (3-60c–d) are. (3-60a–b) could be said in response to "*Jọọn ear ṃōñā ta*? 'What did John eat?'"

(3-60) a. Jọọn e-ar ṃōñā ek.
John 3S-CMPL eat.INTR fish
'John ate fish.'

b. Jọọn e-ar ṃōñā ek eo koṇ-a.
John 3S-CMPL eat.INTR fish the catch-1S
'John ate of the fish I caught.'

4. See Pagotto 1987:489–98 for a discussion of the possible orders in which such sequences may occur.

5. *American Heritage Dictionary,* 1973.

c.	Jo̧o̧n	e-ar	kañ	ek	eo	kon̄-a.
	John	3s-CMPL	eat.TR	fish	the	catch-1S

'John ate the fish I caught.'

d.	Jo̧o̧n	e-ar	kañ	juon	ek.
	John	3s-CMPL	eat.TR	one	fish

'John ate a fish.'

For a sentence to be transitive, the two main requirements are that the verb be transitive and that it have a direct object that is either definite or quantified. The determiner *eo* in sentences b. and c. makes the object *ek* definite, and the numeral *juon* in d. quantifies it. Sentences a. and b. fail to be transitive primarily because their verb *m̧ōñā* is intransitive, but also because in them the word *ek* is something other than the object of the verb. In sentence a. its meaning gets incorporated into the verb so that the translation might more accurately be 'John was fish-eating', while in sentence b. (which implies that John did not consume all of the fish, but only part of it), *ek* is less directly involved in the action than a direct object would be. We will call this role that of CORRESPONDENT (ANOTHER PARTY, NEITHER THE SUBJECT NOR THE OBJECT), an important role that will help us explain other interesting facts of Marshallese grammar (see "Correspondents" on page 235). Some speakers of Marshallese do not accept (3-60b) as being a good sentence, and would say instead (3-60b)′, which (because it includes *ilo* 'at') views *ek* as the LOCUS of the action, rather than the CORRESPONDENT. It could be a response to "Ek ta eo Jo̧o̧n ear m̧ōñā ie? 'Which fish did John eat at?'"

(3-60b)′	Jo̧o̧n	e-ar	m̧ōñā	ilo	ek	eo	kon̄-a.
	John	3S-CMPL	eat	at	fish	the	catch-1S

'John ate at the fish I caught.'

Anaphoric object markers. In some contexts the direct object may be omitted from its position immediately following a transitive verb. When this occurs, an anaphoric object marker is required on the verb. These object markers agree in number with the object that is not expressed in the sentence but is understood from the context, so that the verb has the form *kañe* in (3-61c) but *kañi* in (3-62c). We will see in chapter 6 (6.4.5 on pages 320–21) that in the plural this is true only for nonhuman objects.

(3-61)	a.	Jo̧o̧n	e-ar	kañ	juon	ek.
		John	3S-CMPL	eat.TR	one	fish

'John ate a fish.'

b.	Wōn	eo	e-ar	kañ	ek	eo?
	who	the	3S-CMPL	eat.TR	fish	the.SG

'Who is the one who ate the fish?
'Who ate the fish?'

c.	Jo̧o̧n	e-ar	kañ-**e**.
	John	3S-CMPL	eat.TR-3S

'John ate it.'

(3-62)	a.	Jọọn	e-ar	kañ	ruo	ek.
		John	3s-CMPL	eat.TR	two	fish

'John ate two fishes.'

b.	Wōn	eo	e-ar	kañ	ek	ko?
	who	the	3s-CMPL	eat.TR	fish	the.PL

'Who is the one who ate the fishes?
'Who ate the fish?' [Eng. pl. is either *fishes* or *fish.*]

c.	Jọọn	e-ar	kañ-i.
	John	3S-CMPL	eat.TR-3P

'John ate them.'

Anaphoric markers that get adopted as part of the verb. Anaphoric markers are required in sentences (3-61c) and (3-62c), where no object of the verb is expressed in a noun phrase of its own. But some speakers use them in sentences in which they are not required, such as the preceding a. and b. sentences (which have their objects expressed), so that for them the transitive verb has become *kañe* rather than simply *kañ*. Then they may or may not substitute *i* for *e* in the plural sentences of (3-62'). This means that one can hear a great deal of variation nowadays in transitive verbs of this sort, whether they end in -Ø or *-e* when their object is singular, and whether they end in -Ø, *-e,* or *-i* when their object is plural.

(3-61')	a.	Jọọn e-ar kañ**e** juon ek.	'John ate a fish.'
	b.	Wōn eo e-ar kañ**e** ek eo?	'Who ate the fish?'
(3-62')	a.	Jọọn e-ar kañ**e** ruo ek.	'John ate two fishes.'
	a.'	Jọọn e-ar kañ**i** ruo ek.	'John ate two fishes.'
	b.	Wōn eo e-ar kañ**e** ek ko?	'Who ate the fishes?'
	b.'	Wōn eo e-ar kañ**i** ek ko?	'Who ate the fishes?'

This variation and the reasons for it are discussed in detail in Bender (1984).

Transitive and intransitive counterparts. Although the verbs *ṃōñā* and *kañ* show little resemblance to each other in form, grammatically they are intransitive and transitive counterparts of each other. A few other such pairs showing minimal and unpatterned resemblances are given in table 3-12.

Table 3-12 Transitive and intransitive verb pairs showing minimal resemblance

TRANSITIVE		INTRANSITIVE	
WITH MINIMAL RESEMBLANCE			
kañ	'eat s.'	ṃōñā	'eat'
ilim, inim	'drink s.'	idaak	'drink'
ālim	'bail s.'	ānen	'bail'
WITH CONSONANT DOUBLING, ALTHOUGH UNPATTERNED, IN INTRANSITIVE			
kalbwin	'plant s.'	kallib	'plant'
enōk(e)	'knock s. down'	nenōk[1]	'knock down' (E)
kajitūkin	'ask s.'	kajjitōk	'ask'

1. See 2.4.1 for the rules for pronouncing and spelling out words with initial double consonants in the Ratak (E) and Rālik (W) dialects.

Most transitive verbs have intransitive counterparts that show greater formal resemblance. Tables 3-13 and 3-14 give examples in which the transitive verbs seem to be derived from their intransitive counterparts by adding a suffixal increment. The increment takes three forms, depending on the sounds at the end of the intransitive source. Those that end in a semiconsonant {y,w,h} add {-ik}; those that end in full consonants add *-e,* unless the vowel preceding the full consonant is a high vowel, in which case they add *-i.* Those that add *-e* change it to *-i* when the object of the transitive verb is plural; those that add *-i* use it for both singular and plural objects.

Table 3-13 Adjectival verbs and transitive counterparts

INTRANSITIVE		TRANSITIVE	
LAST VOWEL IS NONHIGH: ADD *-e*			
ban	'be unable'	bane	'be unable to do s.'
bōt	'be disobedient'	bōte, būte	'disobey s.'
kadek	'be poisoned, drunk'	kadeke	'be poisoned by s.'
mijak	'be afraid'	mijake	'fear s.'
būrar	'be smeared'	būrare	'smear s.'
bal	'be covered'	bale	'cover s.'
bukwelep	'be thick'	bukwelepe	'cut s. thick'
jọọḷ	'be salty'	jọọḷe	'salt s.'
pāāt	'be low tide'	pāāte	'strand s.'
pooḷ	'be surrounded'	pooḷe	'surround s.'
LAST VOWEL IS HIGH: ADD *-i*			
luuj	'be a loser'	luuji	'lose s.'
wiin	'be a winner'	wiini	'win s.'
ibwij	'be high tide'	ibwiji	'refloat s.'
lur	'be calm'	luri	'becalm s.'
INTRANSITIVE IS VOWEL-FINAL (ENDS IN {y, w, h}): ADD {-ik}			
abṇōṇō	'be uncomfortable'	abṇōṇōūk	'be made uncomfortable by'
būḷu	'be blue'	būḷuuk	'color s. blue'
kūre	'be grey'	kūreik	'color s. grey'
CONVERSION (NO CHANGE IN FORM)			
lale	'be careful'	lale	'look at s.'

In table 3-13 the intransitive verbs are a type that are referred to as adjectival verbs, from which adjectives are derived, as we will see in 4.4. But there seem to be two different kinds of relations between the pairs of verbs on each row, as brought out by the shading. And there is also some question as to whether the pairs of verbs having to do with tides and the weather are completely parallel to the others. These matters are discussed further in 6.4.5 under "Transitive verbs," beginning on page 316.

Table 3-14 Nonadjectival verbs and transitive counterparts

INTRANSITIVE		TRANSITIVE	
LAST VOWEL IS NONHIGH: ADD *-e*			
alluwaḷọk	'stare'	alluwaḷọke	'stare at s.'
boḷan	'tie'	boḷane	'tie s.'
ejaak	'build'	ejaake	'build s.'
LAST VOWEL IS HIGH: ADD *-i*			
buruṃ	'sweep'	buruṃi	'sweep s.'
riit	'read	riiti	'read s.'
uñur	'touch'	uñuri	'touch s.'
bout	'vote'	bouti	'vote for s.'
raut	'urinate'	rauti	'urinate on s.'
INTRANSITIVE IS VOWEL-FINAL (ENDS IN {y, w, h}): ADD {-ik}			
bu	'shoot'	buuk	'shoot s.'
ajwewe	'whistle'	ajweweik	'whistle at s.'
wia	'buy'	wiaik	'buy s.'
CONVERSION (NO CHANGE IN FORM)			
kinaak	'tattle'	kinaak(e)	'tell on s.'

Tables 3-15 and 3-16 seem to show derivation in the opposite direction, with suffixal material being lost,[6] often together with reduplication or consonant doubling. Note that the transitive verbs *ṃwijit* 'cut s.' and *āte* 'pack s.' appear in both of these tables, being the sources for both nonadjectival and adjectival verbs.

Table 3-15 Transitive verbs and nonadjectival intransitive counterparts

TRANSITIVE		INTRANSITIVE	
THEMATIC {VC} DROPPED			
jañūt	'cry for s.'	jañ	'cry'
poon	'lower sail of s.'	po	'arrive'
jiñūt	'fart on s.'	jiñ	'fart'
ḷōmak	'determine s.'	ḷam	'scheme'
THEMATIC {VC} DROPPED AND INITIAL {C} DOUBLED (W. POSSIBLE V CHANGE)			
tuuj	'dig s.'	tōto[1]	'dig taro (E)'
pukot	'search for s.'	pepok	'search (E)'
tọuk	'mend s.'	tōtọ	'mend nets (E)'
THEMATIC {VC(V)} DROPPED AND REMAINING {CVC} SYLLABLE DOUBLED			
ātoñ	'smell s.'	ātāt	'smell'
buuj	'tie s.'	bubu	'tie a knot'
jeḷate	'loosen s.'	jaḷjaḷ	'loosen'
iñūti	'twirl s.'	iñiñ	'twirl'
ṃwijit	'cut s.'	ṃwijṃwij	'cut'
rọkuj	'scratch s.'	rọkrok	'scoop up'
pọut	'bind s.'	pọpo	'coil up'

6. The final consonant that is lost is sometimes referred to as the THEMATIC CONSONANT.

Table 3-15 Transitive verbs and nonadjectival intransitive counterparts (continued)

TRANSITIVE		INTRANSITIVE	
FINAL {V} DROPPED (IF PRESENT) AND FINAL {CVC} SYLLABLE DOUBLED			
āte	'pack s.'	ātet {yatyẹt}	'pack'
ṃan	'kill s.'	ṃanṃan	'kill'
kad	'throw s.'	kadkad	'throw'
eje	'build s.'	ejej	'build'
baate	'smoke s.'	baatat {bahathat}	'smoke'
FINAL {V} DROPPED (IF PRESENT) AND INITIAL {C} DOUBLED			
kōṇak	'wear s.'	kōkōṇak	'get dressed (E)'
lo	'see s.'	lelo	'see (E)'
kūri	'call s.'	kūkūr	'call (E)'
jiburi	'hug s.'	jijibur	'hug (E)'

1. See 2.4.1 for the rules for pronouncing and spelling out words with initial double consonants in the Ratak (E) and Rālik (W) dialects.

Table 3-16 Transitive verbs and adjectival intransitive counterparts

TRANSITIVE		INTRANSITIVE	
THEMATIC {VC} DROPPED AND INITIAL {C} DOUBLED			
karōk	'fit s.'	kōkar	'be suitable (E)'
THEMATIC {VC} DROPPED AND REMAINING {CVC} SYLLABLE DOUBLED			
deñōt	'spank s.'	deñdeñ	'be spanked'
ṃwijit	'cut s.'	ṃwijṃwij	'be cut'
FINAL {V} DROPPED AND FINAL {CVC} SYLLABLE DOUBLED (± V CHANGE)			
āte	'pack s.'	ātet {yatyẹt}	'be impounded'
baate	'smoke s.'	baatat {bahathat}	'be smoking'
FINAL {V} DROPPED AND INITIAL {C} DOUBLED			
kune	'extinguish s.'	kukun	'be out (E)'
FINAL {V} DROPPED (IF PRESENT) AND {-VK} SUFFIXED (W. POSSIBLE V CHANGE)			
pineje	'cover s.'	penjak	'be covered'
dāpij	'hold s.'	dāpijek	'be fastened'
lim	'fold s.'	limek	'be folded'

Causative transitive verbs. Both nonadjectival and adjectival verbs may also be made into transitive verbs by adding the causative prefix *ka- (kō-, ke-)* (and possibly a suffix as well. Examples are given in tables 3-17 and 3-18.

Table 3-17 Nonadjectival causative transitive verbs

INTRANSITIVE		CAUSATIVE TRANSITIVE	
CAUSATIVE PREFIX, NO SUFFIX			
eañ	'urinate'	keañ	'help s. urinate'
booḷtōntōn	'overflow'	kabooḷtōntōn	'fill s. to the brim'
rōḷọk	'escape'	kōrōḷọk	'allow s. to roam free'

(continued)

Table 3-17 Nonadjectival causative transitive verbs (continued)

INTRANSITIVE		CAUSATIVE TRANSITIVE	
CAUSATIVE PREFIX, {-ey} SUFFIX (AFTER SYLLABLE W. NONHIGH {V})			
ebeb	'shiver'	kaebebe	'make s. shiver'
debokḷọk	'explode'	kadebokḷọke	'make s. explode'
bọọkọk	'use a fork'	kōbọọkọke	'give s. a fork'
CAUSATIVE PREFIX, {-iy} SUFFIX (AFTER SYLLABLE W. HIGH {V})			
dibuk	'penetrate'	kadibuki	'make s. penetrate'
bait	'fight'	kōbaiti	'make s. fight'
CAUSATIVE PREFIX, {-Vk} SUFFIX (AFTER FINAL {y, w, h})			
bukwelōlō	'kneel'	kabukwelōlōūk	'make s. kneel'
kadjo	'fish for *jo*'	kōkadjouk	'take s. fishing for *jo*'
koba	'cohabit'	kōkobaik	'betroth s.'

Table 3-18 Adjectival causative transitive verbs

INTRANSITIVE		CAUSATIVE TRANSITIVE	
CAUSATIVE PREFIX, NO SUFFIX			
dipen	'be strong'	kadipen	'strengthen s.'
bab	'be tight'	kōbab	'tighten s.'
banban	'be weak'	kōbanban	'weaken s.'
CAUSATIVE PREFIX, {-ey} SUFFIX (AFTER SYLLABLE W. NONHIGH {V})			
dujejjet	'be full'	kadujejjete	'fill s.'
dapitōk	'be tangled'	kadapitōke	'entangle s.'
bat	'be slow'	kōbate	'make s. slow'
CAUSATIVE PREFIX, {-iy} SUFFIX (AFTER SYLLABLE W. HIGH {V})			
aruñijñij	'be sleepy'	kaaruñijñiji	'make s. sleepy'
kut	'be crowded'	kọkuti	'make s. crowded'
CAUSATIVE PREFIX, {-ik} SUFFIX (AFTER FINAL {y, w, h})			
dede	'be completed'	kadedeik	'finish s.'
bwebwe	'be stupid'	kabwebweik	'fool s.'
awiia	'wild'	kaawiiaik	'make s. wild'

OTHER VERBS DERIVED FROM VERBS

3.3.3 In the preceding section we were looking at how transitive and intransitive verbs are derived from each other. Now let us look at the relations between other types of verbs. First we will see several other uses of the causative prefix *ka- (ke-, kō)* beyond the deriving of causative transitive verbs in 3.3.2, tables 3-17 and 3-18. These include CAUSATIVE VERBS OF ACQUIRING A QUALITY, CAUSATIVE ADJECTIVAL VERBS, CAUSATIVE VERBS OF TESTING, CAUSATIVE VERBS OF WAITING, and CAUSATIVE VERBS OF CONTROL. Then, in order, other derivations that do not involve the causative prefix: VERBS OF TRACTIBILITY, ANTONYMAL VERBS, DISTRIBUTIVE VERBS, and PLURAL VERBS OF DIMENSION. All are included in this chapter because they all involve a change in form.

Causative verbs of acquiring a quality. These verbs involve acquiring the quality of an adjectival verb. They have the meaning 'cause to V', where V is an adjectival source verb. To cause someone to be fast is to hurry them; to cause oneself to be experienced is to practice; to cause one's lips to be red is to wear lipstick, to cause oneself to be skinny is to diet. This is the thread shared by the examples in table 3-19.

Table 3-19 Causative verbs of acquiring a quality

SOURCE VERB		DERIVED VERB	
CAUSATIVE PREFIX ADDED; NO OTHER CHANGE			
iur	'be fast'	kaiur	'hurry'
mminene	'be experienced'	kamminene	'practice'
būrōrō	'be red'	kabūrōrō	'wear lipstick'
CAUSATIVE PREFIX ADDED; FINAL SYLLABLE REDUPLICATED			
aidik	'be skinny'	kaidikdik	'diet to lose weight'

Causative adjectival verbs. Notice that whereas in sentence (3-63a) it is I, a person, who is sad, in sentence (3-63b) it is the movie that is sad. The movie causes sadness, but we aren't told who has experienced it. That is the shift in viewpoint that comes about for all of the adjectival verbs derived in this way. Examples are given in table 3-20.

(3-63) a. I-lukkuun būroṃōj rainin.
I-be.very be.sad today
'I'm very sad today.'

b. Jab lo ṃupi eṇ bwe e-ka-būroṃōjṃōj.
not see.TR movie that because 3S-CAUS-be.sad
'Don't see that movie because it's sad.'

Table 3-20 Causative adjectival verbs

SOURCE VERB		DERIVED VERB	
CAUSATIVE PREFIX ADDED			
kūtōtō	'be angry'	kakūtōtō	'be anger-provoking'
ṃakoko	'be unwilling'	kōṃakoko	'be bothersome'
mijak	'be afraid'	kaamijak	'be scary'
FINAL SYLLABLE REDUPLICATED; CAUSATIVE PREFIX ADDED			
bwilōñ	'be surprised'	kabwilōñlōñ	'be surprising'
eñtaan	'be in agony'	kaeñtaanan	'be strenuous'
ppaḷ	'be astonished'	kōppaḷpaḷ	'be astonishing'
INITIAL CONSONANT DOUBLED; CAUSATIVE PREFIX ADDED			
jiṃwe	'be straight'	kajjiṃwe	'be strict'
ṃōṇōṇō	'be happy'	kaṃṃōṇōṇō	'be pleasing'
SYLLABLE REDUPLICATED; INITIAL CONS. DOUBLED; CAUSATIVE PREFIX ADDED			
jar	'be broke'	kōjjarjar	'be expensive'
jiñ	'fart'	kajjiñjiñ	'cause flatulence'
mo	'heal'	kammomo	'be a healing agent'

Causative verbs of testing. The source verbs here may or may not be adjectival; the resulting verbs, as in the examples in table 3-21, are verbs of testing. Thus, it would appear that this sort of competition has a time-honored place in island life.

Table 3-21 Causative verbs of testing

SOURCE VERB		DERIVED VERB	
FINAL SYLLABLE REDUPLICATED; CAUSATIVE PREFIX ADDED			
util	'be agile'	kọutiltil	'have an acrobatic contest'
auj	'reach a goal'	kawūjwūj	'play solitaire'
INITIAL CONSONANT DOUBLED; CAUSATIVE PREFIX ADDED			
tilekek	'hide'	kattilekek	'play hide and seek'
FINAL SYLLABLE REDUP.; INITIAL CONSONANT DOUBLED; CAUSATIVE PREFIX ADDED			
dipen	'be strong'	kaddipenpen	'test one's strength'
jerọ	'be a good shot'	kōjjerọro	'have a shooting contest'
pakij	'be able to stay under water'	kōppakijkij	'test ability to stay under water'

Causative verbs of waiting. Certain impersonal verbs (see 5.6.1) having to do with times and tides are converted into intransitive verbs with the meaning 'to wait for' these events. See table 3-22 for some examples.

Table 3-22 Causative verbs of waiting

SOURCE VERB		DERIVED VERB	
iialañe	'be moonrise'	kaiialañe	'wait for moonrise'
aelik	'be a current flowing out'	kaaelik	'wait for the current'
ibwij	'be high tide'	kaibwij	'wait for high tide'
pāāt	'be low tide'	kōpāāt	'wait for low tide
raan	'be daytime'	kōraan	'wait for daylight'
boñ	'be night time'	kaboñboñ	'wait for nightfall'
raelep	'be noontime'	kōraelep	'wait for noontime'
jota	'be evening'	kōjota	'supper'

Causative verbs of control. The source verbs here are not adjectival, nor are the resulting verbs, which seem to have an element of control in their meanings. See table 3-23 for examples.

Table 3-23 Causative verbs of control

SOURCE VERB		DERIVED VERB	
CAUSATIVE PREFIX ADDED			
ttōr	'run'	kattōr	'drive'
bwebwenato	'talk'	kabwebwenato	'make conversation'
FINAL SYLLABLE REDUPLICATED; CAUSATIVE PREFIX ADDED			
añūr	'crave cigarettes'	kaañūrñūr	'refrain from cigarettes'
INITIAL CONSONANT DOUBLED; CAUSATIVE PREFIX ADDED			
bōjrak	'stop'	kabbōjrak	'hold on'
FINAL SYLLABLE REDUP.; INITIAL CONSONANT DOUBLED; CAUSATIVE PREFIX ADDED			
batur	'crave fish'	kōbbaturtur	'refrain from fish'

Verbs of tractability. There are several pairs of adjectival verbs to be found in which one has a tractable meaning ('be easy to V') while the other is intractable 'be hard to V'). For some of these pairs, the source verb is obvious and is given in table 3-24; for others it is less or not at all apparent. And for a few there are no pairs. Only the positive term exists with respect to tractability.

Table 3-24 Verbs of tractability

TRACTABLE		INTRACTABLE	
SOURCE GIVEN ON FIRST LINE OF EACH PAIR OF LINES BELOW			
aik	'tow, pull'		
aikiie	'be easy to tow'	—	
Aḷak	'legendary man; phosphoresence'		
aḷakiie	'be plentiful, easy to find'	aḷakiia	'be scarce, hard to find'
atak	'tow, pull'		
atakiie	'be easy to drag in water'	atakiia	'be hard to drag in water'
mej	'die'		
mejjiie	'be quick to die'	mejjiia	'be slow to die'
jaḷ	'turn, face'		
jaaḷiie	'be easy to turn'	jaaḷiia	'be hard to turn'
kipel	'oblige, instruct'		
kipliie	'be obedient, docile'	kipliia	'be disobedient, obstinate'
ṃweiuk	'goods, property'		
ṃweiie	'be rich, wealthy'	—	
tok	'catch fire'		
tokwiie	'be combustible'	tokwiia	'be incombustible'
NO APPARENT SOURCE			
aḷakiie	'be easy to find'	aḷakiia	'be hard to find'
awiie	'be tame'	awiia	'be wild'
añiie	'be quick when called'	añiia	'be slow when called'
keiie	'be useful, serviceable'	—	
kōiie	'be qualified, worthy'	—	

Antonymal verbs. A number of intransitive verbs are the sources for verbs that have the opposite meaning. They are formed by prefixing {ja-}, which is subject to the rule of low vowel dissimilation (see 2.5.5) when the source verb also has a low vowel in its first syllable, as, for example, in *jettal* 'not leak'. A sampling of antonymal verbs is given in table 3-25.

Table 3-25 Antonymal verbs

		ANTONYM	
kkurere	'always play'	jọkkurere	'seldom play'
rroñroñ	'have good hearing'	jarroñroñ	'be deaf'
ttal	'leak'	jettal	'not leak'
lōke	'believe'	jālōke	'not believe'
keiie	'be strong'	jakeiie	'not be strong'
uwi	'be tasty'	jọuwi	'not be tasty'
kile	'recognize'	jakile	'not recognize'
wōtwōt ~ wōttūwōt	'always rain'	jawōtwōt ~ jawōttūwōt	'seldom rain'

Distributive verbs. There are hundreds of verbs in Marshallese that are DISTRIBUTIVE in form and meaning. They are derived from three main sources: intransitive verbs, transitive verbs, and nouns. We will look at the first two in this section; the third is treated in 3.3.4. The term "distributive" is an attempt to state what a whole constellation of meanings have in common, meanings ranging from "continuative" and "frequentative" to "divided up," "discontinuous," and "diffuse." Most frequently, distributive verbs are formed by doubling the initial consonant and reduplicating the final syllable of the source verb. Here are some examples that show the range of possible meanings. The first group are all derived from intransitive verbs.

(3-64) SOURCE: tōñal 'be sweet' (d-f-Ø)[7]
Ennọ an e**t**tōñal**ñal** [W] / **tō**tōñal**ñal** [E].[8]
'Its pervasive sweetness is delicious.'

(3-65) SOURCE: jọ 'ignite; run, of engines' (d-f-Ø)
E**j**jọ**jọ** injin eṇ.
'That engine gets started often.'

(3-66) SOURCE: llem̧aj 'jerk' (Ø-f-Ø)
Etūm̧ toon aik eo kōn an ellem̧aj**m̧aj** [W] / lelem̧aj**m̧aj** [E].
'The tow line broke because it was jerked too often.'

(3-67) SOURCE: baj 'ride a bus' (d-f-Ø)
Kwōmake baj **eb**baj**baj** [W] / **bō**baj**baj** [E].
'You're on the bus all the time.'

(3-68) SOURCE: jepdak 'crushed in' (d-f-Ø)
E**j**jepdak**dak** neen wa eṇ waan.
'Her/his vehicle always has flat tires.'

(3-69) SOURCE: raelep 'be noon' (d-f-Ø)
E**r**raelep**lep** an ruj.
'He usually wakes up at noon.'

(3-70) SOURCE: jukwa 'use sugar' (d-f-Ø)
Kwōmake **ij**jukwa**kwa** [W] / **ji**jukwa**kwa** [E].
'You use sugar too often.'

---

7. This formula refers to the form of the distibutive verb in comparison with its source: in the first slot, **d** stands for initial consonant doubling, **Ø** for its absence; in the second slot, **f** stands for final syllable reduplication, **i** for initial, and **Ø** for neither; in the third slot, **e** stands for suffixation of *-e/-i,* **Ø** for no suffixation.

8. In chapter 6 we analyze the distributive in this sentence (and those in 3-66 and 3-77) as nouns derived from distributive verbs that have identical forms and meanings (except for the change of verb to noun). That should not prevent their serving here as good examples of various meanings imparted by distributives. In this sentence and those that follow, distributive verbs that begin with double consonants in their basic form, such as {tteñalñal} in this sentence, are spelled out as pronounced and written in both major dialects, Rālik (W) and Ratak (E), when not prefixed with a subject marker—that is, when nonfinite.

(3-71) SOURCE: ṃōrā 'be dry' (d-f-Ø)
Ejino **eṃ**ṃō**rāre** [W] / **ṃō**ṃō**rāre** [E] nuknuk kā aō.
'My clothes are beginning to dry (in certain places).'

(3-72) SOURCE: marok 'be dark; be in darkness' (d-f-Ø)
Ear ruj wōt ke ej **em**marok**rok** [W] / **me**marok**rok** [E].
'He woke as the darkness was vanishing.'

(3-73) SOURCE: jeor 'turn, change direction' (d-f-Ø)
E**j**jeor**eor** wa eo.
'The vehicle keeps turning this way and that.'

The following are derived from transitive verbs. These may reduplicate the first syllable of the source verb rather than the last (d-i-Ø), and the initial consonant is not always doubled (Ø-i-Ø).

(3-74) SOURCE: daṃwij 'lick s.' (d-i-Ø)
Ear bajjek **ed**daṃ**deṃ**wij [W] / **de**daṃ**deṃ**wij ḷọḷe [E] eo.
'He just kept licking the lollipop.'

(3-75) SOURCE: pakiji 'package s.' (d-f-Ø)
Kwōmaroñ ke **ep**pakij**kiji** [W] / **pe**pakij**kiji** pilawā ṇe kijerro [E]?
'Can you put our flour in as many packages as necessary?'

(3-76) SOURCE: jipañ 'help' (Ø-i-Ø)
Koṃwin itok jen jip**jip**añ doon.
'Come let's help each other (and divide up the separate tasks).'

(3-77) SOURCE: rupe 'break, demolish s.' (d-i-Ø)
Eṃōj **ir**rup**rup**e [W] / **rū**rup**rup**e [E] ṃweo.
'The house has been torn down carelessly (with debris left lying all around.'

(3-78) SOURCE: luwajet 'dilapidated' (Ø-Ø-e)
Ejab to an pād kōn an luwajet**e**.
'It didn't stay around very long because it had been in the water too long.'

A smaller number of distributive verbs are formed by another pattern, by suffixing *-e* to the source (Ø-Ø-e), as in (3-78). But this minor pattern is found in only about one-eighth of the more than 800 distributive verbs identified to date. The major pattern of initial-consonant doubling and final-syllable reduplication (d-f-Ø) is clearly the new productive pattern. Note its use with loanwords such as *baj* (3-67), *jukwa* (3-70), and *pakij* (3-75).

Plural verbs of dimension. There is a small group of adjectival verbs that may have a different form when their subjects are plural. All have to do with dimensions that are members of opposite pairs such as large–small, wide–narrow, thick–thin, and long–short. These plural verbs resemble their singular counterparts and differ only in that at least one of their consonants is doubled.

(3-79) a. Emijel bok in.
'This book is thick.'
b. Remijel bok kein.
'These books are thick.'
c. Re**mm**ijel / Remi**jj**el / Re**mm**i**jj**el bok kaṇ.
'Those books are extremely thick.'
d. Ekilep bọọk in.
'This box is big.'
e. Rōkilep bọọk kein.
'These boxes are big.'
f. Rō**kk**i**ll**ep / Rōki**ll**ep bọọk kaṇ.
'Those boxes are really big.'

As these examples show, the plural verbs with doubled consonants are not required to be used with plural subjects, but when used, they give emphasis to the quality of the verb. Table 3-26 gives an exhaustive listing of these plural adjectival verbs together with the adjectives derived from them that appear as modifiers of nouns (see 4.4). The same plural forms may also be used to emphasize the quality of adjectives modifying plural nouns. In (3-80), the only evidence that 'Marshallese youngsters' is plural is the form of *jiddik* as a plural adjective—until this is confirmed by *aer* 'their' (in lit. 'it is great **their** love of outrigger-raising').

(3-80) Likao jiddik in Ṃajeḷ eḷap aer iọkwe kakkiāmem.
'Outrigger-raising [a sport] is a favorite pastime among Marshallese youngsters.'

Table 3-26 Verbs of dimension, adjectives, and the special plurals they share

		VERB	PLURAL	ADJECTIVE
'great, large'		ḷap	-**ḷḷ**ap	ḷap**ḷap**
'lowly, small'	W:	dik	-**dd**ik	dik**dik**
	E:	niñ	-**nn**iñ	niñ**niñ**
'large'		kilep	-**kk**i**ll**ep, -ki**ll**ep	kile**plep**
'small'		jidik	-ji**dd**ik	jidik**dik**
'thick'		mijel	-**mm**i**jj**el, -mi**jj**el, -**mm**ijel	mijel**jel**
'thin'		māni	-**mm**ā**nn**i, -mā**nn**i, -**mm**āni	māni**ni**
'wide'		depakpak	-**dd**epakpak	depakpak
'thin (of cords, etc.); narrow'	W:	aidik	-ai**dd**ik	aidik**dik**
	E:	ainiñ	-ai**nn**iñ	ainiñ**niñ**
'long, tall'		aetok	-ae**tt**ok	aetok**tok**
'short'		kadu	-**kk**a**dd**u, -ka**dd**u	kadu**du**

Bender (1996) includes some evidence that these special plurals are being used less frequently in recent years than they once were.

VERBS DERIVED FROM OTHER PARTS OF SPEECH

3.3.4 There are several types of denominal verbs, that is, verbs derived from nouns. They include denominal distributive verbs, verbs of hunting, and verbs of providing,

Denominal distributive verbs. In 3.3.3 we looked at distributive verbs from verbal sources. There are also a large number that have nouns as their source. These examples give an idea of the range of meanings that are conveyed, including pervasiveness, obsession, sufficiency and even over-sufficiency, multiplicity, discontinuity, dilution, and diffuseness, and even simply aromas. About two-thirds of them follow the d-f-Ø pattern, and one-third the Ø-Ø-e pattern, this being a higher proportion of the latter than for those from verbal sources.

(3-81) SOURCE: teaak 'provisions for a journey' (Ø-Ø-e)
Eteaake wa in.
'We have plenty of food aboard.'

(3-82) SOURCE: ij 'yeast' (d-f-Ø)
Eiijij iiōk eo an.
'His batter came out having too much yeast.'

(3-83) SOURCE: jiip 'jeep' (d-f-e)[9]
E**jj**iip**ipi** an kōnono.
'He's always talking about jeeps.'

(3-84) SOURCE: baid 'smoking pipe, cigarette [from Engl. briar]' (d-f-Ø)
Emake **eb**baid**id** (W) / **bō**baid**id** (E) ļōņe.
'That guy is a chain smoker.'

(3-85) SOURCE: koṃa 'comma' (d-f-Ø)
E**kk**oṃa**ṃa** jaṇtōj ņe.
'That sentence has lots of commas.'

(3-86) SOURCE: wiwi 'fat in turtle shell' (d-Ø-Ø)
E**u**wiwi jọkur in.
'This turtle shell is covered all over the inside with delicious turtle fat.' 'This turtle shell has fat here and there inside it.'

(3-87) SOURCE: armej 'person, people' (Ø-Ø-e)
Earmij**e** ānin.
'This island has lots of people.' 'This island is inhabited.'

9. The suffix is *-i* instead of *-e* when the last vowel of the source is a high vowel.

(3-88) SOURCE: bwiro 'preserved breadfruit' (d-f-Ø)
E**b**bwiro**ro** nuknuk e aō.
'My clothes have scraps of preserved breadfruit on them.'
'My clothes smell of preserved breadfruit.'

(3-89) source: būrōrō 'red' (d-Ø-Ø)
Ej kōṇak juon nuknuk **ib**būrōrō (W) / **bū**būrōrō (E) mejān.
'She is wearing a reddish dress.'

Notice the ambiguity of sentences (3-86) and (3-87), as to whether the item is pervasive, or only present here and there—or, in (3-88), whether there remains simply the odor. This is typical of distributives in many languages.

Verbs of hunting and gathering. Alienable nouns may combine with the causative prefix *ka-* to derive both intransitive and transitive verbs. Intransitive verbs with meanings such as 'look for, hunt, find, gather, collect' are formed by adding the prefix to the names of plants or animals.

(3-90) HUNTING AND GATHERING FLORA AND FAUNA

kōṃakṃōk	'gather arrowroot'
kakeeprañ	'harvest bananas'
kōmā	'pick breadfruit'
ka(lo)wor	'hunt for lobsters'
kōbaru	'hunt for crabs'
kōbale	'fish for flounder'
kalibbukwe	'look for cowrie shells'

This may be done with the names of all plants, fish, and other animals, and with many nouns that refer to things as well:

(3-91) HUNTING AND GATHERING OTHER THINGS

kaat	'look for a hat'
kaaij	'get ice'
kaaik	'look for cedar driftwood'
kōbakbōk	'look for a knife'
kōkane	'gather firewood'
kapilawā	'get bread'
kōkōba	'look for copper'
kōbaḷuun	'meet an airplane'
kōbakōj	'get a bucket'

Verbs of wearing or using. These verbs can be derived from many nouns that refer to articles of clothing or other things that can be viewed as extensions on one's body, such as a cane or spear, or even a canoe in which one sits. A number of them are given in table 3-27. Note that roughly half are loanwords from English. For one-syllable nouns with only two moras (see 2.6.1), the entire word is reduplicated, but for words of three moras, only the last two moras are reduplicated (as, for example, *peenen* 'use a pen' from the three-mora noun *peen* {peyen} 'pen'.

In contrast, there are other nouns that do not reduplicate in forming verbs of wearing. All have more than three moras. These include *baajkōļ* 'bicycle', *pāāñkōļ* 'bracelet', *pālpel* 'head wreath', *jemej* {jeymej} 'slip (from *chemise*', *jodi* {jewdiy} 'zori, go-ahead rubber slippers', *ļobļoba* 'lava-lava', and *ṃarṃar* 'necklace'. For these, the noun, and the verb meaning to wear the noun, have the same form, so that, for example, *ṃarṃar* can be either a noun meaning 'necklace' or a verb meaning 'wear a necklace'. On closer examination, we can see that all of the nouns in table 3-27 have either the form CVC (just the two-mora syllable that will be reduplicated), or they may have preceding this syllable an initial CV, giving the three-mora form (CV)CVC. Those not in the table and listed here do not conform to this formula. All have more than a simple CV preceding the final CVC in their basic form. In some cases, we need to look at the basic form to see this: it is the {w} of {jewdiy} and the {y} of {jeymej} that keep them from fitting the CV-CVC formula of table 3-27.

Table 3-27 Verbs of wearing or using (all nouns have the form {[CV]CVC})

NOUN		VERB	
at	'hat'	atat	'wear a hat'
deel	'fan'	deelel	'use a fan'
doon	'husking stick'	doonon	'use a husking stick'
jiit	'sheet'	jiitit	'use a sheet'
joob	'soap'	joobob	'use soap'
jokoṇ	'cane, crutch'	jokoṇkoṇ	'use a cane or crutch'
jōōt	'shirt'	jōōtōt	'wear a shirt'
juuj	'shoes'	juujuj	'wear shoes'
kaar	'car'	kaarar	'drive a car'
kaļ	'loincloth, diaper'	kaļkaļ	'wear a loincloth'
kañōr	'belt'	kañōrñōr	'wear a belt'
kooļ	'body hair'	kooļoļ	'be hairy'
kọọj	'blanket'	kọọjoj[1]	'use a blanket'
kurob	'baseball glove'	kurobrob	'use a glove'
kuuṃ	'comb'	kuuṃuṃ	'use a comb'
ļaaṃ	'lamp'	ļaaṃaṃ	'use a lamp'
ṃade	'spear'	ṃadede	'use a spear'
mọọr	'bait'	mọọrọr	'use bait'
pet	'pillow'	petpet	'use a pillow'
peen	'pen'	peenen	'use a pen'
piin	'pin; oarlock'	piinin	'wear a pin; use oarlocks'
takin	'socks, stockings'	takinkin	'wear socks'
ut	'flower'	utut	'wear a flower'
wa	'canoe'	wawa	'use a canoe'
waj	'watch'	wajwaj	'wear a watch'

1. Note here the vowel alternation described in 2.5.4.

Verbs of providing. It would appear that transitive verbs with the general meaning of 'provide s. with' or 'permit s. to have' may also be derived from many alienable nouns by the addition of the causative prefix and a transitivizing increment (see "Transitive and intransitive counterparts" on page 154).

(3-92)	a.	kōbaajkōḷe	'let s. ride a bicycle'
		kōbajinjeaik	'take s. along as a passenger'
		kabūrijōōte	'give s. bib-overalls'
		kōjedaujiji	'put trousers on s.'
		kajiñliji	'put an undershirt on (a child)'
		kōjobaik	'let s. sit on a sofa'
		kajokankane	'put a dress on s.'
		kōjorṃōtaik	'make (a child) wear underpants'
		kōkālōklōke bōran	'crown s. with thorns'
		kakutiltili	'put lizards on (an island)'
		kọkwōjkwōje	'provide a feast/communion for s.'
		kōṃakṃōke	'starch s.'
		kanuknuki	'clothe s.'
		kapikniki	'take s. on a picnic'
	b.	kadoonone	'let s. use a coconut husker'
		kajokoṇkoṇe	'make s. use a cane'
		kajuujuji	'put s.'s shoes on for them'
		kōkañōrñōre	'let s. wear a belt/put a belt on for s.'
		kọkurobrobe	'let s. use a glove'
		kakuuṃuṃi	'provide a comb for s.'
		kōḷaaṃaṃwe	'provide a lamp for s.'
		kapeenene	'let s. use a pen'
		kōtakinkini	'provide s. with socks'
		kọututi	'decorate s. with flowers'
		kọwajwaje	'let s. wear a watch'

When we note, however, that a number of the nouns in (3-92a) are things that can be worn, and that the others can be viewed as metaphoric extensions of one's person (including sofas, boat or airplane seats, places at a picnic, or even lizards as being "worn" by an island), we are reminded of the nouns in the preceding section that don't change their form when derived as verbs because they don't fit the formula {(CV)CVC}. Noting further that the examples in (3-92b) contain verbs of wearing whose nouns do fit the formula, we conclude that all of the nouns—those that fit the formula and those that don't—are first converted into verbs of wearing, and that all of the verbs of providing in (3-92) are then derived from these verbs of wearing. Those that fit the formula are reduplicated, and those that don't fit the formula have no change in form. The two types are summarized in table 3-28. Presumably, one could continue to derive transitive verbs of the type in (3-92b) for all of the remaining verbs of wearing in table 3-27.

Table 3-28 Derivation from noun to verb of wearing, to verb of providing

NOUNS THAT REDUPLICATE AND NOUNS THAT DON'T			
ALIENABLE NOUNS			
juuj	'shoes'	jodi	'zories'
INTRANSITIVE VERBS OF WEARING			
juuj**uj**	'wear shoes'	jodi[1]	'wear zories'
TRANSITIVE VERBS OF PROVIDING			
kajuuuju**i**	'provide s. with shoes'	**ka**jodi**ik**	'provide s. with zories'
COMPARISON OF BASIC FORM WITH THE FORMULA {(CV)CVC}			
{jiwij}	(fits)	{jewdiy}	(doesn't fit: X=w)
{CVCVC}		{CVXCVC}	

1. No change in form between noun and verb of wearing.

Verbs of empowerment. A relatively small number of nouns that refer to sources of power or instruments of facilitation may be converted to intransitive verbs of empowerment by the prefixation of *le-* {ley-}, as in (3-92). Example g. shows that these verbs can in turn be transitivized.

(3-93) a. Wa eṇ ej **le**injin.
'That boat has an engine.'

b. Injin eṇ ej **le**tijeḷ.
'That engine uses diesel.'

c. Kwōj **le**wōjḷā ḷọk ñan ia?
'Where are you sailing?'

d. Jitoob eṇ ej **le**jarom.
'That stove uses electricity.'

e. Ḷadik eṇ ej **le**to ñan tallōñ.
'That boy uses a rope for climbing.'

f. E-ḷap an **le**ṃōṇōṇō mour eṇ an.
3s-great its afford.happiness life that his
'He leads a cheerful existence.'

g. E-mọ ḷe eoon eṃ ān-in bwe re-naaj **le**ṃade**ik** eok.
3S-taboo poach.food islet-this because 3P-FUT spear 2S.OBJ
'It is taboo to poach food on this island because you will get speared.' (lit. '… they will use a spear on you')

SUMMARY

3.4 This concludes an introduction to word forms that has focused on the two major parts of speech, nouns and verbs, and some of their major subclasses that differ from each other in form. Chapter 4 will be devoted to noun phrases, and chapter 5 to verb phrases, groupings of words in which nouns and verbs, respectively, stand at the front as heads, followed by other parts of speech in supporting roles. We will learn more about nouns and verbs as we look at their relations with the other words in the phrases they head.

4 Nouns and Their Modifiers

INTRODUCTION

4.1 The basic structure of a noun phrase in Marshallese consists of the head noun followed by attributive modifiers, such as DETERMINERS (4.3), ADJECTIVES (4.4), and PREPOSITIONAL PHRASES (4.5), or by predicational modifiers such as POSSESSIVES (4.6) or QUANTIFIERS (4.7). The RELATIVE CLAUSES (4.8) that also follow nouns as their modifiers are considered to be both attributive and predicational—attributive in the sense that they add descriptive information, and predicational because the head of a relative clause is a predicate (a verb). Nouns are the heads of noun phrases in that they are the single element in the construction that characterizes it and may stand for it as a whole (Matthews 1997).

PRONOUNS

4.2 In this chapter we first introduce pronouns (4.2), a type of noun not mentioned in the last chapter. These include personal pronouns (4.2.1), demonstratives (4.2.2), and interrogative pronouns (4.2.3). Pronouns are typically not followed by modifiers and are, thus, the sole members of their phrases, which, however, behave like other noun phrases in relation to the other elements of a sentence.

PERSONAL PRONOUNS

4.2.1 The Marshallese personal pronouns refer only to humans. Beyond this, they give minimal information, telling us only whether the party being referred to consists of one person (S = SINGULAR) or more than onc (P = PLURAL), and whether the party includes the speaker (1 = FIRST PERSON), or the hearer(s) (2 = SECOND PERSON), or both (1P.INCL = FIRST PERSON PLURAL INCLUSIVE) or neither (3 = one or more THIRD PERSONs instead).[1] Unlike English, with *he* and *she,* Marshallese personal pronouns do not distinguish masculine and feminine.

---

1. 1P.EXCL = FIRST PERSON PLURAL EXCLUSIVE stands for a party that excludes the hearer(s): 'we (but not you)'. See table 4-1, where these grammatical labels are applied to the Marshallese pronouns. Wc may sometimes abbreviate 1P.EXCL to 1P.E (and 1P.INCL to 1P.I) in order to save space.

Absolute and object pronouns. The absolute pronouns are the main set of personal pronouns, and they may serve also as object pronouns. For two of the person-number combinations, 1S and 2S, there are also distinct object pronoun forms, as shown in table 4-1. These object pronouns appear as the objects of transitive verbs or prepositions, but their absolute counterparts may also occur in the same places, with little if any difference in meaning, as shown in (4-1) through (4-3). While there is still a decided preference for the object pronouns following transitive verbs in sentences like those of (4-1) and (4-2), the absolute pronouns are almost equally common following prepositions, as in (4-3). Pagotto (1987:114) provides (4-4) as a spontaneous example from a Marshallese girl, and reports being told that younger speakers show greater tendency to use the absolute forms as direct objects. Because a single set, the absolute pronouns, serve all functions in every combination except 1S and 2S, they are beginning to serve all functions even in these two combinations where separate object pronouns are still available. One can predict that the two distinct object pronouns, *eō* and *eok,* will eventually be replaced everywhere by *ña* and *kwe,* respectively.

(4-1) a. Kwōn jab deñḷọke **eō**.
'Don't hit me.'

b. Kwōn jab joon **ña**.
'Don't put your weight on me.'

(4-2) a. Kwōn kaiur bwe enaaj boñe **eok**.
'Hurry up before it gets dark.'

b. Emaroñ jeptōṃbaik **kwe** ṇa ānin.
'September might still see you on the island.'

(4-3) a. Ear jab eḷtok ñan **eō**.
b. Ear jab eḷtok ñan **ña**.
'S/he didn't pay attention to me.'

(4-4) Iar kaṃuriik **kwe** juon taḷa.
'I lent you a dollar.'

Table 4-1 Absolute and object pronouns[1]

	SINGULAR		SINGULAR		PLURAL		RATAK PLURAL	
	ABSOLUTE		OBJECT		ABSOLUTE		ABSOLUTE	
1.INCL	ña	{gah}	eō	{yẹh}	kōj	{kẹj}		
1.EXCL	—	—			kōm	{kẹm}	kōmmem	{kẹmmẹm}
2	kwe	{k^{w}ey}	eok	{yẹk^{w}}	koṃ	{k^{w}ẹṃ}	kōmi	{kemiy}
3	e	{yẹy}			er	{yẹr}		

1. Object pronouns are shown only where they differ from the absolute forms (in the singular), and Ratak pronouns are shown only where they differ from Rālik pronouns (in the plural).

Further number specification of plural pronouns and person markers. The plural forms of the absolute pronouns can have the elements of table 4-2 added to form compound pronouns with their number further specified. Several of these elements are reduced forms of the corresponding cardinal numeral (see table 4-14), as shown in the table. The resulting combinations are given in table 4-3, with examples in (4-5). As compound pronouns, they fill the same functions as the absolute pronouns. Both dialects show variation in the QUADRUPLE suffix in table 4-2. This variation occurs after all the plural pronouns except for 1.INCL, where only the first variant is found: *kōjeañ* (but not **kōjjeañ*), *kōjmān* (but not **kōjjemān*).

(4-5) a. **Kōjro** joñjoñ.
'Let's see which of us is taller.'

b. **Kōmwōj** dekakḷọk ke kōm roñ an jiñ.
'We all burst into laughter when we heard him break wind.'

c. **Koṃro** ṃōṃōkaj waj bwe eboñ.
'You two go on ahead before it gets dark.'

d. **Erwōj** ar taij inne.
'They were all shooting craps yesterday.'

Table 4-2 Numerical elements of compound plural pronouns

	RĀLIK		RATAK		RELATED NUMERAL	
DUAL	-ro	{-rew}	-ro	{-rew}	ruo	{riwew}
TRIAL	-jeel	{-jẹyẹl}	-jel	{-jẹl}	jilu	{jiliw}
QUADRUPLE	-eañ ~ jeañ	{-yag ~ jẹyyag}	-mān ~ jemān	{-man ~ jẹyman}	emān	{yeman}
MULTIPLE	-wōj	{-wẹj}	-wōj	{-wẹj}	eṃḷapwōj[1]	

1. Meaning 'large community house for extended family of chief and retinue'. Although this word is not a numeral, it seems to contain the same element *-wōj*.

Table 4-3 Absolute pronoun-number compounds[1]

	BASIC	ABSOLUTE	DUAL	TRIAL	QUADRUPLE	MULTIPLE
(W) (E)	{kẹj}	kōj	kōjro	kōjjeel kōjjel	kōjeañ kōjmān	kōjwōj
(W) (E)	{kẹm} {kẹmmẹm}	kōm kōmmem	kōmro kōṃro[2]	kōmjeel kōmjel	kōm(je)eañ kōm(je)mān	kōmwōj
(W) (E)	{kʷẹṃ} {kemiy}	koṃ kōmi	koṃro kōmiro	koṃjeel kōmijel	koṃ(je)eañ kōmi(je)mān	koṃwōj kōmiwōj
(W) (E)	{yẹr}	er	erro	erjeel erjel	er(je)eañ er(je)mān	erwōj
(W) (E)			{rew}	{jẹyẹl} {jẹl}	{(jẹy)yag} {(jẹy)man}	{wẹj}

1. Ratak dialect (E) forms are given only where they differ from Rālik dialect (W) forms.
2. Note that the light *m* expected in this form has assimilated to the heavy *r* that follows.

The elements of table 4-2 may also combine with the subject prefixes of table 3-10 on page 151 to derive subject pronouns that have their number further specified in the same way. The resulting combinations for 1P.INCL and 3P are given in table 4-4, with examples in (4-6) through (4-9). These may serve only as subjects, and the meaning of some (*jero,* for example) seems to include an optative / jussive feature (translated 'Let's ...), as if the helping verb *en* (3.3.1) were also included in the compound. In fact, older forms of the language that are comparable contain this element overtly, suggesting that *jero* may be a contraction of *jenro.* Sources are given for the older attested forms in the table; forms not as yet attested, but expected, are enclosed in square brackets ("[ ]"). Examples (4-6) through (4-8) from folktales contain several of the older forms, including two in which *ro* alone serves as a dual subject instead of *rōro,* and one in which *jel* serves as a trial subject instead of *jejel;* (4-9) gives contemporary examples.

(4-6) Innām ej ba **renjel** wōnarḷọk in pukot jemān. Innām ej ba **renro** kab pikri aje ko. Innām **rejel** etal im kōrā ro rej pikōr aje ko im ba ...
'And he said that the three of them should go toward the lagoon and look for his father. And he said that the two of them should beat the drums. And the three of them went, and the women beat the drums and said ...' (Tobin 2002:302)

(4-7) Raan eo juon ḷadik ro **rejro** ṃōkaj in etal in eọñwōd. Im **ro** ar eọñwōd bajjek iturin āne eo. Ke [ej] tulọk aḷ **ro** ar jerak im ettōr niñaḷọk.
'The next day the boys hurried to go to fish. And they fished a little beside the island. When it was past sunset, they sailed and ran [went] to the north.' (Tobin 2002:183)

(4-8) Irooj eo ej uwaak. Ej ba, "**Jejel** ja pād jidik innām ilo raan kaṇe rej itok **jel** naaj etal ippān jinemiro im jemāmiro."
'The chief replied, and said, "The three of us will remain a little while, and in the days to come, we three will go to your mother and father."' (Tobin 2002:254)

Table 4-4 Subject markers further specified for number

PREFIXES		DUAL	TRIAL	QUADRUPLE		MULTIPLE
je-	1P	jero	jel[1] (< jejel)	jeañ	jemān	jewōj
	+ en	jenro[1]	[jenjel]	[jeneañ]	[jenmān]	[jenwōj]
	+ ej	jejro[1]	[jejjel]	[jejeañ]	[jejmān]	[jejwōj]
re-	3P	ro[1] (< rōro)	rejel[1]	reañ	[remān]	rewōj
	+ en	renro[1]	renjel[1]	[reneañ]	[renmān]	[renwōj]
	+ ej	rejro[1]	[rejjel]	[rejeañ]	[rejmān]	[rejwōj]

1. Tobin (2002): *jel, jejel,* chap. 55, p. 254, col. 2, lines 7–9 (see [(4-8)]); *jejro,* 61:277, 2, 9; *jenro,* 51:231, 1, 19; *rejro, ro,* 39:183, 1, 2–5 (see [4-7]); *renro, rejel,* and *renjel,* 65:302, 2, 3–5 [see (4-6) above].

(4-9) a. **Jero** ḷaitaik ḷọk waini kā.
'Let's haul the copra on the lighter.'
b. **Jeañ** iḷọk in kajjeḷọḷo.
'Let's go see if there's a boat coming.'

Further number specification of noun possessive suffixes. The number elements of table 4-2 may also be added to the possessive suffixes of inalienable nouns given in (3-5) on page 124. Examples are given in (4-10). Note that the 1P.INCL suffix *-d* is assimilated to the following *r* of the *-ro* suffix in (4-10c) and (4-10d): *a-d-ro* becomes *a-r-ro* and *kije-d-ro* becomes *kije-r-ro* (see table 2-19 on page 71). Examples (4-8) and (4-15b) include the 2P.DUAL possessive forms of the words for mother and father.

(4-10) a. Āinjuon **a-er-ro** ḷōmṇak jān doon.
'Those two have differing opinions.'
b. Eṃṃan **a-d-wōj** iiāio.
'It's good for all of us to get together again.'
c. Ej ja joobob eake joob eṇ **a-r-ro**.
'Let him use our soap for now.'
d. Kwōjja wia **kije-r-ro** bwe ijiban.
'You buy our food 'cause I'm a little short of money.'

Summary of personal pronouns. Absolute pronouns can appear as subjects of equational sentences, as in (4-11a); as emphatic subjects of verbal sentences, as in (4-11b); as objects of transitive verbs, as in (4-1) and (4-2); and as objects of prepositions, as in (4-3) and (4-11c). In the last two roles mentioned, as objects, they are in competion with the distinct object pronouns only when the object is 1S or 2S.

(4-11) a. [**Ña**] [ri-jerbal in kien].
'I am a government worker.'
b. **Ña** ij etal kiiō.
'I'm going now.'
c. Kwōmaroñ atōreje tok ñan **ña** / eō?
'Can you address it to me?'

Subject clitics. In two of the person-number combinations, 1P.EXCL and 2P, the absolute pronouns have a form identical with that of the subject prefixes in both dialects, as can be seen in the emphatic sentences of (4-12).

(4-12) a. **Kōm kōm**-naaj etal ñan Teḷap. (W)
b. **Kōmmem kōmmem**-naaj etal ñan Teḷap. (E)
'We (EXCL, EMPH) will go to Telap.'
c. **Koṃ koṃ**-naaj etal ñan Teḷap. (W)
d. **Kōmi kōmi**-naaj etal ñan Teḷap. (E)
'You (PL, EMPH) will go to Telap.'

As noted in connection with table 3-10 on page 151, the prefixes of these two person-number combinations, 1P.EXCL and 2P, behave more like clitics than prefixes. For one thing, they are usually written separately in non-emphatic sentences such as those of (4-13).

(4-13) a. **Kōm** dike bwe ekōbbọọjọj.
'We don't like him because of his overbearing manner.'

b. **Kōmmem** kar ṃōñā ek iṃōn Toni.
'We ate fish at Toni's.'

c. **Koṃ** jab tuṃal bwe koṃ naaj maḷoñ.
'Don't play that keel-haul game or you'll drown.'

d. **Kōmi** ṃōṃkaj ḷọk iṃaan bwe ij baj alowaj wōt.
'You go ahead as I'll be tagging along.'

The fact that they are usually written separately, rather than as prefixes, may reflect their greater phonetic substance: they have at least two consonants, and occupy at least two moras (2.4.2), in contrast to the other person-number combinations, all of which are treated as prefixes and have the form CV-.

Also, they have special forms when joined with *ej* and *en,* as shown in table 3-10 on page 151, replacing the initial *e* of these forms with *i* in *kōmij, kōmin, koṃwij,* and *koṃwin.* There can be no doubt that we are dealing here with subject prefixes rather than absolute pronouns. The *i* in these forms reflects the final high vowels of Proto-Micronesian *kami 'we (EXCL), us' and *kam^{w}u 'you (PL)'. Examples are given in (4-14). In folkloristic material, it is possible to find these special forms further specified as to number, paralleling the 1P.INCL and 3P forms in table 4-4. Examples are given in (4-15).

(4-14) a. **Kōmij** pād wōt in mije eok.
'We will stick with you come what may.'

b. Ear ba **kōmin** kañ ek ko bwe ekin boñ jab lo raan.
'S/he told us to finish the fish because they were too few to be left for the next day.'

c. **Koṃwij** weḷọk ñan ia?
'Where are you going?'

d. **Koṃwin** ajeḷọk mour ko ami ñan Anij.
'Dedicate your lives to God.'

(4-15) a. **Koṃwinro** itok jān ia? (Tobin 2002:254)
'Where might the two of you have come from?'

b. Euwaak ledik ro, "**Kōmijro** itok jān Ep. Ak kwōj maroñ ke kōtḷọk kōmro bwe **kōminro** jepḷaak ñan ippān jinemiro im jemāmiro?"
'The girls answered, "We are come from Ep. But can you release the two of us, so that we may return to our parents?"'

Compound pronouns serve as subject markers. The numerical elements of table 4-2 may combine with the plural absolute pronouns, as displayed in table 4-3. When referring to the subject of a clause, these numerically specified compound pronouns take the place of subject prefixes, fulfilling the general requirement (see the first paragraph of 3.3) that the first verb should always be preceded by a subject prefix. This means that the usual subject prefixes do not appear in the same verb phrase. Several examples are given in (4-16).

(4-16) a. **Kōmro** ar kōkajoor arḷọk.
'The two of us took an excursion to the seashore.'

b. **Koṃro** ṃōṃōkaj waj bwe ebōñ.
'You two go on ahead before it gets dark.'

c. **Erro** jekkar ñan doon.
'They are unsuited for each other.'

Note that none of these contains any form of either the noncompletive *ej* or the optative *en* following the compound pronoun. The same is true of the examples in (4-5). But it is, in fact, possible for *ej* and *en* to be found here, in the position immediately following compound pronouns.

(4-17) a. Erro **ej** kajjibukwi taḷa.
'Each of the two of them has a hundred dollars.'

b. Koṃro **en** jab bwijerro.
'You two shouldn't quarrel.'

c. Erreañ **ej** jab būro-kuk.
'They can't agree among themselves.'

The presence of *ej* and *en* (which seem to contain the 3S subject prefix) here together with compound pronouns such as *erro* and *koṃro* would appear to contradict the statement that the latter take the place of subject prefixes in the verb phrase.[2] This is resolved by recognizing that *ej* and *en* in sentences such as these do not contain the 3S subject prefix, and are simply their basic, unprefixed forms (see table 3-10 on page 151), which have the same shape.[3]

DEMONSTRATIVES

4.2.2 Demonstratives can be both substantive (noun-like) or attributive (adjective-like), as with English *this* in *"This is a book,"* where it is substantive, and *"This book is interesting,"* where it is attributive. In section 4.3 we discuss the adjective-like demonstratives, which function as determiners. Here we present the Marshallese demonstrative pronouns, which are substantive.

They are presented in tables 4-5 through 4-8. These four tables follow the same general organization, with columns for singular and plural, and rows

---

2. Two of the authors were among those who earlier thought that *ej* and *en* always contain the 3S subject prefix (Bender 1969:5, Pagotto 1987:119, Zewen 1977:89). They then had the task of explaining why plural pronouns should be treated as if they were singular, and why first and second person pronouns should be treated as third person. One approach that was used was to assume that a compound pronoun such as *koṃro* should be translated as 'the group of you two', thereby making it possible to interpret it as third person singular.
3. There are other instances in the language of prefixed and unprefixed forms having the same shape: for example, *eṃṃan* is both the basic Rālik form and the 3S form (in both dialects) of the adjectival verb 'good', and *illu* is both the basic Rālik form and the 1S form (in both dialects) of 'be angry' (see the discussion of the Rālik rule on page 53). Double identities such as these are always possible in languages that have REPLACIVE INFLECTION (Matthews 1997).

that sort out the other distinctions common to them all. The basic demonstratives of English would be grouped in a two-by-two system:

	SINGULAR	PLURAL
PROXIMAL	this	these
DISTAL	that	those

The Marshallese system is much more complex by comparison, paralleling the persons of the pronouns in table 4-1, including the inclusive and exclusive distinction relating second person to first. The labels in the first column of each of the four tables 4-5 through 4-8 build on this similarity. In the second column are English translations intended to be helpful: "Close to me, close to you, close to us both, close to a third party, and close to no one in particular." The shaded rows give emphatic (!) demonstratives for those in the row just above. The emphatic demonstratives are used in singling out and emphasizing particular items being referred to: "This one right here," "That particular one right there," and so on.

The basic demonstratives and the focus demonstratives distinguish between human and nonhuman entities in the plural, but not in the singular. This is rare among the world's languages. The reverse is much more common, to make distinctions in the singular that are overlooked in the plural (Bender 1998:60–61). The personal demonstratives distinguish between masculine and feminine in both the singular and plural, using the "man-ḷ" and the "woman-l" referred to in chapter 3 (see "Personal names" on page 120).

The basic demonstrative pronouns appear only in verbless (equational) sentences (see [4-21a] below), where as the head of the second noun phrase, they function as predicates (4-18a) or as subjects of cleft sentences (4-18b), which are described more fully in connection with (4-28). (In the examples in (4-18), the outside brackets indicate the two noun phrases in the equational constructions.)

(4-18) a. [Ri-baaṃ ro jān Roñḷap] [**raṇe**].
'Those are the radiation victims from Roñḷap.'

b. [Jọọn] [**eo** [ear taktōūk eok]].
'John is the one who doctored you.'

The personal demonstratives may appear in sentences that have verbs—(4-19a) and (4-19b)—as well as in equational sentences (4-19c).

(4-19) a. **Ḷōṃaro** rej ebbwā.
'The men are tending the traps.'

b. Ej batini **lieṇ**.
'He's having her as a secret lover.'

c. [Kōjaij] [**lieṇ**].
'She's a knock-out.'

Table 4-5 Basic demonstratives and their emphatic (!) forms

"PERSON"	CLOSE TO:	SINGULAR HUMAN & NONHUMAN		PLURAL NONHUMAN	HUMAN
1.INCL	'us both'	in	{yin}	kein	rein
1.EXCL	'me'	e	{yẹy}	kā	rā
1.EXCL !		iiō	{yiyyẹh}	kākā	rārā
2	'you'	ṇe	{ṇey}	kaṇe	raṇe
2 !		ṇeṇe	{ṇeyṇey}	kākaṇe	rāraṇe
3	'someone else'	eṇ	{yeṇ}	kaṇ	raṇ
3 !		iieṇ	{yiyyeṇ}	kākaṇ	rāraṇ
REMOTE	'the afore-	eo	{yew}	ko	ro
REMOTE !	mentioned'	iuweo	{yiwweyew}	koko	roro

Table 4-6 Personal demonstratives and their emphatic forms

"PERSON"	CLOSE TO:	SINGULAR MASCULINE	FEMININE	PLURAL MASCULINE	FEMININE
1.INCL	'us both'	ḷein	liin	ḷōṃarein	liṃarein
1.EXCL	'me'	ḷōe	lie	ḷōṃarā	liṃarā
1.EXCL !		ḷeiō	liiō	ḷōṃarārā	liṃarārā
2	'you'	ḷōṇe	liṇe	ḷōṃaraṇe	liṃaraṇe
2 !		ḷōṇeṇe	liṇeṇe	ḷōṃarāraṇe	liṃarāraṇe
3	'someone else'	ḷeeṇ	lieṇ	ḷōṃaraṇ	liṃaraṇ
3 !		ḷeieṇ	liieṇ	ḷōṃarāraṇ	liṃarāraṇ
REMOTE	'the afore-	ḷeo	lio	ḷōṃaro	liṃaro
REMOTE !	mentioned'	ḷouweo	luweo	ḷōṃaroro	liṃaroro

Table 4-7 Locative demonstratives and their emphatic forms

"PERSON"	CLOSE TO:	SINGULAR	PLURAL
1.INCL	'us both'	(i)jin	(i)jekein
1.EXCL	'me'	(i)je	(i)jekā
1.EXCL !		(i)jiiō	(i)jekākā
2	'you'	(i)jeṇe	(i)jekaṇe
2 !		(i)jeṇeṇe	(i)jekākaṇe
3	'someone else'	(i)jeṇ	(i)jekaṇ
3 !		(i)jieṇ	(i)jekākaṇ
REMOTE	'the afore-	(i)jo	(i)jeko
REMOTE !	mentioned'	(i)juweo	(i)jekoko

Table 4-8 Focus demonstratives and their emphatic forms

"PERSON"	CLOSE TO:	SINGULAR HUMAN & NONHUMAN	PLURAL NONHUMAN	HUMAN
1.INCL	'us both'	eñin / iin	erkein	errein
1.EXCL	'me'	eñe / iōōe	erkā	errā
1.EXCL !		eñiō / iiō	erkākā	errārā
2	'you'	eñṇe / ieṇe	erkaṇe	erraṇe
2 !		eñṇeṇe / ieṇeṇe	erkākaṇe	errāraṇe
3	'someone else'	eñeṇ / ieeṇ	erkaṇ	erraṇ
3 !		eñieṇ /	erkākaṇ	errāraṇ
REMOTE	'the afore-	eñeo / ieo	erko	erro
REMOTE !	mentioned'	eñuweo / euwoo	erkoko	erroro
INTERROGATIVE PRONOUNS		ewi	erki	erri

The locative demonstratives occur with and without an initial *i* that is the result of their fusion with the preposition *i* 'in, at, on'. In (4-20) two examples are given with this element, and two without.

(4-20) a. Jen kakkije **ijin**.
'Let's rest here.'

b. Ij katōte joor e **ije**.
'I'm fixing the post (in the ground) here.'

c. Imaroñ ke pāāk waj ñan **jeṇe**?
'Can I back up to there?'

d. Joñan an to aṃ pād ānin, kiiō kwe ṃōṃō in **jin**.
'You've been here so long that now you know the place inside out.'

The focus demonstratives occur as the first member of equational sentences. Example (4-21a) is a simple equational sentence, one that consists of two noun phrases that are equated with each other without having any verb like English "be/am/is/are/was/were" standing between. Even without such a verb, the first noun phrase can be said to be the SUBJECT of the sentence, and the second the PREDICATE. (The two noun phrases are enclosed in brackets.) The plural nonhuman determiner *ko* (4.3 on page 185) marks 'the books' as DEFINITE, something both speaker and hearer have in mind from a previous reference. Example (4-21b) says essentially the same thing, but brings the demonstrative into focus in the first position. In the first sentence, *kein* is a basic demonstrative; in the second, *erkein* is a focus demonstrative. Both are 1P.INCL nonhuman.

(4-21) a. [Bok ko] [**kein**].
'The books (referred to earlier) are these.'

b. [**Erkein**] [bok ko].
'These are the books (referred to earlier).'

Focus demonstratives may also occur independently as complete answers to questions, as in (4-22b). In [4-22a], *ewi* is one of the interrogative pronouns included in the bottom row of table 4-8 because of their close relation to the focus demonstratives, and referred to in greater detail in 4.2.3 below. Singular and plural-human examples of focus demonstratives (from Zewen 1977:83) are given in (4-23).

(4-22) a. [**Ewi**] [pinjeḷ eo aṃ]?
'Where is your pencil?'

b. **Eñe**.
'Here it is.'

(4-23) a. [**Eñin**] [bok eo].
'This is the book.'

b. [**Errāraṇ**] [armej in Kōle ro].
'Those are the people from Kili.'

Another place the focus demonstrative pronouns are to be found is in verbal sentences, as the subjects of RESULTATIVE clauses that are introduced by the conjunction *ke* 'that', as in (4-24). Why they are not found in the main clauses of verbal sentences is not clear.

(4-24) a. Epaak tok wōt rak **ke eñin** eañinlur.
'Summer is so near that it's in the breeze.'

b. Eḷap wōt an iọkwe **ke eñeo** ettōr im kōṃṃane wāween eo.
'She loved him so much that she went and did it.'

c. Emake lāj **ke eñṇe** ewaḷọk ilọbwilej.
'He's so mean deep down that it has come out in the open.'

d. Joñan an to an eḷḷaḷḷaḷ **ke eñeṇ** emej wōd.
'The tide has been so low for so long that the corals have died.'

e. Ṃōkajin wōt aer etetal **ke erraṇe rō**tōkeak.
'They walked so fast that they're already here.'

These sentences all have a subordinate clause introduced by the conjunction *ke.* The clause contains a focus demonstrative pronoun followed by a verb with a subject prefix that agrees with the focus demonstrative in number. When the demonstrative is plural, as *erraṇe* in (4-24e) is, the prefix on the following verb is 3P *(rō-)* in agreement. Notice that the English translations of these sentences all introduce the RESULTATIVE with the word "so" followed by an adjective. The main clauses may contain the focus adverb *wōt* in a SUPERLATIVE construction (see page 216), or a SUPERLATIVE construction with *make* (6.5.2), or a MEASURED construction with *joñan* (6.5.1).

The singular focus demonstratives in table 4-8 all contain the consonant *ñ*, but are followed by variant forms that do not. The variant forms tend to be used by older speakers, especially from the Ratak chain. Younger speakers from both chains generally use the first forms given, those that contain the consonant *ñ*.

The personal demonstratives as vocatives. The personal demonstratives that refer to individuals close to the speaker—especially those in the emphatic 1.EXCL row of table 4-6—may be used as intimate terms of address.

(4-25) a. Kwōn jab men rot ṇe **ḷeiō**.
'Don't do that, pal.'

b. Koṃwin kaiur ḷọk **ḷōṃarārā**.
'Step on it, you guys.'

c. Weeak, **liṃarārā.**
'Gracious, girls.'

d. **Ḷōṃare** ebar ita obajañ?
'Now, what's the matter with grandma again?'

More formal and respectful are special vocatives not included in table 4-6 but formed from the roots of the four columns (masculine and feminine, singular and plural) with the vocative *-e* added (see "Vocatives" on page

122): *l̗e* 'sir', *le* 'ma'am', *l̗ōm̗ae* 'gentlemen', *lim̗ae* 'ladies'. Sometimes the bare plural roots are used without the vocative suffix, as in (4-26d).

(4-26) a. Uwọk, āinwōt kwōjeļā injin **ļe.**
'Gee, I didn't know you were a mechanic.'

b. Komm̗ool **ļe.**
'Thank you, sir.'

c. **Ļōm̗ae** eiie rak tok bwe edik ļọk kōto in.
'Men, summer time is near as the wind is fairer.'

d. Lieņ **ļōm̗a** ri-kattoojoj.
'Gentlemen, she's a flirt.'

INTERROGATIVE PRONOUNS

4.2.3 The interrogative pronouns are given in table 4-9. There is a clear relation between the first three in the table and the three columns of focus demonstratives in table 4-8 on page 179, so much so that we have included the interrogatives in the bottom row of that table for ease of comparison. Like the focus demonstratives, they form focused predicates of equational sentences, as in (4-27). *Jete* in (4-27d) follows the same pattern.

(4-27) a. [**Ewi**] [m̗weo im̗ōm̗]?
'Where is your house?'

b. [**Erri**] [ļadik ro nājū]?
'Where are my sons?'

c. [**Erki**] [bok ko am̗]?
'Where are your books?

d. [**Jete**] [oņāān jōōt ņe am̗]?
'How much did your shirt cost?'

Questions with the other pronouns in (4-28) are generally formulated as CLEFT sentences, sentences in which the interrogative pronoun appears as an initial focused predicate with a demonstrative pronoun following as subject. These two pronouns are in an equational relationship, and included with the noun phrase of the second (demonstrative) pronoun is a relative clause. These entities are identified within brackets in the examples that follow. Thus, in (4-28a) *wōn* and *eo* are the two pronouns in an equational relationship ('who' = 'the one'), and *kwaar bouti* ('you voted for [whom]') is the relative clause. The *-i* on *bouti* shows where the interrogative pronoun *wōn* was "cleaved" from and moved to the front; there is an anaphoric relation between *-i* and its antecedent *wōn.* Similarly with sentences b. and c. However, no such anaphoric relation is to be found for the temporal interrogative *ñāāt* in (4-28d); there is nothing later in the sentence that refers back to it.

(4-28) a. [**Wōn**] [eo [kwaar bout**i**]]?
'Who did you vote for?'

b. [**Ta**] [ṇe [kwōj mijak**e**]]?
'What are you afraid of?'

c. [**Ia**] [eo [bao in ej edde **ie**]]?
'Where's this bird roosting?'

d. [**Ñāāt**] [eṇ [wa eṇ ej jerak]]?
'When will the ship sail?'

In (4-28) cleft constructions are used to question direct objects (a. and b.) and locations (c., spatial, and d., temporal). They may also be used to question subjects of verbs (4-29a,b) and objects of prepositions (4-29c). These three sentences also contain anaphoric elements. In the first two, the *e-* of *ej* refers to *wōn* or *ḷōt,* and in the third, the *-e* of *kake* refers to *ta.*

(4-29) a. [**Wōn**] [eṇ [**e**j kōjerbal eok]]?
'Who is employing you?'

b. [**Ḷōt**] [eṇ [**e**j kōjerbal eok]]?
'Who is that man employing you?'

c. [**Ta**] [eṇ [kwōj abṇōṇō kak**e**]]?
'What are you complaining about?'

In general, the male and female interrogative pronouns *ḷōt* and *let* can be used just as *wōn* is, as in (4-29b), and can be viewed as identical to *wōn* except that gender has been further specified. With all three we are asking about humans (like English *who*), and with *ḷōt* and *let* we are asking about humans who are male or female, respectively. The demonstrative pronouns used in the cleft construction may further specify the entity being inquired about as plural, as shown in (4-30b).

(4-30) a. [Ḷōt] [eṇ [ej ekkal eṃ ijeṇ]]?
'Who is that man house-building over there?'

b. [Ḷōt] [raṇ [rej eo̧ñwōd ijeṇ]]?
'Who are those men fishing over there?'

Subjects of verbs and objects of prepositions can also be questioned with the interrogative pronoun in the position normally occupied by subjects of verbs and objects of prepositions, respectively, as in (4-31). However, many speakers prefer the cleft alternatives of (4-32).

(4-31) a. **Wōn** ear būḷo̧ke aḷaḷ eo?
'Who broke the piece of wood?'

b. Kwōj wiaik nuknuk ṇe ñan **wōn**?
'Who are you buying that dress for?'

c. Kwōj kuṇaṇa kōn **ta**?
'What are you contributing?'

(4-32) a. [**Wōn**] [eo [**e**ar būḷo̧ke aḷaḷ eo]]?
b. [**Wōn**] [eo [kwōj wiaik nuknuk ṇe ñan**e**]]?
c. [**Ta**] [eo [kwōj kuṇaṇa kak**e**]]?

Table 4-9 Interrogative pronouns

PREDICATIONAL			
LOCATIONAL			
	SINGULAR	ewi	'Where is ...?'
	PLURAL HUMAN	erri	'Where are ...?'
	PLURAL NONHUMAN	erki	'Where are ...?'
NONLOCATIONAL			
	QUANTITY	jete	'How many? How much?'
	IDENTITY	āt	'And who else?'
NONPREDICATIONAL			
LOCATIONAL			
	SPATIAL	ia	'Where?'
	TEMPORAL	ñāāt	'When?'
	RELATIONAL	teen	'What relation? What location?'
ESSENTIAL			
	NONHUMAN	ta	'What?'
	HUMAN	wōn	'Who?'
	FEMALE	let ~ lita	'Who (female)? (W ~ E)'
	MALE	ḷōt ~ ḷōta	'Who (male)? (W ~ E)'

The same is not true for direct objects of verbs, as the sentences in (4-33) are not accepted by all speakers, and are felt to be "too colloquial."

(4-33) a. ?*Kwaar lo **wōn**?
('Who did you see?')

b. ?*Kwaar roñ **ta**?
('What did you hear?')

The interrogative pronouns *wōn* 'who', *ta* 'what', and *ia* 'where' can also be used to question the possessors of nouns in constructions involving the construct suffix (3.2.6), as in (4-34). Here the interrogative appears after a noun that bears the suffix. The sentences are equational, with initial focused noun phrase predicates followed by demonstrative pronoun subjects.

(4-34) a. [Jokoṇa**n wōn**] [e]?
'Whose cane is this?'

b. [Nōōji**n ia**] [eṇ]?
'Where is that nurse from?'

c. [Bwii**n ta**] [in [ij āt]]?
'What's this odor I smell?'

A relational interrogative. The relational interrogative pronoun *teen* ends in the construct suffix *-n* (3.2.6) and inquires about the relation of the following noun to other entities. If another entity is specified in the question—*lieṇ* in (4-35a) and *Tọọṃ* in (4-35c)—the question is one of relation, usually kinship. If no entity is specified—as in (4-35e)—it becomes a question of location, in which some other entity must be specified in the answer—*tebōḷ* in (4-35f). The relation to that entity is the means of giving the location: 'It's on the table there'.

(4-35) a. [**Teen** [ḷadik eṇ]] [lieṇ]?
'What relation is that boy to that woman?'

b. Nājin.
'Her son. [Her child.]'

c. [**Teen** Ali] [Tọọṃ]?
'What relation is Ali to Tom?'

d. Jātin. [Jātin Ali] [Tọọṃ].
'Younger brother. Tom is Ali's younger brother.'

e. [**Teen** [eo [bok eo ej pād ie]]?
'Where is the book located?'

f. Epād ioon tebōḷ eṇ.
'It's on the table there.'

Instead of the construct suffix *-n* of *tee-n,* one can also use the possessive suffixes (3-5) that go with inalienable nouns such as *tee-* to form queries like (4-36a).[4] Also derived from the same basically interrogative root is the transitive verb *teek* found in (4-36b) together with the reciprocal *doon* 'each other'.

(4-36) a. [**Teeṃ**] [ḷeeṇ]?
'What relation is he to you?'

b. Rej **teek** doon Ali im Tọọṃ?
'How are Ali and Tom related to each other?'

Table 4-10 Determiners and their emphatic (!) forms

"PERSON"	CLOSE TO:	SINGULAR HUMAN & NONHUMAN		PLURAL NONHUMAN	HUMAN
1.INCL	'us both'	in	{yin}	kein	rein
1.EXCL	'me'	e	{yẹy}	kā	rā
1.EXCL !		iiō	{yiyyẹh}	kākā	rārā
2	'you'	ṇe	{ṇey}	kaṇe	raṇe
2 !		ṇeṇe	{ṇeyṇey}	kākaṇe	rāraṇe
3	'someone else'	eṇ	{yeṇ}	kaṇ	raṇ
3 !		iieṇ	{yiyyeṇ}	kākaṇ	rāraṇ
REMOTE	'the afore-	eo	{yew}	ko	ro
REMOTE !	mentioned'	iuweo	{yiwweyew}	koko	roro

DETERMINERS

4.3 The determiners (shown in table 4-10) are identical in form to the basic demonstrative pronouns, but they are found in different places within a

4. Alert readers may have noticed *teen* 'what relation?' listed as an inalienable *noun* in table 3-8, while in this section it is listed as an interrogative *pronoun.* This seeming contradiction is countered if one remembers that as one type of pro-form, pronouns can be viewed as less than fully specified nouns. *Teen* is noun-like in taking the possessive and construct suffixes, but pronoun-like in that *teen* in (4-35a) is a less-than-fully-specified *nājin* of (4-35b); similarly, *teen* in (4-35c) is a less-than-fully-specified *jātin* of (4-35d).

sentence. Pronouns do not appear as attributes of nouns; determiners do. A determiner normally follows the noun it modifies.

Examples given in (4-37) and (4-38) show the three determiners that may be considered definite articles (*eo, ro,* and *ko*) and the fact that in the plural *ro* is used with human nouns, *ko* with nonhuman. The determiners are all listed in table 4-10 on page 185.

(4-37)	a. ajri eo 'the child'	b. ajri ro 'the children'	c. *ajri ko
(4-38)	a. kidu eo 'the dog'	b. *kidu ro	c. kidu ko 'the dogs'

Determiners preceding nouns. Determiners may precede their nouns for emphasis, as the following examples show.

(4-39)	a. Ennọ wōt in juub.' 'This is such a delicious soup.'	<	Ennọ wōt juub in. 'This soup is delicious.'
	b. Etōr wōt ro armej. 'I never saw such gluttons.'	<	Etōr wōt armej ro.[5] 'Those people are gluttons.'
	c. Eḷap wōt ṇe wōt. 'That is indeed a large boil.'	<	Eḷap wōt wōt ṇe. 'That's a large boil'
	d. Eṃōkaj wōt kaṇ wa. 'Those are super fast boats.'	<	Eṃōkaj wōt wa kaṇ.[5] 'Those boats are fast.'

Determiners separated from their nouns. Adjectives and the PARTICULARIZER *jab* may intervene between a noun and its determiner, as shown in (4-40), but usually a determiner comes immediately after the noun.

(4-40) āne aiboojoj jab eṇ
'that beautiful islet over there'

Some nouns are changed in their form by a determiner immediately following. For example, the nouns *leddik* 'girl' and *ḷaddik* 'boy' are one mora shorter when a determiner follows, with their double *d* becoming single: *ḷadik ro im ledik ro* 'boys and girls'. Several alienable nouns fuse with the determiners. Two of these, *eṃ* 'house' and *āne* 'islet', are shown in table 4-11.

The paticularlizer *jab*. As can be seen in (4-40), *jab* is to be found following adjectives and preceding determiners. Additional examples are given in (4-41).

5. The verbs of the b. and d. sentences are impersonal (Class A) verbs, derived from adjectival verbs (Class 3), and *armej ro* and *wa kaṇ*, respectively, are their CORRESPONDENTS. (See the discussion of "Simple Class A verbs with correspondents [A2]" on page 236.) These two sentences could also have adjectival verbs, which would then be *Rōtōr* and *Rōṃōkaj*, with *rō-* as 3P subject marker to agree with the plural determiners of *armej ro* and *wa kaṇ,* their SUBJECTS. When the determiners are singular, as in a. and c., the verbs could be of either class.

(4-41) a. Ejāike wōd **jab** in.
'This particular coral head hasn't got many fish.'

b. Eḷḷaṇtōnana wāto **jab** in.
'This particular spread is grown over with lantana.'

c. Eḷap aō poub ilo raan **jab** kein.
'I am very busy these days.'

There is another *jab,* possibly related, but with different distribution and more clearly locative, to be found only preceding inalienable nouns for the three sectors into which islets are divided, from lagoon to ocean, *arin* 'lagoon side of', *eọọjin* 'interior of', and *likin* 'ocean side of', as in (4-42).

(4-42) a. Ekabokbok **jab** arin Lọto.
'Lọto Island's lagoon beach is sandy.'

b. Ekkaarar **jab** eọọjin ṃwiin.
'There are lots of *kaar* trees in the interior of this piece of land.'

c. Edekāke **jab** likin ānin.
'The ocean side of the island has lots of rocks.'

Finally, there is the generic *jabōn (jabwe)* 'end of, tip of' (see table 3-1) to be found in place names such as *Jabōn-bok* 'tip of the sandspit', a common name for land tracts.

Table 4-11 Demonstratives fused with *eṃ* 'house' and *āne* 'islet'

		eṃ 'house'		**āne** 'islet'	
"PERSON"	CLOSE TO:	SINGULAR	PLURAL	SINGULAR	PLURAL
1.INCL	'us both'	ṃwiin	ṃōkein	ānin	ānekein
1.EXCL	'me'	ṃwe	ṃōkā	āne	ānekā
1.EXCL !		ṃwiiō	ṃōkākā	āniiō	ānekākā
2	'you'	ṃōṇe	ṃōkaṇe	āṇṇe	ānekaṇe
2 !		ṃōṇeṇe	ṃōkākaṇe	āṇṇeṇe	ānekaṇeṇe
3	'someone else'	ṃweeṇ	ṃōkaṇ	āneṇ	ānekaṇ
3 !		ṃweiieṇ	ṃōkākaṇ	āniieṇ	ānekākaṇ
REMOTE	'the afore-	ṃweo	ṃōko	āneo	āneko
REMOTE !	mentioned'	ṃouweo	ṃōkoko	ānuweo	ānekoko

ADJECTIVES

4.4 Adjectives follow the nouns they modify. Most adjectives are derived from adjectival verbs. The verb forms from which the adjectives in (4-43) and (4-44) are derived are given in parentheses at the right. (Dialectal forms of adjectives are given in the order W / E.)

(4-43) a. juon kajjookok **ḷapḷap** (ḷap)
'a big scandal'

b. iien **eṃṃanṃōn / ṃōṃanṃōn** kein (ṃṃan)
'these good times'

c. raan toḷ **utiejej** eo (utiej)
'the high mountain top'

d. ṃōñā **ennọno / nenọno** ko (nnọ)
'the delicious foods'

(4-44) a. Waini **lōñlōñ** eo ekalāik wa eo. (lōñ)
'The great quantity of copra made the boat list.'

b. Tūṃ tok juon utū ilo ra **dikdik** ko. (dik)
'Pick me a flower from the small branches.'

c. [Kōḷanin ṃweiuk **ekkārere / kōkārere** ko] [ṇe]. (kāre)
'That's the column for the miscellaneous.'

d. [Armej **joujuj**] [e]. / [E] [armej **joujuj**]. (jouj)
'S/he's a kind person.'

All of the adjectives in the preceding examples involve final syllable reduplication. Some, like (4-44c) involve initial consonant doubling as well. Others, like *matōk* in (4-45b), involve no change in form. This is also true of verbs like *tutu* 'be wet' and *nana* 'be bad' (4-45c) that are already reduplicated in their basic form. Where the adjective differs in form from the verb, these are given as Code 11 in Abo et al. (1976), and as "stat. adj." in its on-line revision.

(4-45) a. Bao eṇ e**matok**.
'That chicken is fat.'

b. Ikōṇaan wiaik emān bao **matok**.
'I want to buy four fat chickens.'

c. Kwōn jab peejneje armej kōn waj **nana** kaṇe.
'Stop cheating people with those poor quality watches.'

Pro-adjective. As noted in fn. 4 on page 185, pronouns are less than fully specified nouns, and languages sometimes have pro-forms for other parts of speech. In Marshallese, *rot* can be considered a pro-adjective, a less than fully specified adjective that either refers to qualities of the preceding noun as being known by both speaker and hearer, or functions as an interrogative to inquire about them. *Rot* is typically found in a phrase between a noun and a determiner. Whether it refers to a known quality (4-46) or asks about it (4-47) depends on the structure of the sentence in which this phrase occurs.

(4-46) a. [**Ek rot eo** [eppejlọkḷọk]] [ṇe].
'This kind of fish is easy to pierce.'

b. [**Kāāj rot eo** [etare]] [ṇe].
'That's the kind of fishhook that hooks so neatly.'

c. Eḷḷijibjib **ṃade rot ṇe**.
'That kind of spear gets blunt easily.'

d. Emālkwōj **wūno rot eṇ** ñan kinej.
'That kind of medicine is powerful for wounds.'

e. Kappok **mā rot eṇ** ej jab bwijuwewe.
'Look for the kind of breadfruit tree that doesn't have lots of lumps.'

(4-47) a. **Ek rot eṇ** ej aujọjọ ijjuweo?
'What kind of fish is that stirring up the water over there?'

b. **Ṃōñā rot eṇ** kwokōṇaan ṃōñā?
'What kind of food do you like to eat?'

c. **Dān rot eo** kwaar kwaḷkoḷ kake?
'What kind of water did you use to wash with?'

d. [**Mọọr rot ṇe**] [mọọrōṃ]?
'What kind of bait do you have there?'

e. Eor ke aṃ **tuuḷ rot eṇ** ej dikḷọkḷapḷọk?
'Have you got an adjustable wrench?'

Examples (4-46a) and (4-46b) are equational sentences, as shown by their outer pairs of brackets. In each, the first noun phrase includes a relative clause—enclosed in the inner brackets—that further specifies the quality of the *rot* phrase, which becomes the assertion of the sentence. Example (4-47d) is also an equational sentence, but lacking any further specification of the quality of the *rot* phrase, inquires about it.

Sometimes the word *kain,* presumably a loan from English *kind,* is also used together with *rot,* preceding the noun of the *rot* phrase. It may be that the *-n* of *kain* is interpreted as the construct suffix, thereby making *kain bōnbōn* in (4-48a) a noun phrase that means 'kind of arithmetic'—fairly redundant with *bōnbōn rot*—and takes the place of the usual single noun in the *rot* phrase.

(4-48) a. Ña iruwamāejet kōn **kain bōnbon rot in**.
'I'm not familiar with this kind of arithmetic.'

b. Ejjọjọ **kain ek rot ṇe**.
'That kind of fish is always slipping into the sand.'

c. Ejeja **kain wōjke rot in**.
'This kind of tree is scarce.'

d. Kwōn jab wōjak **kain ṃanit rot ṇe**.
'Don't behave that way.'

Rot is also found in a different construction, without a following determiner, but with a following *ke* clause. The examples in (4-49) are assertions rather than questions. It is also possible to precede each of these four sentences with *kain* without changing its meaning appreciably, as shown in (4-49a).

(4-49) a. **Ek rot ke** ejauwi! ~ **Kain ek rot ke** ejauwi!
'What sort of fish is it that is so tasteless!'

b. **Jiṃaat rot ke** ejaje uwaake!
'What sort of smarts is it that can't answer another's question!'

c. **Kajoor rot ke** ejorrāān jāne!
'What sort of strength is it that is put down by another!'

d. **Ṃōṃaan rot ke** eokkworkwor!
'What kind of a man is one who gets scared so easily!'

Finally it should be noted that the expression *men rot kaṇ* (lit. those kinds of things) is used with the catch-all meaning 'you know what' (similar to *da kine* in Hawaiian Creole English) and may be substituted for by *met-torkaṇ,* in which *rot* has been metathesized, and *n* assimilated to *t* unexpectedly (see table 2-19).

PREPOSITIONAL PHRASES

4.5 In addition to determiners, adjectives, and the particularizer *jab,* prepositional phrases are among the attributive modifiers of a noun that follow it in a noun phrase. Example (4-50) shows their relative order.

(4-50)	kidu	kileplep	jab	eṇ	**i**	**turu-n**
	N	Adj	PRTC	Det	P	N
	dog	big	there	that	at	near-3s

'that big dog right there near her'

The last two elements constitute a prepositional phrase. Table 4-12 gives the prepositions of Marshallese. There are three pairs of prepositions that have the same forms, namely *jān, ñan,* and *kōn,* but have different distributions and different meanings. Those labeled "sub-one" deal with "inner relations" within the sentence, and their objects are closely associated with the subject of an intranstitive sentence or the object of a transitive sentence. Those labeled "sub-two" are "outer" by comparison and are more broadly associated with the entire clause or sentence, providing a framework within which to interpret it.[6] Their objects are considered to be CORRESPONDENTS rather than direct objects. Such prepositional phrases often have greater freedom of movement, and can occur at the beginning, to introduce the sentence.

(4-51) a. Ijaje ṃōñā **kōn$_1$ aji.**
'I don't know how to eat with chopsticks.'

b. **Kōn$_2$ an jeḷā būñūmpeḷtak,** ear jab jorrāān.
'Because of his knowing how to fall, he was not injured.'
'He is so nimble that he did not get hurt when he fell down.'

In (4-51a) the object of the preposition *kōn* is *aji* 'chopsticks', which are closely associated with 'I' (the subject of the intransitive verb *ṃōñā* 'eat').

6. We will continue to use the subnumbers 1 and 2 to distinguish these three homonymous pairs of prepositions throughout the remainder of this work. See the discussion of inner and outer CASE RELATIONS in 6.3, beginning on page 284.

The sentence is about "I and chopsticks," and the preposition is *kōn*$_1$, meaning 'with'. This prepositional phrase, *kōn*$_1$ *aji,* cannot be moved to the front of the sentence. In (4-51b), the object of the preposition *kōn* is *an jeḷā būñūmpeḷtak* 'his knowing how to fall', which provides the background for interpreting the main clause, *ear jab jorrāān* 'he was not injured'. Accordingly, the preposition is *kōn*$_2$, translated 'because of', and the prepositional phrase precedes the remainder of the sentence. It could just as well follow.

Table 4-12 Prepositions

DIRECTIONAL			
SOURCE	jān$_1$, jāne$_1$, jāni$_1$ [1]	'from'	
	jān$_2$, jāne$_2$, jāni$_2$	'than, because of'	
GOAL	ñan$_1$, ñane$_1$, ñani$_1$	'to'	
	ñan$_2$, ñane$_2$, ñani$_2$	'for, in behalf of'	
LOCATIONAL			
PUNCTUAL	i	'in, on, at'	
INTERIOR	ilo	'in, inside'	
SURFACE	ṇae	'against'	
NONSURFACE	ṃae, oom	'until'	
ASSOCIATIVE			
MEANS	kōn$_1$; kake$_1$ / eake$_1$; kaki$_1$ / eaki$_1$	'with'	(W / E)
CORRESPONDENT	kōn$_2$; kake$_2$ / eake$_2$; kaki$_2$ / eaki$_2$	'about, because of'	(W / E)

1. The prepositions *jān*$_1$, *ñan*$_1$, *kōn*$_1$ and *jān*$_2$, *ñan*$_2$, *kōn*$_2$ also have forms with *-e* and *-i* that are used in contexts where their objects are omitted, paralleling the anaphoric object markers of transitive verbs (see page 153). Examples are given in (4-52)–(4-54).

The prepositions of prepositional phrases that occur within noun phrases to modify their head nouns are of the inner type. Additional examples are given in (4-52) with their noun phrases enclosed in brackets and their prepositional phrases in boldface.

(4-52) a. Eṃṃan ke [tūrep eo aṃ **ñan$_1$ Amedka**]?
'Did you have a good trip to the States?'

b. Wōn eṇ enaaj ukukot ainikien ilo [tūrep in an **ñan$_1$ Ratak**]?
'Who will interpret for him at every place on his trip around the eastern chain?'

c. [Lōkkūk ro **jān$_1$ Ṃōn-kūbwe**] raṇe tok.
'Here come the female aristocrats from Ṃōn-kūbwe.'

d. [Kumi in al eo **jān$_1$ Ḷora**] ear lukkuun tūtileñeñ ilo jebta eo.
'The singing group from Laura was the most impressive at the song fest.'

e. Aolep [kumi eṇ **ilo kilaaj emān**] boea wōt.
'Class four has nothing but delinquents.'

Anaphoric forms of six prepositions. As shown in table 4-12, the prepositions *jān₁, ñan₁, kōn₁*, and *jān₂, ñan₂, kōn₂* have special forms ending in *-e* and *-i* that are used when no object follows but where one is understood, either from its earlier occurrence or from the broader context. These forms end in *-e* for singular objects and *-i* for plural objects. They parallel the anaphoric forms of transitive verbs (see page 153).

(4-53) a. Ej bōtōktōk **allōñ** ñe laḷ in ej pinej meramin aḷ **jāne$_1$**.
'An eclipse of the moon comes about when the earth blocks off the sunlight.'

b. **Ia** ṇe kwōj kōnnaan tok **jāne$_1$**?
'Where are you calling from?'

c. **Ia** ṇe kwōj kaṃṃweiukiuk **ñane$_1$**?
'Where are you packing your belongings to go to?'

d. Jen iaḷ aidik **jāne$_1$**.
'Let's go away from him one at a time.'

e. Kwōn amān **jāān** kaṇe aṃ bwe kwōnaaj mej **jāni$_1$**.
'Spend your money now because you can't take it with you.'

f. Ear iutūri ḷọk **ñane$_2$**.
'She made *iutūr* for him.'

In (4-53a), *jāne*$_1$ refers to *allōñ,* in (4-53b) it refers to *ia,* as does *ñane*$_1$ in (4-53c). But in (4-53d), the identity of the person referred to is determined by the wider context, as is true also for *ñane*$_2$ in (4-53f). In (4-53e), *jāni*$_1$ is plural because *jāān* is marked as plural by its plural determiner, *kaṇe.* Examples of *kake* and *kaki* are given in (4-54).

(4-54) a. Wā in **ta** eo raar wāik eok **kake$_1$**?
'What kind of shot did they give you?'

b. An wōn ṇe **ṃade** kwōj ṃadede **kake$_1$**?
'Whose spear are you using?'

c. Kwomaroñ ke letok **teeñki** ṇe aṃ bwe in ja romromḷọk **kake$_1$**?
'Can you give me your flashlight so that I can light my way with it?'

d. **Ta** ṇe kwōj ūjō **kake$_2$**?
'What are you grinning about?'

c. Jab inepata **kake$_2$** bwe ikōnālkinṃwio.
'Don't worry about him because he's not with it.'

Examples (4-54a)–(4-54c) are of *kake*$_1$, which refers to the MEANS used in the event described by the verb, while *kake*$_2$ in (4-54d) and (4-54e) refers to the cause or CORRESPONDENT (see page 235) of the event described by the verb.

Although the anaphoric forms of these prepositions *must* be used when the objects of the prepositions are absent from their expected place following the preposition, the same forms are sometimes also used when the objects are present—that is, not anaphorically.

(4-55) a. Ear jobai **kaki**$_1$ / **kōn**$_1$ ek ko koņan.
'He sold (traded with) the fish he caught.'

b. Jab inepata **kake**$_2$ / **kōn**$_2$ niñniñ eo.
'Don't worry about the baby.'

c. Eitok inne im jabneejej tok ñan ña **kōn**$_2$ aer jab kōjeļāik **kake**$_2$ keemem eo.
'She came yesterday and cried on my shoulder about their not letting her know about the birthday party.'

d. Jọọn eñak ta eo en ba **kōn**$_2$ an mejko **kake**$_2$ Jemej ke ear buñ.
'John didn't know what to say because of his embarassment for James when he fell.'

e. Kwōjab inojeik ļọk **jāni**$_1$ wa kein; iaļ in mour ko kein.
'Don't drift away from these canoes; they are your passes to life.'

The substitution of *kake* for *kōn* is more common than either *jāne* for *jān* or *ñane* for *ñan*. In fact, we have no valid examples of the last mentioned, and (4-55e) is the only example we have of *jān* being substituted for when an anaphoric form is not necessary. However, the fact that it is a common proverb gives this sort of substitution a certain historical validity.

The slashes between forms in (4-55a) and (4-55b) indicate that each of these sentences is acceptable with either form. Sentences (4-55c) and (4-55d) are of interest because each contains a prepositional phrase within a prepositional phrase, where what could be a sequence of *kōn*s is avoided by substituiting *kake* for the second instance.

POSSESSIVES

4.6 Alienable nouns are not possessed directly through suffixation, as inalienable nouns are (3.2.2). Instead, to express the possession of definite alienable nouns, Marshallese uses inalienable nouns as predicational modifiers.

(4-56) a. kuuj eo nāji-ṃ
cat DET child-2S
'your (pet) cat'

b. bao ko kije-er
bird DET food-3P
'their chickens (cooked and ready to eat)'

The possessed noun is at the head of the phrase, followed in turn by a determiner (which establishes it as definite) and the modifier (which specifies the possessor and the nature of the possessive relationship). The modifier is sometimes referred to as a possessive classifier, and we will continue this usage, but it should be remembered that it is not the possessed nouns that are being classified (as in languages where a given noun is always used with one and the same classifier). In Marshallese, a possessed noun may be used with different classifiers, depending on the nature of its relation to the possessor, and it is this relationship that is being classified.

Examples of different classifiers with one and the same noun help make the point that it is the nature of the possession that is signified by the choice of classifier.

(4-57)	a.	bao eo kijō	'my chicken (cooked and ready for eating)'
	b.	bao eo nājū	'my chicken (alive and being raised)'
	c.	bao eo aō	'my chicken (frozen shares being divided)'
	d.	bao eo koṇa	'the bird I caught'
	e.	bao eo jibū	'my pet bird' (lit. my grandchild)
	f.	jāān eo aō	'my coin'
	g.	jāān eo nājū	'my special coin' (lit. my child)

The usage in (4-57c) is not common, but one that could occur in a special modern-day situation in which a large package of frozen chicken is being divided equally among several individuals, so that it is really a share that is being referred to. It illustrates a sense in which {haha-} (*aō, aṃ, an, aer,* etc.) can be considered the default classifier, the one most neutral in its connotations, and also the one that serves heavy duty grammatically as the nominalizer of clauses (6.4.1). Although {naji-}(*nājū, nājiṃ, nājin, nājier*) 'child' may be used for pets and treasured possessions (in addition to its basic use for children), it is outranked by {jibi-} (*jibū, jibūṃ, jibūn, jibwier*) 'grandchild' in designating pet birds, as shown by examples (4-57b) and (4-57e). The latter classifier is special among kin terms in being used reciprocally between grandmothers and grandchildren—when a grandchild utters it, it means 'my grandmother'.

The inalienable nouns that serve most often as classifiers are listed in table 4-13. Some of them are among the inalienable nouns whose spelling is exemplified in tables 3-6 through 3-9. Table 4-13 gives spellings for singular possessors (1S 'my', 2S 'your', 3S 'his/her') and for third person plural possessors (3S, 'their') as well. (The spellings of 1P.I, 1P.E, and 2P possessors are omitted, but as can be seen from tables 3-6 through 3-9, they can be predicted from the spelling of 3S, as all four forms have suffixes that begin with light consonants.)

Most of the classifiers in the table are PROPERTIES—TANGIBILE OR ABSTRACT (one of the four types of inalienable nouns listed in tables 3-6 through 3-9), although several are BODY PARTS in their basic sense ('throat', 'chin', 'eye', 'tooth'), and two are KIN terms ('child', 'grandchild'). The SPATIAL OR TEMPORAL ADJUNCTS of table 3-6 are the one type not represented among the classifiers listed in table 4-13.

Table 4-13 Some classifiers of alienable noun possessive relationships

	STEM	1S	2S	3S	3P
GENERAL (DEFAULT)	{haha-}	aō	aṃ	an	aer
THROAT; FAVORITE	{biriwe-}	būruō	būruōṃ	būruōn	būrueer
PANDANUS	{daha-}	daō	daaṃ	daan	daer
EAR ORNAMENT	{diye-}	diō	dieṃ	dien	dieer
NAME	{yata-}	eta	etaṃ	etan	etāer
HOUSE, SHELTER; LAND	{yiṃe-}	iṃō	iṃōṃ	iṃōn	iṃweer
SAUCE	{jaleye-}	jāleō	jāleeṃ	jāleen	jāleer
GRANDCHILD; PET	{jibi-}	jibū	jibūṃ	jibwin	jibwier
PLACE	{jiki-}	jikū	jikūṃ	jikin	jikier
CHIN; CLOSE ADVISER	{jiṃin ñii-}	jimwin ñiū	jimwin ñiiṃ	jimwin ñiin	jimwin ñiier
OINTMENT	{kapite-}	kapitō	kapitōṃ	kapitōn	kapiteer
FOOD	{kije-}	kijō	kijōṃ	kijen	kijeer
SLEEPING GEAR	{kiniye-}	kiniō	innieṃ	kinien	kinieer
CATCH	{kʷeṇa-}	koṇa	koṇaṃ	koṇan	koṇāer
DUTY, CONTRIBUTION	{kʷeṇaha-}	konaō	koṇaaṃ	koṇaan	koṇaer
BOUNDARY (BETWEEN [PL])	{ketaha-}	kōtaō	kōtaaṃ	kōtaan	kōtaer
PLANT	{ketka-}	kōtka	kōtkaṃ	kōtkan	kōtkāer
TRASH	{kupij-}	kupijū	kupijūṃ	kupijin	kupijier
BEVERAGE	{lime-}	limō	liṃōṃ	limen	limeer
BAIT	{maware-}	mọọrō	mọọrōṃ	mọọrōn	mọọreer
EYE; SEEING AID	{maja-}	meja	mejaṃ	mejān	mejāer
OLD, WORN OUT ITEM	{ṃerʷi-}	ṃorū	ṃoruṃ	ṃorun	ṃorwier
FISH BASKET	{ṃara-}	ṃōra	ṃōraṃ	ṃōran	ṃōrāer
NECK ORNAMENT	{ṃare-}	ṃarō	ṃarōṃ	ṃarōn	ṃareer
CHILD, FAVORITE	{naji-, nẹji-}	nājū	nājiṃ	nājin	nājier
TOOTH; EATING AID	{giyi-}	ñiū	ñiiṃ	ñiin	ñiier
BATHING WATER	{wite-}	utō	utōṃ	utōn	uteer
FLOWER	{witi-}	utū	utūṃ	utin	utier
CANOE, VEHICLE	{waha-}	waō	waaṃ	waan	waer
PERSONAL TOOLS, SKILLS	{weja-}	wōja	wōjaṃ	wōjān	wōjāer

Where do classifiers come from? The classifiers are not a closed set of words. Many inalienable nouns are potentially classifiers, because most, if not all,[7] can immediately follow alienable nouns to modify them (with the determiner of the first noun standing in between). Although only two of the classifiers listed in table 4-13 are kinship terms ({naji-, nẹji-} 'child; favorite' and {jibi-} 'grandchild; pet'), the examples in (4-58) show that other kin terms could potentially be included. (The noun phrases with possessive modifiers are in square brackets, and the inalienable nouns are in boldface.)

(4-58) a. Eṃōj an [ḷōḷḷap eo **jiṃṃaō**] kaamṇak eō kōn ijo jikin.
'My grandfather gave me his land.'

b. Jemān ear kaliaik [ḷadik eo **nejin**].
'The father disinherited his son from his land.'

7. The one exception may be the SPATIAL OR TEMPORAL ADJUNCTS of table 3-6.

c. Ear jelpaake [ledik eo **jeran**].
'He put his arm around his girlfriend's waist.'

d. Iar kọbōke [likao eo **rilikū**].
'I wrestled with my cousin.'

e. An bōd eo ak ear ṇaruon [likao eo **jatin**].
'It was his fault but he blamed his brother.'

What is necessary for inalienable nouns like those in boldface to be considered classifiers is that they should be able to stand in this same modifying relationship with a variety of inalienable nouns. For *jiṃṃaō* 'grandfather' in (4-58a), there do not seem to be many possibilities other than *ḷōḷḷap* 'old man' or the male generic *ḷeo*. A bit of variety is possible for the other four words in bold, as they can apply to either males or females—*jati-* 'younger sibling'(4-58e) (and *jei-* 'older sibling'), *riliki-* 'cross-cousin'(4-58d), *nāji-/neji-* 'child'(4-58b)—and various head nouns that serve to specify the gender and give other details about these particular kin. A few of the possibilities are exemplified in (4-59):

(4-59)	a.	ledik eo nejin	'his daughter (a girl)'
	b.	jiroñ eo nejin	'his daughter (adolescent and unmarried)'
	c.	kōrā eo nejin	'his daughter (a woman)'
	d.	likao eo nejin	'his son (a young man)'

The kin term {nik^{w}i-} 'relative' seems an even better candidate for classifier status because of its even greater generality. The examples in (4-60) could be multiplied many times over. These particular examples (all from Abo et al. 1976) happen to have *nukun* modifying demonstrative pronouns, which are already definite, so that a separate determiner is not needed.

(4-60) a. Ej jep ippān [ḷōṃaraṇ **nukun**].
'He's taking his relatives' side.'

b. Ej kōbajaik [ḷeeṇ **nukun**].
'He's making his relative the purser.'

c. Ejeḷā kuṇaan ñan [raṇ **nukun**].
'He takes care of his responsibilities toward his relatives.'

Body parts as classifiers. Four of the classifiers in table 4-13 are body parts. The term for 'throat' (seat of the emotions in Marshallese, much as 'heart' is in English) is extended to include FAVORITES. The terms for 'tooth' and 'eye' are extended as EATING AIDS and SEEING AIDS, respectively. 'Chin' is used for CLOSE ADVISERS, especially to chiefs.

(4-61)	a.	bok eo būruō	'my favorite book'
	b.	armej eo būruō	'my favorite person'
	c.	bōkā eo būruō	'my favorite tide (for fishing)'
	d.	pileej eo ñiū	'my plate'
	e.	jibuun bọọk eo ñiū	'my spoon'
	f.	aji ko ñiū	'my chopsticks'
	g.	mejān det eo meja	'my sunglasses'

h. mejān riit eo meja 'my reading glasses'
i. ļeo jiṃwin ñiū 'my close adviser'

Other seeing aids such as *baikilaaj* 'telescope, binoculars' are usually possessed using the general classifier *aō* 'my', and there is a tendency nowadays to replace *meja* with *aō* for sunglasses and reading glasses as well. Example (4-62) shows this general classifier also being used for an indefinite EATING AID (*ad* '1.P.INCL' + *ro* 'dual' > *arro*) instead of *ñiiro*:

(4-62) Jebjeb tok ṃōk arro bọọk.
'Could you grab me a fork?' (lit. a fork for the two of us)

Miscellaneous classifiers. Several other classifiers deserve mention, especially some that have not always been recognized as such. One is {weja-} 'personal tool, skill, style'. See the examples in (4-63). Additional tools for which it is used include *teeñki* 'flashlight', *kampiutōr* 'computer, *būrintōr* 'printer', *teeprūkotōr* 'tape recorder', *kein jaļjaļ* 'wrench', *kein turoñ* 'diving gear', *mejin in keke* 'portable sewing machine', and for containers such as *tuuļbọọk* 'toolbox', *ainbat* 'iron pot', and *tōptōp* 'foot locker'.

(4-63) a. Ikōṇaan ap jab ṇe wōjaṃ.
'I like your method.'

b. Imaroñ ke kōjerbal pilerab eo wōjaṃ?
'May I borrow your blowtorch?'

c. Ennọ kōmattin jijidiiñ e wōja.
'My broiler cooks real well.'

Except for the more abstract skills or styles, such as in (4-63a), IMPORTED MANUFACTURED ITEMS might be a more general name for the class. However, two seemingly similar items for which it is not used, and for which {naji-, nẹji-} 'child; favorite' is used instead are *retio* 'radio' and *waj* 'watch'. Yet even here there is evidence that the most general classifier, {haha-} *aō, aṃ, an, aer* is sometimes used instead, as in (4-64).

(4-64) a. Ejjorrāānān [waj eṇ **nājin**].
'His watch is always broken.'

b. Ejorrāāṇ anōļin [waj e **aō**].
'The dial of my watch is broken.'

c. Ijook kōn [waj e **aō**] bwe ļam waan bajjek.
'I'm ashamed of my watch, for it is of poor quality.'

Finally, we list here below several additional groups.

Worn-out things, and trash:

(4-65) a. juuj ko ṃorū 'my worn out shoes'
b. jodi kaṇ ṃorin 'his/her old zories'
c. men ko kupijū 'my things for the trash pick-up'

d. diin ek kā kupijū 'these fish bones of mine'
e. bween ṃōñā kaṇ kupijin 'his/her food scraps'

Fruits of one's labors; contributions to a community effort:

(4-66) a. ni ko eddebin 'the coconuts that he husked (W)'
b. waini kein dedebū 'the copra that I husked (E)'
c. ek kā koṇa 'these fish that I caught'
d. wōr kaṇ koṇan 'the lobsters he caught'
e. ni eo kōtkan 'the coconut tree he planted'
f. mā eo kōtkan 'his/her breadfruit tree'
g. jerbal eo koṇaan 'the work that is/was his/her duty'
h. ṃaak ko koṇaō 'the money for my contribution'

Shelters and the land on which they are built:

(4-67) a. Ejaam marok [ṃwiin **iṃōṃ**]?
'Why is your house still dark?'

b. Ḷañ eo erupe [peḷak eo **iṃweer**].
'The storm destroyed their hut.'

c. [Ajjuur eo **iṃōrro**] e.
'Here is our hut.'

d. [Wāto eṇ [etan Bōdao]][**iṃōn** [Capelle raṇ]] .
'The Bōdao land tract belongs to the Capelles.'

In (4-67a), substituting for the alienable noun *eṃ* 'house' followed by the determiner *in* 'this close to us both' is the fused form *ṃwiin* (table 4-11). Example (4-67d) is more complex grammatically than the preceding examples, but shows that the classifier {iṃe-} *iṃō, iṃōṃ, iṃōn, iṃweer* includes words such as *wāto* 'land tract'. In it, the phrase *etan Bōdao* 'whose name is Bōdao' is a relative clause, a type of modifier of nouns to be discussed later in this chapter (4.8), and the *-n* of *iṃōn* is actually the construct suffix (see page 135), giving 'house of those Capelles', but the possessive relation of this sentence could be distilled into the noun phrase *wāto eṇ iṃweer* 'that land tract of theirs', paralleling the definite construction we have been focusing on.

Indefinite possessives. With the exception of (4-62), the possessive constructions in this section up until this point have been DEFINITE noun phrases, referring to people or objects that are known to both the speaker and those spoken to. The words that make them definite are either demonstratives (4.2.2), all of which are inherently definite, or determiners (4.3) that serve to mark their nouns as definite. Remove the determiners and switch the order of the two nouns, so that the possessive classifier becomes the head, and we have INDEFINITE noun phrases.

(4-68) a. eddebin ni 'a coconut/some coconuts he husked (W)'
b. dedebū waini 'a copra nut/some copra I husked (E)'
c. koṇa ek 'a fish/some fish I caught'
d. koṇan or 'a lobster/some lobsters he caught'

e. koņaan jerbal '(some) work that is/was his/her duty'
f. koņaō ṃaak '(some) money for my contribution'

Notice the changes in the English translations between (4-66) and (4-68), where words like "the" and "these" (which are definite markers) have been removed, and that words like "a" and "some" (markers of the indefinite) appear in their stead. More literal translations could have two English noun phrases in apposition; (4-68c) *koņa ek,* for example, would be:

'my catch, a fish' or 'my catch, some fish'
$[\ [\text{my catch}]_{NP}\ [\text{a fish/some fish}]_{NP}\ ]_{NP}$

A good sentence frame for identifying indefinite noun phrases of this sort is to precede them with the existential verb *eor* 'there exists (3S)' (see 5.6.1 on page 239 for further discussion of existential verbs):

(4-69) Eor koņa ek. 'I caught some/a fish.' (lit. there exists my catch of fish)

Summary of possessives. Alienable nouns are possessed by being in the same noun phrase with an inalienable noun that has a possessive suffix. The two nouns are said to be in apposition.[8] A noun phrase of this sort is definite if it also contains a determiner (or a demonstrative); without such a definite marker, it is indefinite. The nature of the possessive relation between these two nouns depends on the inalienable noun that bears the possessive suffix. Such nouns can be said to classify the various possible possessive relationships, and have, therefore, sometimes been called classifiers. There is a tendency in Marshallese today to replace some of the lesser-used classifiers with the most general classifier {haha-} (*aō, aṃ, an, ad, am, ami, aer*).

QUANTIFIERS

4.7 Quantifiers are among the modifiers that may follow the head noun and its determiner in a definite noun phrase. But they precede a possessive modifier when there is one. Taking as an example sentence (4-67b) from the previous section on possessives, and repeating it here as (4-70a), we can note the changes that occur when 'hut' is pluralized and quantified with the numeral *ruo* 'two'. The numeral appears after the noun *peļak* and its determiner *ko,* but before the possessive *iṃweer.*

8. "Apposition" refers to an equational relation. "Ek eo koņa" can be an equational sentence 'I caught the fish; the fish is my catch' or it can be a noun phrase 'the fish I caught'. In either case, it consists of two noun phrases juxtaposed (in apposition), literally 'the fish, my catch'.

(4-70) a. Ḷañ eo erupe [peḷak eo iṃweer].
'The storm destroyed their hut.'

b. Ḷañ eo erup**i** [peḷak **ko ruo** iṃweer].
'The storm destroyed their two huts.'

In these two sentences *peḷak* is definite, as it is followed by a determiner. If, instead, *peḷak* is indefinite, as it is in (4-71), we find that the numeral quantifier again precedes the possessive. (Interestingly, a common way to produce an indefinite in the singular is to use a quantifier, the numeral *juon* 'one'):

(4-71) a. Raar kalōktok [**juon** iṃō peḷak].
'They built me a hut.'

b. Raar kalōk [**ruo** iṃweer peḷak], juon i Rita im juon i Ulika.
'They built themselves two huts, one at Rita and the other at Ulika.'

Comparing the noun phrases in square brackets in (4-70b) and (4-71b), we can conclude that the QUANTIFIER and the POSSESSIVE remain in the same order, whether the noun is definite or indefinite. When definite, *peḷak* stands at the head of the phrase followed by its determiner; when indefinite, it goes without a determiner to "the tail"—to the far side of those two entities that are tied together in a constant order, the quantifier and the possessive. *Ruo* has become the head of the phrase, and it is as if we were saying "They built two (entities), (which were) their shelters, (which were) huts." *Ruo* and the other numerals and quantifiers, which, thus, have the ability to stand at the head of a noun phrase, are considered nouns in Marshallese. There are only a handful of quantifiers other than the numerals, and most of them, like the numerals, are typically indefinite.

(4-72)	aolep	'all'		jet	'some'
	wōj	'many, all'		jejjo	'few'
	jidik	'a little'			

The Marshallese equivalents of certain other quantifiers in English are not nouns, but verbs. These include *jeja* 'few' and *lōñ* 'many'. They may take subject prefixes and appear in syntactic positions defined for verbs, as in (4-73).

(4-73)	E-lōñ	alen-in	bok	ṇe.
	3s-many	page-of	book	that

'That book has many pages.'

Aolep. Examples of *aolep* are given in (4-74). In (4-74d–g) *aolep* heads a phrase (shown in square brackets) in which a noun modifier follows. Examples (4-74g–h) are instances of *aolep* followed by *im,* a construction that is not well understood, but see the discussion of (6-15) on page 277.

(4-74) a. Kwōn kajjouklo̧k mā kaņe ñan$_2$ **aolep**.
'Divide up those breadfruit among everyone.'
'Give everyone a breadfruit.'

b. **Aolep** kajjo mā.
'Each person take a breadfruit.'

c. **Aolep** ej kajjojo lo̧k wōt mā.
'Everybody has a breadfruit.'

d. Eor roro ñan$_2$ [**aolep** kain jerbal].
'There is a chant for any type of work.'

e. Rej ejjālele [**aolep** iien].
'They always eat sauce with their food.'

f. [**Aolep** jurōn m̧wiin] [kōm̧m̧an jān mā].
'All of this house's pillars are made of breadfruit timber.'

g. [**Aolep** ni jekaro kaņ] **im** jejekapenpen (ejjekapenpen).
'The bottles on all those coconut trees being tapped for sap are all less than half full.'

h. **Aolep im** ko jāne bwe ewūdeakeak.
'Everyone ran away from him because he went berserk.'

Wōj. Examples of the quantifier *wōj* are given in (4-75). It seems to be closely related to the MULTIPLE element found in compound plural pronouns (see tables 4-2 and 4-3) such as *kōmwōj* 'we all EXCL' shown (4-75e).

(4-75) a. [Bwijin in armej ro **wōj**] [rā tok].
'Here come several groups of people.'

b. [Ļadik eo] [eņ ibwiljin armej raņ **wōj**].
'The boy is in the midst of all those people.'

c. Bao eo ear loe lep eo lipen ibuļōn lep ko **wōj** ijo.
'The bird found its own egg among the many eggs there.'

d. Kwōn peljoļo̧k ippāer **wōj**.
'Go mix in with all of them.'

e. Kōm**wōj** dekaklo̧k ke kōm roñ an jiñ.
'We all burst into laughter when we heard him break wind.'

Jidik. Examples of *jidik* as quantifier are given in (4-76). Examples of *jidik* as adverb are found in (5-13). It is not clear whether *jidik* in combination with *wōt* (which is generally an adverb), as in the *wōt jidik* of (4-76d–f), should be considered a quantifier or an adverb. We include it here as a quantifier partly because it can be replaced by other quantifiers in the *m̧ōttan wōt* construction, shown in (4-76d), in expressions such as *M̧ōttan wōt juon* 'Just one more' and *M̧ōttan wōt ļalem minit* 'Just five minutes more'.

(4-76) a. Ejjeļo̧k kalijeklo̧k ippān ñan$_1$ **jidik**.
'He has no inclination to bias whatsoever (not even a little).'

b. Jennōbe tok m̧ōk [**jidik** kijō iu].
'Make some *jennōb* for me.'

c. Kwōmaroñ ke ḷatōḷe tok [**jidik** liṃō aebōj]?
'Could you pour me some water with the ladle?'

d. Ṃōttan **wōt jidik** ebar ibeb tok.
'A series of waves will be coming soon (in just a little bit).'

e. Erro baj jibwe doon **wōt jidik**.
'They almost clashed.'

f. Likatōttōt wōt bwe enañin iien ṃupi **wōt jidik**.
'Be patient and stay where you are because it's almost time for the movie.'

Jejjo. Examples of *jejjo* are given in (4-77). It would seem to be related to the numeral *juon* 'one' and its distributive *kajjojo* (see fn. 9 on page 204); *jejjo* has its own distributive, shown in (4-77b).

(4-77) a. **Jejjo** wōt armej ilo āneṇ.
'There are only a few people on that islet.'

b. Eor **jejjojo** ri-Ṃajeḷ Awai.
'There are Marshallese scattered throughout Hawai'i.'

c. An **jejjo** wōt jaṃkat.
'Not very many people can side-kick.'

d. An **jejjo** wōt ṃaanpā.
'The arts of self-defense are known by but a few.'

Definite quantifiers. Two definite quantifiers have been identified (Pagotto 1987:110), and they are homonyms of two of the indefinite quantifiers, *juon* 'one' and *jet* 'some'. While the two are indefinite and have their usual glosses in (4-78), in (4-79) they are definite, and as such, have quite different meanings, both glossed as 'other'.

(4-78)	a. **juon** bok	'a book; one book'
	b. **jet** rūttariṇae	'some soldiers'
(4-79)	a. bok eo **juon**	'the other book'
	b. rūttariṇae ro **jet**	'the other soldiers'

The two juon*s in sharp contrast.* There are two constructions with *āin* 'likeness' that show *juon* in its 'other, different' sense, in sharp contrast with *juon* in its 'unity' sense. In the first two examples of (4-80), *juon* follows *āin* immediately, just as it does *bok eo* in (4-80a), and we get the 'something else' reading, as in 'He's something else' or 'He's one of a kind'. In the last two examples of (4-80), the *āin* phrase is closed by the adverb *wōt* 'only' (see page 215), and *juon* stands alone in the second phrase, asserting the unity of the first. The presence or absence of *wōt* is crucial to the difference.

(4-80) a. [Āin **juon**] jān$_1$ e.
'He's different from him.'

b. [Āin **juon**] aerro ḷōmṇak jān$_1$ doon.
'Those two have differing opinions.'

c. [Āin ḷadik raṇe **wōt**] [**juon**].
'Those two boys are identical.'

d. [Āin**wōt**] [**juon**] ñe kwōj jab etal.
'It's all right if you don't go.'

Definite juon *as sentence opener.* Many statements begin with *juon* followed by a determiner. Quite often the two form an equational sentence.

(4-81) a. [Juon **eo**] [koṇa ajorṃaan].
'I hooked an exceptionally large fish.'

b. [Juon **eo**] [kōrā eor nājin bo].
'The lady has twins.'

c. [Juon **eṇ**] [lowaṇwoṇ].
'There's a busy woman.'

d. [Juon **e**] [kain annor koban jeḷā].
'This is a special kind of knot you'll never learn.'

e. [Juon **e**] [bwijin in ṃọle iar].
'Here's a school of rabbitfish at the lagoon beach.'

f. [Juon **in**] [ear leinjin in wūdkabbweiki].
'Some jerk must have operated this motor (and messed it up).'

The numerals. Table 4-14 gives a basis for determining the common cardinal numerals. Eleven is *joñoul-juon* and 101 is *jibukwi-juon.* The ordinal numerals are formed from the cardinals by putting each in the frame *kein ka___*, as in *kein kajuon* 'first' (lit. thing for making one), *kein karuo* 'second', *kein kajilu* 'third', and so on.

Other numerals. Several archaic numerals are listed in Abo et al. (1976), such as *limakor* 'fifty pairs, fish or copra' and *limadep* 'five thousand', but special methods for counting fish or copra, and other numbers for large quantities are no longer in use or generally known today. The historical picture for Marshallese and sister Micronesian languages is presented by Harrison and Jackson (1983), and Tobin (2002:389) includes a brief report from a resource person at Majuro in 1973 on "The old Marshallese method of counting."

Table 4-14 Cardinal numerals

	UNITS		TENS		HUNDREDS
'1'	juon	'10'	joñoul	'100'	jibukwi
'2'	ruo	'20'	roñoul	'200'	rūbukwi
'3'	jilu	'30'	jilñuul	'300'	jilubukwi
'4'	emān	'40'	eñoul	'400'	eabukwi
'5'	ḷalem	'50'	lemñoul	'500'	limabukwi
'6'	jiljino	'60'	jiljinoñoul	'600'	jiljinobukwi
'7'	jiljilimjuon	'70'	jiljilimjuonñoul	'700'	jiljilimjuonbukwi
'8'	ralitōk	'80'	ralitōññoul	'800'	ralitōkbukwi
'9'	ruatimjuon	'90'	ruatimjuonñoul	'900'	ruatimjuonbukwi
				'1000'	juon taujin

Distributive verbs from numerals. While discussing numerals, distributive verbs derived from numerals should be mentioned. (See "Distributive verbs" on page 162 and "Denominal distributive verbs" on page 165.) As can be seen from (4-83), they are formed by doubling the initial consonant and adding the causative prefix *ka-,* lit. make ones, make twos, and so on.[9]

(4-82)	juon	kajjojo	'one each; each; take turns'
	ruo	karruo	'two each'
	jilu	kajjillu	'three each'
	ḷalem	kōḷallem	'five each'
	joñoul	kajjoñoul	'ten each'
	roñoul	karroñoul	'twenty each'
	jilñuul	kajjilñuul	'thirty each'
	jibukwi	kajjibkwi	'one hundred each'

The most ubiquitous numeral distributive is *kajjojo*; (4-83) gives some examples of its use. Examples of some of the others are given in (4-84).

(4-83) a. Rej **kajjojo** etal.
'They're going one at a time.'

b. Aolep ej **kajjojo** ḷọk wōt mā.
'Everybody has a breadfruit.'

c. Kōjro **kajjojo** tūraip.
'Let's take turns driving.'

d. Bwilijmāāṇ ro rej **kajjojo** waj.
'The police take turns standing guard.'

(4-84) a. Erro ej **karruo** kijeerro pāākin raij ñan$_2$ piiḷtūreep eo ilju.
'They are both getting two bags of rice each to take on the field trip ship tomorrow.'

b. Eṃṃanḷọk **kajjillu** jorṃōta jān$_2$ **karruo** kōnke jilu raan aetokan tūreep in.
'It is advisable to take along three pairs of underwear rather than two, as this is a three-day trip.'

c. Kwaar **kōḷḷalem** ḷọk ke kijen ḷadik raṇ petkōj?
'Did you give five biscuits each to the boys?'

d. Ibaab enaaj kar **kōḷḷalem** tok arro taḷa.
'I thought he would give each of us five bucks.'

e. Raar **kōḷḷaleme** ḷọk ñan maat in.
'They kept taking five at a time from it until it disappeared.'

f. Jar ro rōkijoñ **karroñoul** raṇe.
'They are famous for taking twenty each haul.'

g. En bōjrak aṃ **karroñoulul**.
'Refrain from taking twenty every time'

9. *Kajjojo* is formed irregularly by dropping the *-n* of *juon,* followed by the majority change that created the fourth vowel *{jẹw < jiwe-}* (see 2.5.3) and reduplication of the resultant syllable *[jẹw > jẹwjẹw}*—in addition to the regular doubling of its initial *j*.

RELATIVE CLAUSES

4.8 Relative clauses are among the material that may be included in a noun phrase to modify the head noun. It is possible to consider possessives (4.6) and quantifiers (4.7) as being relative clauses of a verbless, equational variety, as does Sohn (1973). However, in this section we will consider as relative clauses those that are verbal sentences embedded in the domain of an antecedent head noun, and those that are verbless but give information other than that on possession or quantity.

These clauses (1) follow the antecedent noun that they modify, and (2) they often contain some anaphoric element that refers back to the antecedent noun, unless that noun is temporal. If the antecedent noun is temporal, there is divided usage; some speakers do not include an anaphoric element, and some do—see (4-85e) below, where the antecedent is *raan* 'day', a temporal noun. In the examples that follow, the noun phrase and the relative clause within it are both enclosed in square brackets, the antecedent noun is underlined, and the anaphoric element is in boldface:

(4-85) a. [Jōōt e aō [**e**tutu]] ekapiọuk eō.
'This wet shirt of mine makes me chilly.'

b. Kwōn kab piiḷi eō kōn$_2$ [ṃweiuk kā [ij kaduoji**i**]].
'Bill me later for the goods I'm taking out.'

c. Iar lo [ḷadik eo [kwaar leḷọk bok eo ñan**e**$_1$]].
'I saw the boy you gave the book to.'

d. Imeḷọkḷọk bok eo aō ṇa [ijo [jaar kakkije **ie**]].
'I forgot my book there where we rested.'

e. Jọọn ej keememeje [raan eo [ear ilọk jān$_1$ jikin (**ie**)]].
'John remembers the day when he left home.'

f. [Juon kōrā [eta**n** Likaboj]] ear peḷọk ñan$_1$ Iaab.
'A woman whose name was Likaboj drifted to Yap.'

In (4-85a) the *e-* of *etutu* is the anaphoric element that refers back to the antecedent noun *jōōt.* In (4-85b) the *-i* of *kaduoji* refers back to *ṃweiuk.* In (4-85c) the *-e* of *ñane*$_1$ refers back to *ḷadik*; in (4-85d) *ie* refers back to *ijo*; in (4-85e) *ie* (for those speakers who use it) refers back to *raan* (a temporal noun for which usage is divided), and in (4-85f) the *-n* of *etan* refers back to the antecedent noun *kōrā* in a clause that is verbless.

A relative marker. Relative clauses may be introduced by *me*:

(4-86) a. E [juon armej eo **me** [eḷap a**n** jouj]]. [cf. (4-44d)]
'S/he is a person who is very kind.'

b. Ear kañi [mā ko [**me kij**ō]].
'S/he ate those breadfruit of mine.'

c. Ek jọọḷ kab ek ṃōṇakṇak ekkā wōt aer kōṃṃan ilo [aelōñ ko ilikin [**me re**ike ak ejjeḷọk armej in amāni]]. 'Salted and dried fish are rarely made on the outer islands, which have lots of fish but few people to consume them.'[10]

d. Iaar lo [leo [**me** kwaar ire ippā**n**]]. 'I saw the guy you fought with.'

e. Kab lale [jāān ṇe [**me** ij jilkin(**i**) waj ippān ḷōṇe waj]]. 'Make sure you get the money I am sending with him.'

f. Ennọ [iiōk eo [**me** kwaar katakin(**i**) eō raan eo ḷọk]]. 'The recipe you shared with me back then is delicious.'

g. Men [ta ṇe [**me** itulōñ]]? 'What's that at the top?'

h. [Ø [**Me** kwaar letok]]. 'That which you gave me.'

Me is optional in most of these sentences, and can be omitted without altering their meaning appreciably. The anaphoric *-i* on the verbs in the relative clauses of (4-86e) and (4-86f), referring back to *jāān* and *iiōk,* respectively, is also optional (as shown by its being in parentheses). Thus, these are two sentences in which no anaphoric element need be present, even though neither of the antecedent nouns (*jāān* or *iiōk*) is temporal.

Example (4-86g) also has no anaphoric element in its clause, and omits mention of what it is the top of that is being referred to. This must be something in the immediate context that is already clear to speaker and hearer. They could be referring to a list that has just been presented, for example.

When *me* is omitted from sentences in which it is preceded by a noun and its determiner, the determiner must remain if the resulting sentence is also to be acceptable and not appreciaby different in meaning. The determiner is responsible for the antecedent noun being definite. That *armej* is not definite in (4-86a) and that *eo* is not its determiner is shown by the fact that *eo* may be omitted along with *me* without changing the meaning appreciably. This is the demonstrative *eo,* which when present introduces an intermediate level of analysis: [[juon armej][eo **me** [eḷap a**n** jouj]]].

Example (4-86h) is extraordinary in having a zero antecedent, and might be the answer to a question such as *Peen ta eo kwaar jaini jāāk ko kake*$_1$*?* 'What pen did you sign the checks with?' It could also be a question, asking 'Are you referring to the one you gave me?'

---

10. From Bender (1969:299). *Ilikin* here functions as a prepositional phrase that has the preposition *i* incorporated with its object (see 3.2.7). Note that *ilikin* follows the determiner *ko* and precedes the relative clause introduced by *me.* If *ilikin* were an adjective, it would come immediately after the head noun *aelōñ* and precede the determiner *ko.*

Sohn (1973) refers to *me* and its counterparts in sister Micronesian languages as relative markers. He concludes that because they can be omitted without being missed, and because they do not change their shape in reference to what precedes or follows, their only remaining function is to conjoin the two—to serve as "conjunctions" of antecedents and modifying clauses. For Marshallese *me,* this raises the question as to its relation to the conjunction *im/em,* something we will not pursue here.[11]

SUMMARY

4.9 This concludes our examination of noun phrases, which always begin with a head noun that may be followed by modifiers of various sorts. We turn now in chapter 5 to the other major part of speech, verbs, and those elements that are satellite to them.

11. *Im* (and its variant *em*) 'and' are alternants of the relative marker *me,* and may generally be substituted for it. Phonemically, *em* {yem} and *me* {mey} involve a type of metathesis not uncommon in Marshallese, in which the initial and final consonants of one-syllable words are switched. Other examples include *eb* ~ *bwe* {yeb ~ bey} for the homonymous complementizers bwe_1 'so that' and bwe_2 'because' (see table 5-5 on page 232), and *rot* ~ *tor* {r^{w}et ~ ter^w} for the pro-adjective *rot* (see page 189).

5 Verbs and Their Modifiers

INTRODUCTION

5.1 Verbs are introduced in chapter 3, where the emphasis is on word forms, how they may differ from each other by adding prefixes or suffixes, or by doubling a consonant or a syllable. We have seen that the first verb in a sentence is the one that bears a subject prefix (table 3-10) as the finite verb of the sentence (or clause). Other nonfinite verbs may follow, either helping verbs (if the first verb is a helping verb) or other verbs. Some of the other major types of verbs previewed in chapter 3 include transitive verbs and their intransitive counterparts (3.3.2), adjectival verbs (table 3-13), and causative verbs (tables 3-17 and 3-18). They are presented by pairs in tables, with and without a given suffix or other formal feature, showing how one type of verb is derived from another (or in some cases, from nouns), and the resulting differences in meaning.

Here in chapter 5 we will look first at the optional constituents in the domain of verbs: most verbs may occur with ADVERBS (5.2), DIRECTIONALS (5.3), ADVERBIAL PREPOSITIONAL PHRASES (5.4), and ADVERBIAL CLAUSES (5.5). Then we will introduce concepts necessary for a fuller classification of verbs, one that considers not only how they may be derived and differ in form, but also the other sentence constituents they require, and the roles these constituents play. The nine major verb classes of Marshallese are presented, beginning with CLASS A VERBS in 5.6.1, and continuing with the other nonextension classes through CLASS G in 5.6.5. Then, in 5.6.6, the remaining four major classes of verbs (CLASSES D, E, H, and I), all of which are EXTENSION verbs, are considered. Additional subtypes of verbs introduced as part of the classification include IMPERSONAL VERBS, LOCATIVE VERBS, MANNER VERBS, COMPARATIVE VERBS, CORRESPONDENT VERBS, and EXISTENTIAL VERBS.

ADVERBS

5.2 Verbs may cooccur with a relatively small number of words that express uncertainty, time, politeness, degree, direction, and interrogation. Table 5-1 gives a classification of those dealing with everything except direction, which is treated in section 5.3 (see especially tables 5-2 and 5-3).

Interrogative Adverbs

5.2.1 The interrogative adverbs form a fairly simple and basic system. (1) Is something true or isn't it, did something happen or didn't it? **Yes or no? True or false?** Insertion of *ke* at a proper place in the sentence makes it a simple yes-no question. The other three adverb types presume that something did, in fact, happen or that it is true, and deal with the content of the matter, with its substance or its cause. (2) **Why?** There are several ways to ask: *Etke*? *Enta*? Other questions are concerned not so much with cause as with location, either in space (3) **Where?** *Ia*? or in time (4) **When?** *Ñāāt*?

Table 5-1 Classification of adverbs

INTERROGATIVE ADVERBS	
YES-NO QUESTION	PROPOSITIONAL
ke 'yes or no?'	etke, enta 'why'
LOCATIONAL NONTIME	TIME
ia 'where'	ñāāt 'when'
NONINTERROGATIVE ADVERBS	
DEGREE	PROPOSITIONAL
bajjek 'a little, just, only'	bōlen 'maybe'
jidik 'a little'	TIME
wōt 'only'	inne 'yesterday'
POLITENESS	kiiō (W) / kiin (E) 'now'
ṃōk 'please'	ilju 'tomorrow'
DIRECTION (SEE 5.3)	jekḷaj 'day after tomorrow'

The question word *ke*. With a few exceptions, the usual place in the sentence occupied by adverbs is following the nonauxiliary verb,[1] or in an equational sentence such as (5-1c), following the predicate nominal (the second of the two nominals in square brackets).

(5-1) a. Kwōj etal **ke** ñan Awai?
'Are you going to Hawaii?'

b. Kwaar akadeik **ke** bao ko?
'Did you watch the birds to locate their roost?'

c. [Kwe] [ri-kōbaatat] **ke**?
'Are you a smoker?'

Here, the INTERROGATIVE ADVERB *ke* follows both intransitive (5-1a) and transitive (5-1b) verbs. Note that with the latter, it comes between the transitive verb and its noun phrase object. While these examples illustrate the most

1. We underline the nonauxiliary verbs in these examples and others where they are relevant to our discussion of adverbs. The two nominals of equational sentences are each enclosed in square brackets.

common pattern, *ke* is not restricted to these positions. It can appear after an auxiliary verb (5-2a), after the subject of an equational sentence [the first nominal in square brackets in (5-2b)], or at the end of a sentence (5-2c).

(5-2) a. Ej **ke** kōkañōrñōre ļadik eņ?
'Is he letting the boy wear a belt?'

b. [Kwe] **ke** [ri-ānin]?
'Are you from this island?'

c. Kwōj jab mōk in pijļōļō **ke**?
'Aren't you tired of squatting?'

***Ia* 'where' and *ñaat* 'when'.** These two locational interrogative adverbs are found in the position common for adverbs, the one shown for *ke* in (5-1a) and (5-1b). In fact, it is their occurrence in this position that leads us to identify them as adverbs rather than as the interrogative pronouns that have the same shape (see table 4-9),[2] to which they are related derivationally.[3] Examples (5-3c) and (5-3d) show that these two adverbs, like *ke*, can also be sentence-final. However, there is another change that takes place when they appear sentence-finally and the verb is intransitive. Sentence (5-3b) gives the usual order, in which the intransitive verb (*el*) comes first, and the overt noun phrase subject (*bao eņ*) follows it. This order is reversed when *ia* is final, as in (5-3d), so that a final *ia* still immediately follows the verb.

(5-3) a. Kwōnaaj tooke **ñāāt** wa in?
'When are you going to fix this boat?'

b. Ej el **ia** bao eņ?
'Where is that hen making its nest?'

c. Kwōnaaj tooke wa in **ñāāt**?

d. Bao eņ ej el **ia**?

Example (5-3a) shows that an interrogative adverb may appear between a transitive verb and its noun phrase object. However, when the object is a pronoun such as *er* 'they, them', there is some variation in usage. Most speakers prefer to postpone the adverb until the end of the sentence, as in (5-4a) and (5-4c). Some will also accept it in the same position as full noun phrases, immediately following the verb, as in (5-4b) and (5-4d).

2. One of the positions in which their pronoun counterparts are found is as objects of prepositions, as, for example, in *Kwōj etal ñan*$_1$ ***ia****?* 'Where are you going?' and *Kwōj wōnmaan ñan*$_1$ ***ñāāt****?* 'How far do you intend to move up?'

3. Derivations relate words that resemble each other in both form and meaning, but are members of different parts of speech. Sometimes the words resemble each other only partially in form (as, for example, the adjectival verb *nana* 'be bad' and the noun *ri-nana* 'outlaw', where the prefix *ri-* is added by the derivation), and sometimes the resemblance is complete (as, for example, the verb *ṃōñā* 'eat' and the noun *ṃōñā* 'food', or in our discussion here, the adverb *ñāāt* and the pronoun *ñāāt*. This latter type, where no change is made in the form, is sometimes referred to as "zero derivation" or "conversion."

(5-4) a. Kwaar lo er **ñāāt**?
'When did you see them?'

b. Kwaar lo **ñāāt** er?

c. Kwaar lo e **ia**?
'Where did you see her/him?'

d. Kwaar lo **ia** e?

Generally, CLEFT SENTENCES using the interrogative pronouns are preferred to these adverbial interrogatives when the object of the verb is a pronoun.

(5-5) a. **Ñāāt** eo kwaar lo er?
'When did you see them?'

b. **Ia** eo kwaar lo e?
'Where did you see her/him?'

***Etke* and *enta* 'why'.** These PROPOSITIONAL interrogative adverbs are found in a quite different position from other adverbs. They occur only at the beginning of a sentence or clause. The two are fairly interchangeable, although *etke* is unanalyzable and seems more neutral than *enta* when (5-6c) is compared with (5-6b). This may be because *enta* can be analyzed as *en* 'it is to' + *ta* 'what' and in this example may imply that the action is intentional.

(5-6) a. **Etke** kwaar apij ajri eo?
'Why did you pinch the child?'

b. **Enta** kwōj kabūḷāāt aṃ al?
'Why are you singing off key? (please stop it)'

c. **Etke** kwōj kabūḷāāt aṃ al?
'Why are you singing off key?

(5-7) a. Kwōj kabūḷāāt aṃ al ñan$_2$ **ta**?
'What is the purpose of your singing off key?'

b. [**Ta**] [**wūnin a**ṃ kabūḷāāt aṃ al]?
'What is the reason for your singing off key?'

c. [**Ta**] [**wūnin a**ō jetṇaake iọkwe eo arro]?
'Oh, why did I let our love get so deep?'

There are two other ways to ask roughly the same question using the INTERROGATIVE PRONOUN *ta*. In (5-7a) *ta* is at the end of the sentence as the object of the preposition *ñan*$_2$ 'for what purpose'. In (5-7b) where it is sentence initial, *ta* alone constitutes the first nominal of an equational sentence, and the second nominal begins with *wūnin* followed by *aṃ*, a form of the default possessive classifier {haha-} (*aō, aṃ, an, aer*) (see 4.6). Here *wūnin* ends in the construct suffix *-n,* which requires a nominal to follow it. In turn, the nominal *aṃ* introduces a clause that it has nominalized to satisfy this requirement. Thus, *aṃ kabūḷāāt aṃ al* 'your singing off key' (lit. your flatting [of] your singing) in (5-7b) is the nominalized form of *kwōj kabūḷāāt aṃ al* 'you are singing off key' in (5-6b). And the bold portion of

(b) is the constant part of a construction for asking 'why' questions using a nominalized clause in the second part of an equational sentence.[4] Example (c) gives a different form of **a-** {haha-}.

NONINTERROGATIVE ADVERBS

5.2.2 There are some parallels with the interrogative adverbs, with both types having PROPOSITIONAL and TIME subtypes, as brought out in table 5-1.

***Bōlen* 'perhaps'.** The PROPOSITIONAL adverb *bōlen,* like its interrogative counterparts *etke* and *enta,* and unlike other adverbs, occurs only clause-initially.

(5-8) **Bōlen** enaaj itok ilju.
'Maybe he'll come tomorrow.'

***Inne* 'yesterday', *kiiō* / *kiin* 'now',[5] *ilju* 'tomorrow', and *jekļaj* 'day after tomorrow'.** The time adverbs, on the other hand, are usually sentence-final.

(5-9) a. Kwaar aluje ke wāween an kōjọlim̧ **inne**?
'Did you observe the way he fished using the *kōjọlim̧* method yesterday?'

b. Kōjparok am̧ tutu iaar bwe eaolōke **kiiō**.
'Beware of the Portuguese man-o'-war in the lagoon because there are plenty of them at this time.'

c. Inaaj buñi m̧ade e am̧ **ilju**.
'I'll make a handle for your spear tomorrow.'

d. Enaaj kemem **jekļaj**.[6]
'It's his birthday the day after tomorrow.'

Sometimes time adverbs may be moved to the front of the clause for emphasis and/or in contrast with another clause.

(5-10) a. **Kiiō** ijeļā ke kwōj būļabe eō.
'Now I know you're bluffing.'

b. Ejọ kōn kilep ak **kiiō** eaidik.
'He used to be fat but now he is skinny.'

c. Eļap am̧ bōkļap bwe **kiiō** ejabwe.
'You took too much and now there isn't enough.'

d. Ikkein kōbaatat ak **kiin** ijjab.
'I used to smoke, but I don't anymore.'

e. Joñan an to am̧ pād ānin, **kiiō** kwe m̧ōm̧ō in jin.
'You've been here so long, now you know the place inside out.'

4. Note that *am̧* appears in (5-7b) instead of the *kwōj* of (5-6b) (see 6.4.1 for a fuller discussion of clause nominalization).
5. *Kiin* is used primarily in the Ratak.
6. Here is an example of a distributive verb (page 162) derived from *jekļaj* 'day after tomorrow': *Emake **jejekļajļaj** an kōnono*. 'He keeps mentioning the day after tomorrow.'

f. **Jekḷaj** inaaj etal ñan Ḷora.
'The day after tomorrow I will be going to Ḷora.'

More complex time expressions may be built on the time words and appear in their expected positions within the sentence.

(5-11) a. Ear jako **kiin jeṃaanḷọk**.
'He passed away recently.'

b. Rej kātok **kiiō ḷọk jidik**.
'They'll fly here later.'

c. **Kiin wōt** ṇe inaaj kadedeik(i)ḷọk.[7]
Inaaj kadedeik(i)ḷọk **kiin kiin wōt**.
'I shall now finish it.'

d. Iar loe **kiin raan eo ḷọk**.
'I saw him just the other day.'

e. Kwōn itok **kiiō kiiō wōt**.
'Come immediately.'

Degree adverbs. There are three degree adverbs, each with its special role: *bajjek* 'just', *jidik* 'a little', and *wōt* 'only, still'. With some exceptions noted below, they generally follow the verb. **Bajjek 'just'** points to a 'bare minimum', and is often used in dismissive comments, as in (5-12c). In (5-12e) it is used in an equational sentence. It may sometimes follow the prime auxiliary rather than the nonauxiliary verb, as in (5-12f) and (5-12g).

(5-12) a. Rej ito-itak **bajjek**.
'They are just walking around.'

b. Kōmij jejerakrōk **bajjek**.
'We're just sailing around, going no place.'

c. Erro ej iọkwe in kij **bajjek**.
'Theirs is just a puppy love.'

d. Kwōn jab po ippān bwe euttaiḷōṃ **bajjek**.[8]
'Don't be taken in by him because he's constantly so vain.'

e. [Ña] [rūkkatak **bajjek**].
'I'm just beginning to learn.'

f. Ear **bajjek** daṃdiṃwij ḷọḷe eo.
'He just kept licking the lollipop.'

g. Jab illu bwe ej **bajjek** mālijjoñe atūṃ.
'Don't get mad; he's just trying your patience.'

***Jidik* 'a little'.** *Jidik* is a DEGREE ADVERB in addition to being a QUANTIFIER [see (4-76) on page 201]. The first three examples in 5-13 show it in

7. Here the time expression has evidently been cleft (that is, moved to the front for emphasis with the determiner *ṇe* added). An equivalent sentence follows, with *kiin* doubled for emphasis and the time expression in its usual place (without the determiner). The anaphoric *i* 'it' of *kadedeik(i)ḷọk* seems to be optional (as shown by the parentheses).

8. *Uttaiḷōṃ* is a distributive verb derived from *utḷōṃ,* a loanword from English *hoodlum.*

the usual place for adverbs, following the verb (underlined). In (5-13b) it comes between a transitive verb and its object, while in (5-13c) it follows an idiomatic verb-object combination.[9] Example (5-13d) shows the adverb *jidik* modified in turn by the adverb *wōt,* together 'only a little' (lit. a little only); this clause, of which *pir* is the verb, is nominalized in (5-13e), and *jidik* the adverb is replaced by *jidik* the quantifier in a near-equivalent equational sentence, lit. 'A little only (is) its slippage, (that of) the water (level) from the top of the cistern.'

(5-13) a. Dān eo ej ippilpil **jidik** jān$_1$ bakōj ṇe.
'The water is leaking from that bucket.'

b. Kwōn kadukwaḷe **jidik** bōraṃ bwe in lo ṃaan.
'Lower your head a bit so I can see the front.'

c. Ij ja itan wūne meja **jidik** ṃokta jān aō naaj memej (emmej).
'I think I'll get some shut-eye for a while before I go on watch.'

d. Epir **jidik wōt** dān eo jān mejān aebōj eo.
'The water has gone down just a little from the top of the cistern.'

e. [**Jidik wōt**] [an pir dān eo jān mejān aebōj eo].
'The water is down just a little from the top of the cistern.'

***Wōt* 'only; still'.** This is probably the most common and widely distributed of all adverbs. It is found in the usual adverbial position, following verbs, and preceding the objects of transitive verbs as in (5-14a) and (5-14b). The meaning 'still' is often found in the translations of sentences whose subject prefixes are attached to the prime helping verb *ej* 'noncompletive' (3.3.1), as it is in both these examples,[10] and in (5-14c) as well.[11]

(5-14) a. Ke ij tōkeak ḷọk **ej** jejemjeme **wōt** bakbōk eo.
'When I got there he was sharpening the knife.'

b. **Rej** tariṇaeik **wōt** doon.
'They are still fighting each other.'

c. **Jej** jorrāān tok **wōt** jān marripripin ḷañ eo.
'We are still down and out from the damage of the storm.'

Wōt is also found following quantifiers and other nominals, as in the following examples. In (5-15f) it follows the interrogative pronoun *ewi.*

(5-15) a. An jejjo **wōt** kapen.
'Few people know navigation.'

b. Juon **wōt** raanū ṇa iKuwajleen.
'I have been (I was) on Kwajalein only one day.'

9. The original meaning of *wūne* is uncertain. It may be related to *wūn* 'fish scale', so that *wūne meja* would be literally 'put scales over my eyes'.
10. Thus, (5-14a) could also be translated '... he was still sharpening the knife.'
11. Note that (5-14c) shows the relative position of adverbs like *wōt* and directionals like *tok* (which are discussed in 5.3), with directionals coming closer to the verb.

c. Ruo **wōt** wūd e ilo pakij in jikka e kiiō.
'There are only three cigarettes left in this pack now.'

d. Leddik **wōt** rej ejjebaō M̧ajeļ.
'Only girls play *ejjebaō* in the Marshalls.'

e. Nowa **wōt** im bwij eo an raar mour ilo ibwijleplep eo ilo Baibōļ.
'Only Noah and his family survived the great flood in the Bible.'

f. Kwōn keidi m̧ōk ewi **wōt** m̧weo em̧m̧an iaan m̧ōkaņ.
'Please compare which of those houses is best.'

And it is found following prepositions in examples like the following.

(5-16) a. Ejjidikdik jān$_2$ **wōt** aer kar pepeo̧eo̧o̧te.
'It was in shreds after they tore it to pieces.'

b. Jān$_2$ **wōt** am̧ nana, etūm̧ kwōd eo ikōtaarro.
'Simply because you're a harlot, our relationship is dissolved.'

c. Kwōnaaj kalbuuj kōn$_2$ **wōt** kōm̧m̧an kaņe am̧.
'You'll get put in jail as a result of your actions.'

d. Jeitōn ebbweer kōn$_2$ **wōt** ad kōkāliklik.
'We've just about given up because of going to the ocean side so much.'

e. Etūļaar raij eņ kōn$_2$ **wōt** an tar jān joñan am̧ ankaane kijeek ņe.
'The rice is burnt because you overfed the fire.'

f. Kwōn wia ñan$_2$ **wōt** am̧ aikuj.
'Buy just for your needs.'

g. Ej kōnono ñan$_2$ **wōt** kom̧.
'He talking just for you.'

h. Jeitōn abwin make eake$_2$ **wōt** ri-mej eņ.
'We're getting afraid of the dark because of the dead person.'

Superlative constructions with *wōt*. There are several constructions with *wōt* that stress the uniqueness of a certain quality in someone or something. Some are introduced by an adjectival verb bearing the 3S prefix *e-*. Such statements are given additional emphasis by reversing the order of the subject noun and its determiner, as with *laddik eņ* in (5-17c) and *em̧m̧aan eņ* in (5-17d) and (5-17f). Example (5-17e) shows that this "determiner reversal" is not a requirement of the construction.

(5-17) a. Ekōppaļpaļ **wōt** lipopotokun inej eo.
'The arrival of the fleet was very impressive.'

b. Ekajoor **wōt** abōnān ri-anijnij eo.
'The sorcerer has such great powers.'

c. Eaujepaļ **wōt** eņ ļaddik.
'What a gangling boy he is.'

d. Eḷajjuur **wōt** eṇ eṃṃaan.'
'He's such a powerful individual.'

e. Eppānpān **wōt** lijā eṇ.
'She's quite an attractive girl.'

f. Epen **wōt** būruon eṇ eṃṃaan.
'He's such a fearless fellow.'

Even stronger such statements are introduced by *ejjeḷọk wōt* or *ejej wōt,* saying in effect that 'there is no comparison', 'none can compare', and this is followed by an identification of the unique quality and its possessor. Thus, in (5-18a) the quality is the size (*ḷapin* 'largeness of') and the possessor is the ship (*tiṃa eṇ*), which has undergone DETERMINER REVERSAL; in (5-18b) the quality is the embarrassment (*emmālwewe*) possessed by us (-*id* '1P.INCL'). Example (5-18e) also undergoes determiner reversal, while (5-18d) does not.

(5-18) a. Ejjeḷọk **wōt** ḷapin eṇ tiṃa.
'That ship is outstandingly large.'

b. Ejjeḷọk **wōt** emmālweweid kōn$_2$ ṃanōt ko an.
'We were very embarrassed by his behavior.'

c. Ejjeḷọk **wōt** jirūṃlele in iar in ānin.
'The lagoon bottom of this island drops off exceptionally steeply.'

d. Ejjeḷọk **wōt** eddekākā in ḷadik eṇ.
'That boy is really covered with yaws.'

e. Ejjeḷọk **wōt** doebeb in ṇe ajri.
'That's the most mischievous child I've ever seen.'

f. Ejej **wōt** kōjḷọriier ke rej jab ko.
'The fish are so stunned they don't run away.'

Other constructions with *wōt*. *Wōt* may be followed immediately by *jidik* when the verb is 'almost' fully applicable, as in (5-19a–c). After a noncompletive verb (with *ej*) and before *ak*, it sets the stage for the clause to follow (5-19d–f). It is also found in the expression *etan wōt ñe* (lit. its name only as if) as in (5-19g–h), used for 'pretend' situations.

(5-19) a. Enañin ṃōj **wōt jidik**.
'It's nearly finished.'

b. Erro baj taiṃ **wōt jidik**.
'The two of them almost fought.'

c. Ibaj mej **wōt jidik**.
'I almost killed myself.' 'I almost got killed.'

d. **Ej** ettōr **wōt ak** itipiji.
'When he ran, I tripped him.'

e. **Ej** itan mū **wōt ak** rōbuuki im lel.
'As he was craning his neck to see better, he got shot at and hit.'

f. **Ej** jādetok **wōt ak** rōpinniki.
'As he appeared, they threw sand at him.'

g. **Etan wōt ñe** kōjro ej pād Amedka.
'Pretend that we are in the United States.'

h. **Etan wōt ñe** koñak.
'As if you don't know.'

***M̧ōk*, an adverb of politeness.** This adverb is used in imperative sentences to make commands polite, and with the auxiliary verb *en* 'optative' when it expresses a polite command. It generally occurs after the verb, and before its object when the verb is transitive, as in (5-20a) and (5-20b),[12] although it may occur earlier, after the optative auxiliary as in (5-20c) and (5-20d).[13] In (5-20e) and (5-20f) we see traces of what was probably its original meaning of 'try' before it came to be used more widely as a politeness marker.[14] Note that in the latter the helping verb is *naaj* 'will' rather than the optative *en*.

(5-20) a. Bwini **m̧ōk** mā kaņe.
'Please count those breadfruit.'

b. M̧alene tok **m̧ōk** eta ilo jurōn jāje e aō.
'Would you engrave my name on the handle of my machete.'

c. Kwōn **m̧ōk** aiji bōra bwe en jab ebbōj.
'Would you please press some ice cubes to my head so that it doesn't swell.'

d. Kwōn **m̧ōk** jorbañe tok jete oņāān m̧weiuk kaņe.
'How about computing the price of the merchandise for me?'

e. Jen mālejjoñe **m̧ōk** ļōm̧araņ bwe jen jeļā repojak ke ñan jerbal eņ rej jibadeke.
'Let's try giving them a test to be sure they're qualified for the job they've applied for.'

f. Jenaaj elmọkote **m̧ōk** im lale em̧m̧an ke.
'We'll try experimenting with it and see if it works.'

The position following optative forms of *en* like *kwōn* in (5-20c) and (5-20d) is the original position of *m̧ōk* before it became an adverb, when it was simply a verb meaning 'try', and sentences like these meant simply 'Would you try pressing some ice cubes to my head …' and 'Would you try computing the price of the merchandise …'. As *m̧ōk* became more a marker of politeness, it often moved to adverb position by trading places

---

12. Note that in (5-20b) the DIRECTIONAL ADVERB *tok* comes even closer to the verb.
13. The basic form of the optative auxiliary is *en*, which is also the 3S form. Combinations with the other subject prefixes [such as *kwōn* in (5-20b)] are given in table 3-10 (see also 3.3.1 and footnote 2 on page 177).
14. English *try* has developed in a parallel way as *chrai* in Hawaiian Creole English, where reduced to *cha* in *cha come* 'please come' and *cha wait* 'please wait' it functions as a politeness marker (pers. comm., Michael Forman).

with the verb that followed, so that these two sentences could equally well be: *Kwōn aiji* ***m̧ōk*** *bōra* ... and *Kwōn jorbañe tok* ***m̧ōk*** *jete* ... .

DIRECTIONALS

5.3 Directional adverbs, often referred to simply as "directionals," form a highly developed system in Marshallese. There are three simple directionals and four groups of compound directionals. The simple directionals, like the demonstratives (4.2.2), parallel the distinctions between the pronouns to a certain extent: (1) *tok* {tek^{w}} 'toward me',[15] (2) *wōj* / *waj* {wẹj / waj} 'toward you', or (3) *ḷọk* {ḷak^{w}} 'toward a third party, away from both of us'.

The Compound Directionals

5.3.1 The compound directionals are formed by combining certain nouns with any of the three simple directionals. They are best thought of as PAIRED OPPOSITES, that is, for example, 'northward' as the opposite direction from 'southward', or 'upward' as the opposite of 'downward'. Table 5-2 summarizes the combinations with *ḷọk* 'toward somewhere else, toward neither me nor you (neither speaker nor hearer)', in four groups consisting of a total of seven pairs of opposites.

The COMPASS DIRECTIONALS consist of two pairs ('northward: southward' and 'eastward : westward'); the SEA DIRECTIONALS of one pair ('seeward' : 'landward'); the LAND DIRECTIONALS of two pairs ('ocean side' : 'lagoon side' and 'interior' : 'lagoon side'), and the SPACE DIRECTIONALS of two pairs ('upward' : 'downward' and 'forward' : 'backward'). Note that *lik* 'back; outside' is the opposite of both *ar* 'lagoon beach' and *m̧aan* 'forward', and that *ar* is the opposite of both *lik* 'toward the ocean side' and *iooj* / *eọọj* 'toward the interior'. That *iooj* / *eọọj* is not shown as the opposite of *lik* reflects the fact that it is used only when the speaker is at the lagoon side, and not when s/he is at the ocean side.

Fourteen additional directionals that include the meaning 'toward the hearer(s), toward you' can be formed by replacing *ḷọk* with *wōj* / *waj,* and

---

15. Pagotto (1987:195–96) prefers to gloss *tok* as 'toward point of reference', saying that "while it is true that the speaker is often the point of reference, it is not necessarily the case" and refers to the following sentence:

Ḷōḷḷap eṇ ear arrome wōt an armej eo deḷọñ **tok**.
'The old man could hardly recognize the man who came in.'
[The old man indistinctly perceived the man's entrance towards him.]

It is also possible to take the position that someone entering a room is coming toward all its occupants, including the speaker, at least when they first enter. This question, whether a speaker using *tok* is ever excluded from its point of reference, is one that needs further study.

fourteen more that include the meaning ‘toward the speaker’ by replacing it with *tok*. Thus, replacing the *-ḷọk* of *lōn̄ḷọk* ‘away upward’ with *-wōj* yields *lōn̄wōj* ‘upward toward you’, and replacing it with *tok* (which becomes *tak*) yields *lōntak* ‘come upward (toward me)’. Similarly with the other thirteen.

Table 5-2 Pairs of compound directionals: ‘away from speaker and hearer(s)’

COMPASS DIRECTIONALS			
niñaḷọk	rōñaḷọk	(W)	‘northward : southward’
niñeañḷọk	rōkeañḷọk	(E)	
taḷọk	toḷọk	(W)	‘eastward : westward’
takḷọk	toḷọk	(E)	
SEA DIRECTIONALS			
āneḷọk	metoḷọk		‘landward : seaward’
LAND DIRECTIONALS			
likḷọk	arḷọk		‘ocean side : lagoon side’
eọọjḷọk	arḷọk	(W)	‘interior : lagoon side’
ioojḷọk	arḷọk	(E)	
SPACE DIRECTIONALS			
lōñḷọk	laḷḷọk		‘upward : downward’
m̧aanḷọk	likḷọk		‘forward : backward’

Forming those meaning ‘toward the speaker’ is complicated by changes that occur to the expected *tok*; the resulting forms are shown in table 5-3, with the change results shown in boldface type. Some examples in which *tok* is replaced by *tak* are given in 5-21, and some ‘eastward’ and ‘westward’ examples, where it is dropped completely, are given in 5-22.

Table 5-3 Special forms used instead of *tok* in compound directionals that include the meaning ‘toward speaker’

COMPASS DIRECTIONALS			
niña**tak**	rōña**tak**	(W)	‘north/southward to me/us’
niñeañ**tak**	rōkeañ**tak**	(E)	
tak	**to**	(W)	‘east/westward (to me/us)’
tak	**to**	(E)	
SEA DIRECTIONALS			
āne**tak**	meto**tak**		‘land/seaward to me/us’
LAND DIRECTIONALS			
lik**tak**	ar**tak**		‘toward ocean/lagoon side to me/us’
eọọj**tak**	ar**tak**	(W)	‘toward interior/lagoon side to me/us’
iooj**tak**	ar**tak**	(E)	
SPACE DIRECTIONALS			
lōñ**tak**	laḷ**tak**		‘up/downward to me/us’
m̧aan**tak**	lik**tak**		‘forward/backward to me/us’

[The *tak* that remains in (5-22a) through (5-22c) (and in the third and fourth lines of table 5-3) is the one that means 'eastward'.] [16]

(5-21) a. Kwōn bōkkōrāik **metotak** lien.
'Carry her out here to the canoe.'

b. Raar raabe **ānetak** ṃootka eo.
'The automobile was brought ashore on a raft.'

c. Kwōn pirūrrūr **laḷtak.**
'Slip down the tree.'

d. Eṃōraṃrōṃ **laḷtak** tōrerein toḷ eo.
'There was a landslide on the side of the mountain.'

e. Kwōn jutak **lōñtak** ṃōk.
'Please stand up.'

f. Kijak eo euwe lōñḷọk ñan raan tiṃa eṇ; ṃōttan wōt jidik eto **laḷtak**.
'That fellow went on board the ship; he'll get off in a bit.'

(5-22) a. Ej ṃōṃōñāñe **tak** kijeek eṇ (ñan ippād).
'That fire is expanding eastward (toward us).'

b. Kwōn ettōr **tak** bwe in tōpar eok.
'Run eastward (this way) so that I can meet you.'

c. Lio eaar eb **tak** ioon jikin kaloojoj eo.
'The lady danced eastward on the stage (toward the audience).'

d. Rūkowainini ro rej ineek **to** pāākin waini ko aer ñan imōn baun in.
'The copra makers carry their copra westward to this copra shed.'

e. Eajeedeed **to** kopej kaṇe kōn an kōto in pooki.
'The trash scatters westward because the wind blows it (this way).'

f. Aṃ pokpok **to** ejipañ an ajeedeed mej in ñan ippād.
'Your coughing westward helps spread the cold virus (this way).'

Nouns that form the first elements of the compound directionals. As noted above, the compound directionals are formed by combining certain nouns with any of the three simple directionals. The sentences in 5-23 give evidence that the first elements are basically nouns, showing them as objects of prepositions.

---

16. As can be seen from table 5-3, *tok* never appears as such in any of these combinations, either being replaced by *tak,* or simply being dropped following *tak* 'east' and *to* 'west'. The fact that it is omitted in these two directionals, while the meaning of 'toward me; toward the speaker' is still conveyed, indicates that *tok* can be thought of as the "default" directional.

(5-23) a. Eaete ḷọk kōrkōr eo ñan **lik**.
'The current drifted the canoe out to the ocean side.'

b. Erro ar kopāp ḷọk oom **ar**.
'The two of them wrestled all the way up to the lagoon shore.'

c. Ej jebwebwe ekkar ñan **meto** ṇe i **ṃaan**.
'He's steering the boat in accord with the ocean ahead.'

d. Ej itok jān **āne** uweo (ānuweo).
'He came from that island over there.'

e. Ear wōtlọk ñan **laḷ** tata.
'He fell to the very bottom.'

The first elements of the SPACE DIRECTIONALS can also be found as the stems of inalienable nouns, as shown in (5-24a–d).

(5-24) a. Kwōj pād **lōñū** ilo teej eṇ.
'You are above me on the test.'

b. Ipād **laḷ**ūṃ ilo teej eo.
'I scored below you on the test.'

c. Ear pinej **ṃaan**ū.
'He obstructed my view.'

d. Eākilkil **lik**ūṃ.
'The skin on your back is peeling.'

e. [Eñṇeṇe] [**irūk**ūṃ / **irōk**ūṃ].
'It's right there to your south.'

f. [Jaki eo ṇe] [**iūñ**in / **iōñ**in peet ṇe].
'The mat is at the north end of the bed.'

The nominal connections of the first elements of the COMPASS DIRECTIONALS are not so easily established. The basic nouns for 'north' and 'south', respectively, are *eañ* (*iōñi-*) and *rak* (*rōki-*), as shown in table 3-6 on page 130. Their inalienable forms (shown here in parentheses) are illustrated in (5-24e–f) in equational sentences, but these are not the same forms as the first parts of the north-south directionals. The most that can be said is that there is some resemblance between these nouns and their respective forms in the compound directionals: *niña-/ni**ñ**eañ-* and ***rōña**-/ **rōk**eañ-*, more so for 'south' than for 'north'.

It is even more difficult to find the forms *tak* 'east' and *to* 'west' functioning independently as nouns rather than as directionals. The same forms are found with verbal functions involving movement, as in ***takin** aḷ* 'sunrise' and ***to** jān wa* 'get off/down from a vessel'. The following chant would seem to have *to* 'west' in a nominal function, *"Ḷakeke **to**, rooj iekūt, waan Elmọndik."* '*Ḷakeke* (a star) in the west, they (the sailors) stand by, vehicle of the storm called *Elmọndik*.'

Probably the best explanation for the difficulty of finding nouns of the same form and meaning as the first elements of the COMPASS DIRECTION-

ALS has to do with the fact that the noun portions of the other compound directionals can be viewed as their visible destinations: *āne* 'islet', *ar* 'lagoon side', *eọọj* 'interior', *lik* 'ocean side'/'back', *meto* 'sea', *lạl* 'earth', and so on. It is even tempting to view *lōñ* as a modified form of *lañ* 'sky'. Equally visible destinations for the compass directionals are not so obvious. But there is no need that all the compound directionals be derived from present-day nouns of identical form; the compass directionals may be of greater antiquity and may have served as models for the others.

Verbs with built-in directionals. As adverbs, the directionals are considered to be—and are written as—separate words in the adverb position immediately following verbs, except in those cases where the verb is one of a small subset whose stems are obligatorily suffixed with directionals—verbs that have the directionals built in. There is one basic verb that is used only for humans coming and going, and this verb is spelled out in the MED in a number of dialectal forms together with the simple directionals, as, for example, *itok* (W); *wātok, atok* (E) 'come here, of humans'; *ilọk* (W); *wālọk* (W) 'go away, of humans', and so on. The MED shows other such verbs that require directional suffixes by their stems alone, followed by a hyphen, as, for example, *tar-*. The hyphen indicates that they are not complete words without having a directional as suffix; these verbs are listed with their hyphens in table 5-4. Example sentences adapted from Bender (1969:270, 279–80) are given in 5-25. Note that examples (5-25e–f) use *uwe* 'get on board', *tallōñ* 'climb', and *to* 'get off, come/go down', which are verbs that are not in table 5-4 because they may also occur *without* being followed by a directional. For this reason, the compound directionals are written as separate words following these verbs, and not as suffixes.

Table 5-4 Verbs that are obligatorily suffixed with directionals

jekad-	'fling'	lo-	'visit
jieb-	'overflow; erupt'	ḷo-	'be at'
jiraak-	'move; push'	pāl-	'leap, jump, soar'
kā- / ke-	'jump, spring; fly'	tar-	'go on a vehicle or canoe'
leak-	'take; carry, transport'	wan- / wōn-	'walk; go'
le-	'give'	wujlep-	'give freely; surrender'

(5-25) a. Ḷaipen ewanlikḷọk; ṃōttan wōt jidik ewanarwōj.
'Ḷaipen went toward the ocean side; he'll come toward the lagoon beach to you in a little bit.'

b. Ḷaipen etareọọjḷọk; ṃōttan wōt jidik etarartak.
'Ḷaipen drove toward the interior of the island; he'll come (back) to the lagoon side in a moment.'

c. Bao eo ekālōñḷọk ñan$_1$ raan mā eṇ; ṃōttan wōt jidik ekālaḷtak.
'The bird flew up to the branch of the breadfruit tree; soon it will fly back down.'

d. Ewāniñaḷọk; ṃōttan wōt jidik ewārōñawōj. (W)
Ewāniñeañḷọk; ṃōttan wōt jidik ewārōkeañwōj. (E)
'S/he went away northward; s/he'll come southward in your direction in a little bit.'

e. Ḷaipen euwe lōñḷọk ñan₁ raan tiṃa eṇ; ṃōttan wōt jidik eto laḷtak.
'Ḷaipen went up on board the ship there; he'll come back down pretty soon.'

f. Ḷadik eo etallōñ lōñḷọk ñan₁ raan ni eṇ; ṃōttan wōt jidik eto laḷtak.
'The boy climbed up to the top of the coconut tree; he'll come down soon.'

Confirmation for the fact that directionals are built into verbs whose stems are given in table 5-4 can be found in their use with the anaphoric suffix that appears on transitive verbs with missing direct objects (see page 153). Compare the derived directional verbs in (5-26a–b) with those with built-in directionals in (5-26c–d). The anaphoric suffix *-e* appears on the verb *man* 'kill s.' in (5-26b), which is followed by the directional *ḷọk*. However, the anaphoric suffix appears after the directional on the verb *leḷọk* 'give s. away' in (5-26d).

(5-26) a. Kwōn ṃan ḷọk etan jān₁ bok ṇe.
'Cross his name out of the book.'

b. Kwōn ṃan**e** ḷọk jān₁ bok ṇe.
'Cross it out of the book.'

c. Kwōn leḷọk bok ṇe ñan₁ ajri ṇe.
'Give the book to that child.'

d. Kwōn leḷọk**e** ñan₁ ajri ṇe.
'Give it to the child.'

Other uses for directionals. Both simple and compound directionals typically appear with verbs of motion, specifying the direction of the movement of the subjects of intransitive verbs (5-27a–c), or the objects of transitive verbs (5-27d–f).

(5-27) a. Kwōn oktak **tok**.
'Turn around and face me.'

b. Kwōn ajādik **ḷọk**.
'Walk away slowly.'

c. Kwōn ṃōṃkaj **waj**.
'Go on ahead.'

d. Nōōre **waj** kimej ṇe.
'Pull that frond over [toward yourself].'

e. Kwōn kajidaak **tok** wa ṇe.
'Bring the canoe here.'

f. Baiklaaje **tok** ṃōk wa eṇ.
'Take a look at the boat through the binoculars.'

Directionals may also appear with nonmotion verbs, in which case they may add a sense of directed motion (5-28a–c) or may show the direction of an activity and the BENEFICIARY of the action (5-28d–g).

(5-28) a. Wōn in ej ḷōḷāārār (eḷḷāārār) **tok**?
'Who is this making noise on the gravel coming here?'

b. Inaaj aḷkoote **ḷọk** eok.
'You'll share my raincoat with me to your house.'
['I'll raincoat you there.']

c. Kwōn rwe **tok** kobban.
'Stick your hand inside and pull out its contents.'

d. Lōñña̅ **tok** ṃōk.
'Tell me a riddle, please.'

e. Kwōn bōtaik **ḷọk** pilawā ṇe kijen ledik eṇ.
'Put butter on that bread and give it to the girl to eat.'

f. Ij lodideañ **waj** nejiṃ.
'I'm making you a pinwheel.'

g. Kwōmaroñ ke kōbaninnur **tok** arro?
'Can you find some small baskets for us?'

Directionals may also modify the nominal predicates of equational sentences.

(5-29) a. [Ri-eọñōd ro] [raṇe **tok**].
'Here come the fishermen.'

b. [Baḷuun eo] [eṇ **laḷḷọk**].
'There goes the plane downwards.'

c. [Ṃōṃaan eo aō] [ṇe **tok**].
'Here comes my wife's brother.'

Back-and-forth verbs. The paired opposites of the compound directionals (see table 5-2 on page 220) are used to derive intransitive verbs that serve to spice up everyday conversation. The elements that are repeated in some of the verbs in (5-30) are to be found in table 5-4 on page 223, "Verbs that are obligatorily suffixed with directionals." The verb of (5-30b) is the transitive counterpart of that in (5-30a). A person noun derived from a back-and-forth verb is found in (5-30i). As the examples show, many have to do with children and parent-child interaction.[17]

(5-30) a. Jab kōtḷọk an *kāto-ketak / kāto-kātak*.
'Don't let him/her jump around.'
(ka- / ke- 'jump, spring; fly')

17. Extensive assistance from Carmen Alik in assembling these examples is hereby gratefully acknowledged.

b. Kwōnāj *kōkāto-ketake* ḷadik ṇe bajjek innem ejujen wōt im jorrāān.
'You'll keep letting the boy jump around like that and he's going to end up hurting himself.'

c. Ḷadik eṇ, kwōnāj wōtḷọk ñe āindeṇe aṃ *wanlōñ-wanlaḷ*.
'Hey, boy, you are going to fall down if you keep on climbing up and down like that.'
(wan- / wōn- 'walk; go')

d. In kar jeḷā ta eṇ ej kōṃṃane ke eḷak kar *wanlik-wōnar* aolepān rainin.
'I wonder what he is up to; he has been criss-crossing the island all day.'

e. Jab *tarto-tartak* bwe kwōnaaj wōtḷọk ilọjet.
'Stop running around or you'll fall overboard.'
(tar 'go on a vehicle or sailing canoe')

f. Bojin eo ear eọuti im kanooj in kapene tūraṃin kiaaj eo ioon teekin wa eo bwe en jab *dāpilto-dāpiltak*.
'The boatswain securely lashed down the drum of gasoline on the boat's deck so it wouldn't roll about.'
(dāpilpil 'roll')

g. Ri-Amedka rōkijoñ *ito-itak*.
'Americans are great travelers.'
(ito 'go westward'; ita 'go eastward')

h. Kōtḷọke ilaḷ bwe en *tōbalto-tōbaltak*.
'Let him crawl around on the floor.'
(tōbalbal 'crawl, creep; slither')

i. Ri-*niñeañ-rōkeañ* eo eṇ ebōjrak ippān liṃaraṇ tōrerein iiaḷ eṇ.
'The show-off is stopping with the ladies by the roadside.'

j. *Bōklōñ-bōklaḷ! Bōklōñ-bōklaḷ!*
Jolōñ-jolaḷ! Jolōñ-jolaḷ!
'Oopsie daisy! Oopsie daisy!'
(bōk 'bring, take'; jo 'throw')

k. Iọkwe bwe en kar or obwin ej kōjerbal karjin im jemaroñ *bōkto-bōktak*.
'Too bad we don't have a portable kerosene stove.'

l. Jen kūkure (ikkure) *jaṃlik-jōṃṃaan* kōn bọọḷ ṇe nejiṃ.
'Let's play kickball with your ball.'
(jaṃ 'kick'; jaṃlik 'backkick'; jōṃṃaan 'forward kick')

m. Ṃool ke ekadek lieṇ; eban kar *buñto-buñtak* joñan ṇe.
'She must be drunk or she wouldn't fall about like that.'
(buñ 'fall; fall down')

n. Eṃṃan tata *buñto-buñtak* kaṇe an Joe!
'Joe has got the best dance moves!'

o. Ij *reilik-reiṃaan* ilowaan naan kaṇe aṃ im kile ke rōṃṃan im weppān.
'My critical judgment tells me that your ideas are excellent.' (reito-reitak 'look around')

Temporal uses for three directionals. The directional *ḷọk* is often used for time periods that are past (5-31a–c), while *tok* may be used for periods in the future (5-31d–f). Future periods may sometimes also be referred to as being below (5-31g). Two other past examples with *ḷọk* are found in 5-11 on page 214.

(5-31) a. Ear bakke iiō eo **ḷọk**.
'He had the yaws last year.'

b. Ejako raanñanraan eo aō ilo pata eo **ḷọk**.
'I lost my diary during the last war.'

c. Ri-Ṃajeḷ rōjọ kōn ebbadikdik iṃaan mejān doon raan ko **ḷọk**.
'Marshallese used to bow down when walking in front.'

d. Emaroñ jako an Ri-Ṃajeḷ ebbadikdik iṃaan mejān doon iien kaṇe **tok**.
'The Marshallese custom of bowing down when walking in front could disappear in the future.'

e. Iiō eo **tok** juon ear buñ pata eo.
'A year later the war broke out.'

f. Raan ko **tok** ear eṃṃan lañ im kōm ar jerak ñan Likiep.
'The following days the weather was fine and we set sail for Likiep.'

g. Ij kōtmāne bwe inaaj etal ñan Ṃajeḷ iiō in **laḷ**.
'I expect to go to the Marshalls next year.'

Notice that in (5-31e–f), sentences in the past tense with *ear, ḷọk* is used for more recent times, times closer to the present. Interestingly, *ḷọk* can also be used for small deviations from the present into the future, as well as in the past (5-32a–b), depending on the tense.

(5-32) a. Rej tōkeak tok kiin kiin **ḷọk** jidik.
'They should get here any time now.'

b. Raar tōkeak tok kiin kiin **ḷọk** jidik.
'They got here just a little bit ago.'

Ways in which *ḷọk* is different. *Ḷọk* has several functions that are not shared by either *tok* or *wōj*.

Comparisons. *Ḷọk* may occur in the adverbial position immediately following an adjectival verb to indicate an increased state of the verb. This increased state is compared with a lesser state, either implicitly or explicitly. Examples (5-33a–c) imply comparisons between the present state and an earlier state when the individuals were younger, while (5-33d) compares present and future body temperatures. In (5-33e–g) the comparisons are made explicitly with objects of the preposition *jān*$_2$.

(5-33) a. Erūtto **ḷọk** em emmālele **ḷọk**.
'He grew older and became more absent-minded.'

b. Ibwijwoḷā **ḷọk**.
'I'm getting older.'

c. Jerūtto **ḷọk** im ebbanban **ḷọk**.
'We're getting older, and inability seems to be with us all the time.'

d. Nōōj ro raar arkooḷe niñniñ eo bwe en dik **ḷọk** an piba.
'The nurses rubbed alcohol on the baby to reduce its fever.'

e. Ebat **ḷọk** Jọọn **jān**$_2$ ṃokta.
'John is slower than before.'

f. Ejokwajokwe **ḷọk** ānin **jān**$_2$ Likiep.
'The island is more infested with gnats than Likiep.'

g. Ekobbā **ḷọk** aebōj jimāāṇ e aō **jān**$_2$ ṇe aṃ.
'My water cistern holds more water than yours.'

This use of *ḷọk* with adjectival verbs is similar to the comparative degree of English adjectives, often formed by adding *-er* or *more*, as in some of the preceding translations: *old**er**, slow**er**, **more** infested.*

Commands to hurry. Requests for speed, some of them abrupt, seem to have *ḷọk* in the same position in which other directionals are found, following the nonauxiliary verb—the usual position for adverbs, including directional adverbs. Such requests also have the optative verb *en* (or one of its prefixed forms such as *kwōn* or *jen*) as auxiliary verb.

(5-34) a. Kwōn jinṃaiki **ḷọk** pajo ṇe bwe jen eọñōd.
'Hurry up and mash that chum so we can start fishing.'

b. Kwōn kūrepeik(i) **ḷọk** jālele ṇe bwe jen ṃōñā.
'Hurry up with the gravy on the meat so we can eat.'

c. Kwōn raankeik **ḷọk** waini ṇe.
'Hurry up and grate that copra.'

d. Kwōn awōj (wawōj) **ḷọk**.
'Come on, step on it.'

e. Kwōn lipjerjere bajinjea raṇe bwe jen jerak **ḷọk**.
'Hurry those passengers up so we can sail right away.'

f. Kwōn ṇautōn **ḷọk** bwe en tutu.
'Give him some water so he can bathe right away.'

g. Kwōn ānen **ḷọk** bwe enaaj douj wa ṇe.
'Bail faster or the canoe will ship water.'

h. Kwōn anan **ḷọk** bwe jen eọñōd.
'Go ahead and chum so that we can fish.'

i. Kwōn kaikai **ḷọk** bwe jen etal.
'Eat up so we can leave.'

j. Koṃwin kaiur **ḷọk** ḷōṃarārā.
'Step on it, you guys.'

k. Ekwekwe bwe jen etal **ḷọk**.
'Don't stop now; keep at it so we can leave soon.'

Pagotto (1987) identifies *ḷọk* 'hurry, accelerate' as a MANNER DIRECTIONAL, a word different from and a homonym of *ḷọk,* the simple directional, because of its extra element of meaning, calling for a speedy manner. Sometimes it is not easy to determine which of the two is involved. For example, sentence (5-35a) is ambiguous. If *ḷọk* is interpreted as the simple directional, the first translation applies, with its comparative meaning '… so that they will get drier'; if it is interpreted as the manner directional, the second applies, with its element of speed '… so that they will dry faster'. Sentences like (5-35b–c) would seem to confirm Pagotto's analysis; not only are there two different *ḷọk*s, but they may cooccur, and when they do, the manner directional follows the simple directional. But the situation may be even more complex, as will be seen in the next section, where other sequences of *ḷọk* are noted.

(5-35) a. Kwōn atitiik waini kaṇe bwe ren ṃōrā **ḷọk**.
'Smoke those copra nuts so that they will get drier.'
'Smoke those copra nuts so that they will dry faster.'

b. Kwōn jake **ḷọk ḷọk** ajri ṇe.
'Hurry up and hand that child over.'

c. Kwōn jake **tok ḷọk** ajri ṇe.
'Hurry up and hand me that child.'

Continuing activity. Another special use of *ḷọk* is to indicate continuing activity. This is similar to one of the uses of *away* in English. For example, (5-36a) could also be translated as 'The fish sizzled away …'. Sentences (5-36e–g) contain a sequence of *ḷọk*s, and although the first involves continuing activity, there is no indication that the second is the manner directional found in (5-35b). Note that it is translated as *until (till)* in English, and that it is followed by a resultant clause with a finite verb (one with a subject prefix).

(5-36) a. Ettiijij **ḷọk** ek eo ke emat.
'The fish kept sizzling when it was cooked.'

b. Raar ejjebaō **ḷọk** em boñ.
'They played *ejjebaō* till nightfall.'

c. Ear kōb **ḷọk** em po dān.
'He dug until he hit water.'

d. Ta ṇe kwōj ijjitōñtōñe **ḷọk**.
'What is that you keep pointing at?'

e. Ear ḷōmṇak **ḷọk ḷọk** eḷe jān minit ko an.
'He went over his allotted minutes trying to figure out the answer.' ['He kept thinking until he went over his time limit.']

f. Ear kōnono **ḷọk ḷọk** emaat kūtuon im ḷotḷọk.
'She kept talking till she ran out of breath and fainted.'

g. Jej etetal **ḷọk ḷọk** jetōpare.
'We keep walking until we reach it.'

Complementizer with limited distribution. The observations in the preceding section concerning examples (5-36e–g) led us to examine the interchangeability of the second *ḷọk* in a sequence of two with the complementizer *ṃae* 'until'. *Ṃae* proves to be an acceptable substitute for this *ḷọk*.

(5-35) e′. Ear ḷōmṇak **ḷọk ṃae** eḷe jān minit ko an.
f′. Ear kōnono **ḷọk ṃae** emaat kūtuon im ḷotḷọk.
g′. Jej etetal **ḷọk ṃae** jetōpare.

We also tested whether *ḷọk* can substitute for the preposition *ooṃ* 'until'.

(5-36) a. Koṃ naaj kajjoñoulul ḷok **ooṃ** emaat.
Koṃ naaj kajjoñoulul ḷok **ṃae** emaat.
Koṃ naaj kajjoñoulul ḷok **ḷọk** emaat.
'Keep taking 10 each and you won't have any more left.'

b. Wa eo ear kajjoramram ḷọk **ooṃ** raan.
Wa eo ear kajjoramram ḷọk **ṃae e**raan.
Wa eo ear kajjoramram ḷọk **ḷọk e**raan.
'The ship kept flashing light signals until daybreak.'

c. Ear idaak **ooṃ** kadek.
Ear idaak **ḷọk ṃae e**kadek.
Ear idaak **ḷọk ḷọk e**kadek.
Ear idaak **ṃae e**kadek.
'He drank until he was drunk.'

d. Iar ṃōñā wor ḷọk **ooṃ** ṃaal.
Iar ṃōñā wor ḷọk **ṃae i**ṃaal.
Iar ṃōñā wor ḷọk **ḷọk i**ṃaal.
'I ate lobsters till I was absolutely full.'

e. Kwōnaaj ruṃwij bajjek **ooṃ** tūṃ.
Kwōnaaj ruṃwij bajjek **ḷọk ṃae kwo**tūṃ.
Kwōnaaj ruṃwij bajjek **ḷọk ḷọk kwo**tūṃ.
Kwōnaaj ruṃwij bajjek **ṃae kwo**tūṃ.
'You'll keep procrastinating until you're completely lost.'

Modified pronunciation of ḷọk. Finally, a note about the pronunciation of **ḷọk** the directional, which we discovered by noting that a number of example sentences in the *Marshallese On-line Dictionary* (MOD) include a form of the verb **rōre** 'look at' followed immediately by a **ḷọk** that is consistently spelled as **lọk** with a light **l**, making it sound the same as **lọk** 'posterior, buttocks.' Many of these sentences occurred originally in Capelle 2008.

(5-37) a. Ibōk bōra im ḷak **rōre lọk**, ilo juon ḷōḷḷap ioon wab eo.
'I looked up, and when I looked over I saw an old man on the dock.'

b. Iḷak **erre lọk** ilo an Bojin eo tōbal ṃaan ḷọk im jako ḷọk i buḷōn marok ko.
'I watched the Boatswain crawl toward the front of the boat and disappear in to the darkness.'

c. Jen **aktale lọk** irooj eṇ emej.
'Let's go as a group to pay our respects to the dead chief.'

d. Bao eo **ekā lọk** ke erro kar kepaak ḷọk Kapen eo.
'The bird flew away as soon as they got close to the Captain.'

Examples (5-37c–d) are evidence that the fronting of this **ḷ** occurs not only in a **rōre ḷọk** construction, but also following other verbs that end in **e**, and in other front vowels. The consonant assimilation covered in 2.5.1 dealt with the effects of a following consonant on one that precedes. That being discussed here concerns the effect of a preceding semiconsonant (the final {y} associated with all word-final front vowels) on a consonant that follows. It is supported by the tight relation between verbs and the directionals that follow them immediately.

ADVERBIAL PREPOSITIONAL PHRASES

5.4 Here we mention briefly those prepositional phrases that are not required by the verbs of their clauses. Verbs of most types may cooccur with prepositional phrases expressing times, like those in 5-38. These sentences would be grammatical without their prepositional phrases. The prepositions are given in table 4-12 on page 191.

(5-38) a. Iar jitaak **ilo ḷalem awa**.
'I arrived at five o'clock.'

b. Ewōt **ilo boñ**.
'It rains at night.'

c. Ej ṃōñā **jān$_1$ ruo awa**.
'She's been eating since two o'clock.'

Other optional prepositional phrases introduced by the preposition *ñan$_2$* 'for' occur with nonmotion activity verbs and indicate someone on whose behalf or for whose benefit the activity was done.

(5-39) a. Kakili piteto kaṇe **ñan$_2$ jineṃ**.
'Peel those potatoes for your mother.'

b. Iar al **ñan$_2$ President Kabua**.
'I sang for President Kabua.'

Prepositional phrases required by certain classes of verbs are treated in 5.6.

ADVERBIAL CLAUSES

5.5 In (5.6.6) we will consider EXTENSION VERBS, which must be followed by a complement clause. In this section, we look at adverbial clauses that modify the verb optionally. Adverbial clauses are introduced by complementizers, which are displayed in table 5-5. *Bwe* appears twice in the table, as *bwe*$_2$ 'because' and as *bwe*$_1$ 'so that'. The latter is always followed by a form of *en* 'optative', as is seen in (5-40b). *Ke* appears twice, as *ke*$_2$'when, while' (5-41f) and as nonadverbial *ke*$_1$ 'that', which introduces complements of some extension verbs. *Ñe* appears twice, as *ñe*$_2$ 'when, while', and as *ñe*$_1$ 'if'.

(5-40) a. Ikōṇaan idaak wūno **bwe**$_2$ emetak bōra.
'I want to drink medicine because I have a headache.'

b. Idaak ni **bwe**$_1$ **en** kadipen eok.
'Drink coconuts so that they will strengthen you.'

The examples in 5-41 illustrate the use of various other complementizers.

(5-41) a. Ebwe an maroñ **amñe** edik.
'He's quite able despite his age.'

b. **Elaññe** eṃṃan mour inaaj iwōj.
'If I feel alright, I'll be there.'

Table 5-5 Complementizers

ADVERBIAL					
	LOCATIONAL				
	REALIS	POSTERIOR		ṃae	'until'
				ooṃ	'until'
				ḷọk	'until'[1]
		NONPOSTERIOR		ke$_2$	'when, while'
	IRREALIS			ñe$_2$	'when, while'
	NONLOCATIONAL				
	CAUSE			kōnke	'because'
				bwe$_2$	'because'
	NONCAUSE	PURPOSE		bwe$_1$	'so that'
		NONPURPOSE			
			CONDITION	elaññe	'if'
				ñe$_1$	'if'
			NONCONDITION	meñe	'although'
				amñe	'although
NONADVERBIAL					
	FACT			ke$_1$	'that'
	NONFACT			in	'to'

1. See 5-35 and 5-36.

c. **Meñe** emetak neō ak ij kōrwaan ļọk eok.
'Although my feet hurt I'm escorting you there.'

d. Rej jab ennọ mā kaṇe **kōnke** reālkūṃur.
'Those breadfruit are not good because they're from an old tree.'

e. **Ñe**$_2$ eṃōj aō tutu inaaj ṃōñā.
'When I've finished bathing, I'll eat.'

f. Rōbuuki **ke**$_2$ ej duoj tok.
'They shot him when he stepped out.'

g. Jinen ear inoñ **ṃae** ej kiki.
'His mother told him legends until he fell asleep.'

h. Kwōn kajoobobe ke eō **ñe**$_1$ emaat joob e aō?
'Will you let me share your soap if I run out of mine?'

i. Eļap an koṇkoṇ ļeeṇ **ñe**$_2$ ej eọñōd.
'He catches lots of fish when he goes fishing.'

MAJOR VERB CLASSES

5.6 Pagotto (1987) identifies nine major classes of verbs in Marshallese. All nine classes are presented in table 5-6, together with the location of example sentences for each class of verbs. Classes are identified by alphabet letters for ease of reference in the discussion that follows.[18] The table should be referred to for the major characteristics for each class; for example, Class A verbs are not extension verbs, and they are intransitive and impersonal. Class B verbs differ from Class A verbs only in being personal. And so on.

- EXTENSION VERBS are those that must be followed by an inner complement. The four classes with these verbs (classes D & E and H & I are treated together after all the NONEXTENSION classes have been treated.
- TRANSITIVE VERBS are those that must be followed by a direct object that is either definite or quantified (see 3.3.2 on page 152). Most transitive verbs have INTRANSITIVE counterparts that are used in other ways, often with subtle differences in meaning (see "Transitive and intransitive counterparts" on page 154). These two counterparts are always members of different major classes.
- PERSONAL VERBS are those that may bear subject prefixes of any person and number (see table 3-10 on page 151), unlike IMPERSONAL VERBS, which bear only a default 3S prefix *e-* that has no referent.
- ADJECTIVAL VERBS have special characteristics (see table 3-13 on page 155 for examples), including the fact that they are the source for ADJECTIVES (see 4.4 on page 187).

18. The letters match those used by Pagotto 1987.

Table 5-6 Major verb classes of Marshallese

		EXAMPLES
NONEXTENSION		
INTRANSITIVE		
IMPERSONAL	Class A	(5-42)–(5-53)
PERSONAL		
NONADJECTIVAL	Class B	(5-54)–(5-66)
ADJECTIVAL	Class C	(5-67)–(5-72)
TRANSITIVE		
IMPERSONAL	Class F	(5-73)
PERSONAL	Class G	(5-74)–(5-80)
EXTENSION		
INTRANSITIVE		
IMPERSONAL	Class D	(5-81)–(5-82)
PERSONAL	Class E	(5-84)–(5-94)
TRANSITIVE		
IMPERSONAL	Class H	(5-95)
PERSONAL	Class I	(5-96)–(5-98)

CLASS A VERBS

5.6.1 Class A verbs are INTRANSITIVE and IMPERSONAL. Impersonal verbs do not have referential subjects. That is, the implied subject of an impersonal verb does not refer to any entity, event, or state of affairs with referential properties, and is like the empty or "dummy" **it** in English sentences such as "**It** seems that John is sick." The equivalent in Marshallese is the **e-** prefix that marks impersonal verbs as having THIRD PERSON SINGULAR subjects, even when there is no referential PERSON to be marked for an imPERSONal verb. A good example is the meteorological verb *wōt* 'rain' exemplified in (5-42a).

(5-42) a. **E**wōt.
'**It**'s raining.'

b. **E**pāl.
'**It**'s arrowroot-digging time.'

c. **E**dibūkae jikōt?
'In what direction is this *dibūkae* current flowing?

d. Kwōn ņapitōn bwe$_2$ **e**jjeļọk.
'Give him a pillow because he doesn't have any.'
['Give him a pillow because there isn't any.']

The last example has the existential verb *jjeļọk* 'not exist' embedded under a POSSESSED VERB (see "Possessed verbs in ņa." on page 255). Simple class A verbs include, in addition to this one existential verb, meteorological verbs, verbs relating to seasons and other temporal matters, and verbs relating to currents and waves. Other verbs of this same type include *kōto* 'be windy', *detñil* 'be a sunny day without wind', *to* 'be a long time', *jibboñ* 'be morning', *pāāt* 'be low tide', and *buñņo* 'be breaking waves'. All the subtypes of class A verbs are given in table 5-7 together with the location of examples. The classification in the table is from Pagotto (1987), including her letter-number labels for extant types—[A1], for example, the type discussed in this paragraph and exemplified in (5-42), the only subtype of class 1 verbs that does not involve a CORRESPONDENT.

Table 5-7 Subtypes of Class A verbs

		EXAMPLES
NONCORRESPONDENT	[A1]	(5-42)
CORRESPONDENT		
NONEXISTENTIAL		
NONCOMPARATIVE		
NONMANNER		
NONLOCATIVE	[A2]	(5-43)–(5-47)
LOCATIVE		
NONDIRECTIONAL		
NONASSOCIATIVE	[A3]	(5-48a–c)
ASSOCIATIVE	[A4]	(5-48d–e)
DIRECTIONAL	[A5]	(5-49)
MANNER		
NO PREPOSITION	[A6]	(5-50a–b)
PREPOSITION	[A7]	(5-50c–d)
COMPARATIVE	[A8]	(5-51)
EXISTENTIAL	[A9]	(5-52)

Correspondents. The other subtypes of class A verbs are presented in the subsections that follow. Their sentences are more complex, and include a grammatical element called a CORRESPONDENT (first mentioned in 3.3.2. on page 153). The verbs in these sentences typically specify a quality attributed to the nominal with which they cooccur (a nominal is a nounlike word).

(5-43) a. **E**obab tibat eo.
'The teapot is dented.'

b. **E**kankan nuknuk ṇe aṃ.
'Your dress is too tight.'

The nominals that are underlined in these sentences are the CORRESPONDENTS of these impersonal verbs. They might appear to be the subjects of the verbs, as the English translations suggest, and they are in a position that is permissible for the subjects of intransitive verbs, following the verb (although not their usual position before the verb). Thus, the sentences in 5-43 might be construed as having simple personal adjectival verbs (Class C) with postposed subjects. But such an analysis would not be correct.

Subject-verb agreement. This is because Marshallese verbs must AGREE in person and number with their subjects, regardless of whether the subject precedes or follows the verb, as the following examples illustrate (unacceptable sentences are preceded by an asterisk):

(5-44) a. Ajri ro rōkiki. *Ajri ro ekiki.
b. Rōkiki ajri ro. *Ekiki ajri ro.
'The children are asleep.'

Because *ajri ro* 'the children', the subject in (5-44b), is third person plural, the verb *kiki* 'sleep, be asleep' must be marked with the third person plural subject prefix *rō-*. It is incorrect with *e-,* the third person singular prefix. Therefore, verbs such as *kiki* belong to a class of PERSONAL verbs (Class B), which must agree in person and number with their subjects, whether the subject precedes or follows the verb. However, this person-number agreement does not hold between the IMPERSONAL CORRESPONDENT verbs and the postverbal underlined nominals in 5-43. These singular nominals can be made plural with no change in the verb's subject prefix:

(5-45) a. **E**obab tibat ko.
'The teapots are dented.'

b. **E**kankan nuknuk kaṇe aṃ.
'Your dresses are too tight.'

Compare the examples in (5-45) with those in (5-43), whose intransitive stative verbs must agree with their plural subjects, even if the subjects follow the verbs. The examples in (5-45) show that these impersonal verbs can be prefixed with the third person singular prefix *e-* even though the nominal with which they cooccur is third person plural. Nor may these plural nouns precede an impersonal verb prefixed with *e-,* that is, they may not appear in the usual position for subjects of transitive verbs and subjects of personal nonadjectival verbs, before the verb:

(5-46) a. *Tibat eo eobab.
b. *Nuknuk kaṇe aṃ ekankan.

By recognizing that the underlined nominals in (5-43) and (5-45) are the CORRESPONDENTS of the verbs, rather than their SUBJECTS, we can explain the seemingly conflicting facts about person-number agreement between verbs and subjects. The impersonal verbs in these examples cannot have referential SUBJECTS; instead, they have CORRESPONDENTS, and each of them predicates a quality of its correspondent—in this instance, that it is dented, or that it doesn't fit. The personal verbs in (5-44) have referential subjects, but no correspondents.

Simple Class A verbs with correspondents [A2]. The sentences below, like those of (5-43) and (5-45) in the preceding section, involve an impersonal verb and a Correspondent. Verbs of this type are derived from adjectival verbs of class C, and from nouns (see "Denominal distributive verbs" on page 165).

(5-47) a. **E**jeepepḷọk pād eo aerro.
'Their marriage is ruined.'

b. **E**dim juuj ko an.
'His shoes are tight.'

c. **E**bwilọk aḷaḷ ṇe.
'That piece of wood is broken.'

d. **E**dāne oran ko.
'The oranges are juicy.'

e. **E**ddilala rā ṇe.
'That board has many nails.'

f. **E**bbōlōklōk iuṃwin mā eṇ.
'There are lots of leaves under that breadfruit tree.'

Note that the Correspondents *juuj ko* of (5-47b) and *oran ko* of (5-47d) are plural, something that would not be possible if they were the subjects of personal verbs.

Other verbs of this type derived from class C adjectival verbs include *dede* 'be ready', *bur* 'be unripe', *jekapen* 'be less than half full', *iñōkñōke* 'be very decorated', and *ialolo* 'be yellowish'. Other examples with a distributive sense, like (5-47d–f), include *ibbuwakwake* 'be replete with birthmarks', *ike* 'be teeming with fish', and *ekeke* 'be replete with veins'.

Locative verbs [A3, A4]. The locative verbs in this section are impersonal and are followed in their sentences by a CORRESPONDENT and a LOCUS,[19] in that order. The correspondent and locus are both nominals, that is, nouns or words behaving like nouns.

(5-48) a. **E**rerak jaki *ilowaan ṃweo*.
'Mats were all over the floor of the house.'
['There was protection everywhere of mats inside the house.']

b. **E**ṃọk tiṃọṇ *ṇa ippān*.
'He is possessed by a demon.'
['There is entered a demon there with him.']

c. **E**kuk ek ko *ṇa ippān doon*.
'The fish are all gathered together.'
['There is a gathering of fish there with each other.']

d. **E**kane bwiro *ippān wōn*.
'Preserved breadfruit goes with turtle meat deliciously.'
['There is a good mix of preserved breadfruit with turtle meat.']

e. **E**kilōk al eo *ippām*.
'We've memorized the song.
['The song is enclosed with us.']

---

19. Locuses are italicized in these examples.

The LOCUS nominal in (5-48a) is introduced by the INALIENABLE NOUN (see table 3-6 on page 130) *ilowaan* 'inside', and in (5-48b–c) by the locational noun *ṇa* 'there'. The verbs in (5-48d–e) are not only LOCATIVE, but ASSOCIATIVE as well in that they require a locus introduced by the associative noun *ippa-* 'companion; with'.

Directional locative verbs [A5]. Verbs in this subtype of class A locative verbs have their locus further specified with either the direction *ñan*$_1$ 'to' or *jān*$_1$ 'from'. The verbs in (5-49a–b) are nonmotion verbs, whereas the one in (5-49c) is a motion verb derived from the existential verb *or* 'be' (5-52).

(5-49) a. **E**kkar nuknuk kaṇe ñan$_1$ *kwe*.
'Your clothes fit you.'
['It is suited your clothing to you.']

b. **E**jabjab peiū jān$_1$ *raan mā e.*
'I can't reach this breadfruit branch with my hands.'
['It is out of reach of my hands from this breadfruit branch.']

c. **E**or tok armej ñan$_1$ *ṃwiin.*
'Someone is coming toward this house.'
['There are coming people to this house.']

Manner verbs [A6, A7]. The manner verbs in this section are impersonal and are followed in their sentences by a CORRESPONDENT and by a MEANS. The Means nominal may or may not be introduced by the preposition *kōn*$_1$. Without the preposition, the Means precedes the Correspondent (5-50a–b); with the preposition, it follows (5-50c–e).[20]

(5-50) a. **E**arōk *menọknọk* leeṇ.
'That boy is a pack rat (saves any old thing).'

b. **E**kkutaktak *iu* lōḷḷap eṇ.
'That woman is always scraping sprouted coconuts.'

c. **E**obrak wa ko kōn$_1$ *ṃweiuk.*
'The boats are full of trade goods.'

d. **E**ppeddejake ānin kōn$_1$ *mā.*
'This island is covered with breadfruit.'

e. **E**tiljek leeṇ kōn$_1$ *jāān.*
'He is careful with money.'

Other class A manner verbs include *booḷ* 'be full', *jijuurore* 'be full', *jel* 'be grown over (with)', *jure* 'be teeming (with)', and *jok* 'be heavily laden (with) (of boats)'.

Comparative verbs [A8]. Class A verbs that are not existential are typically derived from Class C (adjectival) verbs. As such, they are eligible to

20. The MEANS is shown in italics in these examples.

have comparative verbs derived from them. This subtype compares one nominal with another using the preposition *jān*$_2$ 'than'.

(5-51) a. **E**dik at kā jān$_2$ bōra.
'These hats are too small for me.'
['It is too small of these hats than my head.']

b. **E**kkar nuknuk kaṇe ñan$_1$ *kwe* jān$_2$ ña.
'Those clothes look better on you than they would on me.'
['It is more suited of your clothes than me.']

c. **E**obrakļọk wa ko kōn$_1$ *ṃweiuk* jān$_2$ tūrak ko.
'The boats are more full of trade goods than the trucks.'
['It is more full of trade goods of the boats than the trucks.']

Comparing (5-51b) with (5-49a) (and noting the preposition) shows that *kwe* is the LOCUS, and (5-51c) with (5-50c) shows that *ṃweiuk* is the MEANS.

Existential verbs [A9]. There are only two existential verbs in Marshallese, *ejjeļọk* 'be not, not exist' and *or* (*wōr*) 'be, exist'. (The Ratak counterpart of *ejjeļọk* is *jej*.) Existential verbs are impersonal.

(5-52) a. **Ejjeļọk** raij. (W) **Ejej** raij. (E) [21]
'There is no rice.'

b. **Eor** bōrran (būrarin) ṃōñā ilo nuknuk ṇe aṃ.
'There are food stains on your clothes.'

c. **Ejjeļọk** wōt mōṃanin. (W) **Ejej** wōt mōṃanin. (E)
'There is nothing (that can compare with) its goodness.'

Because the first of the two, *ejjeļọk*, does not *require* a correspondent (as *or/wōr* does), it was introduced at the beginning of 5.6.1 together with other impersonal verbs that do not have corrrespondents. Example (5-52a) shows it with a correspondent; similar examples are found in (5-18) on page 217.

Notice that the nominals interpreted as correspondents in (5-52) are indefinite. Existential verbs cannot occur with definite nouns in Marshallese, as the sentences in (5-53) show.

(5-53) a. *Ejjeļọk ajri eo iṃwiin.

b. Ajri eo ejjab pād iṃwiin.
'The child is not in this house.'

Example (5-53a) shows that a definite noun may not appear with an existential verb; however, the personal locative verb *pād* 'stay' can be used to make an existential-locational statement with a definite noun phrase as subject (5-53b).

---

21. Correspondents are underlined in these and following examples.

This concludes our look at the subtypes of Class A verbs, verbs that are intransitive and impersonal. We turn now to Classes B and C, verbs that are intransitive and personal. Class C verbs are also adjectival; Class B are not.[22]

Class B Verbs

5.6.2 Class B verbs are INTRANSITIVE, PERSONAL, and NONADJECTIVAL. Personal verbs may have subjects of any person and number. The subjects of the sentences are real people (or real things, such as *laḷ in* 'the earth' in [5-54d]). Table 5-8 shows the various *syntactic* subtypes of Class B verbs.[23]

Nonlocative verbs [B1]. In the first three lines of table 5-8, we see that the simplest Class B verbs are not marked for correspondent, manner, or location.

(5-54) a. Ear illu im *limek*.[24]
'She got angry and packed.'

b. Kwōn jab *kūk*.
'Don't bite.'

c. Inaaj *ṃōñā* ilo ḷalem awa.
'I will eat at five o'clock.'

d. Lale bwe kwōn jab *jājḷọk*.
'Be careful you don't slip.'

e. Laḷ in ej *rọọlọl*.
'The earth is spinning.'

f. Kōm ar *ikoeeak* bajjek imeḷan āneo.
'We just sort of roamed around the island.'

There are two basic *semantic* types of Class B verbs: motion verbs, and nonmotion verbs. The Class B verbs in (5-54d–f) are motion verbs; those in (5-54a–c) are nonmotion verbs. Motion verbs involve major changes in position; the smaller, partial motions involved with verbs like PACK, BITE, and EAT do not qualify. Other Class B motion verbs include *jeblaak* 'leave', *oḷọk* 'fall over', *jepjep* 'migrate', *buñ* 'fall', and *ālāl* 'turn over'; nonmotion verbs in this class include *kiki* 'sleep', *jijet* 'sit', *jokutbae* 'wave goodbye', and *lelo* (*ello*) 'see'. Class B verbs that are derived include *kōp-pojak* 'make self ready' (from *pojak* 'be ready') and *jujukwakwa* (*ijju-kwakwa*)'use sugar all the time' (from *jukwa* 'sugar').

22. Refer again to the outline in table 5-6 on page 234.
23. Syntactic types are based on the arrangements of words with each other. Semantic types are based on the meanings of the words.
24. The Class B verbs in these sentences are shown in italics.

Table 5-8 Subtypes of Class B verbs

		EXAMPLES
NONCORRESPONDENT		
NONMANNER		
NONLOCATIVE	[B1][1]	(5-54)
LOCATIVE		
NONDIRECTIONAL		
NONASSOCIATIVE	[B2]	(5-57a–c)
ASSOCIATIVE	[B3]	(5-57d–f)
DIRECTIONAL	[B4]	(5-55) (5-56)
MANNER		
NO PREPOSITION		
NONLOCATIVE	[B5]	(5-58) (5-59)
LOCATIVE		
NONDIRECTIONAL	[B6]	(5-60a)
DIRECTIONAL	[B7]	(5-60b–c)
PREPOSITION	[B8]	(5-61) (5-62)
CORRESPONDENT		
NONASSOCIATIVE		
NONLOCATIVE	[B9]	(5-63)
LOCATIVE		
NONDIRECTIONAL	[B10]	(5-64a–b)
DIRECTIONAL	[B11]	(5-64c)
ASSOCIATIVE		
NO PREPOSITION	[B12]	(5-65)
PREPOSITION		
NONLOCATIVE	[B13]	(5-66a–f)
LOCATIVE	[B14]	(5-66g)

1. Labels used in Pagotto (1987).

Directional locative verbs [B4]. The table also shows that locative verbs are further classified on the basis of direction. Simple (nondirectional) locative verbs are discussed in the next section. All locative verbs require a locus (underlined in the following examples), and the directional locative verbs also require a preposition or other word indicating a direction (double-underlined).

(5-55) a. Ear *kadduoj ḷọk* jān$_1$ U.H.
'S/he graduated from the University of Hawai'i.'

b. Ij *owar* ñan$_1$ eok bwe kwōn jouj in jab baere Jọọn.
'I'm begging you please not to fire John.'

c. Kwōn jab *elḷọk* jān$_1$ e.
'Don't turn away from her.'

d. Aisen ear *etal* ñan$_1$ Awai.
'Aisen went to Hawai'i.'

Verbs like *kadduoj* and *elḷọk* require a locus that is their SOURCE, and others like *owar* and *etal* require a locus that is their GOAL. This information is carried by the prepositions *jan*$_1$ 'from' and *ñan*$_1$ 'to' in 5-55. The absence of this required information makes (5-56b) and (5-56e) sentences that are not well formed, and (5-56c) and (5-56f) only questionably so.

(5-56) a. Aisen ear *etal* ñan$_1$ ia?
'Where did Aisen go?'

b. *Ia eo Aisen ear *etal* ie?
('Where is it that Aisen went?')

c. ?Ia eo Aisen ear *etal* ie ḷọk?
'Where is it that Aisen went?'

d. Wōn eo kwōj *kūttiliek* jāne$_1$?
'Who is it that you are hiding from?'

e. *Jān wōn eo kwōj *kūttiliek* ie?
('From whom are you hiding?')

f. ?Jān wōn eo kwōj *kūttiliek* jāne$_1$?
'From whom are you hiding?'

Other Class B directional locative verbs include *jitḷọk* 'abstain (from)', *ba* 'say (to)', *ejaak* 'evolve (from)', and *elḷọk* 'pay attention (to)'. Motion verbs include *wōtlọk* 'fall (from)', *jājḷọk* 'separate (from)', *ilọk* 'go (to', and *kajju* 'go directly (to).

Nondirectional locative verbs [B2, B3]. Like the directional locative verbs, these verbs also require a locus. They are further subdivided into those that are ASSOCIATIVE (5-57c–f), and those that are not (5-57a–b).

(5-57) a. Kwaar *pād* ke ilo kwelọk eo?
'Did you attend the meeting?'

b. Ni eṇ *ejitpeeḷeḷ* ioon iaḷ eṇ. (*jitpeeḷeḷ* 'lie crosswise')
'That coconut tree is lying across the road.'

c. Wōn ṇe kwōj *rōrā* (*errā*) ippān? (*rōra* 'take sides')
'Which side are you on?'

d. *Kōkejel* (*ekkejel*) ippa. (*kōkejel* 'hang on')
'Hang on to me.'

e. *Epeljo* ek ko koṇa ippān ko koṇan. (*peljo* 'mix in')
'My catch got mixed in with his.'

f. Eḷap aṃ *ṃuri* ippa. (*ṃuri* 'owe')
'You owe me quite a bit.'

Pād is the quintessential locative verb, expressing simply and purely 'be located at'. In (5-57a), 'Were you located at the meeting?'—with meeting being the locus. In (5-57b), it is the 'on of' the road, rather than the road itself, that is the locus.[25] Other NONASSOCIATIVE locative verbs include

25. See 3.2.7 on page 145 for a discussion of "place nouns" like *ioon* 'on'.

waḷọk 'appear', *jokwe* 'live', *peḷaak* 'gather', *kappijinjin* 'put spots on', and *deblọk* 'pass through'.

There seems to be only one word that can serve as locus for ASSOCIATIVE locative verbs, such as those illustrated in (5-57c–f), and that is one of the possessed forms of the inalienable noun *ippa-* 'company'[26] (or its Ratak variant *pepa-*, both listed in table 3-6 among the nouns expressing SPATIAL AND TEMPORAL ADJUNCTS). Thus, one might say that the subjects of associative locative verbs are not alone; they have 'company'.

Manner verbs [B5–B8]. All manner verbs occur with a word indicating the MEANS the verb uses to accomplish what it is doing. One type of manner verb [B8] has a means that is preceded by the preposition *kōn*; the other types [B5–7] (without prepositions) have a means that is an indefinite common noun such as those that immediately follow the verbs in (5-58). The fact that their means is an indefinite common noun makes possible an interpretation that focuses on the activity being performed: 'they are making rolls (using pandanus leaves to do so).'

(5-58) a. Rej *jāljel* maañ.
'They are rolling up pandanus leaves.'

b. Ear *aujek* ṃakṃōk.
'She made starch.'

c. Ej *patpat* raij.
'She is washing rice.'

d. Rej *inene* pāākin waini.
'They are carrying bags of copra on their shoulders.'

Such sentences correspond to those that have been called "incorporated object constructions" in other Micronesian languages such as Kosraean, Mokilese, Pohnpeian, and Woleaian, where the Means is incorporated into the verb, forming a single compound word that cannot be separated by other words, as if one were saying: 'She is starch-making, rice-washing, etc.' Pagotto (1987) shows that Marshallese does not follow this pattern, and gives examples in which sentences like those in (5-58) may have their verb and its means separated, as in (5-59a), which shows that *idaakban* is not a compound meaning 'punch-drinking'. The fact that *tok* cannot be postponed until after *waini* in (5-59b) confirms that *aljek* alone is the verb, as directional adverbs adhere tightly to the post-verbal position. Thus, *aljek* is the verb, and *waini* has not joined it as part of a compound verb.

(5-59) a. Kwōj *idaak* ban **ke**?
Kwōj *idaak* **ke** ban?
'Are you drinking punch?'

26. The *i* of *ippa-* is the locative *i* that has fused with *ppa-*, so that *ippa*, for example, is literally 'in my company', but is often translated as 'with me' in English.

b. *Kwōn *aljek* waini **tok**.[27]
Kwōn *aljek* **tok** waini.
'Gather copra nuts.'

The sentences in (5-58) and (5-59) all have nonlocative manner verbs [B-5]. Those in (5-60) include two types, one (5-60a) that is nondirectional [B-6], and two (5-60b–c) that are directional [B-7] and that specify with the prepositions *jan*$_1$ 'from' and *ñan*$_1$ 'to' whether the locus is source or goal.[28]

(5-60) a. Rej *kattulọk* armej iar.
'They are dunking people in the lagoon.'

b. Rej *kōṃṃan* lodideañ jān$_1$ kōmjān (kōmij in) ni.
'They are making pinwheels from coconut leaves.'

c. Kwōj *aljek* ṃweiuk ñan$_1$ ia?
'Where are you taking those goods?'

We turn now to the type of Class B manner verbs that mark their MEANS with the preposition *kōn*$_1$ [B-8]. (See table 4-12 on page 191, with its note indicating that *kōn*$_1$ has the anaphoric forms *kake*$_1$ and *kaki*$_1$, which are used in contexts where its object is omitted, paralleling the anaphoric object markers of transitive verbs [page 153].)

(5-61) a. Imaroñ ke *kuuṃuṃ* kōn$_1$ kuuṃ ṇe aṃ?
'May I use your comb?'

b. Ij ja *bọọkọk* kōn$_1$ bọọk e aṃ.
'I'll use your box for now.'

c. Kwōn *lōñtak* kōn$_1$ pet ṇe.
'Prop yourself up with that pillow.'

d. Jenaaj *malejjoñ* kōn$_1$ jerbal ko an.
'Let's take his works as examples.'

e. Ta ṇe kwaar *kuuṃuṃ* kake$_1$?
'What did you use for a comb?'

f. Ewi pet eo kwaar *ḷoñtak* kake$_1$?
'Where is the pillow you propped yourself up with?'

The verbs in (5-61a,b,e) are derived from nouns by reduplication, *kuuṃuṃ* 'use a comb' from *kuuṃ* 'comb', and *bọọkọk* 'use a box' from *bọọk* 'box'. The anaphoric form of kōn$_1$ is used in (5-61e–f).

Other Class B manner verbs that require their means to be marked by *kōn*$_1$ include *nine* 'use a container', *peenen* 'use a pen', *anbōro* 'curry favor with', *kakōl* 'show off', and *jobai* 'barter'.

27. An unacceptable sentence is preceded by an asterisk.
28. The noun following each of these verbs is the MEANS, and the LOCUS is underlined.

(5-62) a. Enaaj *nine* (*enne*) kōn$_1$ at e aō.
'He'll use my hat for a container.'

b. An wōn ṇe peen kwōj *peenen* kake$_1$?
'Whose pen are you using?'

c. Kwōn jab *anbōro* kōn$_1$ jāān kaṇe aō.
'Don't use my money to get in good with the girls.'

d. Ej *kakōl* kōn$_1$ nuknuk kaṇ an.
'She's showing off her dresses.'

e. Ear *jobai* kake$_1$ (kōn$_1$) ek ko koṇan.
'He sold the fish he caught.'

Correspondent verbs [B9–B14]. We have met correspondents already in our survey of Class A verbs (see page 235). Some Class B correspondent verbs are associative; some are not.

Nonassociative correspondent verbs [B9–B11]. Transitive verbs in Marshallese must be followed by nouns that are definite or quantified (see 3.3.2 on page 152), yet in (5-63) we see that there are intransitive verbs that may also be followed by definite nouns. These nouns are not their objects, but their correspondents.

(5-63) a. Ear *ṃōñā* ek eo koṇa.
'He ate of my fish'.

b. *Naṃōḷ* tok kijeerro kūrepe.
'Scoop out some gravy for the two of us.'

c. Ear *ṃōñā* ek eo koṇa im iar leḷọk bwe eo ñan Medi.
'He ate of my fish, and I gave the rest to Mary.'

d. *Ear *kañ* ek eo koṇa im iar leḷọk bwe eo ñan Medi.

e. Kwaar *ukōt* kōrkan lowaan ṃwe.
'You rearranged the room.'
'You made rearrangements to the room.'

f. Kajopāl wa ṇe bwe jen *kōttar* wa kaṇ jet.
'Flap the sail because we should wait for the other boats.'

g. Etke kwōj jab *idaak* batin in metak kā ñe emetak bōraṃ?
'Why don't you take these aspirin pills if you have a headache?'

h. Kwōn jab būroñ bwe armej enaaj *mijak* eok.
'Don't talk harshly or people will be afraid of you.'

Although these correspondent nouns are definite, the intransitive verbs (like *ṃōñā* in [5-63a]) force a PARTITIVE interpretation on them, so that the entire fish is not consumed (as it would be if the verb were transitive *kañ*), but only a PART of it. Similarly, with gravy in (5-63b), *some gravy*, a PART of the gravy. A comparison of sentences (5-63c–d) shows that with intransitive *ṃōñā,* there is a remainder to be given to someone else, but with transitive *kañ,* all is consumed and it makes no sense to speak of a remainder. It is easier to see the partitive nature of (5-63e) with the second translation. Other verbs of this type [B-9] are *kōttar* 'wait (for)', *idaak* 'drink (of)', *mijak* 'fear (about) as illustrated in (5-63f–h).

The verbs in sentences (5-64a–b) are also Class B nonassociative correspondent verbs, but they need to have locative [B-10] phrases added, and *bōbrae* in (5-64c) needs a directional [B-11] phrase as well. The partitive nature of the noun correspondents following these verbs may be less obvious, but is nevertheless posited by Pagotto (1987:398).

(5-64) a. Ij *dedoor* (*eddoor*) aō bok ilo tebōḷ eo aō.
'I keep my book in my desk.'

b. Iar *kaddeḷọñ* aō ṃaak ilo pāāñ.
'I deposited my money in the bank.'

c. Kwōn *bōbrae* ḷadik eo jān$_1$ an tutu i ar.
'Keep the boy from bathing in the lagoon.'

Associative correspondent verbs [B12–B14]. These Class B verbs are associated with a correspondent. Those of the type [B12] use forms of *ippa* 'company' to accomplish this without a preposition.[29]

(5-65) a. Inaaj *jebokwōn* ippaṃ.
'I'll spend the night in your company / with you.'

b. Kwōn jab *aerār* ippa.
'Don't touch shoulders with me.'

c. Ej *jep* ippān ḷōṃaraṇ nukun.
'He's taking his relatives' side.'

d. Ḷōṃaro raṇ rej *iāllulu* ippān ek kaṇ.
'Those boys are racing to catch the fish (on the reef).'

e. Ej ilān *idaak* ippān koṃbani eṇ an.
'He's going out drinking with his buddy.'

Those of the type [B13] use the preposition *kōn*$_2$ 'about' before the Correspondent. Example (5-66g) is of the type [B14], which includes a directional locative.

(5-66) a. Iar *taktō* kōn$_2$ peiū.
'I saw the doctor about my arm.'

b. Jab *jājjāj* kōn$_2$ lieṇ pāleeṃ.
'Don't boast about your wife.'

c. Ej *kōḷmānḷọkjeṇ* kōn$_2$ bōd ko an.
'He's pondering his mistakes.'

29. Although one often finds the English preposition 'with' in the translations of these examples, the word *ippa-* found in the examples is a Marshallese relator noun meaning 'company; in the company of'.

d. *Ellotaan* kōn$_2$ piik eo nejin ejako.
'He's complaining about his lost pig.'

e. Eḷap aō *bwilōñ* kōn$_2$ baḷuun eo.
'The airplane amazes me.'

f. Raar joorkatkat ke rej *roñ* kōn$_2$ an po wa eo.
'They mobilized when they heard of the boat's capture.'

g. Koṃ *keeañḷọk* kōn$_2$ naan ṇe ñan$_1$ Arṇo.
'Spread the news over to Arṇo.'

This concludes our look at the subtypes of Class B verbs, verbs that are intransitive and personal, but nonadjectival. We turn now to Class C verbs, which are intransitive, personal, and adjectival.[30]

Class C Verbs

5.6.3 Class C verbs are INTRANSITIVE, PERSONAL, and ADJECTIVAL. They are the verbs from which all adjectives are derived (see "Adjectives" on page 187). They are also the source from which impersonal verbs are derived (see "Simple Class A verbs with correspondents [A2]" on page 236). Table 5-8 shows the various *syntactic* subtypes of Class C verbs.[31]

Nonlocative verbs [C1]. In the first three lines of table 5-9, we see that the simplest Class C verbs are not marked for correspondent, manner, or location. There are a large number of verbs in this simple adjectival class, including verbs such as *piọ* 'be cold', *jide* 'be lucky', *nana* 'be bad', *ṃōk* 'be tired', *ṃōj* 'be finished', *jeñak* 'be covered up', and *ātet* 'be impounded'.

(5-67) a. Taij e*kōjjarjar.*
'Crap shooting is expensive.'

b. Kwōn jab *ṃōṃaelep* (*eṃṃaelep*).
'Don't be too anxious.'

c. Wa eo eṇ e*eọtōk.*
'That canoe is stranded.'

d. I*pooḷ.*
'I am surrounded.'

e. Bao eo eṇ e*ātet* ilowaan oror eṇ.
'The chicken has been put into the coop.'

The verb in (5-67a) is a causative adjectival verb 'cause to be always broke' derived from *jōjarjar* (*ejjarjar*) 'be always broke', a distributive adjectival verb that is itself derived from *jar* 'be broke'.

30. Refer again to the outline in table 5-6 on page 234.
31. Syntactic types are based on the arrangements of words with each other. Semantic types are based on the meanings of the words.

Table 5-9 Subtypes of Class C verbs

		EXAMPLES
NONCORRESPONDENT		
NONMANNER		
NONLOCATIVE	[C1][1]	5-67
LOCATIVE		
NONDIRECTIONAL		
NONASSOCIATIVE	[C2]	(5-68a–e)
ASSOCIATIVE	[C3]	(5-68f–h)
DIRECTIONAL	[C4]	5-69
MANNER		
NO PREPOSITION	[C5]	(5-70h–j)
PREPOSITION	[C6]	(5-70a–g)
CORRESPONDENT		
NONASSOCIATIVE		
NONCOMPARATIVE	[C7]	(5-71b–f)
COMPARATIVE	[C8]	(5-71a)
ASSOCIATIVE		
NO PREPOSITION	[C9]	(5-72a–c)
PREPOSITION	[C10]	(5-72d–e)

1. Labels used in Pagotto (1987).

Nondirectional locative verbs [C2, C3]. These adjectival verbs have a locus, and may also have an associate. Those in (5-68a–e) do not have an associate [C2]; those in (5-68f–h) do [C3]. For these latter, the word *ipp-* 'in the company of' serves as the locus.

(5-68) a. Wōn eṇ e*mmat* i aejet.
'The turtle is on the surface of the ocean.'

b. Ear *keṇaak* ṇa iuṃwin kaar eo.
'He was trapped under the car.'

c. Wa eo eṇ ej *emjak* i ar.
'The boat is anchored close to the lagoon beach.'

d. Eḷap an *miminene* (*imminene*) ilo jerbal in injin.
'He's an experienced mechanic.'

e. E*ṃōkade* ilo piimboñ.
'He is expert at ping pong.'

f. Āne kaṇ re*piro* ippān doon.
'Those islands are joined together.'
(lit. … in each other's company).

g. E*dāpijek* peba ko ippān doon.
'The papers are fastened together.'

h. [Lio e*mmejaja* ippa] [eṇ].
'That's the girl who caught my eye.'
(lit. …the girl who is attractive to me is that one).

Directional locative adjectival verbs [C4]. All locative verbs require a locus (underlined in the following examples), and these directional locative verbs also require a preposition or other word indicating a direction (doubly underlined).

(5-69) a. I*pojak* ñan$_1$ mej in.
'I am immune to the flu.'

b. Jab *jokwōd* jān$_1$ kilaaj.
'Don't be absent from class.'

c. E*jenoḷọk* jan$_1$ mōko jet.
'It was isolated from the rest of the houses.'

d. E*bbarōk* jān$_1$ ri-jorrāān ro.
'He was protected from the hoodlums.'

e. Erro *jekkar* ñan$_1$ doon.
'They are unsuited for each other.'

f. E*ttoḷọk* Wūjlañ jān$_1$ Mājro.
'Ujelang is far from Majuro.'

Manner verbs [C5, C6]. Certain adjectival verbs include a means that is introduced by a preposition [C6], while others have no preposition [C5]. Examples of the former are given in (5-70a–g). The verb *arōk* 'greedy, stingy, miserly' in (5-70h–i) is a good example of a manner verb that does not use *kōn*$_1$ to introduce its means (underlined). In (5-70j) the verb *kūkutaktak* (*ikkutaktak*) 'be always scraping' is a distributive verb (see page 162), reminding us that all distributive verbs are adjectival. Thus, while *kutak* 'to scrape' is not itself adjectival, the distributive verb derived from it is, and *iu* 'sprouted coconut' is the Means that makes it a manner verb.

(5-70) a. Ej *kōmbade* kōn$_1$ lien ippān.
'He is being very careful about his wife.'

b. E*ajjibanban* kōn$_1$ pāākin waini eṇ.
'He was weighted down with a sack of copra.'

c. Eḷap aō *eñtaan* kōn$_1$ aō katak.
'I have a hard time with my studies.'

d. Ij jab maroñ iwōj bwe i*lokjak* kōn$_1$ ajri rā nājū.
'I can't come because I'm tied down with my children.'

e. I*balle* kōn$_1$ nuknuk.
'I have lots of clothes.'

f. E*jab* kōn$_1$ dān.
'It's full of water.'

g. Eḷap aō *atebar* kōn$_2$ an luujḷọk wōt tiim e aō.
'I am impatient because my team keeps losing.'

h. E*arōk* ṃaak ḷeen.
'He is greedy for money.'

i. E*arōk* menọknọk ḷeeṇ.
'He is a pack rat—saves any old thing—even trash.'

j. E*kkutaktak* iu lōḷḷap eṇ.
'That old woman is always scraping sprouted coconuts.'

Nonassociative correspondent verbs [C7, C8]. There are two types of these adjectival verbs, those that are comparative [C8], and those that are not [C7]. Only one example of the latter has been identified to date: (5-71a), in which *ānin* is the Correspondent.

By contrast, the comparative type [C7] can be derived from any other type of personal adjectival verb, as the remaining examples in (5-71) show. In these comparative examples, *kwe* is the Correspondent, and the Correspondent is introduced by *jān*$_2$ 'than'.

(5-71) a. E*jiniet* ānin.
'S/he is familiar with this island.'

b. I*dipen* jān$_2$ kwe. (from [C1])
'I am stronger than you.'

c. I*pojak* ñan$_1$ mej in jān$_2$ kwe. (from [C4])
'I am more immune to the flu than you.'

d. E*ṃōkade* ilo piimboñ jān$_2$ kwe. (from [C2])
'S/he is more expert at pingpong than you.'

e. E*jiniet* ānin jān$_2$ kwe. (from [C8])
'S/he is more familiar with this island than you.

f. Rō*ṃōṇōṇō* kōn$_2$ mupi eo jān$_2$ kwe. (from [C10])
'They are happier about the movie than you.'

Associative correspondent verbs [C9, C10]. Some of these adjectival verbs (5-72a–c) have their correspondent introduced without a preposition [C9], while others (5-72d–e) require a preposition [C10].

(5-72) a. Armejin ṃweeṇ re*ikrooḷ* ippān doon.
'The people of that house are dissatisfied with each other.'

b. Kwaar *lilu* (*illu*) ke ippān?'
'Were you angry with her/him?'

c. Jab *po* ippān bwe enaaj tōlpilouk eok.
'Don't associate with him or he'll lead you astray.'

d. Lio e*būroṃōj* kōn$_2$ leo ippān emej.
'She is mourning her dead husband.'

e. Re*jjānene* kōn$_2$ ṃupi eo.
'They are excited about the movie.'

This concludes our discussion of Class C verbs, and of all INTRANSITIVE verbs except for two classes that are EXTENSION VERBS. But first we need to look at the last two classes of nonextension verbs, TRANSITIVE NONEXTENSION verbs, those that are impersonal, Class F, and those that are personal, Class G

Class F Verbs

5.6.4 Class F verbs are TRANSITIVE and IMPERSONAL.[32] As impersonal verbs, they imply a third person nonreferential actor, and they do not occur with an overt subject. When finite, they are always marked with the third person singular subject prefix *e-*. As transitive verbs, their nonreferential actor is identified as the AGENT, which functions as the grammatical subject.

There is just one type of these verbs [F1]. The seven examples in 5-73 are a good sample. The third line of each gives a more literal translation in which the verb is in quotation marks, and its subject is the word "it"—the "empty it" that is sometimes the subject of impersonal verbs in English. It is called empty because it has no referent: there is nothing in the real world that it can be referring to.

The fourth line of each shows the intransitive counterpart of the transitive impersonal (Class F) verb in the sentence of the first line. Notice that each has to do with a unit of time or space (hour, night or day, month, tide, current, heavens).

(5-73) a. Ij etal kiiō bwe **e***awaūk* eō.
'I'm going now because I'm late.'
[I'm going now because **it** "houred" me.]
(*awa* 'hour; be the hour')

b. **E***pāāte* piiḷ tūreep eo.
'The field trip ship was stranded high and dry.'
[**It** "ebb-tided" the field trip ship.]
(*pāāt* 'ebb tide; be low tide')

c. **E***aete* ḷọk kōrkōr eo ñan lik.
'The current drifted the canoe out to the ocean side.'
[**It** "currented" the canoe out to the ocean side.]
(*aet* 'current')

d. **E***jeḷataeiki* booj jerakrōk eo.
'The sailboat got caught up in the third current zone.'
[**It** "third zoned" the sailboat.]
(*jeḷatae* 'be the third current zone away from an island')

e. Emaroñ *jeptōṃbaik* kwe ṇa ānin.
'September might still see you on the island.'
[**It** might "September" you on the island.]
(*jeptōṃba* 'be September')

32. The labels D and E are reserved for the two classes of intransitive verbs that are extension verbs and will be presented together with the other extension verbs after we have presented all the nonextension verbs. We, thus, follow the usage of Pagotto 1987, where intransitive verb classes are labeled together from A through E, and transitive classes from F through I (see table 5-6 on page 234).

f. Kwōn kāiur bwe **e**naaj *boñe* eok.
'Hurry up before it gets dark.'
[You should hurry because **it** will "night" you.]
(*boñ* 'night; be night')

g. **E**naaj *iiaḷañeiki* kōj ṃokta jān ad tōprak ḷọk.
'We won't make it there before moonrise.'
[**It** will "moonrise" us before we get there.]
(*iiaḷañe* 'moonrise')

CLASS G VERBS

5.6.5 Class G verbs are TRANSITIVE and PERSONAL. Unlike the impersonal verbs of Class F, they allow their AGENT subjects to have the full range of person and number features. Table 5-10 shows the various *syntactic* subtypes of Class G verbs.[33] The various subcategories found in transitive verbs are quite similar to those found in intransitive verbs, as can be seen by comparing table 5-10 with tables 5-8 and 5-9.

Table 5-10 Subtypes of Class G verbs

		EXAMPLES
NONCORRESPONDENT		
NONMANNER		
NONLOCATIVE	[G1][1]	(5-74)
LOCATIVE		
NONDIRECTIONAL		
NONASSOCIATIVE	[G2]	(5-75a–d)
ASSOCIATIVE	[G3]	(5-75e-h)
DIRECTIONAL	[G4]	(5-76)
MANNER	[G5]	(5-77)
CORRESPONDENT		
NONASSOCIATIVE	[G6]	(5-78)
ASSOCIATIVE		
NO PREPOSITION	[G7]	(5-80a–f)
PREPOSITION	[G8]	(5-80g–h)

1. Labels used in Pagotto (1987).

Nonlocative verbs [G1]. In the first three lines of table 5-10, we see that the simplest Class G verbs are not marked for correspondent, manner, or location. They imply just two actants, an AGENT subject, and a PATIENT object.[34]

33. Syntactic types are based on the arrangements of words with each other. Semantic types are based on the meanings of the words.

34. See 6.3 on page 284 for a discussion of case relations that includes AGENT and PATIENT.

(5-74) a. Kwōn jab *kij* peiṃ.
'Don't bite your fingers.'

b. Ear *ikūri* bwebwenato eo.
'S/he distorted the story.'

c. Kwōn *aike* booj eṇ.
'Tow that boat.'

d. Kwōn *dọuk* bwā ṇe.
'Lower that pole.'

e. Kwōmaroñ ke *ineek* pāāk e?
'Can you carry this bag on your shoulder?'

f. Ṇo ej *jeballe* wa eo.
'The waves are rocking the boat.'

Nondirectional locative verbs [G2, G3]. These verbs imply a LOCUS in addition to the AGENT subject and PATIENT object required of all transitive verbs. In addition, they are subdivided based on whether or not they are associative. The LOCUS is underlined in each sentence. Examples (5-75a–d) are not associative, while the word *ippaṃ* 'in your company, with you' shows that examples (5-75e-h) are.

(5-75) a. Iar *kadeḷọñ* ṃaak ko aō ilo pāāñ.
'I deposited my money in the bank.'

b. Kwōn *kate* doon ṇe na i turun bōb eṇ.
'Stand the husking stick in the ground by that pandanus tree.'

c. Kwōn *jiniete* i ānin.
'Show him around the island.'

d. Ṇo e*ubweik* wa eo na ibaal.
'The waves smashed the canoe against the reef.'

e. Kwōn *karōjepe* ḷadik ṇe ippaṃ.
'Take the boy fishing for flying fish with you.'

f. Kwōn *kōjobaik* ḷadik ṇe ippaṃ.
'Let that boy sit on the sofa with you.'

g. Imaroñ ke *ṃuriik* juon taḷa ippaṃ?
'Can I borrow a dollar from you?'

h. *Keidi* ṃōk waḷọk e aō ippaṃ.
'Please compare my results (figures) with yours.'

Directional locative verbs [G4]. The LOCUS implied by these locative verbs is the object of a preposition (*jān* or *ñan*) that indicates whether the locus is the source or the goal of the verb's action. The LOCUS is underlined in the examples that follow.

(5-76) a. Kwōn *ṃane* ḷọk etan jān$_1$ bok ṇe.
'Cross his name out of that book.'

b. Iar *atōreje* lōta eo aō ñan$_1$ ledik eo jera.
'I addressed the letter to my girl.'

c. Kwōn ilān *medeke* jān$_1$ an ilān kōṃṃan tūrabōḷ.
'Go do something to keep him from going and making trouble.'

d. *Kajjuuk* wa ṇe ñan$_1$ Kuwajleen.
'Steer the boat directly to Kwajalein.'

e. Kwōn *jibuuni* jān$_1$ pilej ṇe.
'Spoon it off your plate.'

f. Koṃwin *ajeḷọk* mour kaṇe ami ñan$_1$ Anij.
'Dedicate your lives to God.'

g. *Kōjenoḷọke* raij ṇe jān$_1$ jālele ṇe.
'Separate the rice from the meat course.'

h. *Likūtḷọk* eō ñan$_1$ wa eṇ.
'Carry me over to the ship.'

i. Kwōn *iṃuki* jān$_1$ leen oran ṇe.
'Shake the oranges off that tree.'
(lit. shake from its fruit that orange tree)

Manner verbs [G5]. This is the final subtype of transitive noncorrespondent verbs. In addition to an AGENT subject and a PATIENT object, they imply a MEANS actant that is marked by a preposition. The MEANS is underlined in the examples that follow.

(5-77) a. Kwōn *teiñi* kaar eṇ kōn$_1$ lalem kōḷan in kiaaj.
'Please put five gallons of gas in the car.'

b. Kwōn *kakkinonoik* juub ṇe kōn$_1$ anien bwe en nenọ (ennọ).
'Add some onion to the soup to make it tasty.'
(lit. cause that soup to be replete with onions so that it's tasty)

c. Iar jọuni kōn$_1$ dān im kọruji.
'I splashed water on him to wake him up.'

d. *Kapejlọk* wūno ṇe kōn$_1$ jerpāntain.
'Dilute the paint with turpentine.'

e. Kwōn *kūtbuuj* ajri ṇe kōn$_1$ juon kọọj.
'Cover that baby with a blanket.'

f. Eṃōj aō *kanne* wa eo kōn$_1$ mweiuk.
'I have loaded the ship with trade goods (or provisions).'

Correspondent verbs—nonassociative [G6]. Transitive correspondent verbs imply three case relations: an AGENT as subject, a PATIENT as object, and a CORRESPONDENT. Those that are nonassociative do not mark the Correspondent with a preposition. They are the equivalent of what are sometimes called "di-transitive verbs" in English. Correspondents are underlined in these examples.

(5-78) a. Kwōn *jiroñ* ḷadik eo juon bwebwenato.
'Tell the boy a story.'

b. Ear *naajdik* wa eo juon aod.
'He passed in front of the other boat.'
(lit. he fed the other boat a wake)

c. Kwōmaroñ ke *kaṃuriik* e juon taḷa?
'Can you lend him a dollar?'

d. Kwōn *kaidaak* ajri ṇe ḷalem pil in wūnokwan pokpok.
'Give that child five drops of cough medicine.'

e. Raar kaalooje John juon pija ṃakūtkūt.
'They showed John a movie.'

Possessed verbs in ṇa. Examples of correspondent verbs like those above are not especially numerous, but there is a special set of verbs that cover the same ground in a different way and deserve to be included in the same class, [G6]. They are compounds formed by joining the verb *ṇa* 'provide' with an inalienable noun that identifies in a general way the type of thing that is provided (the CORRESPONDENT)[35] and also, by its possessive suffix, the recipient of that which is provided (the PATIENT). Thus, in sentence (5-78a) the possessed verb *ṇaballier* 'provide them with clothing' is a compound of the verb *ṇa* 'provide' and the inalienable noun *ballier* 'their clothing', made up of the stem *balli-* 'clothing' and the suffix *-er* 'their'. The words *jet nuknuk māṇāāṇ* 'some warm clothes' give further specificity to the general reference to clothing made by the possessed verb. Examples like (5-78b) make it clear that such additional information or modification is not required by possessed verbs for expressing both the PATIENT object and CORRESPONDENT who is provided.

(5-79) a. Kōm ar *ṇaballier* jet nuknuk māṇāāṇ.
'We provided them some warm clothes.'

b. Kwōn etal in *ṇaballiṃ*.
'Go put on your clothes.'
(lit. go provide yourself with clothing)

c. Wōn ear *ṇaetan* wa eṇ?
'Who named that boat?'

d. Wōn enaaj *ṇakijed* ṇa āneṇ ñe jenaaj kowainini?
'Who'll feed us when we go make copra on that islet?'

e. Raar *ṇakọjen* ri-āneo ālkin taibuun eo.
'The islanders were provided with blankets after the typhoon.'

f. Kwōn *ṇapitōn* bwe ejjeḷọk.
'Give him a pillow because he doesn't have any.'

---

35. A number of these same nouns can be found among the possessive classifiers in table 4-13 on page 195.

g. An bōd eo ak ear *ṇaruon* likao eo jatin.
'It was his fault but he blamed his brother.'

h. Iban *ṇaruoṃ*.
'I won't blame you.'

i. Kwōn *ṇautōn* ḷọk bwe en tutu.
'Give him some water so he can bathe right away.'

j. Raar *ṇaoṇāān* ekkar ñan jeḷā eo an.
'He got paid according to his skills.'
(lit. they provided him with pay according to his skills)

Correspondent verbs—associative [G7, G8]. Correspondent verbs that are associative may have a form of the noun *ippa-* 'company' as their CORRESPONDENT [G7], or they may have some other noun introduced by the preposition *kōn*$_2$ 'about' as their CORRESPONDENT [G8]. Numbers (5-80a–f) give examples of the former type, while (5-80g–k) give examples of the latter.

(5-80) a. Inaaj *kaileileik* eok ippa.
'I'll let you string your fish on my stringer.'

b. Kwōn jab *kōtakinkini* ledik ṇe ippaṃ.
'Don't let the girl use some of your socks.'

c. Jab inepata bwe inaaj *kapeenen* eok ippa.
'Don't worry because I'll let you use my pen.'

d. Kwōn *kọuṃuṃi* ippaṃ.
'Let her share your oven.'

e. Kwōn *kajebwebweiki* ippaṃ.
'Let him use one of your paddles.'

f. Kwōn *kajoobobe* ke eō ippaṃ ñe emaat joob e aō?
'Will you let me use your soap if I run out?'

g. Raar jab *kōjeḷāik* ledik eo kōn$_2$ keemem eo.
'They didn't let the girl know about the party.'

h. Rej *aitwe* doon kōn$_2$ men ko.
'They are competing among themselves for things.'

i. *Ājḷore* kōn$_2$ jeḷā kaṇ an ke ej ja mour.
'Exploit what he knows while he's still around.'

j. Anij enaaj *iden-onieik* eok kōn$_2$ nana kaṇe aṃ.
'God will punish your evil deeds.'

k. "Lale kwōmeḷọkḷọk in *kakkōle* Kapen eṇ kōn$_2$ naanin rōjañ eo an ḷōḷḷap eo," irre ḷọk im ba ñan Jema ke ej moot ḷọk Bojin eo.
'"Don't forget to warn the Captain about the Old Man's advice," I said to Father once the Boatswain had left.'

EXTENSION VERBS

5.6.6 Extension verbs are verbs that are extended by an inner complement. The complement generally consists of a second verb, which may be preceded by a complementizer as part of the complement. In (5-81a), *kijerjer* is an extension verb and *in jerak* is the compementizer-verb combination that makes up its complement.

Table 5-11 presents the four classes of extension verbs: classes D and E are intransitive, and H and I are transitive. Not every subtype of extension verb uses complementizers, as the table shows, but those that do use either *in* 'to' or *ke* 'that'. They are listed together with the various adverbial complementizers in table 5-5 on page 232.

Inner infinitival complements [D1]. These extension verbs are IMPERSONAL, and the nominals that follow them are not their subjects, but their correspondents. The complementizer *in* introduces their complements, which as nonfinite verbs (underlined) do not have subject prefixes.

(5-81) a. E*kijerjer* kapen eṇ in jerak.
'The captain is in a hurry to sail.'

b. E*moot* ḷōṃaro in kodia.
'The men have gone to do some serious drinking.'

c. E*kijoroor* likao eo in pālele.
'The young man can't wait to get married.'

d. E*tōkeak* taibuun eo in nitbwilli āneo.
'The typhoon came to devastate the island.'

e. E*kkeilọk* ḷōmaro in kairuj bukwōn eo.
'The men yelled to alert the district.'

f. E*mejki* likao eo in kōnono.
'The boy is too sleepy to talk.'

g. E*jowan* likao ro in jar.
'The young men are too lazy to go to church.'

h. E*mijak* ri-jikuuḷ ro in kajjitōk.
'The students are afraid to ask.'

i. E*jjookok* ke ḷeeṇ in kōnono ñan$_2$ kōjeañ?
'Will his bashfulness keep him from speaking for us?'

Pagotto (1987) found only the first two (5-81a–b) among the example sentences of the MED (Abo et al. 1976); the sentences that follow have since been included in the MOD.

Inner finite complements [D2]. These extension verbs are also IMPERSONAL. Their complements have verbs with subject prefixes[36] and are introduced by the complementizer *ke*.

36. Or the equivalent in verbless sentences, that is, a finite predicate.

(5-82) a. **E***alikkar* ke etōprak jerbal eo an.
'It is clear that he landed the job.'

b. *Ṃool* ke ekane bwiro ippān wōn.
'It is true that preserved breadfruit goes well with turtle meat.'

c. **E**j kab kar *alikkar* ke ej jab [wa kajjirere] [men eo].
'It became clear that this boat wasn't a laughing matter.'

d. "*Alikkar* ke enaaj bar rọọl tok in kọkoṇi kein jerbal kā an," ikar ba ippa make.
'"Obviously he is going to return and put away his tools," I said to myself.'

e. *Alikkar* ke [anidepin Aelōñḷapḷap] [men in].
'It must be a kickball made in Aelōñḷapḷap.'

f. *Alikkar* ke [bwilkōn] [Anidep].
'It's obviously a leaf of the *Anidep* pandanus.'

g. *Ṃool* ke [kwe] [ri-kajjidede].
'It's true that you always guess at the answers.'

h. **E***bajjeet* ke kwokatak.
'That's more like the way to study [implied: you weren't really studying before].'

Table 5-11 The four classes and subtypes of EXTENSION verbs

Class			EXAMPLES
INTRANSITIVE			
NONPERSONAL			
NONFINITE[1]	(COMPLEMENTIZER *in*)	[D1][2]	(5-81)
FINITE[1]	(COMPLEMENTIZER *ke*)	[D2]	(5-82)
PERSONAL			
NONFINITE			
NO COMPLEMENTIZER			
NONAUXILIARY		[E1]	(5-84)–(5-85)
AUXILIARY		[E2]	(5-85)
COMPLEMENTIZER *in*		[E3]	(5-86)
FINITE			
NO COMPLEMENTIZER		[E4]	(5-87)–(5-93)
COMPLEMENTIZER *ke*		[E5]	(5-94)
TRANSITIVE			
NONPERSONAL	(COMPLEMENTIZER *ke*)	[H]	(5-95)
PERSONAL			
NONFINITE		[I1]	(5-96)
FINITE			
NO COMPLEMENTIZER		[I2]	(5-97)
COMPLEMENTIZER *ke*		[I3]	(5-98)

1. Finite verbs have subject prefixes (see table 3-10 on page 151); nonfinite verbs have no subject prefixes.
2. Labels used in Pagotto (1987).

i. "Ekwe *ebajjeet* ke <u>ejijjet</u> ḷọk jidik," Jema eba.
"'Now that seems to be more like it," Father said.'

j. *Aelọkin* ke <u>ej naaj kar itok</u> wōt.
'There was no doubt that he would come.'

k. *Ṃool* ke <u>jeban kōttar</u> jidik.
'Let's wait a little.' [lit. it's true that we can't wait a little]

l. *Alkarkar* ke ijuun eañ <u>erabōḷḷọk</u>.
"'It's quite clear that the north star shines brightly"' [words from a popular song].'

There are, however, deviations from those general expectations in some of these example sentences. Their impersonal verbs (in italics) are not all marked by the expected *e-* prefix: with *ṃool* 'true' it never occurs, with *alikkar* 'clear' it is optional, and with *ebajjeet* 'more like it' in (5-82h–i) it seems to be obligatory. It would not be a surprising development if the minimal person-marking prefix (*e-*) should be dropped altogether from certain impersonal verbs—because it does no marking of real persons for them. (Third person singular [3s] is the least marked person in languages generally, and in some languages it may have a zero marker.)

Nor do their complements all have verbs marked by subject prefixes. Instead, as anticipated in fn. 36, those in (5-82e–g) meet the [D-2] requirement by having the finite predicates of verbless, equational sentences, for example, *ri-kajjidede* in (5-82g). Thus, neither of these seeming deviations should be seen as disqualifying the italicized verbs as bona fide members of [D-2].

Something that most of the members of [D-2] presented here have in common is a positive semantic orientation: *alikkar* 'clear', *ṃool* 'true', *ebajjeet* 'more like it'. Odd verb out in this regard is *aelọk* 'hidden, obscure, invisible, doubtful', a form of which introduces (5-82j). It says literally 'It was doubtful that he would come', yet its translation is positive and says the opposite. This is an instance of SARCASM—where sentences seem to say the opposite of what they mean. Another is given in (5-82k) (from Capelle [2008:1296], where the context can be found). Knowledge of context is always helpful in identifying sarcasm as such, especially in written material. Tone of voice and first-hand participation in the situation are most helpful.

Inner infinitival complements [E1–E3]. These three types of extension verbs are all **PERSONAL**, and may, thus, have any of the subject prefixes. Two of them ([E-1] and [E-2]) have complements that are not introduced by complementizers. The third ([E-3]) has its complements introduced by *in.*

The auxiliary or helping verbs [E2]. This group is special in that it includes all the auxiliary or helping verbs (which have already been presented in ch. 3, beginning on page 151), and it will be discussed first here. It includes both the three prime auxiliaries, and all the nonprime ones as well (see table 3-11 on page 152). The reader is referred to the discussion in ch. 3, which will not be repeated here. That the auxiliaries are all included here is a reminder that they, too, are verbs in Marshallese, a special type of verb that has its own place in this classification, among the extension verbs. Each auxiliary verb must have as its complement extension—without an intervening complementizer—another verb, either another auxiliary verb, or an infinitival verb (one without prefixes), which will end the sequence. Thus, in (5-83) there are three auxiliaries (each followed immediately by its complement), and a final infinitival verb. The complements of the first two auxiliaries have, in turn, their own complements, and the third has as its infinitival complement the adjectival verb deo̧ 'beautiful' [C1] that ends the sequence.

(5-83) E*naaj kar lukkuun* deo̧.
'She would have been really beautiful.'

Nonauxiliary verbs without complementizers [E1]. We now turn to nonauxiliary verbs that, like the auxiliaries, do not take complementizers with their complements. There are many such verbs that are marked to occur with bare[37] nonfinite complements.

(5-84) a. Kwōn *jeļā* ukōt jouj.
'You have to know how to reciprocate favors.'

b. E*jaje* aō.
'He doesn't know how to swim.'

c. Iar *aikuj* kwaļkoļ.
'I had to do the laundry.'

d. I*maroñ* kotak jibuki-lemñoul bo̧un.
'I can lift 150 lbs.'

e. Ear *jino kamminene* katak kūta.
'He started to practice guitar.'

f. Inaaj *kajjioñ* iwōj.
'I'll try to come to your place.'

g. Jej jab *kōņaan* roñjake ri-akwāāl.
'No one wants to listen to people quarrel.'

h. E*bwiden* kadek ak ejjab katak.
'He spends his time drinking rather than studying.'

The word *jeļā* can mean both 'know' or 'know how to', and its antonym *jaje* can also have either meaning, 'not know' or 'not know how'. Examples (5-84a–b) show these words in [E1] contexts where they have the latter meanings. They are to be found with the former meanings in [E4] contexts, in (5-87).

37. That is, those without complementizers.

Example (5-84e) gives a sequence of two [E1] extension verbs in sequence, the second of which also serves as complement of the first. In all of the (5-84) examples, an underlined bare infinitival verb immediately follows the italicized extension verb of which it is the complement.

Several intransitive personal extension verbs have coalesced with the complementizer *in* 'to' so that they now behave like [E1] extension verbs: *itōn* 'come in order to' (< *itok* + *in*), *ilān* 'go in order to' (< *iḷọk* + *in*). These same verbs have also coalesced with the conjunction *im* 'and' to form *itōm* (< *itok* + *im*) 'come and' and *ilām* (< *iḷọk* + *im*) 'come and', which are also [E1] extension verbs. Examples follow:

(5-85) a. Kōjro *itōn* kōaktok nejirro koonin ak.
'Let's go hunt for pet frigate birds.'

b. Kōjjel *ilān* kaalutok kein ad kōṃṃan ṃarṃar.
'Let's (us three) go look for *alu* shells to make head leis.'

c. *Itōm* wōdwōd edouṃ.
'Come chew some cooked pandanus.'

d. *Ilām* eọroñ ta eo raar kūr eok kake.
'Go find out what they were calling you about.'

This coalescence in Marshallese is comparable to English 'to' contraction in verbs such as 'gonna' (< 'going to') and 'wanna' (< 'want to').

Nonauxiliary verbs with complementizers [E3]. These verbs, like those of [E1] and [E2], are intransitive, personal, and require infinitival complements. They differ in that they also require the complementizer *in.*

(5-86) a. I*ṃōk* in jutak.
'I am tired of standing.'

b. Kwōn jab *ṃakoko* in jikuuḷ.
'Don't refuse to go to school.'

c. I*ppat* in etetal ippān.
'I feel unworthy to walk beside her.'

d. Ij kab *ikdeelel* in jikuuḷ.
'I have just decided that I want to go to school.'

e. Ak koṃwij *ḷōmṇak* in jeblaak ñāāt?
'When are you planning on leaving?'

f. Keememej im jab *jokwōd* in jejetok.
'Remember not to neglect writing to me.'

g. Kwōn jab *ṃōṃaelep* (*eṃṃaelep*) in etal eọñōd.
'Don't get carried away by your desire to go fishing.'

h. I*aikuj* in etal.
'I have to go.'

i. Ejjelọk an *maroñ* in kōṃṃan jabdewot.
'He has no power to do anything.'

If we compare (5-84c–d) with (5-86h–i), we see that usage is divided between [E1] and [E3] for both *aikuj* and *maroñ*, that is, whether or not these two verbs require the complementizer *in*. Situations like this with divided usage usually indicate that a change is taking place. Because it seems that the complementizer is already omitted more often than not, we can expect that eventually *aikuj* and *maroñ* will end up only in the [E1] class.[38]

Inner finite complements without complementizers [E4]. There are not many verbs in this class—those that must coocur with a finite clause that is not introduced by a complementizer.[39]

(5-87) a. I*baab* [kwōnaaj kar itok] im iar kōttar.
'I thought you would come and I waited for you.'

b. I*baab* [ejorrāān wa eo waan].
'I thought his car had broken down.'

c. Iar *ba* [ejorrāān wa eo waan].
'I said his car had broken down.'

d. Jej *ba* [kwōj pād wōt iaelōñ ṇe i reeaar].
'We thought you were still on that atoll east of here.'

e. *Lale* [ebuñ ḷọk ajri ṇe].
'Be careful so that the child doesn**'t** fall.'

f. Lale [toon jarom ṇe ejarome eok].
'Be careful that you do**n't** get a shock from that cord.'

(5-87) gives a pair of examples for each of three [E4] verbs: *baab* 'think', *ba* 'say, think', and *lale* 'be careful lest; look at, see'—two of which need further discusson.

Iba *questions.* Examples (5-88a–b) have as their first word the verb *ba* with *i-* 'I' as prefix, but here *ba* is not an example of [E4], because it is not followed immediately by a finite clause, as it was in examples (5-87c–d) above.

What is surprising about initial *Iba* is that when it is followed *immediately* by a finite clause, the word *Iba* is not translated as such, but functions to change the following clause into a yes-no question that has the intonation of a question with *ke*, even though there is no *ke* present. This happens only with the first person singular form *Iba* (not with forms like *Eba* 's/he says', *Jeba* 'we say', *Rōba* 'they say', and so on). The examples in (5-89) provide evidence from the other persons.

38. How can one determine the frequency with which the complementizer is used? One way is to use the MOD (*Marshallese On-line Dictionary*), which contains thousands of example sentences, all of which are organized in its Concordance. Thus, to study the question raised here, one can examine all the sentences with *aikuj* and *maroñ* by finding them in the Concordance. This is how we determined that "the complementizer is already omitted more often than not."

39. The clauses that satisfy this requirement are enclosed in square brackets.

A few more examples of *Iba* questions are given in (5-88c–f). Example (5-88c) gives in its second translation the meaning of the same structure when spoken with a statement intonation. Example (5-88d) has an equational (verbless) clause. We believe these to be instances of *ba* as an [E4] extension verb, though of a special subvariety.

(5-88) a. I*ba* wōt [kwe] [eo iaar lo animrokan] ak ej jab.
'I thought that was you I caught a glimpse of, but it wasn't.'

b. I*ba* wōt [emeḷeḷe kōn an eṃṃajidjid] ke ij kōnono ñane.
'I thought he understood my point because he nodded when I talked to him about it.'

c. I*ba* [ejorrāān wa eo waan]?
'Could it be that his car has broken down?'
'Maybe his car has broken down.' [w. statement intonation]

d. "I*ba* [waan tiṃoṇ] [men eo]?" ikajjitōk ak ejej eṇ euwaak.
'"Is it a ghost ship?" I asked, but no one answered.'

e. "I*ba* [eḷap jọkpej eṇ amieañ]?" irooj eo ekajjitōk.
'"Do you all have a lot of scrap?" the chief asked.'

f. I*ba* [eṃṃan ñe jeañ tar āne waj] im teiñi kōb ṇe adeañ ṃokta jān ad itaḷọk wōt ñan eoonene?
'Should we sail to that island and fill up our water container before heading to the main island?'

(5-89) a. Eba [in etal] a iṃakoko.
'He said for me to go but I didn't want to.'

b. Jeba [en jab tutu iaar] ak eakweḷap.
'We told him to not swim in the lagoon but he insisted.'

c. Kōmba [emaat raij iāneo] ak rejab tōmak.
'We said the island was out of rice but they didn't believe us.'

d. Rōba [rej kowainini ilo wāto eo] im kōmin jab etal ñane.
'They said they were making copra on that piece of land, and we shouldn't go there.'

The various forms of lale. The examples we have seen of *lale* thus far can be glossed as 'be careful lest', in (5-87e–f), where it has a negative cast that can be found in translations of the following clause (in words like "doesn't," "don't", etc.), even though the original Marshallese clause contains no negative element. The negativity can be seen in the translations. Here are some additional examples of *lale* as extension verb [E4].

(5-90) a. *Lale* [bao ṇe ejebwiji eok].
'Be careful that chicken does**n't** cut you with its spurs.'

b. *Lale* [ebbwiroro nuknuk ṇe aṃ].
'Be careful you do**n't** get preserved breadfruit on your clothes.'

c. *Lale* [eitaak bōraṃ].
'Watch that you don't bump your head.'

d. *Lale* [iie ekij eok].
'Watch out for centipedes that they do**n't** bite you.'

e. *Lale* [kwaar kōjjakoko] bwe jenaaj aikuji eok.
'Do**n't** disappear because we might need you.'

When *lale* is not followed immediately by a finite clause, it is not an extension verb and does not have a negative cast. It means simply 'be careful,' and may appear in outer adverbial clauses (not the inner ones that are required to have extensions). In (5-91) there are several examples, wherein bwe_1 means 'so that' and bwe_2 means 'because' (see table 5-5 on page 232). Notice that where these translations are negative, as in (5-91a), the original Marshallese includes a negative element (*jab*).

(5-91) a. *Lale* bwe_1 [kuuj ṇe en **jab** rọkuj eok].
'Be careful that cat does**n't** scratch you.'

b. Kwōn *lale* bwe_2 [erroro].
'Be careful because he is easily angered.'

c. Lale bwe_2 [imaroñ jirillọk im kabwili eok kōn jāje e].
'Watch out because I might accidentally slash you with this machete.'

Another form of *lale* that simply means 'see, look at' is an [E4] extension verb that has indirect content questions as its complements. The same is true of a form of *jaje* 'not know'. The bracketed portions in (5-92a–b) are identical to the direct questions that are given in a.′ and b.′, respectively.

(5-92) a. *Lale* [wōn in eto an ju].
'Let's see who (it is that) can stand on his hands the longest.'

a.′ Wōn in eto an ju?
'Who (is it that) can stand on his hands the longest?'

b. I*jaje* [ia eo ear ilọk ñane].
'I don't know where (it is that) he went.'

b.′ Ia eo ear ilōk ñane?
'Where is it that he went?' / 'Where did he go?'

Lale can also have indirect yes-no questions as its complements of type [E-4], as in (5-93a–b).

(5-93) a. Kwōn kọkwiiki Jọọn im *lale* [ellu ke].
'Provoke John and see if he gets mad.'

b. Kwōn talboone Jọọn im *lale* [ear jiroñ Medi ke].
'Call John and see if he told Mary.'

Inner finite complements with complementizers [E5]. The second main type of intransitive personal extension verbs that requires an extension complement also requires the complementizer *ke*. Examples are given below.

(5-94) a. Eṃōj aō *kallimur* ke [inaaj bar itok].
'I promised that I would come again.'

b. Ij *kile* ippa make ke [eban tōprak jerbal eṇ].
'I can see on my own that that job can never be finished.'

c. Jej *roñ* ke [ewōr taibuun ijōkaṇ].
'We heard that there is a typhoon somewhere out there.'

d. Ejiṃwe wōt aō kar *bōklōkōt* ke [kwōnaaj kar itok].
'My prediction was correct that you would come.'

e. Iar *jeḷā* ke [epād ilo ruuṃ eo].
'I knew of his presence in the room.'

This completes our discussion of intransitive extension verbs. The following section outlines the properties of transitive extension verbs, which occur in two types, personal and impersonal.

Impersonal transitive extension verbs [H]. Thus far only one type of these verbs has been discovered. They require finite complements introduced by the complementizer *ke*.

(5-95) a. E*kainepataik* eō ke [kwaar palele].
'It upsets me that you got married.'

b. E*kabūromōj* kōm ke [rejeblaak ioon waan raun eo].
'It saddened us when they departed on the field trip.'

c. E*kaṃōṇōṇōik* būruōn jemān ke [ej rọọl tok jān tariṇae].
'His return from the war gladdens his dad's heart.'

d. E*kamijak* er ke [rej roñ kōn taibuun eo epaak tok].
'It scared them to hear of the approaching typhoon.'

e. E*kailbōk* eō ke [ij roñ kōn mej eo an ḷadik eo nejin].
'I was shocked to hear of his son's death.'

f. E*kairuj* jukjuk im pād eo ke [ṃōnwa eo ej kōjañ jilel eo ie ilikin āneo āneer].
'It alarmed the community when the warship blew its horn on the oceanside of the island.'

g. E*kaijoḷ* eō ke [ej kōnono kōn pọljej eo].
'His talk about the ripe breadfruit baked in coconut oil gives me an appetite (makes me want to eat).'

Notice that the verbs in all of the examples in (5-95) are not only transitive, but also causative (with the prefix *ka-*) and adjectival.

Inner infinitival complements [I1]. Personal transitive extension verbs with inner nonfinite complements must occur with a clause that is not preceded by a complementizer. The infinitival clause immediately follows the direct object.

(5-96) a. Kwōn *kate* eok [ṃōñā].
'Eat all you can.'

b. Ij *likūt* eok [lukkuun nājū].
'I consider you to be a real child of mine.'

c. Komaroñ itōn ja *jipañ* eō [jerbal].
'Could you come and help me in my work.'

d. Jej aikuj jaruki ṃanit ko ad rōmājkunḷọk im *katakin* ajri ro nājid [leep] ñe re jañin kar jeḷā.
'We must revive some of our waning customs such as *leep* dancing by teaching our children if they don't already know how.'

e. Ta enaaj *kōmaroñ* eō [etetal]?
'What'll enable me to walk?'

f. Kwōn *āñin* Jọọn [bwe en alooj ippaṃ].
'Take John along sightseeing with you.'

g. Rej *āñin* doon [ñan jeraṃṃan].
'They're tagging along toward prosperity.'

Inner finite complements [I2, I3]. These personal transitive extension verbs are further subdivided based on whether or not they require a complementizer. Thus far only one transitive verb has been found to occur with a finite clause not introduced by a complementizer. Two examples of this [I2] verb are given here below.

(5-97) a. Kwōn ṃōk *kajitūkini* ḷōṇe [ear wajjikōt].
'How about asking that man why he came.'

b. Kwōn ṃōk *kajitūkini* [ear pād ia]?
'Inquire of him where he was.'

Examples of [I3], which require the complementizer *ke*, are given next.

(5-98) a. Bwilijmāāṇ ro rej *eṇake* ḷeo ke [e eo ear kọọti ṃani ko].
'The police suspect that he is the one who stole the money.'

b. Ij *jiroñ* eok ke [kwoban tōprak].
'I assure you that you won't make it.'

c. Aolep ro rej eoonpālōñ rej *kwaḷọk* ke [rōkelọk].
'Those that lie and put their arms on their foreheads show that they are lovesick.'

d. Kwaar *karoñ* ke er ke [eor ad kweilọk]?
'Did you inform them that we have a meeting?'

e. Ij *kajineete* eok ke [eañjarjar an lōḷḷap eṇ kōnnaan].
'I'm warning you beforehand that she is an old lady with a sharp tongue.'

Summary of Verb Classification

5.6.7 This concludes our outline of the verb classes of Marshallese. Based on syntactic features inherent in the verbs and contextual features specifying the syntactic frame of the verb, the classes of verbs have been elaborated as shown in tables (5-6)–(5-11). The classification shows the additional elements and arrangments each type of verb requires for its particular sentence environment. Especially notable are:

- The cross-cutting distinctions between TRANSITIVE and INTRANSITIVE, PERSONAL and IMPERSONAL, and EXTENSION and NONEXTENSION classes.
- Classes of IMPERSONAL verbs whose subjects are not to be found in the real world, which help explain number agreement in Marshallese.
- A key player in many clauses (in addition to the SUBJECT and the OBJECT) known as the CORRESPONDENT, whose presence helps explain many puzzles of Marshallese grammar.
- A class of auxiliary verbs (see Class [E2] on page 259).
- An alternative to the incorporated object verbs of certain other Nuclear Micronesian languages (see the Manner verbs [B5–8] on page 243).
- INTRANSITIVE verbs[40] that have a PARTITIVE effect on nouns that might appear to be their objects (see the Correspondent verbs [B9–11] on page 245).

40. Intransitive verbs do not normally have objects.

6 Marshallese Sentences

INTRODUCTION

6.1 In the preceding chapters we have focused on smaller units such as sounds, words, and phrases, and have already looked at a number of example sentences. Now our focus will be on the sentences themselves, and on considerations that apply at the sentence level. We turn first to the basic sentence patterns: those that are VERBLESS (6.2.1), and those that are VERBAL (6.2.2).

BASIC SENTENCE PATTERNS

6.2 The discussion begins with an examination of sentences without verbal predicates (6.2.1) and continues with the various types of verbal sentences (6.2.2).

VERBLESS SENTENCES

6.2.1 Sentences in Marshallese do not always include verbs. Some consist only of two noun phrases, one of which is the subject and the other, the predicate. Cleft, or focused, constructions also consist of two noun phrases, but in clefts, the predicate noun is in initial position and the subject noun phrase includes a relative clause [see 4.8 on page 205].

Equational sentences. Equational sentences in Marshallese consist of two noun phrases. In the examples below, the square brackets are used to identify the noun phrases.

(6-1) a. [Kwe] [ri-ānin].
'You are a person from this island.'

b. [Armej ro rōllotaanan] [raṇ].
'Those are the people who are always griping.'

c. [Tal eo an bukwōn juon] [ṇe].
'That's the procession of mourners from District One.'

d. [Aō bok] [in].
'This is my book.'

Notice that an equational sentence may consist of two simple noun phrases (6-1a) or noun phrases that have internal syntactic structure (6-1b–d). The noun phrase in (6-1b) includes a relative clause, while the first noun phrase in (6-1c) is a definite noun phrase with a possessive construction (see page 193). The first noun phrase in (6-1d) is an indefinite noun phrase with a possessive.

There are no morphological clues that can be used to determine which of the noun phrases in a Marshallese equational sentence is the predicate, and which is the subject. Negating the sentence in some languages may reveal which noun phrase is the predicate, assuming that the positions of the negator and the predicate are parallel in verbless and verbal sentences. In Marshallese, the negator *jab* 'not' is itself an auxiliary verb (see table 3-11 on page 152), so that negating an equational sentence results in the formation of a verbal sentence. Nevertheless, two patterns of negation do appear:

(6-2) a. [Kwe] [ri-kobaatat].
'You are a smoker.'

b. (Kwe) kwōj jab ri-kobaatat.
'You are not a smoker.'

(6-3) a. [Bok eo] [in].
'This is the book'

b. Ej jab bok eo in.
'This is not the book.'

In (6-3b) the negative precedes the first noun phrase, not the second. However, there is some evidence that *ej jab* 'it is not' in (6-3b) negates the whole proposition, not just the predicate.

(6-4) a. [Bok ko] [kein].
'These are the books.'

b. Ej jab bok ko kein.
'These are not the books.'

Consider the pluralized version in (6-4) and note that the negative construction *ej jab* is still marked to agree with a third person singular subject, although neither *bok ko* nor *kein* is singular. Therefore, neither can be the subject of the negative verb *jab*. A more literal translation of (6-4b) would be 'It is not that these are the books.' Similarly, (6-3b) would be 'It is not that this is the book.' Thus, negating an equational sentence does not necessarily provide a foolproof diagnostic for determining the constituent structure of this type of sentence.

However, there is another diagnostic that does offer support for the view that the second noun phrase in Marshallese equational sentences is the predicate, and that is the distribution of certain verbal modifiers. Directional adverbs may appear with nonmotion verbs, adding an element of motion to the meaning of the verb. In these situations, the directional occurs after the verb. Directionals may also have this function in verbless sentences. Compare the verbal and verbless sentences below:

(6-5) a. Kwōn rājetake ḷọk.
'Accompany him there.'

b. [Ri-eọñōd ro] [raṇe tok].
'Here come the fishermen.'

The directional *ḷọk* 'thither' appears after the verb *rājetake* 'accompany s.' in (6-5a). In (6-5b), the directional *tok* 'hither' appears after the second noun *raṇe* 'those'. The position and similar function of the directionals in these two sentences suggest that the second noun in (6-5b) functions as the predicate.

Sentence (6-1c) above—repeated here as (6-6a)—has no directional in its second noun phrase, but a comparison of it with (6-6b), which includes the same demonstrative (*ṇe*), shows the effect of including a directional in the predicate of an equational sentence (note the portions in boldface).

(6-6) a. [Tal eo an bukwōn juon] [ṇe].
'That's the procession of mourners from District One.'

b. [Tal eo an ṃōñā eṇ an Kōppālle] [ṇe **ḷọk**].
'That's the Capelle clan **on its way** to pay its last respects to the deceased.'

These syntactic characteristics correlate with semantic criteria. Rehg (1981:278) describes Pohnpeian equational sentences as two noun phrases, one of which (the predicate) serves to locate or identify the other. Given this definition, the second noun phrases in equational sentences are the predicates in Marshallese. However, as Zewen (1977:82) points out, the order of constituents may be reversed to show emphasis. Emphatic, or cleft, constructions are examples of such predicate-initial constructions.

Cleft sentences. It is possible to emphasize or focus on a noun phrase by placing it at the beginning of a sentence. Such focus constructions, called cleft sentences,[1] consist in Marshallese of an initial predicate noun, and a demonstrative pronoun followed by a relative clause.

(6-7) a. [Bweọ ko] [**kaṇ** rej jojo iaar].
'The coconut husks are soaking along the lagoon beach.'
[lit. 'Those that are soaking along the lagoon beach are the coconut husks.']
< **Bweọ ko** rej jojo iaar.
'The coconut husks are soaking along the lagoon beach.'

b. [Wa eo] [**eṇ** rej kōpopooj**e** ñan an jerak].
'They are doing everything necessary to prepare that canoe for its voyage.'
[lit. 'The one that they are preparing for its voyage is that canoe.']
< Rej kōpopooj **wa eo** ñan an jerak.
'They are doing everything necessary to prepare the canoe for its voyage.'

1. "Cleft" is the past participle of the verb "cleave," implying that a noun phrase has been "chopped" from out of its unfocused sentence position and moved to the front.

c. [Jo̧o̧n] [**eo** iar leļo̧k bok eo ñan**e**].
'John was the one I gave the book to.'
[lit. 'The one that I gave the book to was John.']
< Iar leļo̧k bok eo ñan Jo̧o̧n.
'I gave the book to John.'

Each of the three examples of (6-7) consists of a cleft sentence with its equational structure shown by square brackets, and with two translations—the second more literal—of the Marshallese. This is followed by the nonfocused verbal counterpart (introduced by the "<" sign), with the fronted noun in its original, nonfocused position.

For (6-7a) there is minimal difference between the cleft sentence and the unfocused counterpart, as the focused noun was already at the front. The only change is the addition of the demonstrative pronoun *kaņ* in the conversion of the sentence from verbal to the cleft equational.

For (6-7b) the fronting of the noun is more significant, and an anaphoric *-e* is added to the transitive verb *kōpopooj* in the relative clause of the cleft sentence. This serves as a TRACE of the noun that has been moved to the front of the focused sentence, and helps in its processing.

For (6-7c) the fronting of the noun is most drastic—from sentence-final to sentence-initial—and the preposition *ñan* assumes its anaphoric shape, its *-e* ending serving as a trace of the noun that has been fronted. Thus, it should be noted that cleft sentences are verbless at their top, equational, level. The only verb in a cleft sentence is within the relative clause that is embedded as part of its second, subject portion.

Cleft sentences are commonly used to express content questions with interrogative pronouns (note the preponderance of cleft sentences in the examples of 4.2.3 on page 182 and following).

Most noun phrases may be focused in cleft constructions, regardless of their function within the embedded sentence. One exception is to be found with "ditransitive verbs" of class [G6] (see page 254), whose CORRESPONDENTS cannot be cleft as such. The PATIENT of (6-8a), *ajri,* is focused in (6-8b), but an attempt to focus *bwebwenato*, the CORRESPONDENT, in the same way results in an unacceptable sentence (6-8c). Examples (6-8d–e) show a CORRESPONDENT *bwebwenato* focused in a similar sentence of class [G8] with the preposition *kon*$_2$ 'about' and its anaphor *kake*$_2$.

(6-8) a. Iar jiroñ ajri in bwebwenato eo.
'I told this child the story.'

b. [Ajri eo][**in** iar jiroñ**e** bwebwenato eo].
'This is the child I told the story to.'

c. *[Bwebwenato eo][**in** iar jiron**e** ajri in].
*(This is the story I told this child.)

d. Iar jiroñ ajri in kōn$_2$ bwebwenato eo.
'I told this child about the story.'

e. [Bwebwenato eo]**[in** iar jiroñ ajri in **kake**$_2$].
'This is the story I told this child about.'

Other ways to focus verbless sentences. Another means of focusing the predicate nominal of an equational sentence is to put a nonprime auxiliary verb (see table 3-11 on page 152) at the front of it and place this combination at the front of the sentence, preceding the subject nominal—thus switching their usual positions.

Two auxiliary verbs that can be used in this way are *kar* 'past' and *naaj* 'will (future)'. Each brings its own special contribution to the resulting focused sentence, as the examples show.

KAR-*initial focused sentences.* There follow examples of focused sentences introduced by *kar.* Note that *kar* itself does not have a subject prefix, and that the only verbs that do have a subject prefix are within a relative clause, and not at the top level of either equational nominal.

(6-9) a. [**Kar** āindeeo] [ammān didiakeōk tak ḷọk raan eo ooṃ boñ].
'We kept tacking in this fashion all day as we sailed east until it was night.'

b. [**Kar** iiet tata] [koṇan Toni [iaan ḷōṃaro raar eọñwōd]].[2]
'Tony caught the fewest fish among the men who went fishing.'

c. [**Kar** kadek tata] [Toni ilo bade eo].
'Tony was the most intoxicated at the party.'

d. [**Kar** jerọtata eo] [eṇ ilo tariṇae eo].
'He was a top marksman during the war.'

e. [**Kar** ijekein] [ko [kōm ar pād ie ilo pata eo]].
'These were the places we stayed during the war.'

f. [**Kar** jibūñ wōt] [an ṃōñā].
'He ate a little.'

g. [**Kar** kwe] [āt iaaṃtok]?
'Who was escorting you when you came?'

h. [**Kar** ta] [eo [ḷōḷḷap eo ekar ba]]?
'What was it the old man said?'

i. [**Kar** baj] [abja wōt].
'That's just the way I am.' ('I'm funny that way').

j. [**Kar** baj] [ri-aleak wōt].
'She naturally wears her hair loose on her back so provocatively.'

2. The two nominals of each equational sentence are enclosed in square brackets. In those sentences that have a relative clause, it is also bracketed within the subject nominal, and the finite verb of the relative clause is underlined (including its subject prefix).

k. [**Kar** kijen ri-M̧ajeļ wōt] [ek ñan$_2$ jālele im ñan$_2$ ōn ko [rōaikuji jān$_1$ kanniek]].
'Fish were the only part of the Marshallese diet that provided *jālele* and the nutrients one gets from meat.'

Notice that the translations are all in the past tense, with the exception of (6-9i–j), which can perhaps be attributed to the presence of *baj 'almost, just, superlative',* indicating a more timeless or permanent condition (referred to as NONTEMPORAL INTENSITY in table 3-11). We will have more to say about *baj* below—relevant to its role in these two sentences.

NAAJ-*initial focused sentences.* Next we look at some examples of focused sentences introduced by *naaj* 'will'. They all share a future orientation; the first four are statements, the last five are content questions.

(6-10) a. [**Naaj** āindein] [an nana kōto m̧aan ļọk ñan allōñ in laļ].
'The current unfavorable wind condition is going to persist as is until next month.'

b. [**Naaj** Jọọn kab Pita] [ri-kwaļkwōļ kōnnọ rainin].
'It will be John and Peter to do the dish-washing today.'

c. [**Naaj** kōjro wōt] [ñan jimmiļọkin aō mour].
'It'll just be the two of us till I die.'

d. [**Naaj** jikin iioon doon eo ad] [in].
'This will be our rendezvous.'

e. [**Naaj** kōjka] [wōj]?
'How can I come?'

f. [**Naaj** ta] [am̧ kōpetaklik [ñe inaaj kam̧uriik eok]]?
'What will be your collateral should I give you the loan?'

g. [**Naaj** ta] [wūnoka [ke ijorrāān]]?
'What's the remedy for relieving me of this heartache?'

h. [**Naaj** ie] [wāween aō kōmeļeļeik [ke epokin tōreej]]?
'How will I explain it to him given his utter confusion?'

i. [**Naaj** jete] [buñtōn neem̧ jān ijin ļọk ñan m̧weiien̦]?
'How many steps will it take you from here to that house?'

BAJ-*initial focused sentences.* The role of *baj* in these sentences is quite different from that of *kar* and *naaj* in the two preceding sections. Whereas *kar* and *naaj* continue their function as auxiliaries to bring tense to a fronted predicate nominal, *baj,* as a derived noun itself, serves as the predicate nominal. First, some of the simpler examples.

(6-11) a. [**Baj**] [*adkeelelier*]!
'They are **such** an intractable group!'
(lit. their intractability is superlative)

b. [**Baj**] [*aen̦akūm̧*] ļe.
'Man, you're drenched **to the skin**.'
(lit. your wetness is superlative)

c. [**Baj**] [*adenpein* arin ānin] ḷōṃa.
'Guys, the lagoon side of this island is **teeming** with *adenpe* sharks.'

d. [**Baj**] [*āt* eo pāpijek].
'An **absolute** rascal.'

e. [**Baj**] [*abṇōṇōū* kōn$_1$ an memakijkijtok].
'I'm **so** upset by his frequent visits.'

f. [**Baj**] [*ailparokūṃ* kake$_1$].
'S/he **must** be a burden to you.'

In these sentences, *baj* functions to assert the 'superlativeness' of the subject nominal that follows. This is brought out consistently in the translations, often using words like "such" and "so." Note that the subject nominal often begins with inalienable nouns derived from verbs—such as *abṇōṇō* and *ailparok* in (6-11e–f), respectively.[3] The possessive suffixes of these nouns are often reflected as the subjects of the English translations.

The examples below have the basic structure of those above, followed by a RESULTATIVE clause introduced by the complementizer *ke*$_1$ 'that'. Elsewhere in the sentence, there are no finite verbs with subject prefixes.

(6-12) a. [**Baj**] [*aelọkūṃ*] ke$_1$ iñak ke kwōpād ijo.
'You were **so** well hidden that I didn't notice you were there.'

b. [**Baj**] [*aborū*] ke$_1$ iitōn ban wōnṃaanḷọk.
'I'm **so** impeded that I can't move forward.'

c. [**Baj**] [*aelellọḷūṃ*] ḷe ke$_1$ eñṇe kwọitaak.
'Man, you're **so** impetuous that you've crashed.'

d. [**Baj**] [*aiboojojimi*] ke$_1$ rej ba etami ñan kiin.
'You're all **so** marvelous that they're still mentioning your names to this day.'

e. [**Baj**] [*aiṇokkoūṃ*] ke$_1$ ijakile eok.
'You're **so** light skinned that I didn't recognize you.'

f. [**Baj**] [*aitokūṃ*] ke$_1$ iban lo ioon bōraṃ.
'Your height is **such** that I can't see the top of your head.'

g. [**Baj**] [*ajeḷkāū*] ke$_1$ iaddimejmej.
'I'm **so** weak that I'm lethargic.'

h. [**Baj**] [*akḷañūṃ*] ke$_1$ iḷak tōparḷọk ijo ibbate eok?
'You're **so** preemptive that when I got there you were already there.'

Another initial BAJ? *Baj* appears before other sentences or clauses with the meaning 'successor'. We include examples here so that they can be compared with those above, wherein *baj* denotes 'superlativeness'.

3. These derived nouns (or other nominals) are italicized in the examples; *baj* and words in the translations indicating 'superlativeness' are shown in boldface.

(6-13) a. [Eṃōj ṇe] [kwe], [**baj**] [ña].
'Enough for you; my turn (lit. I am the successor).'

b. Kwōn jerbal em ļak ṃōk, [**baj**] [ña].
'Work and when you're tired, I'll work.'

c. **Baj** lewaj jebwe e bwe$_1$ ij ja kakkije.
'You take the wheel so I can take a rest.'

d. **Baj** letok ṃōk juon jikka?
'Say, how about giving me a cigarette?'

e. [**Baj**] [ña] ṃōk wajwaj kōn$_1$ waj ṇe nājiṃ?
'May I borrow your watch now?'

Sentences (6-13a–c) consist of two clauses each; (6-13b–d) have finite verbs (underlined) in at least one clause. The finite verbs after *baj* in (6-13c–d) do not have subject prefixes, but are IMPERATIVES (see "Commands" on page 279). In each of these sentences, *baj* can be seen as pointing to a 'successor' entity or event in the clause it introduces.

Inappropriate successors. Finally, we note a type of initial *baj* that questions an entity or event that someone has suggested (and to which we are not privy here). The complementizer *ke*$_2$ 'while, when' introduces the contradictory circumstances. The combination *baj ke* is sometimes replaced by the variants *bake* {bahkey} or *make* {mahkey}.

(6-14) a. **Baj ke**$_2$ ejako ṃweeṇ iṃōn?
'How since she's not at home?'

b. **Baj ke**$_2$ emoottok?
'But how can you when she's already here?'

c. **Baj ke**$_2$ enaññinmej?
'How can you when she's sick?'

d. **Bake** ij jerbal?
'But how about my work?'

Does each of the preceding sets of examples show us a different word with a different meaning, each pronounced the same (as HOMONYMS), or are we viewing a single word *baj* that has a broad range of meaning that shows us a different part of itself in different contexts? To take the latter position it will be necessary to find a way to unify the designation of an entity or event as being both SUPERLATIVE and the SUCCESSOR.

Verbless sentences that are not equational. This section on verbless sentences would not be complete without mention of sentences that are not equational and yet have no finite verbs—that is, no verbs with subject prefixes. Note that the examples in (6-15) all begin with *aolep* 'all', which is followed immediately or shortly thereafter by *im* 'and'. With the exception of (6-15f), no finite verbs are to be found in the remainder of the sentence, after *im*. The words between *aolep* and *im* are modifiers of *aolep*.

(6-15) a. **Aolep** armej **im** *iọkwe kōn an lelejkōnkōn (ellejkōnkōn).*
'Everyone likes her because of her appealing personality.'

b. **Aolep im** *kar bar ikōñ im jab kōkeroro.*
'Everyone was silent again and no one spoke.'

c. **Aolep** ro ioon wab eo **im** *ilbōk kōn wāween eo.*
'Everyone on the dock was surprised by it.'

d. **Aolep** men i lowa **im** *kar wāār.*
'Everything inside the boat was sliding around.'

e. **Aolep im** *kar bar kōḷmānḷọkjeṇ im roñjake kōto im wōt ko.*
'Everyone listened to the wind and the rain and thought for a while.'

f. **Aolep im** *ko jāne*$_1$ bwe$_2$ ewūdeakeak.[4]
'Everyone ran away from him because he went berserk.'

IM *as trigger of* SWITCH REFERENCE. It is possible to characterize the role of *im* in the examples of (6-15) as being 'to exempt the verbs that follow it in the clause from the usual requirement of being finite'. "Subject prefixes not needed." There is another interesting phenomenon referred to as "switch reference" that appears in some languages of the world, and it turns out that Marshallese is one of the languages that has it, with the word *im* deeply involved. Basically, when SWITCH REFERENCE occurs, we switch who we are talking about (the subject of our sentence) to someone else with seemingly little or no warning. People who know the language well are not fooled; they know the subject has been switched. But linguists and people trying to learn the language have to work at learning the secret of how to recognize the switch, which involves *im* in a very special context: (1) a transitive verb with its subject prefix, followed by (2) its direct object, (3) *im*, and (4) an intransitive verb without a subject prefix (exempted by *im*?). What newcomers aren't told, the "secret," is that (2), the direct object of the first verb, becomes the subject of the second verb. They naturally assume (encouraged by *im* 'and') that both verbs have the same subject (see table 6-1).

Table 6-1 Example of Switch Reference (unrecognized).

Vtr	DIRECT OBJECT	IM	Vintr
E-idiki	ut eo	im	mej.
'He shook	the flower tree	and	died.'

Examples of sentences with two verbs connected by *im* are given in (6-16). Those in (6-16a–f) qualify for switch reference, as their order is transitive-intransitive. Example (6-16g) contains what must be considered an

4. This sentence ends with a *bwe*$_2$ clause that has the finite verb *ewūdeakeak*, while the preceding sentences have no such clauses. This shows that the scope of *im*'s requirement 'that all following verbs should be nonfinite' has limits that need further study.

idiom *im/em ṃōk*, which does not trigger switch reference. The remaining examples do not qualify; those in (6-16h–i) are both transitive, and those in (6-16j-k) are both intransitive. The discussion of (6-25) on page 284 may give some deeper understanding of what it is about the verb order transitive-intransitive that facilitates the switching of references—that the Patient of the first verb remains the Patient of the second verb.

(6-16) a. Eidiki ut eo **im** mej. (ambiguous)
'He shook the flower tree and it withered.'

b. Eibwiji wa eo **im** peḷọk.
'The tide came up and the canoe drifted away.'

c. Ijelōt bato eo raan tebōḷ eo **em** wōtlọk.[5]
'I bumped the bottle and it fell off the top of the table.'

d. Ekajjidedeiki uwaak eo **im** jiṃwe.
'He made a guess at the answer and got it right.'

e. Kuuj eo ear rakutake jōōt eo aō **em** potak.
'The cat clawed my shirt to shreds.'

f. Rōkuul būrwōn **im** mej.
'He was strangled to death.'

g. Iar pukpukote **em** ṃōk.
'I hunted and hunted for it until I was tired.'

h. Iar kōpeḷ piik eo **im** jibwe.
'I chased the pig and caught it.'

i. Ḷeo ear kaiiouk juon pilawā **im** kañe.
'The man ate a whole loaf of bread.'

j. Ewōtlọk tibat eo **im** pene.
'The tea kettle fell and got dented.'

k. Iar ṃōñā baru **im** iōbaru.
'I ate crab and got poisoned.'

This concludes our discussion of verbless sentences, and other sentences that repress the expected appearance of finite verbs. We turn now to verbal sentences.

VERBAL SENTENCES

6.2.2 The syntactic properties of various types of verbal sentences are the subject of discussion in this section. We look first at simple **statements**, then at **commands**, followed by a description of the form of **questions** in Marshallese. The section ends with a discussion of **conjoined sentences**.

Statements. In a TRANSITIVE clause, the order of constituents is always SUBJECT – VERB – OBJECT, as is shown in (6-17a). In an INTRANSITIVE clause, the unmarked order of constituents is SUBJECT – VERB. Sentence

---

5. *Em* is a variant of *im*. Also, see footnote 11 on page 207.

(6-17b) illustrates the typical sequence of constituents in an intransitive clause. However, Marshallese allows an alternative order in such clauses. It is also possible for the subject to follow the verb, as is shown in (6-17c).

(6-17) a. Ajri eo ear lo kidu eo.
'The child saw the dog.'

b. Ajri eo ej kiki.
'The child is sleeping.'

c. Ej kiki ajri eo. / Ekiki ajri eo.
'The child is sleeping.'

d. Kwōn ajjinono [bwe$_2$ ekiki Baba].
'Speak softly because Father is sleeping.'

e. Kwōn ānen ḷọk [bwe$_2$ enaaj douj wa ṇe].
'Bail the canoe or it will ship water.'

The conditions that govern the variability appear to be discourse related. The sentence in (6-17b) is more likely to be a statement giving information, while (6-17c) is more likely to be a response to a question about the child. The order VERB – SUBJECT is common, though not required, in embedded clauses, as in (6-17d–e).

Commands. Commands in Marshallese may be expressed by using a finite verb without an overt subject and without a subject prefix, where the subject is interpreted as second person singular. In such cases, the verb is treated as being IMPERATIVE. Such imperative verbs are not always initial; they may be preceded by one or more of certain nonprime auxiliary verbs, devoid of any subject prefix, as in (6-18c–e).[6]

(6-18) a. **Letok** pinjel eo aṃ.
'Give me your pencil.'

b. **Lale** niñniñ eo.
'Watch the baby.'

c. "*Kab jujen* **kōjjeḷāiki** ke ān eo e i ṃaan," Jema ebaj ba.
'"And let him know there is land up ahead," Father said.'

d. "*Jab* **inepata** bwe iōōe i ṃur," Bojin eo euwaak.
'"Don't worry, I'm on top of it," the Boatswain replied.'

e. *Kanooj* **iiaake** ek ṇe bwe edidi.
'Be careful in taking the meat off that fish
for it has lots of bones.'

However, not all commands are formulated in this way with imperative verbs. It is also possible to express "mild commands" or more polite com-

6. Nonprime auxiliaries are in italics, imperative verbs in bold.

mands by using a nonimperative form of the verb in a construction headed by the auxiliary verb *en* 'optative'.[7]

(6-19) a. Koṃwin bale uṃ eṇ.
'Cover that oven.'

b. Jen kūbwij juon roñ.
'Let's dig a hole.'

Using the auxiliary *en* to express direct polite commands allows the speaker to specify second person plural addressees (6-19a) or first person inclusive addressees (6-19b), as well as second person singular addressees.

To sum up, the order of constituents in TRANSITIVE clauses is fixed. The subject precedes the verb, and the object follows it. The subjects of INTRANSITIVE verbs usually precede the verb, but may also follow it.

Direct Questions. Two types of direct questions are discussed in this section: yes/no questions and content questions. Forming yes/no questions requires a different strategy from that used in content questions. Yes/no questions are formed using the interrogative adverb *ke*, while content questions require interrogative pronouns, or in some cases, interrogative adverbs (for the latter, see table 5-1 on page 210).

Yes/no questions. The interrogative *ke* is analyzed as an interrogative adverb because it occupies the same syntactic slot as *ñāāt* 'when' and *ia* 'where' (discussed on page 211). The slot is also occupied by noninterrogative adverbs such as *jidik* 'a little' (on page 214) and *ṃōk* 'please' (on page 218). Generally, *ke* follows the nonauxiliary verb or the predicate nominal. For details, see "The question word *ke*" on page 210.

Indirect yes/no questions also include the interrogative adverb *ke* and correspond to English clauses meaning 'if, whether.'[8]

(6-20) a. Kwōn edjoñe ṃōk ṃōñā ṇe ennọ **ke**.
'Taste that food to see **if** it's good.'

b. Etalpeete ṃōk lik ṇe im lale kwōlo **ke** ṃọle eo.
'How about taking a walk over the ocean side reef and see **if** you locate the school of *ṃọle*.'

c. Bwe jejaje koṃro en kar kōṇaan **ke** ṃōñā.
'I didn't know **if** you guys were going to want to eat.'

d. Kwōn wanlaļtak kōjro kōjjemļọk bwe jeñak jen bar **ke** lo doon.
'Come down here so we can spend a few minutes together before we go since we don't know **when** we'll see each other again.'

---

7. *En* is both the 3S and BASIC form of this prime auxiliary. The forms for other persons and numbers (such as *koṃwin* '2P' and *jen* '3S') are to be found in table 3-10 on page 151.
8. Indirect yes/no questions are also referred to in (5-93) on page 264.

e. Kilen jājeik ṃōk e bwe in lale kwōjeḷā **ke**.
'Fence with him so I can see **whether** you're good or not.'

f. Kwōn al tok ṃōk bwe in lale eṃṃan **ke**?
'Why don't you sing so I can **audition** you?'

g. Kwōn ātoñ ṃōk pein eaelel **ke**.
'Smell his hands and see **if** they smell like fish.'

h. Kwōn edjoñe ṃōk iiōk ṇe ennọ **ke**?
'Taste this mixture—**is it** good?'

i. Kwōn joñe jedoujij ṇe dettaṃ wōt **ke**.
'Try the pants on and see **if** they fit.'

j. Kwōn ṃōk bar tallōñ im lale kwōllo **ke** āne i ṃaan.
'Climb up again and see **if** you spot land up ahead.'

Content questions. Content questions are generally formed using three types of interrogative words: interrogative pronouns, interrogative adverbs, and inherently interrogative verbs. The interrogative pronouns are presented in table 4-9 on page 184, and discussed in 4.2.3, beginning on page 182. The interrogative adverbs are covered in 5.2.1, beginning on page 210. In addition, the pro-adjective *rot* is often used interrogatively. See that discussion beginning on page 188.

Two inherently interrogative verbs are *et* 'do what?' and *jaaṃ* 'why persist in?; why still?'. Their use is illustrated here below.

(6-21) a. Ak kwōj **et** wōt ānin?
'So what have you been doing on this island?'

b. Kwōj **ita** ijeṇe?
'What are you doing over there?'

c. Rej **itene** ḷadik eṇ ke_1 eḷap an jañ?
'What are they doing to that boy that he's crying so loudly?'

d. I**jaaṃ** bar metak bar?
'Why did I get a headache again?'

e. 'E**jaam** marok wōt ṃwiin iṃōṃ?
'Why is your house still dark?'

The verb *ita* in (6-21b) is the Ratak (Eastern) dialect variant of *et*, and *itene* in (6-21c) is its transitive form. Notice that *jaaṃ* is an auxiliary or helping verb: in (6-21d) it is followed by another auxiliary (*bar* 'again') and the nonfinite *metak* 'pain'; in (6-21e) by the nonfinite *marok* 'dark'. Notice also that the final heavy *ṃ* of *jaaṃ* becomes light *m* when the following word begins with a light consonant, as in (6-21e).

The word *āt* 'and who else' is another interrogative verb that is related derivationally to an interrogative pronoun of the same form that is often found as the predicate nominal of equational sentences (6-22a–d). Example (6-22e) has *āt* as an interrogative verb, where it is followed by the directional *waj* 'toward you', but it is also possible to use the first person pronoun *ña* instead of the verbal *ij* and produce an equally acceptable equational sentence. Example (6-22f) with initial *kar* is repeated from (6-9g).

(6-22) a. [E] [āt]?
'Who else besides him?'

b. [Koṃro Tony] [āt eo]?
'You and Tony and who else?'

c. [Kwe] [āt eo ijo]?
'Who else was there with you?'

d. [Koṃjel] [āt eo koṃjel kar pād iāneo ke ej bwil]?
'You three and who else were on the island when it burned?'

e. Ij āt waj? / [N̄a] [āt waj]?
'Who else is coming with me?' (addressing someone who is at a different location, as on the phone)

f. [Kar kwe] [āt iaaṃtok]?
'Who was escorting you when you came?'

This concludes the discussion of the syntactic characteristics of questions. We turn now to an examination of conjoined sentences.

Conjoined sentences. Sentences in Marshallese can be conjoined using the conjunctions *im* 'and' and *ak* 'but'. The conjunction *ak* 'but' joins two complete independent sentences, as in (6-23a–d). Note the idiom *im ṃōk* in (6-23d) within one of the conjoined units. Example (6-23e) shows *ak* also occurring sentence-initially and not clearly doing any conjoining with previous discourse; (6-23f–g) show it conjoining words and better translated as 'or'.

(6-23) a. Kwōn jab kōrraat **ak** kwōn jipañ eō.
'Stop being skeptical **and** start helping me.'

b. Ear kamirouk eō **ak** ear jab lo eō.
'She kept an eye out for me **but** couldn't find me.'

c. Eaelọk kiiō **ak** enaaj alikkar tokālik.
'It's invisible now **but** will be revealed later.'

d. Ijeme im ṃōk **ak** ejaje ekkañ.
'I'm tired from sharpening it **but** it won't take an edge.'

e. "**Ak** kwōj et wōt ānin?" Jema ekajjitōk.
'"So what have you been doing on this island?" Father asked.'

f. Ilo aṃ jeḷā ḷe kar ilo allōñ kein, ae ṇe ikōtaan aelōñ in im Likiep ej ae niñaḷọk ke **ak** rōñaḷọk.
'In your knowledge of these months now, is the current between this island and Likiep running north **or** south?'

g. Wāween kōṃṃan jāānkun jān bōb eñin, ñe ej owat bōb, jej aintiini **ak** uṃwini.
'The way to make *jāānkun* from pandanus is, when it is ripe, to boil it **or** bake it.'

We have already met the conjunction *im* (~ *em*) and noted some of its special syntactic properties in section 6.2.1, (6-15) and (6-16). Here, in (6-24a), *im* joins two independent clauses with finite verbs in each clause, just as *ak* did in (6-23a–b). However, when sentences conjoined by *im* 'and' have the same subject and tense, these constituents are not repeated, as shown in (6-24b–c). And when the conjoined sentences do not include an auxiliary verb, the subject prefix appears only on the verb in the first sentence, which is finite—as in (6-24d)—while the verb in the second sentence is nonfinite, and, thus, has no subject prefix. In this situation, the missing subject of the second verb (*bōk* 'take s.') is understood to be coreferential with the subject of the first verb, which bears the subject prefix. Finally, *im* sometimes occurs sentence-initially (6-24e), rather than between sentences, and is sometimes used to conjoin words or phrases (6-24f) rather than sentences.

(6-24) a. Ḷoor eō **im** inaaj kaṃōņōņōik eok.
'Follow me **and** I'll entertain you.'

b. Ear ṃōjjo **em** kakūrañ eō.
'He hid **and** startled me.'

c. Ri-Amedka raar jodiki Kuwajleen **im** pād ie ṃae rainin.
'The Americans invaded Kwajalein **and** have stayed on it ever since.'

d. Ejide **im** bōk jerbal eo.
'He was lucky to get the job. / He was lucky **and** got the job.'

e. **Im** ñe āindein, ekwe iñak jenaaj bar ellolo ñāāt keinikkanin āne.
'And if that happens, well then I don't know when we'll see the island plants and trees, if ever.'

f. [Ri-jiraal waini **im** bwiro eo] [ņe].
'He's the one who is always eating coconut **with** preserved breadfruit.'

Summary of Basic Sentence Patterns

6.2.3 Marshallese has two basic sentence types: verbless sentences and verbal sentences. Verbless sentences include predicate nominals in two types of constructions: equational and cleft sentences. The unmarked order in equational sentences is SUBJECT – PREDICATE. Cleft sentences contain a predicate nominal that appears in initial position. Several nonprime auxiliaries may also introduce predicate nominals focused in initial position, similar to cleft sentences.

The constituents in verbal sentences are typically ordered SUBJECT – VERB – OBJECT, with some variability in intransitive sentences. This order is maintained in yes-no questions, where the adverb *ke*, placed after the predicate, signals the question. Content questions include interrogative pronouns or interrogative adverbs, and may be formulated as verbless sentences with nominal predicates or as verbal sentences.

Finally, sentences may be conjoined by using *im* 'and' or *ak* 'but'.

CASE RELATIONS

6.3 It is possible to add to our understanding of the meaning of a sentence by identifying the VERB as its central unit that relates to each of its NOMINAL units, and to assign a CASE name (from out of an inventory of five) to each of these relations that occur in the sentence. The five case relations are Patient, Agent, Correspondent, Locus, and Means. The last three of these case relations have inner and outer counterparts, with concomitant differences in semantic interpretation.[9] Only the inner case relations are relevant to the classification of verbs. (See "Major Verb Classes" on page 233 and the remainder of section 5.6, in which terms such as CORRESPONDENT, LOCUS, and MEANS figure prominently.)

PATIENT

6.3.1 Patient [PAT] is a case relation that exists with either the subject of an intransitive verb, or the object of a transitive verb. The Patient has been defined as "the perceived central participant in a state or event" (Starosta 1982:4).

AGENT

6.3.2 The Agent [AGT] case relation occurs with the subjects of transitive verbs. The Agent has been defined as "the perceived external instigator, initiator, experiencer, or (volitional or nonvolitional) controller of an event or state" (ibid.).

(6-25) a. Niñniñ eo ej kiki.[10]
[PAT] [–trns]
'The baby is sleeping.'

b. Ajri eo nājū enañinmej.
[PAT] [–trns]
'My child is sick.'

c. Niñniñ eo ekōṇaan kidu eo.
[AGT] [+trns] [PAT]
'The baby likes the dog.'

d. Aliksa eṃane piik eo.
[AGT] [+trns] [PAT]
'Aliksa is slaughtering the pig.'

e. Kako eo ejebwiji kako eo juon.
[AGT] [+trns] [PAT]
'The rooster kicked (spurred) the other rooster.'

---

9. See the discussion of inner and outer prepositions beginning on page 190.
10. [–trns] and [+trns] serve as abbreviations for intransitive and transitive, respectively.

CORRESPONDENT

6.3.3 Inner Correspondents [COR] are implied by certain verbs and nouns (see "Correspondents" on page 235). Such correspondents are interpreted as having an intimate connection with the Patient implied by the verb, as in (6-26a–c), although the second person singular Patient subject of the imperative verb in (6-26c) is unexpressed. No such connection is to be found in (6-26d), where the impersonal verb implies a nonreferential Patient [see (5-52) on page 239]. The nonassociative comparative verbs of class [C8] (on page 250) imply a Correspondent marked by the preposition *jān*$_2$ 'than', as in (6-26e–f).

(6-26) a. Ledik eṇ ej jijet ippān jinen.
[PAT] [–trns] [COR]
'That girl is sitting with her mother.'

b. Jab kaidaak ḷadik ṇe pia ṇe limō.
[+trns] [PAT] [COR]
'Don't make the boy drink my beer.'

c. Naṃōḷ tok kijerro kūrepe.
[–trns] [COR]
'Scoop out some gravy for the two of us.'

d. Ejjeḷọk armej ilo ṃōn jar eo.
[–trns] [COR] [LOC]
'There were no people in the church.'

e. Ejiniet ānin jān$_2$ kwe.
[–trns] [PAT] [COR]
'S/he is more familiar with this island than you are.'

f. Eaemedḷọk jota jān$_2$ jotenin.
[–trns] [PAT] [COR]
'It was cooler last evening than this evening.'

The associative correspondent verbs of class [B13] use the preposition *kōn*$_2$ 'about' before the Correspondent, as in (6-27a). Certain semantic types of verbs also mark their inner Correspondent with *kōn*$_2$ 'about'; this is true of PERCEPTION VERBS like *roñ* 'hear', *bwilōñ* 'wonder', *lōmṇak* 'think', and *emḷọk* 'reminisce' (6-27b–e), and of VERBS OF INFORMATION like *katak* 'learn', *jiroñ* 'tell s.', *kōnono* 'speak', and *kojeḷāik* 'inform s., let s. know' (6-27f–i).

(6-27) a. Etke kwōj jab taktō kōn$_2$ bakke ṇe neeṃ?
[–trns] [COR]
'Why don't you see the doctor about that ulcer on your leg?'

b. Rej mijak ke rej *roñ* kōn$_2$ taibuun eo epaak tok.
[–trns] [COR]
'It scared them to hear of the approaching typhoon.'

c. Iar kanooj *bwilōñ* $kōn_2$ jibai eo an ri-jibai eo.
[–trns] [COR]
'I was amazed by the magic trick performed by the magician.'

d. Ej juon ri-karejar ejeḷā *ḷōmṇak* $kōn_2$ ro jet.
[–trns] [COR]
'He is a cooperator, considerate of others.'

e. Ij idpeenen im *emḷọk* $kōn_2$ kiddik ko arro.
[–trns] [COR]
'I toss and turn reminiscing about those little things we used to do.'

f. Rej *katak* $kōn_2$ mour ilo jikuuḷ.
[–trns] [COR]
'They're studying biology in school.'

g. Iar *jiroñ* eok $kōn_2$ kweḷọk eo.
[–trns] [PAT] [COR]
'I notified you about the meeting.'

h. Ekaijoḷ eō ke ej *kōnono* $kōn_2$ pọḷjej eo.
[–trns] [COR]
'His talking about the ripe breadfruit baked in coconut oil gives me an appetite.'

i. Eitok inne im jabneejej tok ñan ña kōn
aer kar jab kōjjeḷāik $kake_2$ keemem eo.[11]
[AGT] [+trns] [COR]
'She came and cried on my shoulder yesterday saying they did not let her know about the birthday party.'

Relator nouns are a small class of inalienably possessed nouns (shown in table 6-2 on page 287) that function to mark inner case relations, including Correspondent and Locus. Associative correspondent verbs like those of class [B12] use forms of the relator noun *ippa-* 'company' as the Correspondent, as in (6-28a). The same is true of adjectival verbs of class [C9], as in (6-28b).

11. This speaker uses *kake*$_2$ as a variant of *kōn*$_2$.

Table 6-2 Relator nouns

TERMINUM		
INTERIOR	lowa-	'inside'
NONINTERIOR	tōrerei-	'side'
NONTERMINUM		
VERTICAL		
CARDINAL	ioo-	'top'
NONCARDINAL	iuṃwi-	'under'
NONVERTICAL		
INTERIOR	kōtaa-	'between'
	bwiliji-	'among'
	būlōn	'middle of'
	eoḷapa-	'center'
NONINTERIOR		
AXIAL		
CARDINAL	ṃaa-	'before'
NONCARDINAL	āliki-	'after'
	ḷokwa-	'after'
NONAXIAL		
ASSOCIATION	ippa-	'company'
	iaa-	'company'
NONASSOCIATION	turu-	'near'

(6-28) a. Ri-niñeañ-rōkeañ eo eṇ ebōjrak ippān liṃaraṇ tōrerein iiaḷ eṇ.
[PAT] [–trns] [COR]
'The show-off is stopping with the ladies by the roadside.'

b. Jej jab ṃōṇōṇō ippān ri-kaaeñwāñwā.
[–trns] [COR]
'We're not crazy about people who are responsible for noise.'

Outer Correspondents give the "external target or evaluative frame of reference for the state or action as a whole" (Starosta 1982:18). In Marshallese, outer Correspondents are marked by the prepositions *ñan*$_2$ 'for', *jān*$_2$ 'because of', and *kōn*$_2$ 'because of'. Some examples follow in (6-29).

(6-29) a. Iar al ñan$_2$ Mede.
[–trns] [COR]
'I sang for Mary.'

b. Ebar baūjō kōn$_2$ an tab.
[–trns] [COR]
'He's giddy again from drinking.'

c. Jān$_2$ wōt aṃ nana, etūṃ kwōd eo ikōtaarro.
[COR] [–trns] [COR]
'Simply because you are a harlot, our relationship is ended.'

The Correspondents in (6-29a–b) are considered to be outer because neither verb (*al* 'sing' nor *baūjō* 'be giddy') requires a Correspondent. The verb *tūṃ* 'be ended' in (6-29c) requires an inner Corrpondent, filled by *kwōd* 'relationship', so that the other Correspondent in the sentence, required by *jān*$_2$, can only be the outer Correspondent.

LOCUS

6.3.4 Certain classes of nouns in Marshallese function as case markers. One such class is that of LOCATIONAL NOUNS. They can be interpreted as Locus nominals without additional prepositions as case markers. The locational noun *Ṃajeḷ* 'Marshalls' is interpreted as a Locus in both sentences in (6-30a–b). The verb *pād* 'stay' in (6-30a) always implies a Locus, but *ejjabaō* in (6-30b) does not. Thus, the Locus in (6-30a) is an inner Locus, while that in (6-30b) is outer.

(6-30) a. Ej pād wōt Ṃajeḷ.
[–trns] [LOC]
'He's still in the Marshalls.'

b. Leddik wōt rej ejjabaō Ṃajeḷ.
[PAT] [–trns] [LOC]
'Only girls play *ejjabaō* in the Marshalls.'

Locational nouns need not always be interpreted as having the Locus case relation. The examples below show them in other case relations. In (6-31a) the locational noun *Ṃajeḷ* is the Patient subject of the verb *pād* 'stay'. The locational noun *āneṇ* 'that island' in (6-31b), as a possessive attribute of the inalienably possessed relator noun, is assigned the Correspondent case relation by *ioo-* 'on top of'. In (6-31c) the locational relator noun *tōrerei-* is interpreted as the Patient of the verb *ḷāik* 'file s.'. But when locational nouns are not assigned specific case relations, their unmarked interpretations are as Locus actants, as in (6-30a).

(6-31) a. Ṃajeḷ epād i turun ikkwetōr.
[PAT] [–trns] [LOC]
'The Marshalls are situated near the equator.'

b. Etōpar ioon āneṇ.
[–trns] [COR]
'He reached the island.'

c. Ḷāik jidik tōrerein.
[+trns] [LOC]
'File down the edges.'

d. Ḷōḷḷap eo jiṃṃaō ekaamṇak eō kōn$_2$ ijo jikin.
[AGT] [+trns] [PAT] [MNS]
'My grandfather gave me his land.'

The inner Locus case relation is assigned to nominals that are interpreted as the source, goal, location, or orientation of the Patient. Locative verbs imply Locus actants, and are of two types: directional (6-32a) and simple (6-32b). In the former, the verb *eļtok* 'pay attention' requires a sister like *ñan*$_1$ marked for direction and goal, and a Locus nominal like the pronoun *eō* 'me'. In the latter, the verb *pād* 'stay' requires a Locus actant without intervening preposition.

(6-32) a. Ear eļtok ñan$_1$ eō.
[–trns] [LOC]
'He paid attention to me.'

b. Iar pād Awai.
[–trns] [LOC]
'I was in Hawai'i.'

Outer Locus actants are not required by verbs, and are interpreted as the general temporal or spatial setting of the action or state expressed by the verb. In (6-33a) the relator noun *iuṃwin* 'under of' is interpreted as a Locus actant that provides the location of the fallen squashed fruit. The preposition *ilo* 'at' provides a temporal outer Locus—as it is in sentence-initial position, where generally only outer Locuses are to be found. In (6-33b) the prepositional phrase *ilo boñ* 'at night' is interpreted as the outer Locus, specifying the temporal setting of the state expressed by the impersonal verb *wōt* 'rain'. It is not required by the verb *wōt* 'rain'. Two more examples of sentence-initial outer Locuses are given in (6-33c–d): the first includes the preposition *ilo* 'at' and the compound noun *ṃantin Ṃajeļ* 'Marshallese custom'; the second is the relator noun *ālikin* 'after of'.[12]

(6-33) a. Ilo iien rak eo, ear eppedejdej iuṃwin aolep mā.
[LOC] [–trns] [LOC]
'During the summer there was squashed ripe breadfruit under all the breadfruit trees.'

b. Ej wōt ilo boñ.
[–trns] [LOC]
'It rains at night.'

c. Ilo ṃantin Ṃajeļ, emọ aluej ñe ej or irooj.
[LOC] [–trns]
'It's forbidden to be singing up above when there is a chief around, according to Marshallese custom.'

d. Ālikin aō wōtlọk, iar pitpit.
[LOC] [–trns]
'After I fell, I got a good rub-down.'

MEANS

6.3.5 Inner Means is defined as the "perceived immediate effector of an event or state; the external entity [that] impinges most directly and immediately on

12. The relator nouns are found in table 6-2 on page 287.

the Patient," and outer means is the "abstract path by way of which an external influence impinges on the situation" (Starosta 1982:21).

In Marshallese, both inner and outer Means are usually marked by the preposition *kōn*$_1$ 'with'. In (6-34a) the verb is impersonal and requires both a Correspondent and a Means, while (6-34b) has a manner verb of class [B8]. The verb in (6-34c) assigns the Means relation directly to the common noun *pia* 'beer' without need for the preposition *kōn*$_1$ 'with'. Both sentences are considered examples of inner Means.

(6-34) a. Ejure ānin kōn$_1$ bao.
[–trns] [COR] [MNS]
'This island is teeming with birds.'

b. Ij ja bọọkọk kōn$_1$ bọọk e aṃ.
[–trns] [MNS]
'I'll use your box for now.'

c. Ejab kōṇaan idaak pia.
[–trns] [MNS]
'He didn't want to drink beer.'

There follow two examples of outer Means. Their verbs do not require Means actants. Yet outer Means actants are possible with most verbs that express an activity, where the nominal assigned the Means case relation is interpreted as either INSTRUMENT or CAUSE. In (6-35a) *aō piọ* 'my cold' is interpreted as the CAUSE of the state *ebeb* 'be shivering'. In (6-35b) *jibuun* is interpreted as the INSTRUMENT by which the action of eating is accomplished.

(6-35) a. Eḷap aō ebeb kōn$_1$ aō piọ.
[–trns] [COR] [MNS]
'I'm so chilly I'm shivering.'

b. Jab kañ ek ṇe kōn$_1$ jibuun.
[+trns] [PAT] [MNS]
'Don't eat that fish with a spoon.'

Summary of Case Relations

6.3.6 The inclusion of case relations in a grammar makes it possible to capture significant generalizations about the syntactic properties of various nominals, as well as their syntactic-semantic relationships to the key verbs, prepositions, and nouns with which they occur.

The inventory of case relations in Lexicase (the system used in Pagotto 1987 and followed here) is limited to five: Patient, Agent, Correspondent, Locus, and Means. All five are realized in Marshallese, and exhibit the semantic properties ascribed to them within the theory. They are marked by grammatical devices such as word order and inflection, as well as mechanisms that include features such as prepositions and noun classes.

Certain case relations have been shown to have an inner vs. outer distinction. This distinction has semantic and syntactic consequences. Semantically, inner case relations are closely associated with the Patient implied in the case frame of a verb. Inner case relations subcategorize verbs and nouns, and must be included as implicational features of the relevant verbs and nouns. Outer case relations, on the other hand, are typically associated with the event or state as a whole. This semantic relationship is not encoded in the case frames of verbs or nouns.

DERIVATION

6.4 Derivation is a word formation process available to speakers of most, if not all, languages to create new words and to extend the syntactic range of already-existing words. It creates new words by analogy with an existing word. In some derivations, the new word will have a different form, having undergone a morphological change such as affixation or reduplication. With other derivations, the new word will be identical in form with the existing word. No morphological change will have taken place, but the syntactic range of the word will have changed—so that it can be used in new places.

For example, in (6-36a) the first *ṃōñā* is an intransitive verb meaning 'eat'. (We can recognize it as a verb by the subject marker *rej* preceding it.) The second *ṃōñā* is actually the second part of the compound noun *jikin ṃōñā* 'dining hall' derived from the two words that make it up.[13] (We can recognize it as a noun by the determiner *eo* that follows it.) In (6-36b) ***ṃōṃōñāñe*** **(*eṃṃōñāñe*)** is a distributive verb meaning 'eat all the time'. It has been derived from *ṃōñā* with two types of morphological change, initial-consonant doubling,[14] and final-syllable reduplication. In (6-36c) *ṃōñā* 'food' is a noun derived from *ṃōñā* 'eat' without any morphological change. (We can recognize it as a noun by the determiner *ko* that follows it.)

(6-36) a. Rej *ṃōñā* ilo *jikin ṃōñā* eo.
'They are eating at the dining hall.'

b. Eṃōj ṇe aṃ ***ṃōṃōñāñe*** (***eṃṃōñāñe***)?
'Why don't you stop eating all the time?'

c. Mā ej juon iaan *ṃōñā* ko eḷaptata an ri-Ṃajeḷ kōjerbale.
'Breadfruit is one of the foods that Marshallese use most.'

---

13. By analogy with other compounds such as those discussed in 3.2.9 on page 148.
14. Initial-consonant doubling has had different results in the two major dialects. The original result survives as the Ratak dialect form, but this was further modified to produce the Rālik dialect form that is shown in parentheses (see 2.4.1 on page 52).

Much of Marshallese derivation is already treated in chap. 3 with its emphasis on morphology—"Marshallese words and their forms"—but this does not include instances of derivation involving no morphological changes. These latter will be a major focus here in chap. 6 because of their importance in sentence formation, but we will also include a systematic review of derivations that involve morphological change.

First we look at words in other lexical categories that are derived from verbs. These include both nouns and adjectives.

Deverbal Nouns

6.4.1 With the exception of the prime auxiliaries,[15] all verbs, both transitive and intransitive, are potential sources of abstract nouns. They can form indefinite common abstract nouns without any change in form.

(6-37) a. Intransitive verb source
Kwōn lale **aṃ** *jijet.*
'Watch the way you are *sitting.*'

b. Transitive verb source
Eḷap **aṃ** *jājek* eok.
'You boast too much.'
[It is big **your** *bragging* about yourself.]

c. Transitive verb source (with anaphoric suffix)
Ebbōjbōj pein ālikin **aer** *lōke.*
'His arm was swollen all over after he got stung.'
[It is swollen all over of his arm after **their** *stinging him.*]

d. Personal adjectival verb source
Eḷap **aō** *wūdiddid* kōn$_2$ **aō** *piọ.*
'I'm so cold I'm shivering.'
[It is big of **my** *shivering* because of **my** *being cold.*]

e. Impersonal correspondent verb source
Ḷeo eṇ ej ñijlọk kōn **an** *metak* bōraṇ.
'He is groaning from his headache.'
[That man is groaning because of **its** (impersonal) *hurting* of his head.]

The source verbs are nominalized—derived into abstract nouns: 'sitting' instead of 'sit', 'bragging' instead of 'brag', and so on. There is a morphological change of *-ing* between the English translations, but none between the Marshallese verbs and nouns: *jijet* remains *jijet*, *jājek* remains *jājek*, and so forth.

In these sentences there is another replacement. What would have been the subject of the source verb is the possessor of the derived noun: '**they** sting' becomes '**their** stinging'. This is accomplished with various

15. The prime auxiliaries (*ej*, *ar*, and *en*) are not eligible, as they are inherently finite, always occurring inflected with a person marker, while derivations involve only uninflected forms.

forms of the default possessive classifier *aō, aṃ, an, aer,* and so on (see table 4-13 on page 195).

Such combinations are an extremely common way of forming complex sentences: a nominalized verb preceded by a form of the default possessive classifier. Further examples are given in (6-38) showing each of the possible forms of {haha-}, which are in boldface; the nominalized verbs are in italics.

(6-38) a. Eḷap **aō** *piọ* kōn$_2$ kōto in.
'I am chilly because of this wind.'
[It is great my chilliness …]

b. Eḷap **aō** *addiṃakoko* rainin im iabwin jerbal.
'I'm sluggish today and don't feel like working.'
[It is overwhelming my sluggishness today and I …]

c. Eḷap **aṃ** *bōbabubu* (*ebbabubu*).
'You're always lying down.'
[It is considerable your lying down.]

d. Eḷap **aṃ** *bōbajbaj* (*ebbajbaj*).
'You ride the bus frequently.'

e. Eḷap **an** *bab* nuknuk kaṇ ej kiiji.
'The clothes she sews are always tight.'

f. Eḷap **an** *kōkōb* (*ekkōb*) bakbōk e.
'This knife is quite dull.'

g. Eṃṃan **ad** *kar* lioeo ṇa ilo juon wōt jikuuḷ.
'It's good that we all got together in one school.'
[It is good our having all gotten together …]

h. Emṃan **ad** *aluje* an ri-Pikinni raṇ ṃōñā kōn aji.
'It was good to watch the Pikinni people eating with chopsticks.'

i. Eṃōj **am** *jekakaik* bōb ko.
'We have made chips out of the pandanus.'
[It is finished our making chips …]

j. Ekkā **aer** *jālele* ek ippān mā.
'They often eat fish with breadfruit.'
[It is frequent their eating fish with breadfruit.]

k. Ekōjkan **aer** *naaj ṇawāween* jorrāān eo ewaḷọk kōn$_2$ **aer** *akōjdate* doon?
'How are they going to deal with the damage caused by their hating each other?'
[How will it occur their finding a way to deal with …]

The derived nouns we have been looking at thus far all occur in sentences together with a form of the default possessive {haha-}. However, possessives are not obligatory, as the following sentences show:

(6-39) a. Eṃōj nuuji eok.
'You are in the news.'
[It is finished of (the) putting you in the news.]

b. Ekar ļap jejeurur (ejjeurur) ke_2 ej bwil m̧weo.
'There was a great commotion when the house burned.'

c. Eļap piọ rainin kōn kōto in.
'There's lots of chilliness today because of this wind.'

d. Em̧ōj kōḷḷāik waj oņeam̧.
'You've been paid your wages.'
[It is finished of the paying you your wages.]

e. Em̧ōj jekakaik bōb ko.
'The pandanus have been made into chips.'

f. Ekkā jālele ek ippān mā.
'Fish is commonly eaten with breadfruit.'
[It is usual eating fish as an accompaniment to breadfruit.]

In (6-39a) *nuuji* 'news' is an abstract noun derived from a transitive verb and the Patient *eok* 'you'. It appears as the Correspondent of the impersonal verb *m̧ōj* 'be finished'. In (6-39b) the derived abstract noun is the verb 'be excited', which functions as the Correspondent of the impersonal correspondent verb *ļap* 'be big'. None of the sentences in (6-39) contains any form of the possessive found in the sentences of (6-38). In fact, those in (6-39c–f) were adapted from sentences in (6-38) by removing the possessive.

A second type of deverbal nominalization creates nonabstract (concrete) common nouns. Instead of being possible for all verbs (except nonprime auxiliaries), it applies only to intransitive nonextension personal verbs (Class B). The pairs of lexical items in (6-40) show the semantic relationships between the intransitive verbal sources and the resulting derived nouns.

(6-40)	m̧ōñā	'eat'	m̧ōñā	'meal, food'
	jerbal	'work'	jerbal	'task, job'
	kōm̧m̧an	'make'	kōm̧m̧an	'deed, action'
	ļōmņak	'think'	ļōmņak	'thought, idea, plan'
	al	'sing'	al	'song'

These derived nouns have the full range of syntactic behavior that is chacteristic of common nouns, as the examples in (6-41) show.

(6-41) a. Raar waaki ļọk *m̧ōñā* nenọno (ennọno) **ko**.
'They passed up the delicious foods.'

b. Ear kam̧ōj aolep *jerbal* **ko**.
'She finished all the tasks.'

c. Kwōnaaj kalbuuj kōn wōt *kōm̧m̧an* **kaņe** am̧.
'You'll get put in jail as a result of your actions.'

d. Ejenolọk kōn *ļōmņak* **kaņ** an.
'His ideas make him different from others.'

e. Am̧onikaik tok m̧ōk *al* **ņe**.
'How about playing that song on the harmonica for us.'

In these sentences, the derived nouns all appear with determiners, a syntactic environment possible only for common nouns. In (6-41a) *m̧ōñā* is the direct object of the transitive verb *waaki* 'to pass without partaking', the final *-i* of which agrees with *m̧ōñā,* which is marked as plural by its determiner *ko.* (The noun and determiner are separated by the adjective *nenọno/ennọno.*) Examples (6-41b–e) all have their determiners immediately following the derived noun.

The nouns thus derived may undergo further derivations. Like other common (alienable) nouns, they may appear as inalienably possessed nouns (see "Nouns Derived from Verbs" on page 141 and note also from the examples in (3-23) that the nouns thus derived are *i*-stems).

They may also appear as compound nouns with the construct suffix (see "The construct suffix with alienable nouns" on page 137 and "Compound Nouns" on page 148).

(6-42) a. *jijet*-in ri-M̧ajeļ
'the (way of) sitting of the Marshallese'

b. *kiki*-in jipenpen
'the sleeping of a sea cucumber'

c. waan *tulọk*
'submarine'

These examples from Zewen (1977:57) show that a deverbal noun may appear as either the head noun of a compound (6-42a–b) or as the attributive noun in a compound noun (6-42c).

All the derivations presented thus far in this section on deverbal nouns have involved no morphological change. There is one derivation of verbal nouns that does involve morphological change, and that is the derivation of PERSON NOUNS, for which see 3.2.4 on page 139.

DEVERBAL ADJECTIVES

6.4.2 Simple personal adjectival verbs are potential sources of adjectives. As (6-43) shows, there are four patterns: no morphological change (a), final syllable reduplication (b), initial-consonant reduplication (c), and both initial-consonant and final-syllable reduplication (d).

(6-43) a.	utiej	'be tall'	utiej ~ utiej**ej**	'tall'
	jājim̧aat	'not be smart'	jājim̧aat	'not smart'
	pidodo	'be soft'	pidodo	'soft'
	kūre	'be grey'	kūre ~ **kū**kūrere	'grey (E)'
b.	kōkañ	'be sharp (E)'	kōkañ**kōñ**	'smart (E)'
	meọ	'be sour'	meọ**eo**	'sour'
	kajoor	'be strong'	kajoor**or**	'strong'
	riab	'be false'	riab**eōb**	'false'

c. pirōkrōk	'be braided'	**pi**pirōkrōk	'braided (E)'
depakpak	'be wide'	**de**depakpak	'wide (E)'
dāndān	'be watery'	**de**dāndān	'watery (E)'
d. potak	'be torn'	**pe**potak**tak**	'torn (E)'
kadu	'be short'	**kō**kadu**du**	'short (E)'
būḷu	'be blue'	**bū**būḷu**ḷu**	'blue (E)'

There does not seem to be any way to predict from the form of the source words which of these four patterns is to be followed, and considerable variation obtains. See further discussion under ADJECTIVES in 4.4 on page 187 and under "Plural verbs of dimension" on page 163.

If all adjectives are derived from adjectival verbs, then Marshallese does not have a lexical category of original adjectives. But the existence of adjectives like *utiej* and *kūre*—and others in (6-40a) that, like them, show no morphological change—leaves open the possibility that they were originally adjectives and the ones upon which others were modeled. The truth of the matter remains an open question, one that may possibly be settled when more of the history of all the Nuclear Micronesian languages is known.

This concludes our review of instances of deriving **out of** the verbal category. We turn now to instances of deriving **into** the verbal category.

DENOMINAL INTRANSITIVE VERBS

6.4.3 With the possible exception of adjectival verbs mentioned above, Marshallese verbs are derived only from nouns or from other verbs. Here we examine the nominal sources of intransitive verbs, first those that involve no morphological change, then those that do.

Nonlocative intransitive verbs. These verbs are formed from common noun sources in three different ways. We consider each in turn. The first way is discussed in connection with (6-44) through (6-48).

(6-44) rōjep 'fishing method' — rōjep 'to fish using this method'
rojeri 'rosary prayer' — rojeri 'say the rosary'
teiñwa 'telephone' — teiñwa 'use the phone'
kaaj 'playing cards' — kaaj 'play cards'

(6-45) a. Kwōnañin kati ke *kaaj* kaṇe?
'Have you cut the cards yet?'

b. Ḷōṃaro raṇ rej kaaj.
'The men are playing cards.'

The examples in (6-45) illustrate the differences in distribution of the source noun and the resulting intransitive verb. The noun *kaaj* 'card' in (6-45a) appears with a definite determiner *kaṇe* 'those'; in (6-45b) *kaaj* appears as an intransitive verb meaning 'play cards' following the noncompletive prime auxiliary *rej*.

Many nouns that are derived into the verbal category as intransitive verbs are subject to further derivation as transitive verbs (see page 316). In (6-46) below, the first form given is the source noun, which is followed by the intransitive verb derived from it in this section and the transitive verb that can be derived from it in (6-85) on page 316—like those in table 3-14 on page 156.

(6-46)	a.	buwat	'slingshot'
		buwat	'use a slingshot'
		buwat**e**	'hit s. with a slingshot'
	b.	būḷāwut	'plywood'
		būḷāwut	'install plywood'
		būḷāwut**i**	'put plywood on s.'
	c.	dila	'nail'
		dila	'use nails'
		dila**ik**	'nail s.'

Some other nouns derived as intransitive verbs are subject to further derivation as causative transitive verbs of the sort shown in table 3-17 on page 157.

(6-47)	a.	būraj	'brush'
		būraj	'use a brush'
		kabūraj**e**	'make someone brush (their teeth)'
	b.	kadjo	'method for catching *jo* (goatfish)'
		kadjo	'use the method for catching *jo*'
		kōkadjo**uk**	'take s. fishing for *jo*'
	c.	ajerwawa	'opening allowing drafts'
		ajerwawa	'have openings allowing drafts'
		kaajerwawa**ik**	'permit drafts in a house'

(6-48) a. Kwōn *buwat**e*** bao eṇ.
'Hit that bird with your slingshot.'

b. Eṃōj *būḷāwut**i*** tōrakin ruuṃ in.
'The ceiling of this room has been covered with plywood.'

c. Kwōn *dila**ik*** rā ṇe.
'Nail that board.'

d. ***Ka**būraj**e*** ajri raṇ.
'Make the children brush their teeth.'

e. Ia eo ear ***kō**kadjo**uk*** eok ie?
'Where did he take you pole fishing for goatfish?'

f. Kwōn jab ***ka**ajedwawa**ik*** ṃwiin.
'Don't let a draft into this house.'

Intransitive adjectival verbs. The second way in which intransitive verbs are created from common nouns is one that derives adjectival verbs of class [C1]. As with those of the first way, there is no morphological change.

(6-49)	joñọ	'fish odor'	joñọ	'have a fishy odor'
	rilojet	'sickness'[16]	rilojet	'have the sickness'
	bok	'blister'	bok	'have blisters'
	dile	'barnacle'	dile	'have barnacles'

(6-50) a. Ejoñọ peiṃ.
'Your hands are fishy.' ~ 'You have fishy hands.'

b. Erilojet ḷōḷḷap eṇ.
'That old man has the sea-ghost sickness.'

c. Ebok peū kōn an to aō jabōḷ.
'I have a blister on my hand from shoveling so long.'

d. Edile kapin wa eṇ.
'The boat has barnacles underneath.'

Usually these derived verbs can be translated as 'have N'. They can be subject to further derivation, and typically are changed to impersonal correspondent verbs of class [A2] (see page 236).

Intransitive verbs of attendance. The third way of creating intransitive verbs from common nouns creates verbs that are interpreted as 'attend, go to N'. Usually the nouns are loanwords from English. We assume that this is the direction of the derivation, as the borrowed words do not function as verbs in English.

(6-51)	būreek	'brig, jail'	būreek	'go to jail'
	jikuuḷ	'school'	jikuuḷ	'go to school'
	ṃupi	'movie'	ṃupi	'go to the movies'
	kuḷab	'club'	kuḷab	'go to a club'

(6-52) a. Taktō eo ear kakilen eō.
'The doctor examined me.'

b. Kwaar taktō ke inne?
'Did you go to the doctor yesterday?'

Taktō in (6-52a) is a common noun that functions as the Patient subject of the auxiliary *-ar* 'completive'. It is interpreted as the Agent of the embedded verb *kakilen* 'examine s.' by the general rule that associates missing subjects of infinitives with the Patient implied by the verb in the next higher clause. In (6-52b) *taktō* is a nonfinite intransitive motion verb meaning 'go to the doctor', commanded by the auxiliary *-ar* 'completive'.

Intransitive directional motion verbs. Certain common nouns serve as sources for these verbs, which are typically interpreted as 'go as a N (to)', or 'go by N (to)', and require a directional adverb (usually *ḷọk* 'toward a third party') and a locative goal.

(6-53) a. meej 'mate'
meej … ḷọk 'go as a mate'

16. Believed to be caused by sea-ghosts (cf. *lọjet* 'ocean, sea')

b.	baja	'purser'
	baja ... ḷọk	'go as a purser'
c.	baj	'bus'
	baj ... ḷọk	'go by bus'
d.	iaḷ kadu	'shortcut'
	iaḷ kadu ... ḷọk	'take a shortcut'

Example (6-53d) shows that compound nouns are also potential sources of derived directional verbs. The sentences below show a source noun (6-54a) and a corresponding derived directional verb (6-54b) in their respective syntactic environments.

(6-54) a. Ij jañin lo jiip eo waan.
'I haven't seen his jeep yet.'

b. Raar jiip ḷọk ñan$_1$ tawūn.
'They went to town by jeep.'

Jiip 'jeep' in (6-54a) is a definite common noun that functions as the direct object of the transitive verb *lo* 'see s'. In (6-54b) the derived intransitive directional motion verb *jiip* 'go by jeep' is commanded by the prime auxiliary *-ar* 'completive'.

Impersonal intransitive verbs. Here the sources are temporal or meteorological nouns that derive intransitive impersonal noncorrespondent verbs (Class [A1]).

(6-55) det 'sunshine' — det 'be a sunny day'
pāāt 'low tide' — pāāt 'be low tide'
aemed 'coolness' — aemed 'be cool'

(6-56) a. Ear būreek boñ.
'He got put in jail last night.'

b. Jab pepedikdik (eppedikdik) bwe$_2$ eboñ.
'Don't be slow because it's almost night.'

In (6-56a) the noun *boñ* 'night' sets the temporal location of the action and is interpreted as the outer Locus (see [6-33] on page 289). In (6-56b) *bōñ* 'be night' is a finite impersonal verb with a third person singular subject marker *e-*. Thus, on the one hand, it exhibits nominal properties in so far as it can be assigned a case relation, whereas, on the other, it has a property that is restricted to verbs—being assigned a subject prefix.

These derivations, like the others we have looked at thus far in 6.4.3, do not involve any morphological change. We turn now to some that do.

Intransitive causative verbs. These verbs are derived from common nouns by adding what is often referred to as the causative prefix *ka-* and may have the meaning 'hunt, gather, collect N'.

(6-57)	aij	'ice'	**ka**aij	'get ice'
	at	'hat'	**ka**at	'look for a hat'
	eḷbōn	'elephant'	**ka**eḷbōn	'hunt elephants'
	bakōj	'bucket'	**kō**bakōj[17]	'get a bucket'
	bale	'flounder'	**kō**bale	'fish for flounder'
	baḷuun	'airplane'	**kō**baḷuun	'meet an airplane'
	baru	'crab'	**kō**baru	'hunt for crabs'

The sentences below illustrate the syntactic environments of the source noun (6-58a) and the related causative verb (6-58b).

(6-58) a. Ekōṇaan ṃōñā aij.
'He wants to eat ice.'

b. Iar etal in **ka**aij.
'I went to get ice.'

In (6-58a), *aij* 'ice' is an indefinite common noun interpreted as the Means nominal of the intransitive manner verb *ṃōñā* 'eat'—see (6-34c) on page 290. The derived causative *kaaij* 'get ice' in (6-58b) appears in the infinitival clause commanded by the verb *etal* 'go' (class [E3] on page 261).

See "Verbs of hunting and gathering" on page 166 for further examples.

Denominal distributive verbs. Distributive verbs are derived from several sources: from both transitive and intransitive verbs, and from nouns. Those from verbal sources have already been treated in 3.3.3 on page 162, and those from nominal sources in 3.3.4 on page 165. Here we briefly consider only the latter, noting the patterns of morphological change involved in their derivation, and the unpredictability of the pattern that is followed for a given noun.

(6-59)	a.	boraañ	'sting ray'
		bōboraañ**añ** (**eb**boraañ**añ**)[18]	'be full of sting rays'
		jọọḷ	'salt'
		jejọọḷ**ọḷ** (**ej**jọọḷ**ọḷ**)	'be salty'
		buwak	'birthmark'
		būbuwak**ak** (**ib**buwak**wak**)	'be full of birthmarks'
	b.	bōb	'pandanus'
		bōb**e**	'be full of pandanus'
		buwak	'birthmark'
		buwak**e**	'be full of birthmarks'
		dān	'water'
		dān**e**	'be juicy'

17. The low vowel of the *ka-* prefix is subject to low-vowel dissimilation (see 2.5.5 on page 92), as can be noted in the last four examples of (6-57), where *ka-* becomes *kō-*.

18. To save space with these forms that involve initial consonant doubling, where the E and W dialects have different pronunciations for unprefixed forms, we follow the MOD solution as exemplified in table 2-16 on page 56.

c. bar — 'rock'
barbare — 'be rocky'

bok — 'sand'
bokboke — 'be sandy'

jọọḷ — 'salt'
jọọḷọḷe — 'be salty'

The three patterns exemplified here involve initial consonant doubling and final syllable reduplication (a), suffixation of *-e* alone (b), and both reduplication and suffixation (c). But the existence of words like *jọọḷ* 'salt' and *buwat* 'wart' that show variation in the patterns followed makes it clear that there are no obvious criteria determining the pattern for each source noun. The sentences in (6-60) show that the source noun and the derived verb appear in different syntactic environments.

(6-60) a. Ebooḷ kōn$_1$ *dān*.
'It is full of water.'

b. Ij kañ oran e bwe$_2$ *edāne*.
'I'm eating this orange because it's juicy.'

Many nouns that are the sources of derived intransitive distributives are associated with flora and fauna. These derived distributives are eligible for further derivation into the class of impersonal correspondent verbs (page 326).

Verbs of wearing or using. Intransitive verbs may be derived from nouns that refer to wearing apparel or other items of close personal use. They require Patients that are human. Verbs thus derived have the meaning 'wear or use N'. Any noun that is not more than three moras long—fitting the form {(CV)CVC}—will have its final syllable reduplicated in deriving the verb. When verbs are derived from longer nouns that belong to this semantic class, there is no morphological change. The same form is retained. See table 3-27 on page 167 for a listing of forms that undergo morphological change and those that don't.

(6-61) a. Kwaar wiaik ia *waj* ṇe nājiṃ?
'Where did you buy your watch?'

b. Ij jab kōṇaan *wajwaj*.
'I don't want to wear a watch.'

Waj 'watch' in (6-61a) exhibits the syntactic behavior appropriate for nouns, being marked as definite by the following deteminer and being interpreted as the Patient of the transitive verb *wiaik* 'buy s.'. The derived intransitive verb *wajwaj* 'wear a watch' in (6-61b) is the inner infinitival complement of the extension verb *kōṇaan* 'want' (class [E1] on page 260).

Verbs of empowerment. Whereas the intransitive verbs derived in the previous section and glossed as 'use N' require Patients that are human, there is no such requirement on the verbs derived here, which may also be glossed as 'use N'. The derived verb includes the prefix *le-*.

(6-62)	injin	'engine'	**le**injin	'use an engine'
	karjin	'kerosene'	**le**karjin	'use kerosene'
	wōjlā	'sail'	**le**wōjlā	'use a sail'

Notice that both borrowed words as well as words native to Marshallese can be the sources of derived verbs of empowerment. The sentences below illustrate the syntactic environment of the source noun (6-63a) and the derived verb (6-63b).

(6-63) a. Eor ke aṃ karjin?
'Do you have any kerosene?'

b. Jitob eṇ ej **le**karjin.
'That stove uses kerosene.'

Karjin 'kerosene' in (6-63a) is an indefinite common noun that functions as the predicational attribute of the inalienably possessed noun *aṃ* 'yours'. In (6-63b) the derived verb *lekarjin* 'use kerosene' is an infinitive commanded by the prime auxiliary *ej* 'noncompletive'.

See the earlier section on verbs of empowerment on page 301 for more example sentences and further discussion.

Summary of section 6.4.3. This concludes our discussion of intransitive verbs that are derived from nouns. We have seen that while some derivational processes entail changes in the shape of the source word, others do not. The morphological processes incorporated in the denominal derivations that have been discussed in this section are prefixation (verbs of empowerment), suffixation (distributive verbs), reduplication (verbs of wearing or use, distributive verbs), and initial consonant doubling (distributive verbs).

While the derivations do not always involve morphological changes, all the processes that derive denominal verbs have syntactic consequences, including at least a change of lexical category. These processes also involve semantic changes, some of which are unpredictable.

Once the denominal verbs have been derived, they are potential sources of further derivations, which are the subject of the next section.

Deriving within the Verbal Category: Semantic Derivations

6.4.4 The function of derivational processes discussed in the previous sections is to change the lexical categories of the source word to derive a new lexical item. Those discussed in this section do something different. Both the source and derived words are verbs. Thus, the derivations discussed here do not change the major lexical category (the "part of speech") of the source verb, but they do change its semantic category.

These semantic derivations also entail changes in morphology that function as overt signals of the semantic changes. Four such derivational processes are discussed, and are referred to by the type of verb that they derive: antonymal verbs, distributive verbs, causative verbs, and adjectival verbs.

The source and derived verbs related by these four processes have identical argument structures and syntactic frames. That is, the number and types of case relations implied by the source and derived verbs do not change, nor do their syntactic properties. Only the inherent semantic characteristics of the verb or the semantic features of its implied case relations are altered.

Antonymal verbs. Intransitive verbs are potential sources of these verbs, which have the opposite meaning of their source counterparts. The derived verbs are prefixed with the basic form *ja-* and have a semantic feature[19] that NEGATES the semantic features of the source verb. The pairs of lexical items in (6-64) below illustrate both the range of syntactic verb types that are potential sources of antonymal verbs and the semantic relationships that hold between source and derived pairs.

(6-64) a. Personal distributive verbs [B1], [C1]

kukurere (ikkurere)	'always play'
jọkkurere	'seldom play'
roroñroñ (erroñroñ)	'have good hearing'
jarroñroñ	'be deaf'

b. Simple intransitive verbs [B1]

tōtal (ettal)	'leak'
jettal	'not leak'
lōke	'believe'
jalōke	'not believe'

c. Personal adjectival verbs [C1]

keiie	'be strong'
jakeiie	'be not strong'
uwi	'be tasty'
jọuwi	'be not tasty'

d. Intransitive extension verb [E1]

kile	'recognize'
jakile	'not recognize'

e. Impersonal distributive verb [A1]

wōttūwōt	'always rain'
jọwōttūwōt	'seldom rain'

These verbs were first introduced in table 3.3.3 on page 158. Notice that both personal and impersonal verbs are subject to antonymal derivation. These examples show that the meaning of the derived verb is completely predictable, which is one of the characteristics of totally productive derivations. Antonymal verbs, however, fall a bit short; they cannot be derived from all the intransitive verbs of Marshallese.

19. This feature is shared with the negative auxiliary verb *jab* 'not' and the response word *jaab* 'no', both of which resemble the antonymal prefix *ja-* in form.

Distributive verbs. Distributive verbs derived from other verbs receives initial discussion in 3.3.3, beginning on page 300.[20] Here the variety of morphological patterns to be found is exemplifed for those from intransitive sources.

(6-65)	a.	jālele	'eat sauce'
		jejālele (**ej̧**jālele)	'always eat sauce'
		idimkwi	'be easily angered'
		i**d**dimkwi	'be edgy'
	b.	jijet	'sit'
		jijijet**jet** (**ij̧**jijet**jet**)	'keep sitting'
		kōto	'wind'
		kōkōtoto (**ek**kōto**to**)	'always be windy'
		ajādik	'walk slowly'
		a**j̧**jādik**dik**	'sneak'
	c.	badik	'bow down'
		badik**dik**	'humble oneself'
		addimej	'be feeble'
		addimej**mej**	'be sickly'
		lelo (ello)	'see'
		lelo**lo** (ello**lo**)	'be unfaithful'
	d.	eọọt	'be striped'
		eọọt**ọte**	'be striped all over'
		bok	'have a blister'
		bok**boke**	'have blisters all over'
	e.	inōknōk	'be decorated'
		inōknōk**e**	'be decorated all over'
		bok	'have a blister'
		bok**e**	'have blisters all over'

No obvious phonological or morphological conditions appear to trigger which of the morphological possibilities apply in any particular derivation. The stative verb *bok* 'have a blister' has two possible patterns: *bokboke* (6-65d) and *boke* (6-65e). Moreover, source verbs with similar morphological shapes may follow different patterns; for example, *jālele* 'eat sauce' (6-65a) uses initial consonant doubling, while *inōknōk* 'be decorated' (6-65b) uses suffixation with *-e*. Notice also that the semantic relationships between the source and the derived distributive are not always predictable.

The potential sources of verbs derived in this way can be found in all the major branches of intransitive Marshallese verbs.

20. Those derived from nouns are discussed in 3.3.3 on page 165 and in 6.4.3 on page 300.

(6-66) a. Simple intransitive verbs [B1]

dokwōj	'snap'
dedokwōj**kwōj** (**ed**dokwōj**kwōj**)	'continue snapping'
būñlik	'sail out of lagoon'
būbuñlik**lik** (**ib**buñlik**lik**)	'make many voyages'
buñlọk	'fall'
būbuñlọk**lọk** (**ib**buñlọk**lọk**)	'always fall'

b. Personal adjectival verbs [C1]

maroro	'be green'
memaroro (**em**maroro)	'be greenish'
piiñ	'be pink'
pipiiñ**iñ** (**ip**piiñ**iñ**)	'be very pink'
lilu (illu)	'be angry'
lilu**lu** (illu**lu**)	'be easily angered'

c. Personal manner verb [B5]

kōjak	'make jokes with'
kōkōjak**jōk**	'always make jokes with'

d. Personal adjectival locative verb [C2]

eojaḷ	'be scattered'
eojaḷ**jaḷ**	'be scattered all over'

e. Personal extension verbs [E3]

pojak	'be ready (to)'
pepojak**jōk** (**ep**pojak**jōk**)	'keep getting ready (to)'
tabur	'hesitate (to)'
tōtabur**bur** (**et**tabur**bur**)	'always hesitate (to)'

f. Impersonal noncorrespondent verbs [A1]

buñṇo	'be breaking surf'
būbuñṇo**no** (**ib**buñṇo**ṇo**)	'be many waves'
kōdọ	'be cloudy'
kōkōdọ**dọ** (**ik**kōdọ**dọ**)	'be cloudy all over'

g. Impersonal correspondent verbs [A2]

joñọ	'be fishy'
jejoñọ**ñọ** (**ej**joñọ**ñọ**)	'smell all over of fish'
bōbool (ebbool)	'be swollen'
bōbool**ol** (ebbool**ol**)	'be swollen all over'

These examples not only illustrate the various classes of intransitive verbs that may derive distributives, they also show the range of semantic relationships between the source and derived verbs.

Transitive verbs are also potential sources of distributive verbs. Their patterns differ from those of intransitives in that the initial syllable of transitive verbs is often the target of the reduplication instead of the final syllable.

(6-67)	a.	bukwe	'cut s.'
		bukbukwe	'cut s. carelessly'
		jibwe	'hold s.'
		jibjibwe	'fondle s.'
		jalate	'take s. apart'
		jaljalate	'take s. apart carelessly'
		rupe	'break s.'
		ruprupe	'tear s. down carelessly'
	b.	deñōt	'spank s.'
		deñdeñōt**e**	'spank s. all over'
		buuj	'tie s. in a knot'
		bubuuj**i**	'tie s. in a knot carelessly'
	c.	kij	'bite s.'
		kūkijkij (**ikkij**kij)	'chew s.'
		jibwe	'hold s.'
		jijibjibwe (**ijjib**jibwe)	'fondle s.'
		rupe	'break s.'
		rūruprupe	'tear s. down carelessly'
	d.	tūṃ	'pull s.'
		tūtūṃtūṃ**i**	'keep pulling s.'
		karōk	'arrange s.'
		kōkarkarōk**e** (**ekkar**karōk**e**)	'arrange s. carelessly'

The choice of the suffixed vowels in (6-67b) and (6-67d) is conditioned by the height of the last vowel in the stem; transitive verbs with stem-final high vowels are suffixed with *-i*; those with nonhigh vowels are suffixed with *-e*. The morphological patterns followed by the derivations are not predictable. Notice that both *jibwe* 'hold s.' and *rupe* 'break s.' may follow either b. or d. Many transitive verbs permit such doublets.

Causative verbs. Although causativization often produces verbs with different syntactic features, in this section we will look at four derivations in which there are no syntactic consequences, and only the semantic features of the source verb are changed—as well as its form, because minimally, each derivation includes the prefixation of *ka-* 'causative'. This, and any other morphological change, is marked by boldface in the groupings of the examples given for each derivation.

Causative adjectival verbs. (See the treatment of these verbs in 3.3.3 on page 159.) As the name promises, these derived verbs are adjectival, as are some—but not all—of their source verbs. The source verbs of the first three groups in (6-68) are adjectival; the last two source verbs of group (6-68d) are nonadjectival. But in every instance, the kind of entities that can be the Patient of the derived verb is different from the kind of entities that can be the Patient of the source.

(6-68) a. mijak — 'be afraid'
kaamijak, **kaam**mijakjak — 'be scary'[21]

kūtōtō — 'be angry'
kakūtōtō — 'be anger-producing'

b. bwilōñ — 'be surprised'
kabwilōñ**lōñ** — 'be surprising'

pepaḷ (eppaḷ) — 'be amazed'
kōppaḷ**paḷ** — 'be amazing'

c. jiṃwe — 'be correct'
kajjiṃwe — 'be corrected'

ṃōṇōṇō — 'be happy'
kaṃṃōṇōṇō — 'be pleasing'

d. jar — 'be broke'
kōjjar**jar** — 'be expensive'

jiñ — 'fart'
kajjiñ**jiñ** — 'be gas-producing'

mo — 'heal'
kammo**mo** — 'be a healing agent'

The sentences in (6-69) illustrate the differences between the source and derived verbs.

(6-69) a. Joñan aō *pepaḷ* (*eppaḷ*) ikar aḷḷañ.
'I was so amazed my mouth was hanging open.'
[The measure of my amazement was such that my mouth was hanging open.—a RESULTATIVE]

b. Eḷap an ***kōppaḷpaḷ*** kōl ko nājin.
'His tricks were amazing.'

In (6-69a) *pepaḷ* (*eppaḷ*) 'be amazed' is a personal intransitive adjectival verb that has been nominalized with a first person singular form of the default possessor. The derived causative *kōpaḷpaḷ* 'be amazing' in (6-69b) is used impersonally (3s implied) of the Correspondent *kōl ko nājin.*

Causative verbs of testing. This process creates nonadjectival verbs that refer to testing the quality or competing in the activity expressed by the source verb (which may be either adjectival or nonadjectival).

(6-70) a. tilekek — 'hide'
kattilekek — 'play hide and seek'

b. util — 'be agile'
kọutil**til** — 'have an acrobatic contest'

auj — 'reach a goal in a game: go out'
kaawūj**wūj** — 'play solitaire; attempt to "go out"'

---

21. Both variants include unexplained doubling of the prefix vowel.

c.	dipen	'be strong'
	kaddipen**pen**	'test one's strength'
	jerọ	'be a good shot'
	kōjjerọ**ro**	'have a shooting contest'
	pakij	'be able to stay under water'
	kōppakij**kij**	'test ability to stay under water'
	jide	'be lucky'
	kajjide**de**	'depend on chance'
	taḷe	'have sex appeal; be popular'
	kōttaḷe**ḷe**	'attempt to be popular w. the opposite sex'

The meanings of some of these derived words are literally 'test V', where V represents the meaning of the source verb. Others may be less clearly testing, but there is always an element of striving toward some goal, even if it involves competing with oneself in solitaire, or hiding oneself better than others hide themselves.

Causative verbs of control. Here we see a derivational relationship between nonadjectival verbs. Nothing about the source verb changes except its meaning and, of course, its shape. An element of control or restraint is introduced into the meaning, and the causative prefix *ka-* is added (plus reduplication and/or initial consonant doubling) in some of the groupings of examples below.

(6-71)	a.	tōtōr (ettōr)	'run'
		kattōr	'drive a vehicle'
		bwebwenato	'talk'
		kabwebwenato	'make conversation'
	b.	añūr	'crave cigarettes'
		kaañūr**ñūr**	'refrain from smoking cigarettes'
	c.	**bōjrak**	'stop'
		kabbōjrak	'hold on'
	d.	batur	'crave fish'
		kōbbatur**tur**	'refrain from eating fish'

These verbs were first introduced in chap. 3 on page 160.

Causative verbs of acquiring a quality. Here nonadjectival verbs are derived from adjectival source verbs. The meaning of the derived verb can generally be expressed as 'cause to V', where V represents the quality expressed by the adjectival source verb. Acquiring the quality sometimes requires an element of discipline and/or perseverance. But it also sometimes seems to go to the head of the person acquiring the quality.

(6-72)	a.	iur	'be fast'
		kaiur	'hurry'
		miminene (imminene)	'be experienced'
		kamminene	'practice'

	būrōrō	'be red'
	kabūrōrō	'wear lipstick'
b.	aidik	'be skinny'
	kaaidik**dik**	'diet'
c.	kilmeej	'be black'
	kakkilmeej**ej**	'blacken'
	ļap	'be big'
	kōļļap**ļap**	'exaggerate'
	tooj	'be conspicuous'
	kattooj**oj**	'show off, be a show-off'
	jiṃaat	'be smart'
	kajjiṃaat**at**	'act smart; put on airs'
	jeraṃōl	'be lonely'
	kōjjeraṃōl**ṃōl**	'exude loneliness'
	to	'be a long time'
	katto**to**	'linger'
	tōñal	'be sweet'
	kōttōñal**ñal**	'apply diabetic medicine'
	ñaj	'fragrant'
	kōññaj**ñaj**	'apply aromatic ointments'

The four sections on causative verbs are summarized briefly in table 6-3.

Table 6-3 The derivation of causative verbs[1]

CAUSATIVE VERBS …	SOURCE VERB	DERIVED VERB
	±	+
Adjectival Verbs	jar 'be broke'	kōjjarjar 'be expensive'
	±	–
Verbs of Testing	util 'be agile'	koutiltil 'acrobatic contest'
	–	–
Verbs of Control	ettōr 'run'	kattōr 'drive'
	+	–
Verbs of Acquiring a Quality	iur 'be fast'	kaiur 'hurry'

1. Plus and minus signs indicate whether either the source verb or the derived verb is adjectival.

Verbs of tractability. Verbs with contrasting positive and negative values for a feature of 'tractability' are derived from certain nonadjectival verbs.

(6-73)	a.	atak	'tow, pull'
		atakiie	'be easy to drag in water'
		atakiia	'be hard to drag in water'

b.	aik	'tow'
	aikiie	'be easy to tow'
	aikiia	'be hard to tow'
c.	jaḷ	'turn, face'
	jaḷiie	'be easy to turn'
	jaḷiia	'be hard to turn'
d.	jo̧	'ignite, start an engine'
	jo̧wiie	'be easy to start'
	jo̧wiia	'be hard to start'
e.	kipel	'oblige, instruct'
	kipiliie	'be obedient, docile'
	kipiliia	'be disobedient, obstinate'
f.	mej	'die'
	mejiie	'be quick to die'
	mejiia	'be slow to die'
g.	tok	'burn'
	tokwiie	'combustible'
	tokwiia	'incombustible'

The contrasting verbs are marked by the suffixes *-iie* 'with ease' and *-iia* 'with difficulty', but the derived verbs sometimes undergo unpredictable morphological changes such as the doubling of the final consonant of *mej* in (6-73b), and the change of vowel quality of *kipel* in (6-73d).

However, there are also pairs of seemingly derived verbs for which no source verb exists. Verbs like these may, in fact, have provided the pattern upon which the derivations are based.

(6-74)	a.	aḷakiie	'be easy to find'
		aḷakiia	'be hard to find'
	b.	añiie	'be quick when called'
		añiia	'be slow when called'
	c.	awiie	'be tame'
		awiia	'be wild'

One or two adjectival verbs that end in what appears to be the positive tractable suffix have also been spotted, where words with the form of the expected negative counterpart have not been attested: *keiie* 'be useful; be of great help'; *kōiie* 'be strong; be well qualified'.

This concludes our review of semantic derivations. We turn now to syntactic derivations across the nine major verb categories introduced in chap. 4.

Deriving within the Verbal Category: Syntactic Derivations across Major Categories

6.4.5 The categories of verbs referred to here are the nine major verb classes of Marshallese that were introduced in chap. 5, beginning on page 233, and portrayed in table 5.6. They will be referred to here by the letters[22] of their class names, for example, [B1] for Class B: Intransitive Nonadjectival verbs. Arrows drawn between categories represent the direction of the derivation. Section headings refer to the type of verb being derived.

In chap. 3 we compared a number of transitive and intransitive counterparts. Here in chap. 6, as we consider their derivation more closely, we will find that some intransitive verbs are derived from transitive verb sources, while for other intransitive verbs, it is the other way around: they are the sources for deriving other transitive verbs. In the first two sections that follow, we will learn why this is so.

Intransitive verbs. The source verbs for deriving these verbs are the sort of transitive verbs that have been called strong verbs or thematic verbs (Bender 1984:445–51). The verbs in this group exhibit characteristics that reflect developments in the history of Marshallese. Thematic transitive verbs, for example, typically end in a stem-final vowel and consonant that do not appear in the intransitive form, e.g., *deñōt* 'hit s.', *deñdeñ* 'hit'. The retention of the final VC (vowel consonant) sequence of this stem (*-ōt*) is the result of an earlier transitive suffix *-a* protecting the final VC of the verb from the historical processes of final consonant deletion and later final vowel deletion that affected the unprotected intransitive stem.

This analysis proposes that the current relationship between verbs such as *deñōt* 'hit s.' and *deñdeñ* 'hit' is established through detransitivization. The evidence for this direction of derivation is morphological. The intransitive counterparts of these thematic and strong verbs are often morphologicaly more complex (reduplicated) forms. If the intransitive verb is treated as the source, then predicting the final VC of the transitive verb is impossible.

For this reason, there are two detransitivizing derivations that take thematic transitive verbs as their sources. Their data were first surveyed in tables 15 and 16 in chap. 3, where it was noted that they were moving in the opposite direction with respect to transitivity. Both find their sources in [G1]; the first derives [B1] verbs, the second [C1].

Detransitivizing [G1] → [B1]. This derivation removes the implied Patient from the transitive verb, and reinterprets the former Agent as the Patient of the intransitive verb. This reanalysis of the case relations is illustrated in the sentences of (6-75).

(6-75) a. Niñniñ eo ejañūt jinen.
[AGT] [+trns] [PAT]
'The baby is crying for his mother.'

22. Or, where relevant, by letter-number combinations with numbers greater than one, for one of their subcategories: e.g., [B9].

b. Niñniñ eo ejañ.
[PAT] [–trns]
'The baby is crying.'

Counterparts of representative verbs grouped according to the morphological changes involved are presented in (6-76).

(6-76) [G1] → [B1]

a.	jañ**ūt**	'cry for s.'	jañ	'cry'
	po**on**	'lower sail of s.'	po	'arrive'
	jiñ**ūt**	'fart on s.'	jiñ	'fart'
	ļōm**ak**	'determine s.'	ļam	'scheme'
b.	tu**uj**	'dig s.'	tōto (etto)	'dig taro'
	puk**ōt**	'search for s.'	pepok (eppok)	'search'
	tọ**uk**	'mend s.'	tōtọ (ettọ)	'mend nets'
c.	āt**on**	'smell s.'	ātāt	'smell'
	bu**uj**	'tie s.'	bubu	'tie a knot'
	jeļ**at**e	'loosen s.'	jaļjaļ	'loosen'
	iñ**ūt**i	'twirl s.'	iñiñ	'twirl'
d.	ṃan	'kill s.'	ṃan**ṃan**	'kill'
	kad	'throw s'	kad**kad**	'throw'
	eje	'build s.'	ej**ej**	'build'
	baate	'smoke s.'	baat**at**	'smoke'
e.	kōṇak	'wear s.'	**kō**kōṇak (**ek**kōṇak)	'get dressed'
	lo	'see s.'	**le**lolo (**el**lolo)	'see'
	kūri	'call s.'	**kū**kūr (**ik**kūr)	'call'
	jiburi	'hug s.'	**ji**jibur (**ij**jibur)	'hug'

The thematic VC of the transitive verbs, which are lost in the derivation of their intransitive counterparts, are shown in boldface in (6-76a–c). In (6-76d–e) no such VC is lost, but final syllable reduplication takes place in d. and initial consonant doubling in e.

Two forms show low vowel dissimilation (2.5.5 on page 92): *ļōmak* ~ *ļam* in (6-76a) and *jeļate* ~ *jaļjaļ* in (6-76c). Two others show high-mid vowel alternation (2.5.3 on page 78): *tuuj* ~ *tōto* (*etto*) and *pukōt* ~ *pepok* (*eppok*) in (6-76b).

While the morphological patterns in (6-76) account for most of the related transitive and intransive verbs, certain verbs are marked by unpredictable morphological changes (6-77a) or suppletion (complete replacement) (6-77b).

(6-77)	a.	kalbwin	'plant s.'	kallib	'plant'
		enōk	'knock s. down'	nenōk (ennōk)	'knock down'
		kajitūkin	'ask s.'	kajjitōk	'ask'
	b.	kañ	'eat s.'	ṃōñā	'eat'
		ilim	'drink s.'	idaak	'drink'
		ālim	'bail s.'	ānen	'bail'

Although the morphological shapes of the verb pairs in (6-77) are unpredictable, the semantic-syntactic relationship follows the same pattern as in (6-76), and the derived intransitives include only a Patient that corresponds to the Agent of the source verb. As Pagotto (1984) notes, "These detransitivization processes [this one and the one we will turn to next] are unique among the derivational processes in the grammar of Marshallese in so far as they remove or reinterpret case relations implied by the source verb. All other syntactic derivations either add case relations or clausal complements to the matrix of the derived verb."

Detransitivizing [G1] → [C1]. This second detransitivizing derivation also applies to thematic or strong transitive verbs to derive intransitive verbs that are adjectival. Here the implied agent of the source transitive verb is removed from the input model. The original implied Patient is not affected by the derivation, and is retained by the derived intransitive adjectival verb. The semantic-syntactic relationship between the derived adjectival and the source transitive is illustrated in (6-78).

(6-78) a. Ḷeo ear deñōt eok.
[+trns] [PAT]
'He spanked you.'

b. Kwōn jab bōt bwe$_2$ kwōnaaj deñdeñ.
[PAT] [–trns]
'Don't be naughty or you'll get spanked.

The verb pairs in (6-79) below illustrate the morphological and semantic relationship between verbs involved in this derivation. They fall into the same groups as in (6-76), except that no verbs have yet been found for the first group, the one in which the thematic VC is dropped, and nothing is added in forming the derived verb. We show this group as a placeholder for ease of comparison, and also for filling if one is yet found.

(6-79) [G1] → [C1]

a. —	—	
b. kar**ōk** 'fit s.'	kōkar (ekkar)	'be suitable'
c. deñ**ōt** 'spank s.'	deñdeñ	'be spanked'
d. baate 'smoke s.'	baatat	'be smoking'
e. kune 'extinguish s.'	kukun (ikkun)	'be out'

Not all Marshallese verbs show this syntactic-semantic relationship with the morphological consequences shown here. Certain transitive verbs have morphologically distinct adjectival forms, sometimes referred to as perfective forms (Abo et al. 1976:xxi), many of which end in *-ak* or *-ek*. A few of them are given in (6-80), where we continue to embolden thematic C or VC.

(6-80)	pin**ej**e	'cover s.'	pen**j**ak	'be covered'
	em**je**	'anchor s.'	em**j**ak	'be anchored'
	peọ**ọt**	'tear s.'	po**t**ak	'be torn'
	dāp**ij**	'hold s.'	dāp**ij**ek	'be fastened'
	lim	'fold s.'	limek	'be folded'
	kub**ōl**	'bend s.'	kob	'be bent'
	rupe	'break s.'	rup	'be broken'

In (6-77a–b) we have a residue of forms from the [G1] → [B1] detransitivization that did not fit into any of the five main types of morphological change identified for that rule. Here again in (6-80) we have a residue of forms for the [G1] → [C1] detransitivization, including an additional type that may have involved an *-ak* or *-aki* suffix, which appears in some instances to have preserved the earlier -VC thematic suffix, or the consonantal portion thereof.

These two detransitivizing derivations account for the fact that certain intransitive verbs have both an adjectival (stative) and a nonadjectival reading. Sometimes the two are identical in form (6-81a–b), and sometimes the *-ak* suffix (or the consonantal portion thereof) appears in the adjectival form, as we see in (6-81c–e).

(6-81)	a.	ṃwij**it**	'cut s.'	
		ṃwijṃwij	'cut'	[B1]
		ṃwijṃwij	'be cut'	[C1]
	b.	āte	'pack s.'	
		āte	'pack'	[B1]
		ātet	'be impounded'	[C1]
	c.	uk**ōj**	'turn s. over, topple s.'	
		ukok	'turn over, topple'	[B1]
		ok**j**ak	'be turned over, toppled'	[C1]
	d.	uk**ōt** ~ uk**ot**	'change s., translate s.'	
		ukok	'change, translate'	[B1]
		ok**t**ak	'be changed, translated'	[C1]
	e.	eb**aje**	'scatter s.'	
		ebeb	'scatter'	[B1]
		eb**j**ak	'be scattered'	[C1]

Detransitivising [G1–G2] *verbs to create Correspondent verbs that are partitive.* This derivation is more pinpointed than the two preceding, producing intransitive verbs that may be followed by definite nouns that are not their objects, but their Correspondents. Here we give a few examples of a range of partitive verbs derived in this way. The transitive source verb is given in square brackets at the end of the sentence. This detransitivizing applies to both inherently transitive verbs (like the ones in the preceding two derivations) or to transitive verbs derived from intransitive verbs in derivations that we will consider in the next major section below.

(6-82) a. Simple partitive verb [G1] → [B9]

Rejjañin *jejjet* ek ko. [*jit**ūk***]
[–trns] [COR]
'The fish hasn't been cleaned the fish yet.'

b. Directional partitive verb [G1] → [B11]

Kwaar *lilik* (*illik*) kuṇaaṃ ñan₁ bade eṇ. [*lik**ūt***]
[–trns] [COR] [+drcn]
'You contributed to the party.'

c. Locative partitive verb [G2] → [B10]

Ear *dedoor* (*eddoor*) an bok ilo tebōl eo. [*door*]
[–trns] [COR] [LOC]
'He kept his books on the table.'

Although the English glosses do not always reflect it, each of the derived verbs in (6-82) has a partitive reading. Other examples and a detailed discussion of the syntactic-semantic properties of partitive verbs are found in (5-63) on page 245.

Detransitivising [G1–G4] *verbs to create Manner verbs with Means nominals.* This derivation, like the preceding one, is pinpointed toward deriving intransitive verbs of manner that are followed by a Means nominal that is an indefinite common noun not marked by a preposition. These are the equivalents of incorporated object verbs in certain other Micronesian languages (see the discussion of [5-58] on page 243), which for the examples below would be verbs of "fish-stringing," "cement-buying," and "people-dunking." The manner verbs below are derived from a number of different transitive verb sources; the source verbs are given in square brackets at the end of each sentence.

(6-83) a. Simple manner verb [G2] → [B5]

Rej *ilele* ek. [*ile**ek***]
[–trns] [MNS]
'They are stringing fish.'

b. Directional manner verb [G4] → [B7]

Kwaar wia tok jimeeṇ jān₁ ia? [*wiaik*]
[–trns] [MNS] [+drcn]
'Where did you buy that cement?'

c. Locative manner verb [G2] → [B6]

'Rej *kattulọk* armej i ar.' [*katulọk*]
[–trns] [MNS] [LOC]
'They are dunking people in the lagoon.'

Deriving intransitive verbs from impersonal verbs. The final derivation process that forms intransitive verbs does not involve detransitivization. Rather, in this last derivation an intransitive impersonal verb is the source of a corresponding personal adjectival verb. As such, it will then also be eligible as a source verb for being derived as a transitive verb as well.

(6-84) Impersonal source [A1] → [G1]

a. ṃōḷō 'be cool' ṃōṃōḷoḷo (eṃṃōḷoḷo) 'be cool all over'

b. Eṃṃan an ṃōṃōḷoḷo (eṃṃōḷoḷo) iarin ānin.
'It's nice that the whole lagoon side of this islet is cool.'

The derived intransitive verb *ṃōḷō* 'be cool' ceases to be an impersonal meteorological verb and can now be used personally with a variety of subjects, including a part of the islet, as in (6-84b). Another impersonal meteorological verb *lur* 'be calm' underwent similar derivation to become eligible as a personal [C1] intransitive verb for the derivation to transitive verb found in (6-87b).

Transitive verbs. In this section, transitive verbs are derived by adding particular suffixes to intransitive verbs. Three phonologically conditioned patterns of suffixation are possible:

a. *-e* is added to a consonant-final verb whose last vowel is non-high
b. *-i* is added to a consonant-final verb whose last vowel is high
c. {-ik} is added to a vowel-final verb (thus, *-ik* / *-ūk* / *-uk*)
d. occasionally the source and derived verbs are homophonous.

The first two derivation groups have sufficient in common to permit their being presented together. For both, the case frame of source verbs is altered by reinterpreting its implied Patient as the implied Agent of the derived transitive, to which is added a new implied Patient.

(6-85) Nonadjectival sources [B1] → [G1]

a.	alluwaḷọk	'stare'	alluwaḷọke	'stare at s.'
	boḷan	'tie'	boḷane	'tie s.'
	ejaak	'build'	ejaake	'build s.'
b.	riit	'read'	riiti	'read s.'
	uñūr	'touch'	uñūri	'touch s.'
	bout	'vote'	bouti	'vote for s.'
c.	bu	'shoot'	buuk	'shoot s.'
	ajwewe	'whistle'	ajweweik	'whistle at s.'
	wia	'buy'	wiaik	'buy s.'
d.	kinaak	'tattle'	kinaak	'tell on s.'

(6-86) Adjectival sources [C1] → [G1] [+human]

a.	ban	'be unable'	bane	'be unable to do s.'
	bōt	'be disobedient'	bōte	'disobey s.'
	kadek	'be poisoned'	kadeke	'be poisoned by s.'
	mat	'be satiated'	mate	'be satiated by s.'
	mijak	'be afraid'	mijake	'fear s.'
b.	wiin	'be a winner'	wiini	'win s.'
	luuj	'be a loser'	luuji	'lose s.'
c.	abṇōṇō	'be uncomfortable'	abṇōṇōūk	'be made uncomfortable by'
d.	lale	'be careful'	lale	'look at s.'

Another group of adjectival sources has a different outcome. Whereas the derivation rule for the group in (6-86) above contains instructions for reinterpreting the implied Patient of the source verb as the Agent of the derived verb, the rule for the group in (6-87) below does not mention the Patient, so that the Patient subject of the source verb remains as the Patient object of the derived verb.

(6-87) Adjectival sources [C1] → [G1] [–human]

a.	bal	'be covered'	bale	'cover s.'
	būrar	'be smeared'	būrare	'smear s.'
	bukwelep	'be thick'	bukwelepe	'cut s. thick'
	būñal	'be dusty'	būñale	'make s. dusty'
	jọọḷ	'be salty'	jọọḷe	'make s. salty'
	pooḷ	'be surrounded'	pooḷe	'surround s.
b.	lur	'be calm'	luri	'becalm s.'
	mouj	'be white'	mouji	'whiten s.'
c.	būḷu	'be blue'	būḷuuk	'color s. blue'
	kūre	'be grey'	kūreik	'color s. grey'

Why are there two different derivations for adjectival verbs? Verbs from these two groups [(6-86) and (6-87)] are presented together in table 3-13 on page 155 separated by a difference in shading. The juxtaposing of the two groups raises at least two questions: (1) how best to describe the nature of the contrast, and (2) the reason for its existence—why the bifurcation?

A possible answer to the first question in terms of case relations is available above—that some Patients of intransitive source verbs abandon that role to become Agents of their transitive counterparts, while others seem content to continue being Patients, trusting that proper agents will be found.

The second question attempts to go deeper, and the most that we can offer now is to note the semantics of the first group of adjectival verbs: 'be envious', 'be disobedient', and so on. This requires Patients who are human, or at least animate. The same is not true of the second group. Remembering that the first are Patients who become Agents of their derived transitives, one can then ask what are the qualities we expect of our Agents, and look again at the definition quoted in 6.3.2 on page 284, "the perceived external instigator, initiator, experiencer, or (volitional or nonvolitional) controller of an event or state." That sounds like someone who is animate, if not human. And it is our reason for labeling the first group [+human]: intransitive adjectival verbs whose Patients have human qualities, and whose derived transitives will have Agents with the same qualities.

Dealing with apparent semantic-syntactic conflicts. Several of the verbs in (6-86) might seem to have semantic and syntactic considerations in conflict—to be pulling in different directions. Yet they furnish evidence that it is morphosyntactic (and not semantic) features that are the crucial factors in defining transitivity. Example sentences are furnished for three such pairs below.

(6-88) a. Jọọn eabn̄ōn̄ō.
[PAT] [–trns]
'John is uncomfortable.'

b. Jọọn eabn̄ōn̄ōūk kijak eṇ.
[AGT] [+trns] [PAT]
'John is disturbed by that guy.'
'John distrusts that guy.'

(6-89) a. Jọọn ekadek.
'John is poisoned / drunk.'

b. Jọọn ekadeke ek eo /dānnin kadek eo.
'John got poisoned by the fish / drunk on the liquor.'
'John succumbed to the fish / to the liquor.'

(6-90) a. Jọọn emat.
'John is satiated.'

b. Jọọn emate raij eo.
'John was satiated by the rice.'
'John stuffed himself on the rice.'
'John ate his fill of the rice.'

Notice that in the a. sentences *Jọọn* is the Patient, the nominal interpreted as being in the state expressed by the verb. The verbs in the b. examples are marked [+trns] as a result of the derivation process that also marks each verb with a transitive suffix. In the transitive constructions, *Jọọn* is assigned the Agent case relation but is semantically the undergoer of the state. Similarly, the semantic roles of the patient objects are atypical in so far as they are interpreted as the entities that brought about the states, not as affected entities.

This section is adapted from Pagotto (1987:440–43), who notes that such apparent semantic-syntactic conflicts are also found in English sentences such as the following:

(6-91) a. John underwent an operation.
b. John had a fit.
c. John caught a cold.
d. John suffered a seizure.
e. John survived the hurricane.

In these sentences, 'John' is the agent subject of a transitive verb, but semantically, 'John' is the entity affected by the action expressed by the verb. The semantic difficulties posed by the Marshallese constructions in the b. examples above can be minimized by providing glosses that are more in keeping with the syntactic facts. This we have tried to do in the second translation given for each of the b. examples of (6-88)–(6-90).

Examples of some pinpointed derivations. Features of source verbs not specifically mentioned in derivation rules are assumed to be retained by the derived verb.

(6-92) a. Directional locative verbs [B4] → [G4]

kajju	'go (to)'	kajjuuk	'steer s. (to)'
baar	'guard (from)'	baare	'prevent s. (from)'

b. Nondirectional locative verbs [B2] → [G2]

kat	'stand (in)'	kate	'stand s. (in)'
ubwe	'smash (on)'	ubweik	'smash s. (on)'

c. Locative associative verb [B3] → [G3]

ṃuri	'have a debt (with)'	ṃuriik	'have a debt of s. (with)'

d. Impersonal verbs [A1] → [F1]

awa	'be an hour'	awaik	'be an hour on s.'
allōñ	'be a month'	allōñe	'be a month on s.'
aet	'be a current'	aete	'sweep s. away in current'

e. Extension verb [E5] → [I3]

eṇak	'suspect'	eṇake	'suspect s.'

These pairs of verbs show that inherent features of source verbs are retained by the derived transitives. The characteristics of derived impersonal transitive verbs (6-92d) are described in 5.6.4 on page 251. An example of the transitive extension verb *eṇake* 'suspect s.' is given in (5-98) on page 266.

Three derivations that apply to all transitive verbs. All three of these derivations have to do with regulating the use of two transitive suffixes, *-e* and *-i* (see page 154). The function of the first derivation, DR-33,[23] is to regularize the stems of transitive verbs by analogy with the verbs derived from intransitive verbs and exemplified in (6-85a–b), (6-86a–b), and (6-87a–b) above. It applies to certain thematic and strong transitive verbs (see the first paragraph of this section on page 316) and to transitive verbs derived in (6-85c), (6-86c), and (6-87c), all of which are consonant-final. It changes neither the semantic nor the syntactic features of these verbs, only their morphological shape. The rule is written formally in Pagotto 1987 as follows:

(6-93) DR-33

[+trns]	→	[+trns]
a. [–hi]C]	→	[–hi]C*e*]
b. [+hi]C]	→	[+hi]C*i*]

The rule simply adds an *-e* to transitive verbs whose stems end in a nonhigh vowel followed by a consonant (a) or an *-i* to transitive verbs whose stems end in a high vowel followed by a consonant (b). The morphological changes entailed by the rule are illustrated in (6-94) below, grouped according to the two patterns of the rule.

(6-94) a.

deñōt	deñōte	'hit s.'
kañ	kañe	'eat s.'
lo	loe	'see s.'

23. For these three derivations we use the labels from Pagotto 1987:645–56).

b. ṃwijit ṃwijiti 'cut s.'
kūr kūri 'call s.'
ļwōjāik ļwōjāiki 'spank s.'

The verbs in (6-94a) are thematic or strong verbs, including the suppletive *kañ* 'eat s.' (*ṃōñā* 'eat'). The verbs *ṃwijit* 'cut s.' and *kūr* 'call s.' in (6-94b) are also inherently transitive verbs, while *ļwōjāik* 'spank s.' is derived as in (6-85c) from *ļwōjā* 'spank'.

The suffixed and unsuffixed forms in (6-94) have exactly the same syntactic distribution, that is, wherever the unsuffixed form can appear, so can the suffixed form, including with overt Patients of any kind. They are in free variation and have no difference in meaning.

The function of *-e* and *-i* in DR-34 and DR-35 is to provide anaphoric information concerning a missing direct object. Like DR-33, DR-34 also suffixes *-e* or *-i* to transitive verbs, but only under certain conditions: (1) that an overt direct object does not appear in the sentence, and (2) that the direct object is nevertheless interpreted as a third person singular entity. (6-95) shows only the morphological portion of DR-34, which differs only slightly from DR-33, but the full rule, including its syntactic portion, ensures that even if the transitive source verb already ends in an *-e* or an *-i*, the derived verb will still have the proper suffixation when the above syntactic conditions are satisfied.

(6-95) DR-34
a. [–hi]C(*e*)] → [–hi]C*e*]
b. [+hi]C(*i*)] → [+hi]C*i*]

The sentences below provide examples of the different syntactic contexts appropriate to these source and derived verbs. In each set of examples the (a) sentence includes a transitive verb with an overt Patient, and the (b) sentence shows the same verb without its direct object.

(6-96) a. Kwōn jurōke baib ṇe ṇa ijeṇe.
'Stand the pipe over there by you.'
b. Kwōn jurōke ṇa ijeṇe.
'Stand it over there near you.'

(6-97) a. Kwaar eọroñ ke jinōṃ?
'Did you respond to your mother?'
b. Kwaar eọroñe ke?
'Did you respond to her?'

(6-98) a. Iar kadjouk jo e.
'I caught this goatfish by pole fishing.'
b. Iar kadjouki.
'I caught it by pole fishing.'

Jurōke 'stand s.' in (6-96a) is a transitive verb derived as in (6-85a). In (6-96b), the Patient does not appear overtly, but the shape of the verb does not show any change, as is indicated by DR-34a. The verb *eọroñ* 'respond to s.'

is an inherently transitive verb that cooccurs with an overt Patient in (6-97a). When a third person singular Patient is missing, the verb appears with the suffix *-e* (6-97b). Finally, in (6-98a), the verb *kadjouk* 'pole-fish s.' appears with its Patient *jo* 'goatfish'. When the Patient is missing (6-98b), the verb is suffixed with *-i* (DR-34b).

A similar derivation is required to suffix verbs with anaphoric elements that refer to missing third-person plural nonhuman Patients.[24] The morphological portion of its rule is given in (6-99). The rule applies only under two conditions: (1) that the derived verb does not occur with direct objects referring to human beings, and (2) that it not occur with singular direct objects.

(6-99) DR-35

a. C(*e*/*i*)] → [C*i*]

b. [C*e*] → [C*ei*]

The majority of verbs follow the (a) component, which adds the *-i* suffix to source verbs with final consonants, or replaces a final *e* or *i* with *-i*. Three monosyllabic strong verbs are suffixed by the pattern shown in DR-35b: *je* 'write s.' → *jei*, *kwe* 'scratch s.' → *kwei*, and *me* 'chew s.' → *mei*.

The sentences below illustrate each of the possible syntactic forms for a strong verb not suffixed with *-e* or *-i*, where the distinctions are evident (6-100), and then for a derived transitive verb with a stem-final high vowel, where the distinctions are neutralized (6-101).

(6-100) a. Kwōn ṃan kijeek ṇe.
'Extinguish that fire.'

b. Kwōn ṃane kijeek ṇe. [DR-33a]
'Extinguish that fire.'

c. Kwōn ṃane. [DR-34a]
'Extinguish it.'

d. Kwōn ṃani kijeek kaṇe. [DR-35a]
'Extinguish those fires.'

e. Kwōn ṃani. [DR-35a]
'Extinguish them.'

(6-101) a. Ej addikdiki waj ṇe aṃ. (6-85)
'He's got his eyes on your watch.'

b. Ej addikdiki. [DR-34b]
'He's got his eyes on it.'

c. Ej addikdiki waj kaṇe aṃ. [DR-35a]
'He's got his eyes on your watches.'

d. Ej addikdiki. [DR-35a]
'He's got his eyes on them.'

---

24. Third-person plural human Patients of transitive verbs may not be omitted. They may, however, be realized as the pronoun *er* 'they'.

The relevant derivations are shown at the right margin. The inherently transitive verb *m̧an* 'kill s.' (6-100a) may appear in (6-100b) with an *-e* suffix as a result of the stem-extending derivation DR-33a. It may also take an *-e* suffix to mark an anaphoric Patient (6-100c). Finally, DR-35a adds an *-i* suffix to the verb and allows it to cooccur with a third person plural nonhuman Patient (6-100d), or to interpret such a Patient if it is missing (6-100e).

Similarly, a derived transitive verb such as *addikdiki* 'look at s.' is subject to the same derivations, with the exception of stem-extension DR-33, since it is already suffixed with *-i*. Notice, however, that the morphological shape of the verb does not change as the result of any of the derivations that apply. In the absence of additional context, the distinctions between (6-101b) and (6-101d) are neutralized. Thus, given the isolated sentence *ej addikdiki,* the missing Patient may be either third person singular (human or nonhuman) or third person plural nonhuman. However, such ambiguities are unlikely to arise in connected discourse.

Causative transitive verbs. The semantic derivation of four causative verbs has already been discussed in 6.4.4 beginning on page 306 and summarized in table 6-3 on page 309. Those derivations did not change the syntactic class of their source verbs. Here we consider the causative derivations that relate verbs across the major syntactic classes. It should be emphasized that only intransitive verbs can be the sources for these derivations. No transitive verbs are input to causativization.

Source verbs may be either adjectival or nonadjectival. Adjectival verbs lose this feature in the derivation, and the semantic feature causative is added to derived verbs. The Patient of the derived verb corresponds to the Patient of the source verb. Because the derived verb is marked transitive, an implied Agent is added to its case frame. Four morphological changes are possible: (a) simple prefixation of *ka-* or one of its phonologically-conditioned alternants, (b) *ka-* prefixation and suffixation of *-e* to sources with stem-final nonhigh vowels, (c) *ka-* prefixation and suffixation of *-i* to sources with stem-final high vowels, and (d) *ka-* prefixation and suffixation of {-ik} to sources whose stems end in vowels. Intransitive verbs derived from nouns are also subject to this transitive-causative derivation (see [6-47] on page 297).

(6-102) Nonadjectival sources [B1] → [G1]

a. eañ — 'urinate (children only)'
   keañ — 'help s. urinate'

   boo̧ļtōntōn — 'overflow'
   kabooļtōntōn — 'fill s. to the brim'

   rōļo̧k — 'escape'
   kōrōļo̧k — 'allow s. to roam free'

b. ebeb — 'shiver'
   kaebebe — 'make s. shiver'

deboklọk 'explode'
kōdeboklọk**e** 'make s. explode'

bọọkọk 'use a fork'
kabọọkọk**e** 'give s. a fork'

c. dibuk 'penetrate'
kadibuk**i** 'make s. penetrate'

bait 'fight'
kōbait**i** 'make s. fight'

d. bukwelōlō 'kneel'
kabukwelōlō**ik** 'make s. kneel'

kadjo 'go pole fishing'
kōkadjo**uk** 'take s. pole fishing'

koba 'cohabit'
kakoba**ik** 'betroth s.'

(6-103) Adjectival sources [C1] → [G1]

a. dipen 'be strong'
kadipen 'strengthen s.'

bab 'be tight'
kōbab 'tighten s.'

banban 'be weak'
kōbanban 'weaken s.'

b. dujejjet 'be full'
kadujejjejet**e** 'fill s.'

dāpitōk 'be tangled'
kadāpitōk**e** 'entangle s.'

bat 'be slow'
kōbat**e** 'make s. slow'

c. aruñijñij 'be sleepy'
kaaruñijñij**i** 'make s. sleepy'

kut 'be crowded'
kọkut**i** 'make s. crowded'

d. dede 'be completed'
kadede**ik** 'finish s.'

bwebwe 'be crazy'
kabwebwe**ik** 'call s. crazy'

awiia 'be wild'
kaawiia**ik** 'make s. wild'

Notice that in each case the Patient implied by the intransitive verb (its subject) corresponds to the Patient of the derived transitive verb (its direct object). As has been noted earlier, features of the source verb not specifically relevant to the derivation are assumed to be retained by the derived counterpart. Thus, more specifically pinpointed causative-transitive verbs may be derived from corresponding verb sources, as the examples in (6-104) show.

(6-104) a. Locative verbs [B2] → [G2]

deḷọñ 'enter (into)'
kadeḷọñ 'deposit s. (into)'

b. Directional verbs [C4] → [G4]

jenoḷọk 'be separated (from)'
kōjenoḷọk**e** 'separate s. (from)'

Impersonal sources. Impersonal intransitive verbs are also the sources of causative-transitive verbs. An intransitive verb with a nonreferential Patient becomes a simple transitive verb (with a new referential Patient). The morphological changes are identical to those of the previous derivation, except for simple prefixation of *ka-*, which marks the derivation of *intransitive* causatives from impersonal sources in (6-107), the next derivation below.

(6-105) Intransitive impersonal sources [A1] → [G1]

a. bōbōl (ebbōl) 'be light on'
kabbōl**e** 'light s.'

b. būbūtūktūk (ibbūtūktūk) 'be spraying all over'
kabbūtūktūk**i** 'make s. spray all over'

c. dekāke 'be rocky'
kadekāke**ik** 'make s. rocky'

kōkōtoto (ekkōtoto) 'be windy'
kakkōtoto**uk** 'expose s. to wind'

The following examples illustrate that the morphology and the semantics of verbs derived in this way are relatively predictable.

(6-106) a. Lale koṃ ar *kabbōle* ḷaaṃ ṇe bwe$_2$ rōnaaj lo kōj.
'Don't light the lamp or it will give away our position.'

b. Kwōn jab *kabbtūktūki* tok dān ṇe bwe jetutu.
'Don't spray the water because we'll get all wet.

c. Jab *kakkōtotouk* eok.
Don't expose yourself to the wind.

Impersonal verbs may also be causativized to derive personal *intransitive* verbs. This derivation entails only the prefixation of *ka-*, or one of its phonologically conditioned variants.

(6-107) Impersonal verb sources [A1] → [B1]

a. iialañe 'be moonrise'
kaiialañe 'wait for moonrise'

b. aelik 'be a current flowing out'
kaaelik 'wait for a current flowing out'

c. ibwij 'be high tide'
kaibwij 'wait for high tide'

d. pāāt 'be low tide'
kōpāāt 'wait for low tide'

Additional examples are to be found in table 3-22 on page 160.

Causative derivations that change subclass membership. The causativizing transformations we have been looking at in this section result in derived verbs that belong to the same syntactic subclass as the corresponding source verb. For example, in (6-92b) on page 319 an intransitive locative verb [B2] forms a causative-transitive locative [G2].[25] However, there are two other causative derivations that add syntactic features that result in derived verbs of syntactic subclasses different from the corresponding source verbs.

(6-108) Intransitive [B1] → locative transitive [G2]

a. tulọk 'bathe'
katulọk 'submerge s.'

b. babu 'lie down'
kōbabu**uk** 'put s. down on'

Only these two examples with their two morphological patterns have been found so far. Further investigation is likely to provide examples that will fill out the morphological component so that it resembles the patterns found in the other causative rules that derive transitive verbs. Here follow example sentences of these two derived verbs.

(6-109) a. Katulọk neeṃ ilojet.
'Dip your feet in the (lagoon) water.'

b. Kwōn kōbabuuk niñniñ ṇe ṇai raan peet ṇe.
'Put the baby down on the bed there.'

The final causative derivation derives the Marshallese equivalent of ditransitive verbs from intransitive verbs. The source Patient remains together with a new Agent and a new Correspondent in the features of the derived verb. Examples are provided in (6-111) below.

(6-110) Intransitive [B1] → ditransitive [G6]

a. idaak 'drink'
kaidaak 'make s. drink s.

b. ṃuri 'have a debt'
kaṃuri**ik** 'make s. owe s.; lend s. s.'

The causativization of *idaak* 'drink' in (6-110a) is particularly interesting since it clearly shows that the intransitive form of the verb is the source of the derived causative transitive. It could not be a transitive source, as *idaak* 'drink' has a suppletive transitive form *ilim* / *inim* 'drink s.'

25. The arabic numeral portions of the class labels indicate subtypes, e.g., the 2 of [G2].

(6-111) a. Kaidaak ajri ṇe ḷalem pil in wūnokwan pokpok.
[+trns] [PAT] [COR]
'Give that child five drops of cough medicine.'

b. Eṃōj an Jọọn kaṃuriik Toni juon taḷa.
[AGT] [+trns] [PAT] [COR]
'John lent Tony a dollar.'

This concludes our study of the derivation of causative transitive verbs. We turn now to the derivation of impersonal verbs.

Impersonal verbs. Marshallese includes a number of verbs that are inherently impersonal, such as the temporal, meteorological, and existential verbs included in class A, beginning in 5.6.1 on page 234. However, many adjectival verbs are derived into this syntactic class by the following derivation.

(6-112) Simple adjectivals [C1] → [A2]

a. Nuknuk kaṇe aṃ rōtooj.
[PAT] [–trns]
'Your clothes are quite loud.'

b. Etooj nuknuk kaṇe aṃ.
[–trns] [COR]
'Your clothes are quite loud.'

The personal adjectival *tooj* 'be conspicuous, be loud' in (6-112a) appears with a third person plural Patient *nuknuk* 'clothes' and is marked with the third person plural subject prefix *re-*. The derived impersonal *tooj* in (6-112b) exhibits the characteristics ascribed to impersonal verbs. It implies a nonreferential actor, which is marked by the third person subject prefix *e-*. Notice that *nuknuk* 'clothes', which functions as the Patient of the personal adjectival in (6-112a), is assigned the Correspondent case relation by the derived impersonal in (6-112b).

This derivation applies not only to simple adjectivals (Class [A1]) such as *tooj* 'be conspicuous' in (6-112) above. All the various subclasses of non-Correspondent adjectivals are potential sources of derived impersonals.

(6-113) a. Directional source [C4] → [A5]
Ekkar nuknuk kaṇe ñan$_1$ kwe.
'Your clothes fit you.'

b. Nonassociative locative source [C2] → [A3]
Ekuk ek ko ṇa ippān doon.
'The fish are all gathered together.'

c. Associative locative source [C3] → [A4]
Ekane bwiro ippān wōn.
'Preserved breadfruit goes with turtle meat deliciously.'

d. Manner source [C5] → [A6]
Ekkutaktak iu lōḷḷap eṇ.
'That old woman is always scraping coconuts.'

e. Manner source [C6] → [A7]
Ejok wa eṇ kōn₁ waini.
'The boat is full of copra.'

Each of the example sentences in (6-113) contains an impersonal adjectival verb that has been derived from a particular syntactic subtype of personal adjectival. The relevant features are retained by the derived verb.

The derivations we have looked at in this section are all zero-derivations. They involve no change in morphological form.

Extension verbs. The final syntactic derivations that relate verbs across major categories involve the formation of extension verbs. Like the derivations in the preceding section, they are zero-derivations, involving no change in morphological form.

As discussed in 5.6.6, beginning on page 257, extension verbs require clausal complements that typically contain a finite or nonfinite verb, and may or may not be introduced by a complementizer preposition (either *ke*₁ 'that' or *in* 'to'). While there are verbs that are inherently extension (such as *baab* 'suppose'), many other verbs are derived into one of the extension classes [D, E, H, or I] by the derivations presented in this section. Four distinct general derivations are required to derive the four possible types of complement structure (see table 5-11 on page 258).

Nonfinite clause without complementizer. The sentences below illustrate syntactically different extension verbs derived according to this derivation.

(6-114) a. Intransitive source [B1] → [E1]
Kwōn etal ormej.
[PAT] [–trns]
'Go wash your face.'

b. Transitive source [G1] → [I1]
Kwōn jipañ eō iuni kaar e.
[AGT] [+trns] [PAT]
'Help me push this car.'

The complements of these derived extension verbs consist of infinitival verbs with no complementizer preposition. In each of these sentences, the missing subject of the embedded infinitive is associated with the Patient implied by the main verb. More examples can be found in (5-84) on page 260 and in (5-96) on page 265.

Nonfinite clause with complementizer. In this derivation the nonfinite complement required by the extension verb must contain a complementizer preposition. Such derived verbs are illustrated in the following sentences.

(6-115) a. Intransitive source [B1] → [E3]
Kwōj *ḷōmṇak* in jibwili ñāāt ṃakṃōk eṇ?
'When do you intend to mold the arrowroot starch?'

b. Adjectival source [C1] → [E3]

I*mijak* in etal ñan Amedka.
'I'm afraid to go to America.'

c. Impersonal source [A2] → [D1]

E*kijerjer* kapen eṇ in jerak.
'That captain is impatient to sail.'

Each of these derived extension verbs is satisfied by the complementizer preposition *in* 'to' and the infinitival verb. More examples can be found in (5-86) on page 261 and in (5-81) on page 257.

Finite clause without complementizer. The sentences below illustrate syntactically different extension verbs derived according to this derivation.

(6-116) a. Intransitive source [B1] → [E4]

Ear *ba* koṃwin kañ ek ko.
'He said you should eat the fish.'

b. Adjectival source [C1] → [E4]

Lale kwoaṃaik peiṃ.
'Be careful you don't hammer your finger.'

c. Transitive source [G1] → [I2]

Kwōn ṃōk *kajitūkini* ḷeṇe ear wajjikōt.
'How about asking that man why he came?'

The verbs in (6-116) are derived from nonextension source verbs, and each is satisfied by the finite verbs of its complement clause. See the discussion of "Inner Finite Complements Without Complementizers [E-4]" beginning on page 262 and of "Inner Finite Complements [I2, I3]" on page 266.

Finite clause with complementizer. This is the final general derivation for deriving extension verbs. These typically cooccur with finite clauses that include a complementizer preposition.

(6-117) a. Intransitive source [B1] → [E5]

Raar *roñ* ke$_1$ enaaj itok.
'They heard that he would come.'

b. Intransitive [+drcn] source [B4] → [E5]

Kwōn *ba* ḷọk ñan Mama ke$_1$ ij jab etal.
'Tell Mama that I'm not going.'

c. Transitive source [G1] → [I3]

Ij *jiroñ* eok ke$_1$ koban tōprak.
'I assure you that you won't make it.'

d. Impersonal source [A2] → [D2]

Ejej wōt *kōjḷọriier* ke$_1$ rej jab ko.
'The fish were so stunned that they didn't run away.'

Each of the extension verbs in these sentences has retained the syntactic features of the corresponding source verb. In each case, the requirements added by the derivation are satisfied by the clausal constituent that includes both the complementizer *ke*$_1$ 'that' and a finite predicate. For further examples see (5-82) on page 258 and (5-98) on page 266.

Impersonal counterparts of certain personal adjectival verbs. Finally, two pinpointed derivations relate certain personal adjectival verbs and their impersonal extension counterparts. One derives impersonal intransitive counterparts, while the other derives an impersonal nonadjectival transitive extension verb.

(6-118) a. Adjectival [C1] → [D2]
Ṃool ke$_1$ ekane bwiro ippān wōn.
'It's true that preserved breadfruit goes with turtle meat deliciously.'

b. E*alikkar* ke$_1$ etōprak jerbal eo an.
'It is clear that he landed the job.'

Impersonal *ṃool* 'be true' and *alikkar* 'be clear, obvious' are derived from their personal adjectival counterparts so that they now require finite clauses as complements introduced by the complementizer *ke*$_1$.

The second derivation that forms impersonal extension verbs from personal adjectival source verbs involves causativization. The same sort of complement is required as in the previous derivation. A single example is given here.

(6-119) E*kabūroṃōj* eō ke$_1$ kwaar pālele.
'It makes me sad that you are married.'

Further research may uncover examples that will complete the full range of patterns typically associated with causative-transitive derivations, as in (6-103).

This concludes the discussion of the syntactic derivations that relate Marshallese verbs across the major syntactic categories. We have seen that the majority of derivations add new case relations and/or syntactic features, deriving transitive verbs, causative-transitive verbs, impersonal verbs, and extension verbs. However, unlike most other syntactic derivations, intransitivization removes or reinterprets a case relation implied in the case frame of the source transitive verb. While most syntactic derivations entail prefixation or suffixation or both, two such processes do not. The formation of impersonal and extension verbs are examples of zero-derivation.

SUMMARY OF DERIVATION

6.4.6 Derivation is a word-formation process that allows a speaker to either create or understand new words based on analogy with preexisting words. Marshallese makes use of derivational processes to relate words from one syntactic category to words in another, or to relate different words in a single lexical category.

Derivational relationships often entail changes in morphological shape, especially those that relate words in different semantic categories and verbs across the major syntactic classes. In these instances, the source and derived words can readily be seen to be distinct lexical items. However, even when derivations do not alter the shape of the lexical items, the source and derived words are still considered to be different lexical items, each with its own separate lexical entry. Even though such an analysis may result in a large number of distinct (but related) entries for a single morphological shape, it allows us to capture generalizations about all verbs within a particular syntactic class, and to capture generalizations between different semantic classes by referring to the relationships established by the derivations. It also allows us to account for sporadic semantic shifts in one of the two related items as a consequence of the assumption that each lexical entry has its own history.

Our approach in this section has centered on verbs. Marshallese nouns can be derived from verbs. They can be abstract (6-37) or concrete (6-40), with no change in the morphology of the source verb. Some verbs also derive a particular semantic class of nouns known as person-nouns and marked with the prefix *ri-*. Certain Marshallese verbs are also the potential sources of adjectives, which derivation often involves some overt morphological change, especially reduplication.

Some derivations produce a variety of verbs from noun sources without affecting the shape of the lexical item in question (6.4.3), while others show overt morphological changes. Derivations also relate both verbs of different semantic classes (6.4.4) and those of different syntactic classes (6.4.5). We have stopped short of including the derivation of verbs in different subcategories within a single syntactic class, all of which are zero-derivations. These are discussed in Pagotto (1987:688–722).

MISCELLANY

6.5 There are several topics having to do with key words in certain constructions that we wish to include before closing out this reference grammar.

MEASURED CONSTRUCTIONS

6.5.1 The key word here is *joñan* 'its extent, extent of'. It is related to the intransitive verb *joñjoñ* 'measure; compare size; try on clothes', and its transitive counterpart *joñe*, as in the following examples:

(6-120) a. Ḷeo ej ri-joñjoñ nuknuk eṇ.
'He's the one who takes people's measurements for clothes.'

b. Iar joñe jōōt eo.
'I tried the shirt on.'

c. Kōjro joñjoñ.
'Let's see which of us is taller.'

d. Joña wōt kwe.
'I am the same size as you.' 'We are the same size.'

e. Ej jab joñāer wōt juon.
'They are not on a par.'

f. Joñan wōt juon.
'Equal.'

g. Ewi joñan?
'How much should it be?'

h. Eḷap jān$_2$ joñan.
'More than enough.'

i. Ejjeḷọk joñan.
'Unexcelled.' [lit. 'Nothing else has its measure.']

j. Ejjeḷọk joñan kūkdikdik (ikkidikdik) in raan ko arro.
'One cannot enumerate the little things we did in days gone by.'

The forms beginning with (6-120d) are inalienably possessed nouns: *joña* 'my size', *joñaer* 'their sizes', and *joñan* 'his/her/its size'.

Here follows a sampling of the MEASURED CONSTRUCTION with *joñan*.

(6-121) a. *Joñan an* kajjiṃwe ear kōmọ an lio nājin alwōj pija.
'He was *so* strict he forbade his daughter to see movies.'

b. *Joñan an* lilu (illu) ekilbūrōrō.
'He got *so* mad he turned red.'

c. *Joñan aō* pepaḷ ikar aḷḷañ.
'I was *so* amazed my mouth was hanging open.'

d. *Joñan aer* koñil, raar jab bar rọọl.
'The extent of their alienation was *such* that they didn't return.'

e. Ke ledik eo ej ba jaab *joñan an* mejān balu.
'He had *such* a hurt expression on his face when the girl said no.'

f. Enana ñe ej ḷe jān$_1$ *joñan ad* ineeṃṃan.
'It's not good to be *too* easy going.'

There are dozens of such sentences in the MOD that can all be found and examined by using its concordance. In the measured construction, *joñan* is followed by a form of the default possessive classifier *aa-*, as in the sentences of (6-121), and the meaning is generally SUPERLATIVE and RESULTATIVE.

SUPERLATIVE CONSTRUCTIONS WITH *MAKE*

6.5.2 The word *make* 'alone, unaccompanied' is often translated as 'self', as in (6-122) below, where *make* follows a personal pronoun or other person marker, or a form of *ippa-* 'in the company of'.

(6-122) a. Kwōn jab kaaruñijñiji *eok make.*
'Stop making yourself sleepy.'

b. Kwōn jab kōjekkar *eok make.*
'Don't make a fool of yourself.'

c. Ikar roñ an kōnono *ippān make.*
'I heard him talking to himself.'

d. *E*ar *make* tok.
'He came alone.' 'He came by himself.'

e. Jej kōttar wōn ke_2 *jemake*?
We're all alone so who are we waiting for?

e. *I*j kile *ippa make* ke_1 eban tōprak jerbal eṇ.
'I can see on my own that that job can never be finished.'
'I myself can see that that job can never be finished.'

Notice that there is no semantic element of SUPERLATIVE in these sentences, and also that the syntactic position of *make* seems to be determined by what it follows, not by what it precedes.

Examples of *make* in SUPERLATIVE CONSTRUCTIONS can be found in (6-123), where *emake* is often sentence-initial. What becomes clear is that here—unlike in (6-122) above—*make* is an auxiliary or helping verb, derived into class [E2]. Example (6-123c) contains a sequence of six auxiliaries, with *make* being the first. The indication of the superlative is italicized in the translations.

(6-123) a. E*make* jijipiijij (ijjipiijij) aḷap eṇ.
'That old man is *always* preaching.'

b. E*make* juwaḷōñḷōñ.
'He's *such* a show-off.'

c. E*make* naaj kar baj lukkuun ātin jorrāān.
'He would have *really* had it.'

d. E*make* jab metak neeṃ aṃ jintōb im etetal.
'It doesn't seem to hurt your feet *at all* to walk around barefoot.'

e. Ijā, e*make* baj ṃōṃan (eṃṃan) an lur.
'Goodness, it's *so* nice and calm.'

f. Kwō*make* ājmour.
'You are *so* healthy.'

g. "Re*make* naaj ilbōk ñe rōbar lo kōjmān," iba.
'"They are going to be *so* shocked when they see us," I said.'

The possibility that *make,* with its 'alone, unaccompanied' approach to being superlative, might use only the singular and not be possible in the plural is laid to rest by example (6-123g).

Rather different examples of *make* in SUPERLATIVE CONSTRUCTIONS are found in (6-124), where *make* is preceded by a form of *ej* 'noncompletive' and followed by *wōt* 'only; still' as, for example, *ej make wōt* in (6-124a–f) below. *Rej* in (6-124g–h) and *kōmij* in (6-124i) are the 3P and 1P.INCL forms of *ej*, respectively.

(6-124) a. Kōrā eṇ *ej make wōt bōbōk (ebbōk)* iaan kōrin ānin.
'That woman is the nosi*est* on this island.'

b. *Ej make wōt ñak* aitwerōk.
'He*'s special* in that he never wants to get into controversies.'

c. *Ej make wōt jāllulu* tata.
'*No one is* as patient as (s)he is.'

d. *Ej make wōt depakpak* an riab.
'His exaggerations are *out of this world*.'

e. Ri-jāmminene ro raṇ *ej make wōt ruṃwij* aer jerbal.
'Those inexperienced workers are *awfully* slow in doing their work.'

f. *Ej make wōt.*
'He/she/it is *the one and only*.'

g. Kōrein Likiep *rej make wōt jeḷā āj* deel amiṃōṇo.
'Women of Likiep are *renowned* makers of fan handicraft.'

h. Ṃōṃaanin Mājej *rej make wōt ṃōkade* ilo jurbak.
'Men of Mājej Island are *famous* tap dancers.'

i. "[Kōmij make wōt] [Ri-ṃaanpā rainin ilo aelōñ kein]," Saimon Latdik eba.
'"We're *the remaining members* of the clan in the islands with the traditional martial arts skills," said Saimon Latrik.'

In these sentences, the portion of the translation indicating the superlative has been italicized, as has also the Marshallese portion to be examined to determine its status as verb phrase—except for (6-124i), which appears to be a candidate for being an equational sentence.

Make, following *ej* and preceding a nonfinite verb, seems to be in the position of an auxilliary, except for the intrusion of *wōt*, which hardly qualifies as an auxiliary. If we conclude that these are valid verb phrases, the role of *wōt* will have to be as modifier of *make*. We have already seen in 5.2.2 (on page 215) that *wōt* has a wider distribution than most adverbs (following quantifiers and prepositions, for example), and so it may be that we have just discovered another such spot, as it seems to be present here only when accompanying forms of *ej.* The sentences where they occur (6-124) all express continuing states, something not true for all of the sentences in (6-123).

Whether there is any precedent for a form of *ej* occurring in a nonverbal sentence—*kōmij* in (6-124i)—we can note its presence in the negative sentences of (6-3) and (6-4) on page 270.

Concerning the question as to how statements with *emake/remake* (6-123) and those with *ej make wōt* (6-124) differ from each other, we can note that the latter seem to be used for noncompletive and continuing states without exception, while the former seem open to both alternatives.

Index